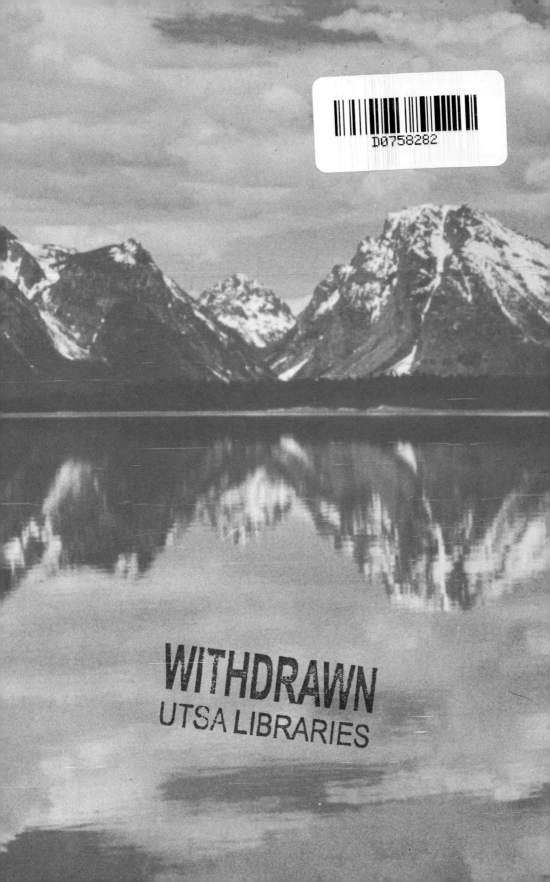

OUTDOOR RECREATION PLANNING

ALAN JUBENVILLE
The University of Wyoming

1976   W. B. SAUNDERS COMPANY

Philadelphia • London • Toronto

W. B. Saunders Company: West Washington Square
Philadelphia, Pa. 19105

12 Dyott Street
London, WC1A 1DB

833 Oxford Street
Toronto, Ontario M8Z 5T9, Canada

Front cover illustration courtesy of J & W Planning and Research Institute, Laramie, Wyoming.

Front endpaper—Yankton Boat Basin, Omaha, Nebraska (courtesy of U.S. Army Corps of Engineers).

Back endpaper—Mt. Moran, Jackson Lake, Grand Teton National Park (courtesy of the author).

Outdoor Recreation Planning   ISBN 0-7216-5228-X

Last digit is the print number: 9   8   7   6   5   4   3   2   1

To my wife
JO

ABOUT THE AUTHOR

Alan Jubenville, originally from southeastern Virginia, has had many varied professional experiences from the Appalachian Mountains and the Midwest to the Northern Rockies and Alaska. He has worked with federal and state agencies and a private consulting firm.

Alan has a B.S. degree in forest management from North Carolina State University (1952), a M.S. degree in silviculture-ecology from West Virginia University (1964), and a Ph.D. degree in wildland recreation from the University of Montana (1970). After completing the Ph.D., he became the state outdoor recreation extension specialist at the University of Illinois. He later returned to the West to accept a teaching and research position at the University of Wyoming.

Since that time, Alan has conducted several state and federal research projects, and has engaged in several private consulting (planning) opportunities. He teaches outdoor recreation planning and management courses at the graduate and undergraduate levels. And he is also the senior planner in the J & W Planning and Research Institute.

PREFACE

This book is written both as a text and a professional reference. It attempts to present planning in a logical, understandable sequence for the planner and for the professional who may employ a consultant to do the specific planning tasks. The book is based on an accumulation of personal experiences, research findings, and contact with other professionals. Probably the greatest influence is Dr. S. S. Fressell, colleague and former graduate advisor,

This book has a dual purpose as a text. It may be used for area, regional or systems planning, using Parts 1 through 3 and Part 5. Part 4 is also necessary to the understanding of specific behaviors that would be incorporated in area or regional planning. Also, Part 4 and Chapter 11 can be used in conjunction with landscape design material to teach outdoor recreation site planning.

·The author attempts to develop a foundation for planning, including visitor behavior, before proceeding with specific planning techniques and guidelines. Part I outlines a framework, or a perspective, for planning from the social psychological foundations and historical perspectives to the steps in the planning process and the basic elements of the planning model. Then specific concepts—management, social, and resource factors are discussed.

Part II, *Economics of Outdoor Recreation Planning,* explains supply-demand relationships in the total process. Specific means of improving demand projections and effective supply are presented. Lastly, cost-benefit analysis is discussed as a means of investment analysis in planning.

Part III focuses on the various levels of planning—nation-wide, state, region, area, and site. Also, it covers methods of evaluating the resource for recreation purposes. The last chapter analyzes the role of recreation in land-use planning and presents techniques for controlling land uses.

Part IV summarizes the user needs and planning guides for specific sites. The various sites, from campground to wilderness areas, are presented in separate chapters. Many line drawings for site development are presented.

Part V is a collection of reports and examples to complement the previous reading. It is imperative that examples are available to give the reader a practical orientation to planning.

In summary, the book is not presented as the ultimate in planning theory and application. It is not the panacea for all existing problems. Hopefully, after reading the book, you will have a better understanding of planning principles, concepts, and guidelines. Thus, for you, it should be a point of departure—a base to build on, to plan, as well as to seek to improve the concepts and strategies. Yes, the future is yours.

CONTENTS

Part 4

GUIDELINES FOR SITE AND FACILITY PLANNING

PART 1

THE PLANNING PROCESS

> The planning process has as its objective the accomplishment of premeditated goals and is primarily concerned with providing technical information for decision making and for plan implementation and control. Obviously the planning process is a subpart of the decision making process, since information is being provided to decision makers. Also it is a subpart of the administrative process, because plan implementation and control are important parts (steps) of the process.
>
> B. L. DRIVER: *Elements of Outdoor Recreation Planning*, 1970.

The preceding statement is somewhat complex, perhaps befitting the complexity of the recreation planning process and all its ramifications; but when boiled down, it becomes evident that recreational planning is not done as an entity unto itself. It is part of the comprehensive planning relating to all real or potential land uses—from the urban and industrial developments to the harvesting or extracting of renewable and nonrenewable natural resources.

The difficulty with past recreation planning efforts has been the abdication of responsibility by the park and recreation professionals for reasons of political expediency, the lack of understanding of leisure needs, or the lack of professional preparation to develop the leisure services to meet

1

these needs. Future efforts, if they are to be effective, not only must be integrated into the total planning scheme but also must reflect human values and needs.

The first step has to be the development of a logical framework within which planning can be effective. Development of philosophies and concepts is an important tool of the framework. This is essentially what is presented in Part I, The Planning Process. It focuses on a definition of planning and the steps involved in order for it to be effective.

The historical perspectives offer insights into the development of modern park and recreation planning concepts and some of the carry-over effects from early park and conservation movements as well as early national legislation.

Probably as important as any idea presented in this first part is that plans are for people. The ultimate success of planning is dependent upon meeting the needs of people. Plans must not be stereotyped and inflexible. Society is ever-changing, and plans must be flexible to meet the changes. Plans give goals and directions—not bureaucratic dogma that is to be exalted or followed blindly. This and other important concepts such as quality of use, carrying capacity, functionality of design, and so on are also explored.

Finally, basic planning models are presented to show what is involved in recreation planning. Subsystems are discussed in terms of their role and their interrelationships with other subsystems. Where possible, realistic examples are provided to give depth and meaning to the discussion.

CHAPTER 1

FOUNDATIONS OF OUTDOOR RECREATION PLANNING

Societal roles and demands of the individual are great and extremely complex; consequently, his attitudes, behavior, and life style are extremely complex and difficult to understand. Probably the least understood aspect of his behavior is his participation in outdoor recreation. For this reason, to plan adequately for the needs of the outdoor recreationist, we must describe normal behavior and try to understand it.

This chapter will focus on the general behaviors of the outdoor recreationist and possibly how these patterns are formed. The foundations presented are also a basis for further discussion in other parts of the book.

A DEFINITION OF RECREATION

If we are properly to plan for various recreational experiences, we must ask, "What is recreation?" *Webster's New International Dictionary* (second edition) defines recreation as "refreshment of the strength and spirits after toil; diversion; play; also a mode or means of getting diversion." This definition is reasonably complete in that it includes extrinsic values—recreation is an activity that occurs after work and rejuvenates us, making us better workers and citizens. The definition also includes intrinsic values involving participation in satisfying recreational experiences, i.e., play for inherent enjoyment and not for what it may do for us later.

As indicated in the preceding definition, there are characteristics of recreation that the planner should recognize: nonwork activity, replenishment of spirits, change from the routine, pleasure, etc. The term "constructive activity" should be added as a characteristic, constructive in its effect on the user, and also in its nondestructive effect on the participation of others and the resource setting. The last characteristic in the list should be defined as spontaneity, in which the participant may spontaneously pursue new situations as they arise. This condition gives the participant maximum freedom of choice in guiding his own leisure behavior.

The preceding philosophical definitions seem appropriate as they focus on the recreation activity and its social ramifications. This focus needs to be interpreted in some behavioral framework for the planner. Since planning is aimed at providing satisfying experiences to meet human needs, it seems important to refine the definition in terms of human behavior, rather than merely with nebulous philosophical terminology. Driver and Toucher[8] developed five postulates about recreation and the behavioral aspects:

1.   Recreation is an experience that results from recreational engagements. Most human behavior is goal-oriented, and a person's responses are instrumental in obtaining some goal-object or need satisfaction. The observable behavior is directed by personal motivations toward the achievement of a goal-object. In recreation, the person pursues a goal-object to satisfy some psychological motivation. There are many motivations for explaining recreational behavior—for instance, affiliation, exploration, dominance, achievement, and so on. The basic motivation/satisfaction model is discussed in Chapter 5.

In summary, our society has become leisure-oriented. Work is a means to support the leisure behavior patterns one develops. It seems that the future will further magnify this leisure orientation. Thus, the planner will have to focus more on the total recreational experience. What is it that people are seeking? How do they participate? What satisfactions are derived? The planner will then become the catalyst facilitating the movement of the recreationist, from motivations to satisfactions and ultimately, to personal benefits.

2.   Recreational engagements require a commitment by the recreationists. Recreation requires a commitment of energy, time, and personal resources, including money. This type of commitment requires the recreationist to develop a formal or informal course of action.

For example, the backpacker may commit psychic energy through special interest organizations to promote the establishment of wilderness and back-country hiking opportunities. He will also commit physical energy in conditioning his body and in the actual backpacking experience. Backpacking generally requires larger blocks of time; thus, the backpacker must possibly forego other pursuits, recreational or otherwise, to pursue his chosen course of action. The resource commitment seems obvious, since certain types of equipment must be purchased.

Figure 1-1 Active participation in auto-oriented camping (photo by USDA Soil Conservation Service).

3. Recreation engagements are self-rewarding. In contrast to work, which is generally pursued for income to meet other goals (although other psychological and physiological benefits may be derived), recreation is an end in itself. In fact, a very large part of our lives is spent either planning, pursuing, or reminiscing about recreational experiences. Consequently, much of our personal resources is spent on recreational objects (such as campers, trucks, and backpacks) and services (such as food, lodging, and entertainment).

These experiences are rewarding, not punishing; they have net positive values. Otherwise people would naturally tend to gravitate away from negative experiences to more positive ones. For example, a goat hunt in Alaska may have many negative factors—black flies, foul weather, and so forth; however, the positive factors of natural beauty, isolation, serenity, challenge, or whatever must outweigh the negative ones if the hunters are to find the experience rewarding. Otherwise, people may hunt goats elsewhere or seek an entirely new experience.

4. Recreation engagements require the recreationist to make personal and free choices. Implicit in the idea of free choice are: (1) that an array of opportunities exists from which a suitable choice can be made, (2) that the person is free and able to choose, and (3) that he is free and able to

participate after the choice. Many people may choose an activity but are unable to follow through because of constraints of time, money, information deficiencies, and other factors.

5.   Recreation engagements occur during nonobligated time. Obligated time is a block of time during which we are bound by a sense of urgency or importance to continue a given course of action, such as work, civic activities, and household chores. Generally we do not feel free to change that course of action; however, there is a varying degree of personal commitment to those things that bind us temporally, e.g., occupational work versus repairing a sink.

The remaining blocks of time should be considered unobligated, during which a person may feel free to pursue his own course of action and to change that course of action if he wants. Unobligated time may be, psychologically, the last bastion of freedom. However, none of us is ever totally free of roles, expectations, and other social ambiguities. More importantly in terms of planning, the recreationist feels fewer constraints of time and the allocation of the time, and greater freedom of thought and action than in other social roles.

RECREATION AS A TOTAL EXPERIENCE

The recreation experience is often considered as the actual participation in an activity. We know that human behavior is more complex than merely a chance participation in a single activity at a given site. Yet the planner has often developed recreational experiences that focus only on a single on-site activity. The experience is much broader than this and is separated into five distinct chronological phases:[5]

ANTICIPATION
↓
TRAVEL TO
↓
ON-SITE EXPERIENCE
↓
RETURN TRAVEL
↓
RECOLLECTION

1.   *Anticipation.*   Anticipation, including planning, is the first phase of the total experience. It may last only a brief period for more spontaneous participation, or it may require extended periods of time for more lengthy trips. Anticipation is a very necessary and desirable part of the experience because it allows the person the opportunity to plan the trip physically and to prepare himself mentally for the experience.

The primary input from the planner during the anticipation stage is information. Proper and sufficient information should lead to adequate planning and later satisfactory participation. If the information is incorrect (such as an overstatement of the attractiveness of the area) or is insufficient for proper planning, then the anticipation stage may lead to disappointment and frustration.

Furthermore, many people may find the anticipation stage as satisfying as the actual on-site experience, e.g., the fisherman who spends the winter making a balanced bamboo fly rod. Also, some people never advance beyond this stage because of social, economic, or environmental constraints.

2. *Travel To*.   Travel to the site is required; the monetary cost, time, uncertainties, and inconveniences can greatly affect the amount of travel and enjoyment one receives. Many visitors value the travel as an integral part of the experience, while others see it as a necessary nuisance. The types of travel routes and their condition and the availability of services and intermediate recreational opportunities can greatly affect the quality of the experience. If great inconveniences are encountered, the trip may be aborted, or at best the satisfactions derived from the experience may be lowered, even if the on-site experience was a high quality one.

Planning on a regional basis can improve circulation patterns and services. The major problem is one of coordinating action by both public and private agencies.

3. *On-Site Experience*.   This is the actual participation phase; the activities in which one engages, the resource setting, the services, facilities, and travel (on and between sites) make up the whole on-site experience.

Proper area and site planning can facilitate visitor satisfaction with the on-site experience. In area planning, proper circulation patterns between sites should be developed, and closely related opportunities can be clustered together in a complex, or incompatible opportunities can be adequately separated. In site planning, we can ensure adequate services and facilities while facilitating normal travel and behavioral patterns for a given site.

4. *Return Travel*.   The routes and services may be the same, but the recreationist is psychologically different. He may be tired, his anticipations are different, and his reflections now cover his on-site experience. His needs for information and services may be different, and we should attempt, if possible, to provide for these needs. Perhaps such a provision would require a minimal expansion of existing planning efforts. Some agencies have been so concerned with drawing people to certain attractions that they have not focused on the return trip.

5. *Recollection*.   After the experience, people recall many of the important aspects. They share these with friends, relatives, and associates. It is a way of revisiting the location and reliving the experience. Interest-

ingly, human recall tends to blot out or neutralize the negative aspects and accentuate the positive.

RECREATION—A PERSONAL COMMITMENT

A personal commitment is necessary if one is to pursue many outdoor recreation opportunities. Many people desire to participate but find it difficult to overcome their fears of uncertainty, insecurity, and so on. To overcome these, a person needs a sense of commitment and willingness to learn. No one has been a good mountain climber, or a good backpacker, or a good fly fisherman in just one or two outings. In addition, generally very few supervised recreational programs are designed specifically to develop the outdoor skills. The development is initiated by the outdoor recreationist—he seeks the advice of experts, joins a special interest club, practices the necessary skills, and, as his confidence builds, explores new ways of improving his skills. In sum, he eventually finds his niche in the pursuit of various opportunities.

The personal commitment, providing there are no major constraining factors such as money, time, or availability of opportunity, is measured by:

1. *Freedom of Choice.*   Freedom of choice is essential if a person is to have a real commitment to a given pursuit. If a person is told he must do something or feels constrained by economics, personal or family relations, and so on, then his commitment will be limited.

2. *Effort Extended.*   If a person feels total dedication, then he will extend maximum effort to develop and then perfect the necessary skills. If a person is interested in many varied pursuits, then his dedication and subsequent effort are going to be less for any single activity. Since outdoor recreation activities are generally not promoted or developed as supervised programs, they must be initiated by the recreationist. Thus, the effort extended should reflect the degree of commitment.

3. *Allocation of Time.*   Time is a unique resource.[8] More and more time is being allocated to leisure—longer vacations, weekends, and holidays; yet there are more alternatives for the use of this time than ever before. Thus, although he has more time, a person must choose wisely how he will spend it. The amount of time spent on any one pursuit should reflect the relative importance and personal commitment he accords to it.

The amount of money spent and the gadgetry accumulated do not necessarily reflect commitment. The trailer camper is not more dedicated than the tent camper because he spent $7000 for the trailer instead of $200 for a tent. These are basically different pursuits, and each participant may be very dedicated in his own way. Similar examples could be developed for the guided and unguided hunter, the wilderness horseman and hiker, and others.

TOWARD A LEISURE-ORIENTED SOCIETY

Life Goals. The American people are the most leisure-oriented society in the history of mankind. No longer are we caught in the web of the Christian work ethic. Our life goals are directed to the attainment of certain leisure patterns, or leisure life style. Work is used as a means to an end—primarily leisure of one form or another.

People spend more of their real income and unobligated time on recreational pursuits than ever before. Still there is pressure for more time and money to devote to those pursuits. Even family life style, including family size, purchase of equipment, location of residence, selection of friends, and other components, is often dictated by recreational interests.

Time Budget. A time budget reflects how people allocate their time. It consists of the following:[7]

> Total Time
>   less subsistence time (eating, sleeping, etc.)
>   less existence time (work and related activities)
> ──
> Free or Unobligated Time

Unobligated time is divided into three basic categories:

1. *Daily.* Daily periods of unobligated time may come before school or work, during lunch and coffee breaks, or in the late afternoon and evening. The total time may equal an average as much as 6 hours; however, it is generally fragmented into small time periods which limit the activities that one can pursue.

An increase of the daily periods of unobligated time would probably not cause much increase in outdoor recreation participation because of the still limited and fragmented nature of the time. Thus, it would largely be used inefficiently, and by the end of the year, one might hardly recall having increased unobligated time.

2. *Weekly.* The weekend has traditionally been the weekly period of unobligated time. It allows participation in nearly all opportunities not possible during the week. Thus, surges in attendance at local recreation areas occur on the weekend. The push by the American worker has recently been to increase weekly periods of unobligated time so that he may participate in activities on a regular basis rather than have to wait for the longer vacation period. Nationally, several holidays have been shifted to make 3-day weekends; some firms even periodically offer 3-day weekends to their employees. There has also been some interest in a 32-hour work week. Even if the hours are not reduced, some people would prefer the 4-day, 40-hour work week. This schedule allows the person to travel to more distant recreational areas. Consequently, given sufficiently large

blocks of time, a major limiting factor becomes the amount of discretionary income.

One of the major problems is scheduling if family members have different work weeks, or if certain services are not available during the odd times. We would probably have to restructure the work week on a national basis to minimize scheduling problems.

3. *Annual.* Vacation time is allocated on an annual basis, usually during the summer. For the worker, the paid vacation is an important fringe benefit that is generally allotted on the basis of his length of service. "In 1929, the average length of vacation was 0.37 weeks, and rose in 1959 to nearly 3 times that, or greater than 1.0 weeks."[6] Today the average length of vacation is about 2.25 weeks, and it is slowly rising to a possible 4–6 week average by the year 2000.

The timing of the vacation is important. More and more students are vacationing during the summer instead of joining the seasonal labor force. Also, most workers take their vacations during the summer. This situation has generally caused overloading of existing recreational developments and a decrease in visitor satisfaction. Many employers are encouraging employees to take vacations during the other three seasons. The main problems in scheduling during those seasons are the timing of the public school year and the availability of services. Some schools are going to year-round scheduling so a student can take his vacation any time during the year. Also, some services are staying open during the fall and winter where there is sufficient demand.

Discretionary Income.   Income is divided into existence, subsistence, and discretionary—the same divisions as the time budget. Theoretically, the discretionary income is spent on unobligated time. Unfortunately, it does not work out that way, but according to Clawson and Knetsch,[6] much of our income is discretionary. A person may feel that he has little alternative to the way he spends his money; yet the person generally finds a way to support those pursuits that he finds important.

The percentage of disposable income of the average household spent on outdoor recreation equals about 5 percent. This percentage is fairly standard for a variety of incomes, educational levels, and occupations. However, not all expenditures for recreation fall into the recreation category. Some are included under the categories of food, clothing, automotive (and travel), and home operation. Thus, the 5 percent is extremely low.

Recently, with high inflation and reduced energy resources, discretionary income has been reduced, a condition that has affected the recreational buying power. Some economists feel that this is a long-term trend; thus, purchasing recreational equipment and traveling medium and long distances should be greatly reduced. This consideration should not affect total participation, but it may change the manner of participation to local travel and less dependency on the recreational vehicle.

RECREATION AS A SERVICE

Outdoor recreation is too often perceived as a product, resource, or other physical entity. It should be more appropriately viewed as a social service system in which programs are designed to meet human needs. It can also be viewed as a subsystem which provides important inputs into the total social system—the social well-being of the nation. These inputs can help maintain the integrity or homeostasis or promote the growth and development of individual members of our society, or both.[8]

In outdoor recreation planning, there are three basic inputs—the visitor (his behavior, motivations, and perceptions), the resource (its potential and limitations for recreation), and management (planning and management of programs to meet the needs of the visitor). The first consideration should be the needs of the visitor, because the other two inputs (resource and management) only take on value as they relate to the provision of recreational opportunities to satisfy human needs. Thus, recreation in any form should be viewed as *an essential social service*.

THE FUTURE

The first part of the chapter is really a preview of the future. We are a leisure-oriented society that depends very much on the personal vehicle for participation. With increased unobligated time, the demand for participation should continue to rise at a rapid rate.

The mode of participation has to change, though, if discretionary income goes down and energy resources remain scarce. Personal mobility will decline; in fact, some observers feel that personal mobility has already begun to decline. We will become more dependent on mass transportation, take shorter personal travels, and become content with advance scheduling of sought-after experiences, perhaps as much as one year in advance. In addition, because of these new conditions, people will begin to seek satisfying substitute experiences closer to home.

How do you feel about the future? What will outdoor recreation be like in the year 2002? As a planner, what should your role be?

SELECTED READINGS

1. Arnold, M. D. 1970. "A Look to the Future—Recreation in America and the West," *Rocky Mountains–High Plains Park and Recreation Journal*, 5(1).
2. Brightbill, C. K. 1961. *Man and Leisure: A Philosophy of Recreation*. Englewood Cliffs, New Jersey: Prentice-Hall, Inc.
3. Brockman, C. F., and L. C. Merriam, Jr. 1973. *Recreational Use of Wildlands*. 2nd Edition. New York: McGraw-Hill, Inc.
4. Brown, W. W. 1971. *Islands of Hope*. Washington, D.C.: National Recreation and Park Association, Chapters 1–3.

5. Clawson, M. 1963. *Land and Water for Recreation*. Chicago: Rand McNally and Company.

6. Clawson, M., and J.L. Knetsch. 1969. *Economics of Outdoor Recreation*. Baltimore: The Johns Hopkins Press.

7. de Grazia, S. 1964. *Of Time, Work, and Leisure*. Garden City, New York: Doubleday and Co., Inc. (Anchor Books).

8. Driver, B.L. (ed.). 1970. *Elements of Outdoor Recreation Planning*. Ann Arbor, Michigan: University of Michigan.

9. Huizinga, J. 1955. *Homo Ludens: A Study of the Play Element in Culture*. Boston: Beacon Press.

10. Jensen, C.R. 1973. *Outdoor Recreation in America*. Minneapolis: Burgess Publishing Company.

11. Larrabee, E., and R. Meyersohn (eds.). 1958. *Mass Leisure*. Glencoe, Illinois: Free Press.

12. Murphy, J.F. (ed.). 1974. *Concepts of Leisure: Philosophical Implications*. Englewood Cliffs, New Jersey: Prentice-Hall, Inc.

13. Texas A&M University. 1967. *Proceedings of the First Recreation Management Institute*. College Station, Texas: Texas A&M University, Sections 1–8.

14. University of Montana. 1966. *Proceedings of the Recreation Planning Conference*. Missoula, Montana: University of Montana.

CHAPTER 2

THE PLANNING FRAMEWORK

In establishing a framework, the first step is to define planning so that we may delimit the steps and activities associated with the entire process. What is planning? *Webster's Third New International Dictionary* defines "planning" as "the act or process of making or carrying out plans." Probably a good operational definition is that planning is a deliberate attempt to focus our thinking on a specific problem or problems in order to create rational means of solving them or to achieve established common goals or objectives. This definition offers certain parameters or elements common to any planning process, such as establishment of objectives, coordination, and perhaps projection of needs or circumstances.

THE PLANNING PROCESS

Regardless of the type of planning, the basic steps are the same; chronologically, these steps are:

1. *Establishment of Objectives.* This step is paramount to the process; we must have some common or agreed upon goals. Objectives are the foundation for planning. We have no direction and no means of measuring success or failure unless we establish the objectives to be accomplished.

The importance of this step can be illustrated by a vacationer who starts out with no destination or preparation. He has no means of evaluat-

13

ing his progress or the accomplishment of the aims of his vacation. One could argue that an evaluation is not important; the only thing that is important is whether he enjoyed himself. In this instance the vacationer would be called an opportunist—one who takes advantage of present situations to further his immediate interests. However, he may be unable to take advantage of situations unless he comes prepared. Alas, the poor vacationer cannot go boating on the lake unless he has a boat or climb the mountain unless he has his mountaineering equipment. Furthermore, he may not be able to do either even if he has the equipment because he may not be skilled in either activity.

And so it is with planning. We must establish goals in order to give direction and purpose to the planning effort, to prepare ourselves for the basic issues and tasks at hand, and to measure our progress or success.

2. *Projection into the Future.* A basic tenet in the planning process is that we must be able to predict the future in order to provide the goods and services demanded by people. Because of the cultural complexity of our present society and the associated socioeconomic and environmental factors affecting human behavior, it has been difficult to project future human needs with a high degree of reliability. This difficulty does not mean that projection should be abandoned. On the contrary, planning that proceeds from reasonable projections of future needs provides valuable input—with a higher degree of reliability than mere guesswork.

Because of the lower reliability of projection, planning to meet human needs has often *not* been very successful. Five years may be a desirable upper limit for projection until more sophisticated projection techniques are developed. This limit means that plans will have to be updated on a short, regular time interval. Thirty-year projections of needs certainly seem unrealistic for the relatively new and dynamic field of outdoor recreation. Mission 66 of the National Park Service and Operation Outdoors of the U.S. Forest Service are examples of failure to project needs even for a relatively short period of time. In both cases, future recreation participation on our public domain lands was severely under-projected. However, had these projections not been made, the development deficit would have been even greater.

3. *Development of Course of Action.* This step is the selection of the best course of action to meet the objectives and the specific needs associated with objectives. In making these selections, the courses of action are separated into priority classes and spread over the entire planning projection period, the higher priority needs being accomplished first.

This procedure requires maximum professional expertise in deciding how best to allocate existing resources. The first two steps are essentially free of constraints; the answers involve what is needed and how much. At this point, the planner must show great resourcefulness and imagination in selecting a course or courses of action that best meet the needs of people over time, yet stay within the available fiscal and physical resources.

4. *Coordination of Actions.* People rarely recognize agency boundaries when pursuing a particular activity. Thus, coordination of planning actions is essential to total planning. Services offered by an agency and even by offices within a given agency must be integrated to ensure adequate coverage for the entire service population without duplication or voids in the service. This section should perhaps be called "coordination and cooperation" because coordination entails the cooperation of concerned agencies and organizations.

Too often in any large-scale planning, the agency that initiates the planning action feels that other agencies should cooperate with it. This feeling may accentuate petty differences; the atmosphere should be one of mutual respect and an honest attempt to work out major differences, i.e., cooperation for mutual benefits. If planning proceeds without coordination, then a major element of the plan is lost. On public domain lands in the past, coordination of actions has been almost absent; consequently planning has been fragmented along agency lines. We end up with duplication, voids, and poorly placed facilities that seem totally out of concert with the needs of people and lack continuity of purpose and opportunity.

5. *Flexibility of Plans.* Plans are tools to be used with caution and wisdom. They are not dogma that must be rigidly followed to ensure "consistency" of decision making. Many unforeseen events will occur, and it will take strong leadership to bridge these adverse conditions.

Plans are no better than the leadership to implement and administer them. It is easy to follow blindly the course charted in the plans, but such action is doomed to failure if planners are unwilling to bend to meet changing needs. Plans are goals and courses of action to achieve the goals; the strong leader understands this and chooses appropriate courses of action according to the particular circumstances, keeping in mind the agreed upon goals. In sum, plans complement or enhance administrative decision making; they do not supplant it.

A second area of flexibility is the periodic plan revision. This is important not only in terms of collecting new base information for the revision of the plan, but also in terms of totally reassessing goals. As time and needs change, goals must reflect these changes. There is no standard time interval; it is based on the reliability of the data and the rapidity in which social and technical changes occur. Probably the best approach is one with a variable interval where the monitoring systems of social and physical environment indicate a need for goal reassessment, or charting new courses of action. But because of the lack of sophistication in our monitoring systems and ease of administration and budgeting, we generally choose a known interval, commonly five years.

CHARACTERISTICS OF THE
OUTDOOR RECREATION PLANNER

According to Branch:

> The test of an intellectual discipline is whether it has a
> structure of theory, principles, techniques, and substantive con-
> tent sufficiently distinct to be more appropriately identified with
> it than another field. Another important factor is whether there is
> a history of situations and a need in the real world to which this
> discipline is more responsive than others.[6]

Outdoor recreation planners are employed by federal, state, and local
governments and by private enterprise, including park and recreation
planning consulting firms. This type of commitment to the improvement of
recreation planning and the resulting leisure services is increasing at a rapid
rate. The agency and the general public are becoming aware of the need for
the professional planner.

The outdoor recreation planner must face many varied and unique
problems in terms of both the social aspects of recreation (such as behavior, perception, and motivation) and the physical aspects of the environment (such as site quality and human impact). However, if we were to
identify characteristics that would distinguish the outdoor recreation planner from other types of planners, we would discover five basic differences.

1. *Behavioralist in Terms of Human Behavior.* No planning for
visitor use or accommodation should proceed without a basic understanding of who would use the service/facility—their backgrounds, attitudes,
and values, all of which are integrated to mold the behavior of the individual. Too many sites and facilities go unused today not because there is
little demand for recreation but because they do not fulfill the behavioral
needs of the visitor.

A primitive auto campground may go unused because it is poorly
located, or the demand is for more modern trailer campgrounds, or the
primary activities are day-use only. We may find that hardening the
campsites in a backcountry area (pit toilets, tent pads, rustic tables, etc.)
completely eliminates many of the original users, even though visitation
increases. Or a poorly placed comfort station may not be used, greatly
affecting the sanitation of the campground. As an outdoor recreation
planner, one must strive to understand visitor behavior and those pertinent
factors which affect behavior.

We must also understand behavior for another reason—how to modify
behavior subtly to protect the site or the visitor and yet have minimum
disruption of the recreational experience. At times, we may want to discourage certain behavior or at least modify it. This type of management is
difficult without some understanding of behavior and the possible consequences of decisions.

I have talked with administrators about how to eliminate trail bikes in the backcountry without continuous enforcement patrols. Two factors always seem to accompany the problem. There are no places or trails designated for the trail bike enthusiast, and the entrance trails in the backcountry are attractive to trail bikers, even the inexperienced ones. Generally the trails are 4 to 6 feet wide with low gradient. Why not make the trail narrow with varying gradients, placing a steep gradient at the beginning? Perhaps have the first part of the trail traverse a steep rock outcropping, using steep, sharp angle switchbacks.

In terms of normal behavior, you have eliminated the trail bike enthusiast. However, if you do this, then you assume an obligation of providing for the behavioral needs of the trail biker elsewhere within your jurisdiction, if at all possible.

These examples show that it is of utmost importance to strive to understand the behavior of the various user groups. If we fail to do this, we have no real basis for outdoor recreation planning.

2. *Natural Scientist in the Understanding of the Natural Resource Base.* The second major component of the recreation experience is the resource setting in which the activities take place. Certain types of activities require certain types of natural settings. The reasons why individual visitors choose particular places will vary, but nevertheless the resource setting is important to them. Thus, the planner has the responsibility to develop planning strategies to protect the resource from massive deterioration.

He must understand the maintenance of natural resources. How much use can vegetation sustain without reducing its vigor or general health? What types of soils are more suited to medium or heavy levels of use? What effects will our plans have on sustaining the fish and wildlife populations, prime outdoor recreation attractors?

Much of our past planning has failed to integrate behavioral needs and maintenance of the resource base. In the past, sites such as campgrounds and fishing access points have been developed where there was a junction of a road and a waterway. This type of place suited the behavior of people so the site was developed as the ideal location, without any regard to possible effects of visitor use on the soil, vegetation, and water runoff. Many of these sites eventually show loss of vegetation and sheet erosion until they are no longer attractive to the visitor and are affecting the fishery because of stream siltation. More suitable, stable locations that meet the behavioral needs of the visitor could probably be found through resource inventories.

In hilly or mountainous country, many lakefront developments are placed on alluvial fans where streams enter the lake. It is cheaper to gain access via the stream bed and develop where the road approaches the lake. However, alluvial fans are extremely unstable and are subject to periodic flooding. By not understanding the resource and the potential effects of visitor use, development on such places as alluvial fans can be economically and ecologically disastrous.

3. *Designer in Terms of Fitting Developments to the Landscape*. Developments fitted to the landscape are generally more aesthetic, more economical, and more environmentally sound. And these developments are more pleasing as a recreational environment. Furthermore, management and maintenance are reduced if we try to maintain existing vegetation rather than reintroducing native or exotic species.

A good illustration appeared in a magazine article in Michigan several years ago. Two developers planned adjacent housing developments in an oak-hickory woods in a new suburb of Lansing. Developer No. 1 removed all trees, put in streets and laid out the lots to meet his planning specifications. The other developer, No. 2, staked out his streets and removed the trees only in the right-of-way; then he staked out the lots.

When No. 1 sold a lot, he built the house and then landscaped with nursery stock. When No. 2 sold a lot, he staked out the foundation and removed all trees within the stakes, plus any adjacent hazard trees or others the buyer wanted removed. Because of increased care, No. 2 had to charge higher prices. When No. 2 developer had sold all of his lots, No. 1 had sold less than 25 per cent. An analogy could be drawn for public recreation developments in terms of visitor usage.

4. *Aesthetician in His Sensitivity Towards the Landscape*. Probably none of the preceding differences could be fully developed unless the planner had a sensitivity towards maintaining the natural landscape. Aesthetics and natural beauty are becoming important to urban dwellers as they see the last vestiges of the natural landscape give way to the bulldozer. This attitude change, although a bit too late, appears to reflect a change in value systems in which a quality environment is worth more than whatever gain could be gouged from the landscape. Thus, we are beginning to see more trail systems, green belts, and quiet areas within our urban landscape.

This change of attitude is not limited to the urban landscape. The underlying problem in the clearcutting controversy in the Bitterroot Valley of western Montana was whether the aesthetics and natural beauty of the forested landscape—valued highly by the people of the area—would be maintained. The quality of the visual environment was important, more important than the economics of timber harvesting. Large, symmetrical openings were incongruent with the natural landscape; smaller, irregular ones would appear as natural openings in the forest.

Large recreational developments on the natural landscape such as Canyon Village in Yellowstone National Park also appear to be incongruent parts of the landscape. If we are to maintain our appreciation of the landscape, then we must overcome our infatuation with recreation technology—the attitude that allows people to say "We have a parcel of land, so let's develop it," or "We can put any development anywhere."

5. *Generalist in Terms of Land-Use Philosophy*. The entire spec-

trum of recreational uses, from the urban park to the wilderness area, should be recognized as important and legitimate forms of recreation. The planner should remain objective and attempt to provide for varied needs within the scope of the plan. To do otherwise would eliminate important parts of the recreation spectrum that we should provide for.

Also, the outdoor recreation planner must recognize that recreation is just one of the many uses of our resources and landscapes. Recreation must compete favorably and coordinate with other land uses. In other words, recreation is not an end; it is a means of satisfying social and psychological needs—a benefit to people. But the other resource uses also offer human benefits.

PLANNING PHILOSOPHY

What are plans and what are they supposed to accomplish? Are plans an end in themselves, or are they the means to an end? We need to develop some basic philosophy and understanding of plans—what they can do and what they should not do.

The Dusty-Shelf Approach. We implement the dusty-shelf philosophy when we have a plan that meets program, organizational, or governmental requirements, but it just collects dust on the shelf—the "we've complied with the law" attitude. The unfortunate part of the philosophy is that compliance takes precedence over needs.

There are two basic causes of the dusty-shelf approach. The first is stereotyping the planning process through substituting bureaucratic policy for specific policy relating to particular local needs or circumstances. In other words, the plan is merely a reiteration of doctrine from the agency's policy and procedures manual without due consideration of particular needs or innovative ways of meeting the needs. However, this policy insures the instant success of the plan (within the agency) in that its content will measure favorably with the agency's barometer—the policy and procedures manual.

The adage "If you've seen one, you've seen them all" would hold true for this approach. The results of this type of planning are stereotyped campgrounds, picnic areas, and other types of sites and facilities, regardless of the circumstances.

The second basic cause is the responsible park and recreation professional's lack of involvement in the planning process. It may seem easier to hire a consultant to do the plan or to ask the engineering section of your agency to plan the road location and site development, but the resulting plans may not and often don't meet the needs of the visitor.

The person in charge of the local district should be aware of local conditions and special problems unique to that locale. Even if a private consultant or specialist from the regional office of the agency is called in, he must be made aware of the particular situation, what is needed, and where.

An Illinois Park District contracted a consultant to design an outdoor education center, but without specifying local conditions and needs. The resulting plan was of little benefit; the costs were too high and the physical facilities were not designed for child education programs.

The engineering section of a state park system developed a plan for relocating and enlarging a sewage treatment system on one of the state parks, without consulting the superintendent. It was to be relocated in an open field next to the parking lot of one of the more heavily-used sites. By engineering criteria it may have been perfect, but recreationally and aesthetically it was a disaster. Both plans were relegated to collecting dust on the shelf.

Plans Don't Work—People Do.   As stated by Rettie:

> I think part of this frustration with the planning process is based on a continuing misunderstanding of what the planning process and plans are all about. Plans are not decisions— although some plans make the mistake of flying under false colors on this score. Plans should be *guides* and *decision-making tools* to help make decisions among various opportunities and competing alternatives. Plans make it more possible to allocate usually scarce resources among competing uses. [*emphasis added*][10]

Plans do not make decisions; they give goals to be accomplished and direction in achieving the goals. Even though the plan outlines the overall direction, daily decisions must be made in order to effect the plan's implementation and the periodic adjustment necessitated by changes in circumstances. Not only should plans give direction, but they should be "the primary mechanism for institutionalizing the process of change."[10]

Thus, planning is a continuing process, from inception to implementation and then to periodic review. Because it is a continuing function, we must have intrinsic flexibility to change goals or direction or to increase existing recreational opportunities to meet expanding visitor needs.

Limited Resource Base for Planning.   Buckminster Fuller has characterized earth as a spaceship with finite resources.[11] In terms of mineral supply and sources of energy for human benefit, we base our planning on the probability of improved future extraction and processing technology and on continued exploration. Thus, we allocate these resources on the basis of unknown factors in our ability to supply what is demanded. We continue with these assumptions, even though we face periodic, short-lived crises.

Outdoor recreation cannot proceed on those assumptions. We cannot simply go out and find more recreational lands. We can do some reshaping of the landscape to make a particular site more suitable for certain types of development. However, we have not created more recreational resources (land); we have merely changed the character of the recreational opportunities available on that site—a matter of shifting the resource from one recreational opportunity category to another without increasing total amount available.

For example, a road could be constructed into a wilderness area to "create" new, auto-oriented campgrounds. This may be an admirable goal, but the opportunity ledger remains balanced. It is merely replacing one form of recreation, wilderness camping, with another, auto camping.

The public seems to be insatiable in its demand for more outdoor recreation opportunities. Future projections by the Bureau of Outdoor Recreation indicate that total participation (in number of occasions) will spiral from the 4,282 million occasions in 1960 to 10,128 million in 1980 and to 16,846 million by 2000.[8] Even if we fall short of the 16,846 million, the planner will have difficulty in providing these opportunities simply because the amount of land for outdoor recreation is decreasing.

Not only is participation increasing, but it is increasing faster in the more resource-oriented categories, e.g., wilderness, hiking, etc. (Table 2–1). These types of opportunities require greater spacial allocation per unit of visitation. Thus, while demand for opportunities is escalating, the resulting spatial demands appear to be accelerating even faster.

The existing supply is diminishing at an alarming rate. Our public lands

TABLE 2–1 TRENDS IN HIKING AND RELATED TRAIL USES IN THE UNITED STATES, BASED ON NUMBER OF OCCASIONS

Activity	Percent Change	
	1960–1965	*1960–2000*
Hiking	47	368
Nature Study	19	180
Walking	82	356
Wilderness	68[1]	859[2]
Camping	62	447
Driving for Pleasure [3]	8	146

Table developed from Bureau of Outdoor Recreation, 1967. *Outdoor Recreation Trends.* Washington, D.C.: U.S. Government Printing Office.

[1]*Outdoor Recreation Resources Review Commission. Outdoor Recreation for America.* Washington, D.C.: U.S. Government Printing Office, 1962, p. 220.
[2]Robert C. Lucas. 1971. "Natural Amenities, Outdoor Recreation, and Wilderness," *Ecology—Economics—Environment,* R.W. Behan and R.M. Weddle, (eds.). Missoula, Montana: Montana Forest and Conservation Experiment Station, University of Montana. p. 143.
[3]Driving for pleasure is used as a comparison to show an apparent trend of driving less and spending more time away from the automobile, which in part may account for the large increases in hiking participation.

also provide other resource values such as timbering, mining, and other uses that tend to be incompatible with most forms of recreation, at least for a given period of time. These resource values then reduce the total acreage available to recreation or other similar uses. As timber and mineral needs increase, a greater portion of the existing land base will likely be allocated to these uses—further reducing the possible land base for recreation.

The planning picture is also complicated by heavy use and abuse of much of the existing quality recreational sites, destroying the very resource base we want to maintain and expand. Overuse, although proceeding somewhat more slowly, is just as deadly as the bulldozer. Consequently, the recreationist is contributing to the ever-diminishing supply.

Finally, we must consider the potential in terms of productivity. The most productive lands in the United States have already been allocated to intensive land uses such as farming, urban developments, and industrial complexes. Thus, historically, outdoor recreation has been limited to the lesser productive lands. Even on these lands, the least productive in terms of animal and plant life (an indicator of their ability to sustain recreational use) appear to be the most attractive—the alpine basin, the unique rock outcropping, the semi-aquatic ecosystem around mountain lakes. Thus, the prospects for increasing productivity and recreational use through cultural site treatments (such as fertilization or introduction of exotic woody species) appear to be slight. Only hardening of the site (gravel or hard surfacing, facility development, etc.) offers any opportunity for increasing the visitor-use capacity of the resource, but this type of treatment may completely change the type of recreation opportunities offered on the particular site. If hardening of sites were continued, the more resource-oriented portion of the outdoor recreational planning spectrum would slowly vanish.

MULTIPLE USE AS A PLANNING TOOL

Multiple use is a land use planning concept in which all uses, generally wood, water, recreation, fish and wildlife, and grazing, are given equal consideration in the planning process. All of these may not be compatible on any given acre; thus, we may have a dominant use or mix of uses on any particular area. Therefore, effective multiple-use planning must be done on a large-scale basis, rather than on the basis of the individual acre or small parcel of land. Balance can only be achieved through a systems approach, balancing resources with human needs on a regional or even national basis. This way we can encourage a given mix of uses on a piece of land based on what the land can best give to the system.

If a parcel of land has unique natural features and scenic wonders, its best contribution may be for human enjoyment of these natural amenities. Deep, fertile soils, coupled with optimum growth conditions, may be best suited to timber production. A mountainous, roadless area may be best suited to sustaining unique wildlife populations such as bighorn sheep. The system, in terms of human needs, can then be balanced through internal adjustments if they are needed. Lands allocated to recreation can be shifted to timber management, range management to wildlife production, and so forth, to achieve the best allocation of our limited resources. In sum,

> The concept is a meaningful one when applied to areas large enough to provide sufficient latitude for periodic adjustments in use to conform to changing needs and conditions. Each small area need not be used for more than one purpose, and the combination of uses to be chosen need not be that which gives the greatest dollar return or the greatest unit output. If multiple use were applied to every acre of forest land, it would result in travesty of good forest management.[14]

Inherent in the application of the multiple-use concept is the awareness of the dynamic physical and social environments and the human aspects of deciding on alternatives. The physical and biological environment is constantly changing because of natural forces, i.e., wind, fire, precipitation. Planning must account for these changes rather than assume a static situation.

Social needs and values change more rapidly than the physical and biological phenomena, placing greater need on the monitoring and understanding of social changes and how to incorporate them into resource planning. There is no substitute for knowledge of social needs and the willingness to incorporate the varied needs into the total planning process

Really multiple use can be equated to the leadership that directs the planning. If the leadership is not interested in the broad regional and national implications, then planning will probably focus on

> a narrow commercial interpretation, dismissing all factors that are neither measurable nor purchasable. Still others have been known to distort multiple use into a green light for exploitation. In this case, its goal is not accepted other than personally— "society" is relaced by "me" or "us."[4]

All of us are at times guilty of this type of planning effort—supplanting our own goals for those of society. Multiple-use planning in the past has been fragmented on a discipline basis, i.e., recreation, watershed, timber. The integration of planning was through overlays to determine places of conflict and then realignment of the uses to minimize conflict. This "smoothing-over" of the edges may minimize conflict but in no way assures that the results will meet the needs of society. To overcome the problem, multiple-use planning must be done by an interdisciplinary team, the team composition determined by the specific needs of the planning region.

SELECTED READINGS

1. Behan, R.W. 1971. "Natural Resources, People, and the Quality of Life," *Ecology Economics Environment,* R.W. Behan and R.M. Weddle (eds.). Missoula, Montana: Montana Forest and Conservation Experiment Station, University of Montana. pp. 3–27.
2. Behan, R.W. 1972. "Wilderness Purism—Here We Go Again," *American Forests,* 12: 8–11.
3. Bolle, A.W., *et al.* 1970. *A University View of the Forest Service.* U.S. Senate Document No. 91–115.
4. Bolle, A.W., and E. Hannum. 1966. "The Multiple-Use Administrator." Unpublished manuscript on file, Forestry Library, University of Montana.
5. Branch, M. 1970. *Comprehensive Urban Planning: A Selected Annotated Bibliography With Related Materials.* Beverly Hills, California: Sage Publishers.
6. Branch, M. 1966. *Planning: Aspects and Application.* New York: John Wiley and Sons, Inc.
7. Brooks, L. 1968. "Multiple-Use Aspects: Recreation Implications," *Proceedings of the Annual Meeting of the Canadian Institute of Foresters.*
8. Bureau of Outdoor Recreation. 1967. *Outdoor Recreation Trends.* Washington, D.C.: U.S. Government Printing Office.
9. Clark, W.F. 1966. "Why Land-Use Planning, Part I," *Montana Business Quarterly,* 4(1): 35–43.
10. Driver, B.L. (ed.). 1970. *Elements of Outdoor Recreation Planning.* Ann Arbor: University of Michigan.
11. Ewald, W.R., Jr. (ed.). 1968. *Environment and Change: Next Fifty Years.* Bloomington: Indiana University Press.
12. Ewing, D.M. 1969. *The Human Side of Planning.* Boston: The Macmillan Co.
13. Gutenschwager, G. 1971. *Planning and Social Theory: A Selected Bibliography.* Council on Planning Librarians Bibliography. No. 179.
14. Kozicky, E.I. 1963. "Forest Wildlife Management—The Job Ahead." Address to 5th American Forest Congress, Washington, D.C.
15. Lowenthal, D. 1962. "Not Every Prospect Pleases," *Landscape,* 12(1): 19–22.
16. Outdoor Recreation Resources Review Commission. 1962. *Outdoor Recreation for America.* Washington, D.C.: U.S. Government Printing Office.
17. Palmer, J.E. 1967. "Recreational Planning—A Bibliographical Review," *Planning Outlook* (Journal of Town and Country Planning, University of Newcastle, England), 2: 19–69.
18. Sessoms, H.D. 1964. "New Bases for Recreation Planning," *Journal of the American Institute of Planners,* 30(1): 26–33.
19. Taylor, N.D. 1966. "Why Land-Use Planning, Part II," *Montana Business Quarterly,* 4(1): 44–53.
20. University of Montana. 1966. *Proceedings of the Recreation Planning Conference.* Missoula, Montana: University of Montana.

CHAPTER 3

HISTORICAL PERSPECTIVES OF PARK AND OUTDOOR RECREATION PLANNING

EARLY PARK PLANNING

Parks and outdoor recreation planning originated in early historical times; however, tracing the historical path is very difficult because there is no concerted movement—only fragments of history that we pool together and call the beginnings. Planning is more easily identified in the history of the United States, but even then some of the actions for planning and preserving open space are difficult to capture in any detail. Because of this, methods and motivations associated with planning are sometimes difficult to comprehend.

Modern park planning has only been in existence a short time—since the latter part of the nineteenth century. People, politicians, and planners always seem to *react,* rather than act. We never seem to be interested in preserving or conserving the valued resource until it is nearly depleted. It was not until the turn of the century that we began a concerted movement to preserve open space. And not until after the exploitation period of the early 1900s did some begin to feel that the natural resource base was finite. People only became important in the planning process when people began to crowd the cities. Later, with increased mobility, people began to seek refuge from the cityscape as the open space was consumed by industrial development and the automobile. In the last decades, people have become increasingly important in the planning process, even in the rural and wildland environs.

Planners have now realized that it takes a coordinated planning effort at all levels of government to provide a quality life, quality in the social, psychological and environmental aspects of *life, liberty, and the pursuit of leisure.*

EARLY PARKS—THE PRE-CHRISTIAN ERA

Early Asiatics of Mesopotamia are credited with initiating the park idea. These parks were an interspersal of woodland, vineyard, and ponds with well designed trail systems and an emphasis on maintaining natural aesthetics.[8] These open spaces were for the ruling, land-holding aristocrats' private, leisured enjoyment. The emphasis was strictly aesthetic enjoyment; the more difficult physical tasks were handled by peasants.

Gothein[8] credits the Sumerian King Gudea, about 2340 B.C., with initiating the first planned park-like landscape. These parkscapes became more elaborate in succeeding centuries with greater emphasis on formal landscape development and management. Still, aesthetics was the primary purpose of the landscape. The Hanging Gardens of Babylon (800–900 B.C.) exemplify this period of planning. Flowers and other exotic vegetation were introduced to the parkscape in the successive centuries.

In ancient Greece, parkscapes emphasized aesthetics and physical conditioning. Recreational facilities became a part of the parkscape— gymnasiums, hippodromes, and academies. Thus, parks were no longer merely places for aesthetic appreciation; programs attempted to condition body and mind as one. Out of this grew a love for competition and spectator sports and a development of architectural styles and themes for major sporting events.

The Roman Empire also shared many of these sports or recreational values, and it, too, developed facilities as monuments to god and man. They probably had more influence than other cultures on the early history of park planning because they "borrowed" many ideas and carried them throughout the known western world. They, too, influenced our city planning with their beautiful open spaces in the cities and villas (suburbs) near the outskirts of towns.

THE CHRISTIAN ERA THROUGH THE RENAISSANCE

The emphasis on aesthetic enjoyment and physical activity, primarily for the noble or ruling class, continued. Greater emphasis began to be placed on recreational facilities, probably because of Greek influences and the export of ideas by the Romans. More stadiums, gymnasiums, and race courses were constructed, and we even find the rudiments of ball fields and play areas. On the other hand, the hunting parks of the nobility became more elaborate, more intensively developed, and more intensively managed—with the introduction of exotic animal species such as elephants, lions, and giraffes.

Basically there was little change in parkscapes during early Christian times, except that the number of sports arenas and hunting grounds increased. At the fall of the Roman Empire (the beginning of the Middle Ages), the park declined in importance. Many of the parkscapes (the lands of the nobility) were acquired by orders of monks who maintained them, but because of the monks' seclusive habits, they were unable to further the park idea.

Gradually some of the nobility began to reacquire larger estates, and in the fourteenth century the emphasis began to shift back to formal gardens and the associated aesthetics. Also, during this period of time the people of Italy began to develop parks for the commoner. These parks were formally designed with walks, resting places, and statues. Probably the greatest influences on the "parks for people" concept were the monks who gave up some of their solitary habits to work for the benefit of all society.

The Renaissance brought interesting changes in leisure patterns and in park planning. In the 1500s and 1600s many modern types of facilities began to emerge—aviaries, fish ponds, summer homes, the weekend hideaway, and others. Other outdoor individual sports facilities, such as tennis courts, fowling courts, field archery courses, and playgrounds, were developed. Frequently these settings were beautiful with man-made aesthetics from statues, exotic vegetation, and fountains. Many of these very same ideas are commonplace today in larger urban and state parks.

The formal park design of the Renaissance years became the vogue in England, but by the latter part of the 18th century the formal design had been replaced by more informal, natural conditions. Natural aesthetics began to take precedence as the use of the parkscape switched to the commoner. This informality later affected park planning in the United States and continental Europe.

EARLY PARK PLANNING IN THE UNITED STATES

The first American parkscape is traced to the Boston Commons in 1634, and in 1640, these open spaces were given protection from further encroachment. In the same period, the Massachusetts Bay Colony set aside through the Great Ponds Act almost 90,000 acres of natural bodies of water for fishing and fowling.

William Penn advanced the commons idea (common open space)

when he decreed that ten acres of open space would be dedicated in the center of the new city of Philadelphia, and eight acres for each quarter of the town in residential development.

General James Oglethorpe in 1733 was more lavish in his design of park and open space for the city of Savannah, Georgia. He depicted large open spaces for common public uses and parkways lined with native trees. He even went to the trouble of saving many of the larger trees in the original town development.

Conceptually, this type of park planning reached a new level in the design of Washington, D.C. (then called Federal City), known as the city of the future where urban man and nature might live in harmony. The plan was drawn by Major L'Enfant under the guidance of George Washington and Thomas Jefferson, and generously provided for large parks and pleasuring gardens.

Unfortunately, most of the early parks gave way to other urban land uses, public abuses, and commercial pressures; they had no permanence in the new country. Other parks and parkscapes were planned, but none was more significant than Central Park.

THE CENTRAL PARK STORY

The Central Park story is interesting because of foresighted planning. Many present planning concepts stem from the Central Park plan and the later works of Mr. Fredrick Law Olmsted. Actually, William Cullen Bryant, the writer who captured nature in poetry, developed the idea as early as 1836 that New York City should reserve the finest woodland left where the residents could find respite from the urban landscape and enjoyment of pastoral life. However, it was not until July 3, 1844, that Bryant made this suggestion publicly as an editorial, "A New Park," in the *Evening Post*. He had traversed the island searching for the ideal parkscape and recommended Jones Woods as the site for the new park. Jones Woods was still relatively intact, and as fast as the city was growing, it might encircle the tract within the next decade or so. A year later, after a visit to London and its beautiful parks, Bryant became even more convinced of the need for a "central reservation" that people could enjoy on a continuous basis.

His repeated editorials brought the project before the public. Another advocate emerged in 1848, Andrew Jackson Downing, who wrote an article in the *Horticulturalist* entitled "A Talk About Public Parks and Gardens." He was displeased that people were so enamored with the commercial metropolis at the expense of other human values.

In 1851, Ambrose C. Kingsland, supported by the *Evening Post*, was elected mayor of New York City and favored the establishment of a public park. On April 5, 1851, Mayor Kingsland sent a historic message to the Common Council of the City stating that much of the open space set aside in the early 1800s was being lost and that the city needed to acquire more lands and formally dedicate them in perpetuity. He posed the problem, and it was up to the people to decide when, where, and how much. The Commons Committee on Lands and Places, to whom the problem was referred, reported favorably on the issue and recommended Jones Woods. However, opposition to the taking of Jones Woods immediately developed. Some wanted no park at all, while others felt that Jones Woods was too small for a large but growing city. Even Bryant began to feel that it was too small. Downing protested the site and the size and proposed the following in the *Horticulturalist* (August 1851):

> Looking at the present government of the city as about to provide, in the People's Park, a breathing zone, and healthful place for exercise for a city of half a million souls, we trust they will not be content with the limited number of acres already proposed. Five hundred acres is the smallest area that should be reserved for the future wants of such a city, now, while it may be obtained. Five hundred acres may be selected between 39th Street and the Harlem river, including a varied surface of land, a good deal of which is yet waste area, so that the whole may be purchased at something like a million dollars. In that area there would be space enough to have broad reaches of park and pleasure-grounds, with a real feeling of the breadth and beauty of green fields, the perfume and freshness of nature. In its midst would be located the great distributing reservoirs of the Croton aqueduct, formed into lovely lakes of limpid water, covering many acres, and heightening the charm of the sylvan accessories by the finest natural contrast. In such a park, the citizens who would take excursions in carriages, or on horseback, could have the substantial delights of country roads and country scenery, and forget for a time the rattle of the pavements and the glare of brick walls. Pedestrians would find quiet and secluded walks when they wished to be solitary, and broad alleys filled with thousands of happy faces, when they would be gay. The thoughtful denizen of the town would go out there in the morning to hold converse with the whispering trees, and the wearied tradesmen in the evening, to enjoy an hour of happiness by mingling in the open spaces with "all the world."
>
> The many beauties and utilities which would gradually grow out of a great park like this in a great city like New York, suggest themselves immediately and forcibly. Where would be found so fitting a position for noble works of art, the statues, monuments and buildings commemorative at once of the great men of the nation, of the history of the age and country, and the genius of our highest artists? In the broad area of such a verdant zone would gradually grow up, as the wealth of the city increases winter gardens of glass, like the great Crystal Palace, where the whole people could luxuriate in groves of the palms and spice trees of the tropics, at the same moment that sleighing parties

glided swiftly and noiselessly over the snow covered surface of the country-like avenues of the wintry park without. Zoological Gardens like those of London and Paris, would gradually be formed, by private subscription or public funds, where thousands of old and young would find daily pleasure in studying natural history, illustrated by all the wildest and strangest animals of the globe, almost as much at home in their paddocks and jungles, as if in their native forests; and Horticultural and Industrial Societies would hold their annual shows there, and great expositions of the arts would take place in spacious buildings within the park far more fittingly than in the noise and din of the crowded streets of the city. [16]

(Author's note: The preceding work gave great impetus to the park and open space planning movement. Likely Andrew Jackson Downing would have been the designer of Central Park, except that he drowned a year later in the Hudson while rescuing his mother-in-law in a steamboat disaster.)

The final recommendations for the park called for a more central location or central park idea. However, the *Evening Post* began to push for two parks—Jones Woods and Central Park. Bryant even suggested a series of parks to be developed over a period of time. The Board of Aldermen, however, adopted the Central Park theme and secured state legislative authorization to acquire the land on July 21, 1853. At the same time, the legislature passed a separate act for the acquisition of Jones Woods by the city. Opposition was so great to the two-park development that the Jones Woods Act was repealed in April 1854, losing a splendid opportunity for the development of a waterfront recreation site complex.

The period 1853 to 1856 was spent in actually acquiring the 624 acres of land from 59th to 106th Streets between Fifth and Eighth Avenues. In mid-1855, support was garnered to reduce the size of the park on the Fifth and Eighth Avenue sides and reserve a portion for villas. Although the measure was passed by the council, it was vetoed by Mayor Wood, who felt the necessity for the great park and that any reduction in size would limit its effectiveness.

On February 5, 1856, the state supreme court confirmed the report from the city's Commissioners of Estimate and Assessment. The amount paid to the landowners was $5,069,693, of which $1,657,590 was paid to adjacent landowners for loss of property value.

The years from 1856 to 1858 were difficult times, with many political battles over the potential park development. Contrary to belief, Central Park was not immediately designed and developed; it was held in political limbo for over two years. What development took place was unplanned; however, fortunately, the land was maintained mostly in a custodial state. The final plan for Central Park resulted from public competition —a competition that originated through political compromise.

On May 19, 1856, the Common Council adopted an ordinance giving the management of Central Park to a board of park commissioners, consisting of the mayor and the street commissioner. The new board was to have full authority to determine the development plan, to actually lay out the gardens, and to hire sufficient personnel to operate the park.

A few days later, Mr. Egbert L. Viele was appointed by the park board as its chief engineer to manage the park operations. Since 1853, Mr. Viele had secretly been preparing a preliminary topographic land survey and a general development plan for Central Park. Ironically, the plan was published in the first report of the Board of Park Commissioners, apparently tacitly accepted at the time of Mr. Viele's appointment. Little money was appropriated; thus, Viele's plan was never implemented. And on April 17, 1857, the state legislature passed an act for "the Regulation and Government of the Central Park in the City of New York." The reason for such a movement was the lack of progress and the corruption and inefficiency of the politicians in charge. The central authority was removed from the city government and vested in an independent commission, the Board of Commissioners. The new board appointed Mr. Viele as chief engineer on June 16, 1857, and at the same time adopted a resolution to advertise a planning contest in which monetary rewards would be paid for the four best park designs.

Party politics were still a part of the planning process for the newly appointed board. Even with the many squabbles, progress was being made—laborers were being hired and the position of superintendent was created. The man who filled the new position would be primarily an administrative officer to the chief engineer to oversee the maintenance and operations of the park.

Probably no one was better qualified for the position than Fredrick Law Olmsted. Olmsted had an intense interest in the out-of-doors and had developed skills in boating, camping, and so on. As a young man, he spent many hours thinking, dreaming, and studying the outdoors and how it affected man. He also devoted much time to reading about people and nature, philosophy and agriculture, the science and art of landscape gardening. He then became a farmer, raising the traditional agricultural and horticultural crops, and practiced landscaping gardening as well. As time passed, he turned more of his attention to landscape design and became a friend and colleague of Andrew Jackson Downing, the respected horticulturist and proponent of the Central Park idea.

History is not clear whether the meeting between Fredrick Law Olmsted and a park commissioner at a seaside inn was by chance or design; however, the result was that Olmsted applied for the superintendency. He was warned to develop some political support before applying. This he did when he submitted an application. Even with some political drawbacks, Olmsted was appointed as the superintendent of Central Park on September 11, 1857.

On the same day, the Board of Commissioners approved the final plan for the Central Park design competition. The rules were:

1. The board would choose the best four designs.
    a. First place $2000
    b. Second place $1000
    c. Third place $ 750
    d. Fourth place $ 500

2. All designs were to become property of the board.

3. The space was 770 acres, 2½ miles long by ½ mile wide. About 150 acres were to be reserved for the Reservoirs of the Croton Waters.

4. Development should be limited to the expenditure limit of 1.5 million dollars set by the legislature.

5. Four or more crossings from east to west must be made between 59th and 106 Streets.

6. A parade ground of 20–40 acres should be included, with arrangements for spectators.

7. Three playgrounds of 3–10 acres should be included.

8. A site for a future exhibition/concert hall should be reserved.

9. A site for one principal fountain and one prospect tower should be reserved.

10. Grounds should be reserved and designed for a 2–3 acre flower garden.

11. Space should be reserved for a winter area.

12. The designs should be to the scale of 1 inch equal to 100 feet.

13. Designs should be in India ink and sepia, with no colors.

14. Each design should be accompanied by a concise written description, and the designer's name in a sealed envelope.

Interestingly, Frederick Law Olmsted deliberately avoided the competition because his superior, Mr. Viele, was to enter the plan he had

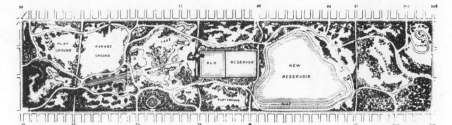

Figure 3–1 *Greensward,* the selected plan for developing Central Park, designed by Olmsted and Vaux in 1858. The park is elongated between 59th and 106th Streets.

developed several years earlier. However, Mr. Viele boasted of his own plan while indicating indifference to others of his staff entering the competition. Thus, Olmsted changed his mind and accepted an earlier invitation by Calvert Vaux to collaborate on a plan for Central Park.

Although his superintendent's duties consumed most of the days, Olmstead spent nights and weekends working with Vaux on the design of the park. Even midnight walks were taken to observe the land and to discuss possible courses of action. Their work was finally completed under the title of *Greensward* (Figure 3–1) on the last day of the competition.

There were thirty-five plans submitted, and on April 28, 1858, after careful review, the commissioners awarded first prize to number 33, *Greensward,* because of its innovative design techniques beyond the rules established for the competition.

Central Park — An Interpretation

Many concepts that are a part of the present park and recreation planning effort were incorporated in the Olmsted and Vaux plan for Central Park. Although many appear very subtle in their use and some were never fully explained by the two designers, this section will attempt to interpret the *Greensward* plan.

Planning to Meet Human Needs

1. Planning should be based on well-defined objectives. Developments have no basis for existence unless their objectives are founded on human values—the welfare of the people. And at any particular time, one can only measure success by reflecting on the established objectives. Olmsted and Vaux felt that Central Park was a single, coordinated work of art that should be "framed upon a single, noble motive."[16]

2. Leisure needs are continuous, rather than intermittent. Most people in the United States live within the urban environs, and Olmsted and

Vaux foresaw this condition in New York City. Many of these people would live out their entire lives within these urban environs of buildings and paved streets and smog; and, if it were not for large, planned open spaces, these people would find no visual and healthful respite. Others can only find temporary relief through weekend holidays and vacations. Olmsted and Vaux stated:

> that millions upon millions of men were to live their lives upon this island, millions more to go out from it, or its immediate densely populated suburbs, only occasionally and at long intervals, and that all its inhabitants would assuredly suffer, in greater or lesser degree, according to their occupations and the degree of confinement to it, from influences engendered by these conditions.[16]

3. All uses are not necessarily compatible. In the Central Park plan, interrelationships of activities and supporting facilities were considered. Any particular parcel of land developed for recreational uses cannot be all things to all user groups. Certain uses are compatible and interdependent and should be planned to enhance these characteristics, whereas other uses are not compatible and are independent, and should be spatially separated to minimize conflict and confusion. Ideally the planner should develop harmony in order to maximize social benefit to the user public while minimizing the social costs involved in providing for those recreational uses.

4. Recreation is for all social classes. The *Greensward* plan allayed the fears of many that the park was to be designed for the upper social classes when the plan description stated, "the primary purpose of the Park is to provide the best practicable means of healthful recreation for the inhabitants of all classes."[16]

This was the beginning of modern park planning, relating particularly to the urbanist. Many planning and design techniques came from this humble beginning. However, the greatest lesson to be learned—to plan to meet specific human needs—somehow has been lost in our greed to consume land and its natural features in the name of urbanization and progress.

Natural Aesthetics and Environmental Perception

1. Park and recreation planning should present an antithesis to man-made objects, particularly the effects of urbanization. Efforts should be made to minimize the visual effects of existing developments within and along the periphery of the parks. Wherever landscape manipulation is necessary, one should make it appear as natural as possible, and all physical improvements necessary to provide access, activities, and services should blend with the natural landscape features.

2. Plan the layout around existing landscape features, rather than using modern heavy equipment to manipulate the landscape to the demands of the plan. Olmsted wrote, "interfere with its easy, undulating outlines, and picturesque, rocky scenery as little as possible . . . how

important they felt to be the subordination of architectural and engineering features to the predominate rural character.''[16] This idea distinguished *Greensward* from the other plans. Unfortunately many planners have not learned this principle, and consequently many beautiful sites have become victims of the bulldozer. This practice in turn creates other resource management problems such as erosion, reestablishment of vegetation, disruption of visual harmony, and others.

3. Landscape perception is important in adapting plans to human needs. Olmsted believed in screening to hide incongruent elements of the landscape and to create an illusion of unlimited open space (without man-made development) even in high-density urban areas. Thus, one could create environs that appear larger than they really are. On the other hand, one can shrink the psychological (perceived) size by allowing incongruent and unwanted elements.

4. Variety and contrast of scenery are important to environmental perception. What is important is how people perceive a landscape or landscape element. Thus, Olmsted felt that the landscape elements were only important as they affected people. Contrast would give greater depth perception, better definition of form (size and shape) and spatial relationships. Variety would give the suggestion of unlimited range of landscape conditions while relieving visual monotony through constant change.

Recreational Planning Must Mirror Management

1. Employ natural features to separate use patterns. The two planners envisioned Central Park as a place with distinct land features which, if properly utilized in the design, could tend naturally to segregate different use patterns, particularly the potentially more conflicting ones. Natural vegetation and bold land features were used to separate activities and to encourage certain movement patterns from one scene/activity setting to another.

2. Separate potentially conflicting modes of travel. This principle is not utilized by many outdoor recreation planners; yet, because of modern means of recreational travel, we have greater potential for conflict than we did a century ago. Amazingly foresighted, Olmsted and Vaux observed that problems:

> both in our own streets and European parks, led to the planning of a system of independent ways [travel routes]; 1st, for carriages; 2nd, for horsemen wishing to gallop; 3rd, for footmen; and 4th, for common street traffic requiring to cross the park. By this means it was made possible even for the most timid and nervous to go on foot to any district of Park designed to be visited, without crossing a line of wheels on the same level, and consequently, without occasion for anxiety or hesitation.[16]

3. Planning should reflect programs to be offered, and the basic division was into programs for children and adults. Family recreation is

desirable and should be fostered to promote family cohesiveness; however, children have their special needs in their interaction with each other and their environment (the requirements of the social and educational growth of the child). Thus, special programs should be planned for the child beyond the offerings to family and adults. These needs were incorporated into the *Greensward* plan as described in the accompanying report:

> Children will come to the Park in large numbers while yet too young to have the tastes and habits with regard to which its arrangements are generally designed, and localities in which they can be more particularly cared for are thus desirable.[16]

4.   Development of a park system is necessary to provide for a variety of recreational needs, a system that should be integrated with the other social service systems. Olmsted and Vaux felt that New York City should expand the park operations and develop a coordinated system of park properties. Furthermore, they felt that this system should be integrated with the other public service delivery systems of the city. Unfortunately, this concept was not implemented, but it did establish the idea of a totally integrated planning system—something we are still striving to accomplish!

Design Techniques in Recreation Planning

These techniques have been summarized by Frank A. Waugh (1918) as the Olmstedian principles:

1.   Preserve the natural scenery and if necessary restore and emphasize it.
2.   Avoid all formal design except in very limited areas without buildings.
3.   Keep open lawns and meadows in large central areas.
4.   Use native trees and shrubs, especially in heavy border plantings.
5.   Provide circulation by means of paths and roads laid in wide-sweeping curves.
6.   Place the principal road so that it will approximately circumscribe the whole area.

OUTDOOR RECREATION AND LAND USE PLANNING—A HISTORICAL PERSPECTIVE

Many events have influenced the history of outdoor recreation in the United States. Probably none is more important than the establishment of Yellowstone National Park in 1872. Even though other similar events preceded it, this event was probably the most significant one because it established the procedure of dedicating *large* parcels of land for public benefit, use, and enjoyment. Other types of public lands were later to evolve out of this concept.

Development of the Concept (1850–1891). Most people during the early 1800s felt that land and the other resources were unlimited. In fact many resources presented barriers to westward expansion and the development for man's use. Consequently many resources were destroyed, overused, and exploited in taming the land and molding it to agricultural practices, development, and later urbanization. However, a few people were concerned about the exhaustibility of many of our resources. Generally it was the philosophical writer and the poet, such as Thoreau and Marsh, who attempted to create an awareness of the inherent aesthetic and cultural qualities of nature and the need to preserve nature for the enjoyment of all the people. Through their efforts, many of the negative attitudes toward nature began to wane, and a few staunch supporters began to push for establishment of areas for the protection of the natural qualities and for public enjoyment.

The first thrust was the Yosemite Grant Act of 1864, which turned over to the state of California the Yosemite Valley and the Mariposa Grove of Big Trees for preservation and recreational use. The language of the Yosemite bill established an intent (use and preservation) which was incorporated into the Yellowstone Park Act and later statutes. The Yosemite Grant later became the heartland of Yosemite National Park.

Even though the language and concept had been developed earlier, the Yellowstone National Park Act established legal precedence for preserving large acreages for public benefit, use, and enjoyment. Several national parks—Sequoia, General Grant, and Yosemite—were established in the late 1800s, using Yellowstone National Park as the model. This activity stimulated interest in other types of public land uses—water, wildlife, forestry, and so on. In 1881, the Federal Division of Forestry was established in the Department of Agriculture to advise on national timber and land policies. However, it was not until 1891 that we established public forest lands under the Forest Reserve Act. The first was the Yellowstone Timber Reserve and was administered by the General Land Office of the Department of the Interior—with advice from the division of Forestry. This event was the culmination of the development of the public land use concept for the American public, even though the size of public use lands has grown considerably since then. The successive stages reflect changes in planning and management strategies as applied to these lands.

Custodial Stage (1891–1930). The first public reserves were in the west because most of the lands in the eastern part of the United States had been claimed for private ownership. Several large reserves were established in the west. For the most part, recreation was not considered an important component of the administration because of the isolation of the large populations in the east and the need to develop the economies of local communities. Consequently little concern was given to any land use planning or to recognize recreation as a legitimate use of public lands.

These reserves were transferred to the Forest Service (the old Forestry Division and the later Bureau of Forestry) in 1905 and renamed National Forests. However, lack of interest in land use planning and development of recreation opportunities continued; the administration of the lands was primarily custodial in the use and protection of the public lands, but not in terms of management to sustain certain qualities and resources.

Thus, this period in outdoor recreation planning is affectionately called the "crapping can planning stage," since the only concern was in providing outhouses for the visitor. There was no concern for the development of recreational opportunities, accessibility, or comfort-convenience for him.

These attitudes slowly began to change. Leopold[12] and Marshall[13] advanced ideas about the need for preserving the wilderness and managing the lands for public use. Cleveland,[3] a national forest employee, saw the value of recreation for the health and well-being of the public. This type of agency philosophy, coupled with the Weeks Act (the purchase of land for National Forests in the east) boosted the image and the need for recreation. But little concern was given to recreation until Frank A. Waugh's report, "Recreation Uses of the National Forests," the first official U.S. Forest Service study of recreation. The report recognized recreation as one of the major uses of national forests. Even then very little money was allocated to recreation planning development.

In 1925, at the insistence of Chief Forester Greeley, the Forest Service adopted a policy of integrating recreation with other land uses to guide the development of recreational facilities. This policy was further augmented by the Recreation and Public Purposes Act of 1926 (P.L. 69–386), which recognized recreation as a legitimate use of public lands along with uses such as timber, minerals, and grazing. Later legislation supplemented this statute; however, a significant result of the custodial stage was that people began to see the need for planning and the potential role of outdoor recreation on the public lands.

Welfare Development Stage (1930–1950). The stock market crash of 1929 certainly curtailed any development plans initiated during the 1920s; however, with the onset of the Great Depression, several governmental public works programs were started. The more intensive programs were the Civilian Conservation Corps and the Works Progress Administration. These intensive recreational development programs were not the result of increased demand or foresighted planning. Generally, these were make-work projects to put people to work so those seeking employment could maintain some minimal family earnings. Furthermore, attempts were made to keep rural residents in a rural setting by developing road, building, and recreational facility projects on public lands near rural residents. It was essential that the projects be developed on public lands for the long-run

Figure 3–2 Typical recreation facility developed as a CCC project, Fort Clark, Colorado (photograph by Bureau of Outdoor Recreation, Mid-Continent Region, Denver, Colorado).

benefit of the general public. Interestingly, many projects were oriented to the development of roads and auto-related facilities, even though automobile use was still very minimal.

Many of the present recreation facilities on public domain lands were developed during this period. Much emphasis was placed on obtaining native material—logs, stone, and so forth; consequently, many of the projects are very rustic in appearance and blend well with the landscape. Some masonry and hand-hewn beams are characteristic of the structures, items which are too expensive for present-day public development.

This period was also the beginning of recreation management planning. Because of the increase in public recreation, some of the more favored places were becoming overused. As indicated in 1930 by E.P. Meinecke, a U.S. Forest Service plant pathologist who studied the effects of recreational use on vegetation, root damage and soil compaction were affecting the growth and vigor of the trees. Also, loss of ground vegetation and subsequent erosion were causing serious loss of site productivity.

From these types of studies, the Forest Service began to formulate management planning guidelines to minimize the damage. The guidelines basically included an analysis of site factors such as soil, vegetation, and weather that a planner should consider in locating a development on a particular site. Other considerations were design features to control use and minimize site maintenance, such as a well-planned road system and placing each development on a fixed site coordinated with the road system. Essentially, this type of feature involved hardening the site to handle large numbers of visitors with minimum long-term effect on the site.

Thus, although this period is the beginning of recreation planning on the public domain, one should remember that the planning was totally resource oriented with no regard for the needs of the visitor, his normal behavior, or the quality of the experience offered him.

Mass Use and Development Stage (1950–1970). World War II helped America overcome the problems of the Great Depression. It brought the country out of its economic woes and united the American people. However, it was not until the late 1940s that we began to recover completely and flex our industrial might. Thus, by 1950 the American life style had drastically changed and would change even more in the next two decades. Americans cast off their economic austerity and sought more and better consumer goods and new forms of recreation to match their new life styles.

Because of this new prosperity, Americans enjoyed more money, more leisure time, and greater personal mobility. These factors created a phenomenal increase in recreation participation, far beyond the capacities of the existing facilities. Crash programs were developed to modernize existing facilities and to add new ones.

The two most noteworthy planning efforts, because of their magnitude, were Mission 66, initiated by the National Park Service in 1956, and the Operations Outdoors Programs initiated by the U.S. Forest Service in 1958. Both of these programs were to meet with minimal success because of poor demand projections of recreational needs and haste in properly locating the developments. Demand for recreational opportunities continued to spiral and planning was further complicated by the rapid expansion of the recreational vehicle market—snowmobiles, trail bikes, and self-contained campers. Thus, the gap between demand and supply has continually widened since the early 1960s, and the greatest emphasis has shifted to the new challenge—the recreational vehicle.

The planning problems were not only with recreation but also with other land uses such as water, timber, mining, agriculture, and urbanization, and with the interaction of these uses in terms of conflict and incompatibility. The problem became one of how to integrate these uses while providing for the total needs of the American public. This problem has become more acute as demand for the various uses has spiraled, while the resource has stabilized or dwindled. Thus, resource managers faced with scarce resources must rationalize a priority system for allocation. Even broader than this, they must look at the total environment and the effects of planning decisions on the physical and mental well-being of mankind. They cannot afford to destroy our life support systems, our open spaces, or our visual landscape harmony without deleterious effects on the American society. In the late 1960s many people, particularly the young, asked themselves about the long-term effects of our life style. These types of questions motivated some to seek new values and meanings of life. These new values seemed to focus on a quality environment—both socially and ecologically.

Quality of Life Stage (1970–present). The quality of the environment (ecologically and sociologically) has received greater emphasis in the 1970s than ever before in our history. Since we have become an urbanized technological society, technology has governed the direction of events as indicated in Figure 3–3; many people want to change this direction.

The last spontaneous social change not caused by technology was the American Revolutionary War. The greatest cultural change since then was the urbanization of the latter 1800s, caused by the Industrial Revolution. Cultural and ecological changes have been taking place since then, caused by the exploitation of new-found technology. Leisure patterns, particularly in the 1950s and 1960s, changed drastically because of the technological changes in the recreation equipment industry—the self-contained trailer, the motor home, the trail bike, the all-terrain vehicle, the snowmobile, and other lesser-known equipment. All of these had their social and ecological impact on modern man and his leisure behavior.

Our society, particularly the younger segment, is questioning the idea that technology should control the destiny of mankind. These people feel that modern man should be the cause rather than an effect. The system should be humanized to return dignity to man, rather than to the machine, and that man should live in harmony with nature.

Some long-term trends in leisure patterns seem to be emerging. People are driving their automobiles less and walking or hiking more. The emphasis seems to be going to the nonvehicular and self-reliant types of activities, usually participated in by small groups. Because of the trends of stable resource base and increase in population, greater emphasis must be placed on intensive planning before development (social and resource systems) and on management after the development.

In sum, "quality" has become a byword of the 1970s to express our feelings about the American life style and the environment in which we live. A parallelism in outdoor recreation planning is that "quality" should also be the byword for the American leisure style and the environment in which we play.

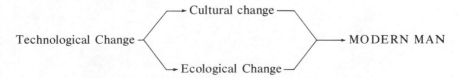

Figure 3–3 Modern man: a product of technological change.

SELECTED READINGS

1. Brockman, C. F., and L. C. Merriam, Jr. 1973. *Recreational Use of Wild Lands*. 2nd Edition. New York: McGraw-Hill Book Co.
2. Bureau of Land Management. 1962. *Historical Highlights of Public Land Management*. U.S. Department of Interior.
3. Clawson, M. 1968. *The Land System of the United States*. Lincoln, Nebraska: University of Nebraska Press.
4. Cleveland, T. 1910. "National Forests as Recreation Grounds" *Annals of the American Academy of Political and Social Science*, 35 (2): 241–247.
5. Doell, C.E., and G.B. Fitzgerald. 1954. *A Brief History of Parks and Recreation in the United States*. Chicago: Athletic Institute.
6. Doell, C.E., and Louis F. Twardzik. 1973. *Elements of Park and Recreational Administration*. Minneapolis: Burgess Publishing Company.
7. Fabos, J.G., O.T. Milde, and V.M. Weinmayr. 1968. *Fredrick Law Olmsted, Sr.* Amherst, Massachusetts: University of Massachusetts Press.
8. Gotheim, M.L. 1928, *A History of Garden Art*. Vol. I, II. New York: Dutton Publishing Co.
9. Huth, H. 1957. *Nature and the American*. Berkeley, California: University of California Press.
10. Ise, J. 1961. *Our National Park Policy*. Baltimore: The Johns Hopkins Press.
11. Lee, R.F. 1972. *Family Tree of the National Park System*. Philadelphia: Eastern National Park and Monument Association.
12. Leopold, A. 1925. "The Last Stand of the Wilderness," *American Forestry and Forest Life*, 31: 599–604.
13. Marshall, R. 1930. "The Problem of Wilderness," *Scientific Monthly*.
14. Maughan, O. 1934. *Recreational Development in the National Forests*. Syracuse, New York: New York State College of Forestry. Technical Publication No. 45.
15. Nash, R. 1968. *The American Environment: Readings in the History of Conservation*. Reading, Massachusetts: Addison-Wesley Publishing Company.
16. Olmsted, F.L., Jr., and T. Kimball. 1970. *Frederick Law Olmsted, Landscape Architect, 1822–1903*. Vol. I, II. New York: Benjamin Blom, Inc.
17. Padover, S.K. (ed.). 1946. *Jefferson and the National Capitol*. Washington, D.C.: U.S. Government Printing Office.
18. Reed, H.H., and S. Duckworth. 1967. *Central Park: A History and A Guide*. New York: Potter.
19. Waugh, F.A. 1918. *Recreation Uses on the National Forests*. Washington, D.C.: U.S. Forest Service. Misc. Publication No. 462.

CHAPTER 4

THE PLANNING MODEL

There is a need to organize any planning effort so that the proper data inputs are developed for each specific situation, and so that the outputs are analyzable in terms of decision making. Development of *planning models* is necessary to ensure organization of the entire planning effort and to enhance the decision making by making it more objective and more consistent in application. However, the model does not make the decision; the planner must take the output and temper it with professional judgment. The model merely gives the planner a means of handling large amounts of data and integrating large numbers of variables in the decision making.

To develop a systems planning model, the planner starts with the selection of a general paradigm and then adapts it to the specific situations (from the general to the specific). Once this is done, the planner must decide what variables are important as inputs into the model. He must remember that some variables may be important but are not controllable in terms of their effects on the visitor or the resource. After the variables are selected, the planner must determine the best method of measurement in order to integrate these variables into the model. The final steps require analyzing the data, possibly through computer programming for certain outputs, and the outputs then become the prime bases for the final decision.

DEVELOPMENT OF A BASIC PLANNING MODEL

A planning model is a symbolic representation of the relevant aspects of a real situation. Also, inherent in a model is a series of connected and identifiable relationships that indicate possible results of a given action. Models will vary considerably in their description of events and their sophistication in measuring them. Nevertheless the planner will better understand the important relationships and develop the plan accordingly.

The model should be representative of particular planning situations, and the total planning environment should be included—social, ecological, and service variables. And, finally, any model framework should show primary and secondary inputs to produce a given output.[4] The framework is:

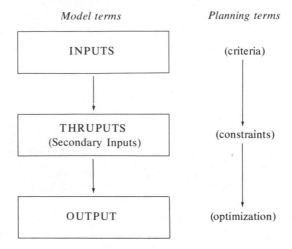

Figure 4-1   Planning model framework.

The output is the optimization of the recreation experience or experiences for a given area. The thruputs are constraints on the recreation system to provide maximum benefits to the total user population; examples are the resource and service limitations. The inputs are the criteria that the planner determines to have the greatest effects on the particular recreation experience or experiences. In the input and thruput steps, components, variables, and interrelationships must be developed. Environmental perception would be a component in the input (criteria) step, and hazard perception would be a variable under this component. The measurement and weighting of this particular variable must be relative to the output (recreation experience), because hazard perception will vary considerably for the picnicker, camper, and backpacker. For an example of a planning model using the above framework, see Chapter 5, page 64.

The optimization model is preferred over the maximization model because of the tremendous array of recreation experiences for which one must plan; certain inherent conflicts between many types of opportunities; the "inefficiency" in certain types of opportunities, in terms of allocation of planning time, funds, and recreational space; and the lack of sophisticated measuring devices to determine the benefits derived from planning actions.

The optimization model reflects a need for quantitative analysis of behavior and its environmental effects and for each criterion to be measured on an interval scale. However, outdoor recreation planning has not developed to that level of sophistication. Thus, the model should be called an "improvement model" where the measurements are relative values (good, better, best) of each criterion and the planning decisions are based on the interrelations of the criteria developed through systems analysis.

The last element of model building is verification, or model validity. Model validity refers to the correspondence of the model to the real situation, including the components and variables, their depicted relationships, and assumptions. Model verification is extremely important and should be continuously reassessed in light of new research findings, planning experiences, and change in planning strategies or philosophies.

STEPS IN THE PLANNING PROCESS

It seems essential to elaborate on the planning process in order to understand some of the potential subsystems and the chronology of outdoor recreation planning.

Establishment of Objectives. Establishment of objectives is the foundation for any type of planning. It is especially critical in outdoor recreation planning because of increase in demands, increase in population, and decrease in the total land for recreation opportunities. There are several inputs which can be used in the establishment of objectives, and these should be evaluated individually for inclusion in the planning effort.

1. *Behavioral and Demand Studies.* Demand studies are necessary to establish the trends in participation rates and possible "classical" demand in terms of a latent desire to participate in certain activities or leisure styles. These should be done on a regional and nationwide basis and must then be adapted to specific areas based on a knowledge of the potential user groups and their behavioral norms.

The problem with direct application of demand statistics to planning is that the planner has no way of converting the rates of participation into the allocation of space for certain types of recreational activities. The only way the planner can properly allocate space is to combine participation rates with the behavioral requirements of the particular user population. Thus, we must determine the behavioral norms in terms of the way people participate, i.e., size of territory, personal space, social interaction, service requirements. For example, the hiker from eastern New Jersey may have quite different behavioral norms and subsequent spatial needs in his hiking experiences than a person from western Wyoming.

In sum, demand studies are necessary to establish the use trends, but the allocation of space for certain types of recreational developments must be adjusted based on the behavioral needs of the various user groups. Thus, the combination of the two can be used as one of the bases for establishing objectives for *regional* and *area* planning (Chapter 10, Regional and Area Planning).

2. *Public Opinion.*   Involvement of public opinion in the planning process has become mandatory in our society, regardless of whether the planning is in the public or private sector. Various methods have been devised to encourage this type of input, since it can give the planner an idea of the current interest in the area and the attitudes of the user public about the potential of the area for certain types of activities and land uses.

Measurement of public opinion is extremely difficult; some problems of measurement can be overcome, although others are not as controllable. Thus, the planner should be cautious in using public opinion that has been typically gathered in a very fragmented way and not correlated or validated with other user data.

3. *Potential of the Area.*   The potential of the resource to provide certain opportunities must be evaluated, because such an evaluation establishes the range of potential opportunities (objectives). Certain types of uses can be eliminated from further consideration if the land features or other elements are not suitable for those types of developments. An example might be drawn from the experience of a person seeking a wilderness experience in a pristine environment, yet in a place where the resource areas are small with developed road systems. Or there may be a demand for winter sports in a place where the snow conditions and the length of the season are not conducive to them.

It then becomes the responsibility of the agency to assess the potential and limitations of an area and make these known to the public.

4. *Enabling and Secondary Legislation.*   Legislation can delimit the range of possible land use objectives for a given agency. Also, the agencies' interpretations of the statutes can further restrict possible land use alternatives. For example, the basic tenets of national park policy — use versus preservation — are a part of the original National Park Act of 1916 and were further interpreted by Secretary of the Interior Frank K. Lane in a letter dated May 13, 1918. The ideas were later refined in a letter by Secretary of the Interior Hobert Work on March 11, 1925. Interestingly, each park has its own enabling act (secondary legislation to the original 1916 act), and these acts may vary greatly from some aspects of the 1916 act's intent. Political tradeoffs and other antecedents affect the final draft of the statutes that authorize each national park; consequently, the secondary legislation can severely restrict the ensuing planning.

The U.S. Forest Service is in a similar situation. The original enabling acts identify certain roles in relation to resource management. These roles have been further delimited by subsequent legislation such as the Multiple Use Act of 1960, the Wilderness Preservation Act of 1964, and others.

Thus, each land management agency has certain roles to play in provisioning for certain types of land uses, including outdoor recreation. Regardless of how the roles are developed, the basic foundation is legislation and the result is a delimiting of the scope of planning.

Coordination of Planning.   Coordination of planning is essential to the success of the overall planning effort. With increasing participation and scarce resources, proper coordination can minimize duplication of development and reduce the voids in provisioning for recreational opportunities.

There are three types of coordination:

1. *Intra-agency.*   Coordination is sometimes difficult to achieve even within an organization; however, it is particularly necessary because most administrative boundary lines do not reflect boundaries of participation patterns. In addition, with coordination, the agency can extend its efficiency and effectiveness in the allocation of the organizational fiscal and natural resources.

2. *Interagency.*   Agencies must cooperate in planning since the recreationist ordinarily does not recognize agency boundaries in his activity participation. Too often in the past, agencies have been provincial in recreation planning without regard to the role of other agencies.

3. *Private Sector.*   The private sector contains almost 70 per cent of the total land base and must contribute more to the recreation resource base. Much of the planning data is developed by public agencies, some of which should be coordinated with the private sector to encourage various types of commercial recreation development.

Projection of Needs.   The planner must project the activity and behavioral needs of the recreationist in order to provide the desired types of areas, sites, and facilities. Too often the planner is satisfied with mere projections of activity patterns; however, he should also evaluate behavior in terms of the way people participate in a given activity. Merely projecting the demand for camping is insufficient. One needs to know the specific types of camping behavior—tent or RV, long-term or central, family or group, multiple or single activity, and so on.

Furthermore, the planner should understand the recreation experience—the user satisfaction and benefits derived from the experience, and the motivations and perception that molded the particular behavior.

Implementation of Plans.   The previous steps should enable the planner to determine the best alternatives of programs, sites, and facilities. Once these alternatives are selected, a time schedule should be initiated to establish a priority of development. The planner should then follow up with timely supervision to ensure that the developments are on schedule, facilities are properly located, and construction meets specifications.

Reevaluation of Plans.   Planning is a continuing process. Societal needs change, and facilities become obsolete because of changes in behavior. Consequently the planner needs to foresee these changes and adjust planning techniques and strategies accordingly. This continuous reevaluation of existing plans is called "plan maintenance."

TOWARD A RECREATION PLANNING MODEL

The following basic planning models develop the components, variables, and relationships of outdoor recreation planning. Several approaches are presented to expose the reader to a broad spectrum of planning models.

Concentric Circle Model. The concentric circle model defines the limits of the planning system by identifying the basic components and their relationships:

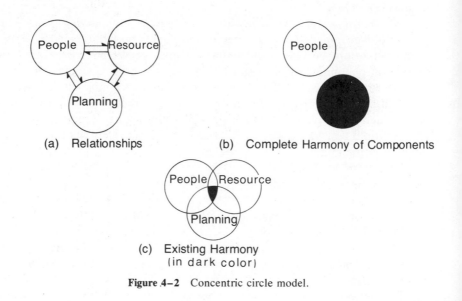

(a) Relationships   (b) Complete Harmony of Components

(c) Existing Harmony
(in dark color)

Figure 4–2 Concentric circle model.

The basic model components are people, resource, and management, each component affecting the other two (Figure 4–2[a]). The components are shown as concentric circles because they are separate systems by themselves, or subsystems of the model. The resources are the natural resources such as the land, water, air, flora, fauna, and natural agents that constitute the recreational environment. The interrelationships of the resources determine the characteristic appearance and stability of the particular resource setting. This situation affects the types of recreational experiences that can be provided.

The people (users) component is the social subsystem for which we are planning. The motivations and perceptions of people are the products of the world in which they live; these vary according to the conditions under which they live. Thus, there is a continuum of recreational needs that must be satisfied through planning.

Planning, as indicated in Figure 4–2(b), is the component that develops harmony between the people and the resource—to provide for the recreational needs of people while minimizing the effects of the user on the resource. In reality there is only a small degree of harmony between the visitor, the resource, and the planning (Figure 4–2[c]). More sophisticated planning can improve the performance, but there will never be total harmony (a situation where there is no uncertainty or unknown in the planning process).

User-Resource Relationship Model. This model requires an assessment of leisure needs and resource capability to provide various recreational opportunities on an area basis (Figure 4–3). The visitor needs and resource potential are interpreted in a proposed *area-wide plan.* There are three basic steps:

1. *Identify Recreation Users and Resources.* Leisure needs are analyzed on both bases in terms of existing activity participation patterns (commonly called "macro-behavioral patterns)" and expressed interests in other unavailable activities, or modifications of existing ones. User groups are then formed on the basis of having similar recreational activity (existing or desired) requirements. These are cross-classified with social and economic characteristics to define the user group further. In theory, we determine not only what is demanded but who is demanding it.

The resource base is analyzed for two purposes. First, we must identify the environmental stability and scenic qualities of the landscape. We must evaluate the environmental elements such as soil, vegetation, hydrology, and so on and the possible effects recreational and other potential land uses have on maintaining the landscape. We must also evaluate the landscape personality in relation to the scenic and natural qualities that attract the visitor.

Once this step is completed, we can proceed to the measurement of the physical qualities of various sites to determine their suitability for providing various recreational opportunities. There are guides for making determinations for sites such as campgrounds, winter sports development, and others. The important point to remember is that the landscape personality (environmental stability, and scenic and natural qualities) and the suitability of a given resource area determine the *potential* supply of resource-oriented recreational opportunities.

2. *Estimate Recreation Demand and Supply.* The next step is to compare demand with existing supply (already developed sites) and potential supply developed in Step 1. In recreation planning, we are continuously dealing with a shortage of opportunities relative to demand. Thus, we can expect a sizable gap between existing supply and demand. After this gap is identified for the particular planning region or area, the planner should

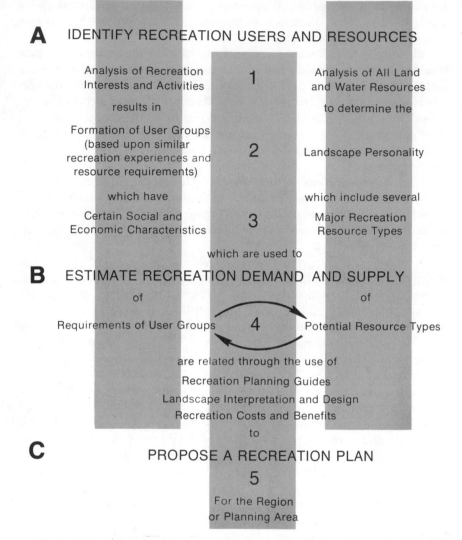

A IDENTIFY RECREATION USERS AND RESOURCES

Analysis of Recreation   1   Analysis of All Land
Interests and Activities   and Water Resources

results in   to determine the

Formation of User Groups
(based upon similar   2   Landscape Personality
recreation experiences and
resource requirements)

which have   which include several

Certain Social and   3   Major Recreation
Economic Characteristics   Resource Types

which are used to

B ESTIMATE RECREATION DEMAND AND SUPPLY

of   of

Requirements of User Groups   4   Potential Resource Types

are related through the use of

Recreation Planning Guides
Landscape Interpretation and Design
Recreation Costs and Benefits

to

C   PROPOSE A RECREATION PLAN

5

For the Region
or Planning Area

Figure 4–3 A diagram of user-resource relationships. This model was developed by Anderson, K. R., 1959. *A User-Resource Recreation Planning Method* Loomis, California: National Advisory Council on Regional Recreation Planning.

develop a priority system of project development to meet the higher priority recreational needs.

3. *Develop a Proposed Recreational Plan.*   The requirements of the various user groups and the recreational potential of the resource are integrated on a regional or area level to offer the maximum variety of opportunities, relative to demand, within reasonable travel distance for the user groups. The recreational planning guides and landscape interpretation indicated in the model refer to planning policy that attempts to account for

normal behavior patterns of a user group, that incorporates legislative or legal requirements, and that projects the service and environmental constraints of a given resource type.

Previously, we determined what types of opportunities would be preferred by whom (Step 1) and then the potential of the resource to provide for these opportunities (Step 2). This last step attempts to determine the best location (*where*) for the opportunities based on *what* (activities) are demanded, *who* is demanding them, and *types* of resource limitations in the area.

Systems Planning Model.   The basic systems model expands the concentric circle model to include specific variables and their interrelationships (Figure 4–4). The major subsystems are the visitor, the resource, and the planning, which are interrelated through either cause and effect relationships or developed management programs. It is not a closed system; many *external* variables affect internal variables and relationships. The planner must recognize the external variables and their possible effects on the internal relationships. For example, leisure behavior patterns may be drastically changed by the reduction of available energy resources

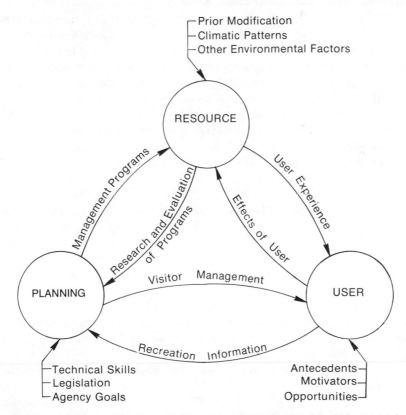

Figure 4–4 The outdoor recreation systems planning model. This model is an adaptation of one used by S.S. Frissell, University of Montana, Missoula, Montana.

(primarily in the form of petroleum products). This type of change could affect the systems planning and thus should be monitored and evaluated for its possible effects.

Also, the planner should discriminate between controllable and noncontrollable variables. Controllable variables are those that can be manipulated to produce a given effect, or desirable outcome. For example, the site may be hardened to handle the increased visitor impact. Or the visitor management program can be altered to encourage better dispersal of recreation use over a given area, particularly if the first program (hardening of the site) was not a desirable alternative.

Noncontrollable variables are those which can not be manipulated directly to produce a given outcome. However, they should still be accounted for in the planning process because they can affect planning programs. The backgrounds of the visitors and their leisure needs are generally not controllable, although planners may control certain on-site behaviors; yet these form *the primary input* in the planning process. Cyclic weather patterns are not controllable but must be accounted for in planning a particular area. We could develop enclosed facilities or encourage use during the better weather periods, however.

1. *Subsystems.*   The following are descriptions of the subsystems:

a.   *Resource.*   The resource base is a separate subsystem that is molded by factors external to the model. It is composed of the soil, water, flora, fauna, and abiotic elements of the particular environmental setting. Its natural characteristics and adaptability for recreation opportunities are affected by cyclic climatic patterns, natural processes (such as fire, insects, flooding, etc.), and prior land use modifications by man.

b.   *User.*   The user is the key element in the planning process. It is for him that we develop programs and plans to provide for basic user satisfactions and benefits. The external effects are best summarized as leisure needs—needs that are derived from personal motivations, perceptions, and situational antecedents.

c.   *Planning.*   Planning refers to the organizational element that is responsible for planning, developing, implementing, and supervising various outdoor recreational programs designed to meet the needs of the particular user groups. The planning job is to provide the maximum quality of recreational experience that is consistent with the basic needs of the user groups, the role of the particular agency, and the capabilities of the resource to provide this quality on a continuous basis. The external influences are the qualifications of the technical staff, agency philosophy, prior legislation such as the agency enabling act, and subsequent secondary legislation (Wilderness Act of 1964, etc.).

2. *Interaction of Subsystems.*   The basic interactions (interrelationships) are:

a.   1)   *User × resource.*   The user effects on the resource are significant; however, some planners discount this situation as having any real effect on the quality of the recreational experience of the present user population. In the short run, their opinion may be valid, but ideally we should be attempting to provide high quality experiences on a sustained yield basis, which includes maintenance of the site quality and productivity.

There are three primary user effects on the recreational site — resource deterioration through normal recreational behavior, resource and facility destruction through depreciative behavior, and facility deterioration. Depreciative behavior refers to deviant behavior that affects the quality of the site or the experience of other visitors. Examples are hacking on trees, removing ground vegetation, driving a vehicle over sensitive vegetation, and so on, causing deterioration through other than normal use. If the planner recognizes these effects, he can develop programs to reduce the amount of deterioration.

The following is a list of examples of user effects and possible planning programs to combat them:

(1) *Resource deterioration*
    (a) Soil erosion in picnic unit — harden central part of unit.
    (b) Trail deterioration — harden trail; develop water diversion structures; restrict number and types of trail users; reroute trail; etc.

(2) *Depreciative behavior*
    (a) Vandalism of facilities — relocate development; redesign facility; assess motivations for vandalism.
    (b) Intentional destruction of vegetation or other natural elements — provide outlets such as "hack trees" (poles); improve information and education program.

(3) *Facility deterioration*
    (a) Snow damage to shelters — redesign or relocate shelters.
    (b) Rapid deterioration of wooden structure — redesign for disassembly and storage; select different construction materials; use different preservation processes.

a. 2) *Resource × user.* This factor is commonly called the user perception, since the user derives certain satisfactions and benefits from the resource setting. These satisfactions and personal benefits may include a better understanding of nature and the natural processes that produce the resource setting. The natural aesthetics and how people perceive the various elements of the landscape are important to the planner if he is to maintain the visual continuity of the landscape, and, at the same time, minimize the visual impact of a specific development.

The visitor may also receive satisfaction from the relatively undeveloped landscape through visual relief from the urbanscape, physical and mental challenges relative to the visitor's needs, and recreational skills development.

b. 1) *Resource × planning.* Man's presence, even on a regulated basis, causes a certain amount of site deterioration. Thus, the planner, as an integral part of the recreation resource planning team, must assist in continuously evaluating the effects of the user on the resource by monitoring resource management programs, and assessing resource capabilities. These types of information can then be used in revamping existing planning guides and management programs.

b. 2) *Planning × resource.* Using the data obtained through research and evaluation, resource planning and management programs can be developed and periodically reevaluated in terms of protection of the site and the visitor from resource hazards. Examples of such programs include irrigation to improve heartiness of ground vegetation, removal of overstory vegetation because of hazard to the visitor, or reduction of the spread of insect and disease attacks.

c. 1) *User × planning.* The primary subsystem is the user, for ultimately the total planning system is developed solely for his benefit. However, certain types of recreation information are needed about the user in order to properly plan recreation areas, sites, and facilities. This type of information is obtained through legislation, informal and formal public communications, and user research.

Legislation such as the Wild and Scenic Rivers Act is enacted to provide uniform approaches to planning and management. Public communications may include public hearings, pressure group politics, and political pressures, all of which may affect planning decisions. Thus, it is sometimes difficult for the planner to understand the final decisions on a given planning project if tradeoffs are made at higher administrative levels with no explanation about the public communications that affected the decision.

Even though some communications may unfavorably affect the technical aspects of planning, it is still important that all channels of communications with the public and the various special interest groups remain open, because communications is a two-way process. To eliminate, selectively, communications with selected user groups would destroy the concept of total systems planning.

     c. 2) *Planning* × *user*. Feedback through the recreation information management program can assist in the proper development of visitor management programs, such as information and education, visitor services, and user management. User management includes any program designed to manage the social experience of the individual or the effects of the visitor on the resource, or both. Thus, it is imperative in visitor management that we understand the normal behavioral needs of the visitor, and also how the visitor use might affect the resource base.

SELECTED READINGS

1.   Anderson, K. R. 1959. *A User-Resource Recreation Planning Method*. Loomis, California: National Advisory Council On Regional Recreation Planning.
2.   Branch, M. C. 1966. *Planning: Aspects and Application*. New York: John Wiley & Sons, Inc.
3.   Buzzell, R. D. 1964. *Mathematical Models and Marketing Management*. Cambridge, Massachusetts: Harvard University Press.
4.   Chadwick, G. F. 1971. *A Systems View of Planning*. New York: Pergamon Press.
5.   Chubb, M., and P. Ashton. 1969. *Park and Recreation Standards Research: The Creation of Environmental Quality Controls for Recreation*. National Recreation and Park Association. Technical Report No. 5.
6.   Driver, B. L. 1970. *Elements of Outdoor Recreation Planning*. Ann Arbor, Michigan: University of Michigan.
7.   Ewing, D. W. 1969. *The Human Side of Planning*. Boston: The Macmillan Company.
8.   Hart, W. J. 1966. *A Systems Approach To Park Planning*. Morges, Switzerland: International Union for the Conservation of Nature and Natural Resources. Supplementary Paper No. 4.
9.   Jubenville, A., and G. R. Peel, Jr. 1973. *A Pilot Study of Modeling the Snake River Float Trip, Grand Teton National Park*. Laramie, Wyoming: University of Wyoming.
10.   Krutilla, J. (ed.). 1972. *Natural Environments: Studies in Theoretical and Applied Analysis*. Baltimore: The Johns Hopkins Press.
11.   Taylor, J. L. 1971. *Instructional Planning Systems*. Cambridge University: Cambridge University Press.
12.   VanMeter, J. R. 1970. *A Framework for Outdoor Recreation Planning*. Illinois Department of Conservation.

CHAPTER 5

CONCEPTS IN RECREATION PLANNING

There are many concepts used in the total planning process; the ones presented in this chapter are those with which the student of recreation planning should be familiar. These concepts are divided into three areas: management, social, and resource.

MANAGEMENT PLANNING CONCEPTS

Planning Mirrors Managements. This concept is variously called "management by design" or "functional planning." One cannot plan a site for one type of behavior and manage for another. Thus, the planner, in consultation with other staff members, must decide on the specific objectives for which a site will be managed, basic management policies consistent with the objectives, and specific design criteria based on the expected normal behavioral patterns.

For example, suppose we want to develop a transient (enroute) campground in order to provide maximum access and service for the visitor as he is traveling to and from his vacation destination. If we design it as a forest campground or locate it away from the through routes, then it will not suit the needs of the transient camper, no matter how we manage it.

Another example is the wilderness trail. Many wilderness trails are designed as wide, flat trails which are attractive not only to the hiker but also to the trailbiker. Thus, at times, it becomes impossible to manage only for hiking experiences when we have no effective way of eliminating trail bikes. If the trail design had accounted for the management problem, then perhaps it could have been rerouted over a large rock outcropping with sharp switchbacks along the trail, or perhaps natural obstacles (downed trees, rocks, etc.) could be used as design features to discourage the nonhiker traffic.

Quality of Use. Quality of use refers to how people treat the landsape. If people treat the landscape with respect and attempt to minimize their effects on the resource, there is a high quality of use. Thus, we can handle a large number of people with minimum deterioration of site quality. If quality of use is low, then we can only handle a small number of people. In sum, our planning and management effort is no better than the attitudes and behavior of the visitor. Thus, the success of planning and management is somewhat dependent on the information and education programs. However, this is not the simple answer to high quality of use. In the long run, year-round environmental education programs at the community level may give insight into consequences of certain types of behavior, which in turn may cause the individual visitor to change his attitudes and subsequent behavior. Although the information and education program for an agency may cause a visitor not to engage in destructive acts in one place, there is no assurance that he will not do so somewhere else.

Experience Buffer. The experience buffer is a philosophy of recreational land use planning that would buffer a person's recreational experience by providing proper transition from one experience to another. This transition can take two forms. First, the transition can be one of buffering the change in recreational experience, using appropriate change in landscape elements. It would seem inappropriate to start a wilderness trail head 100 yards off a U.S. highway, for example, because there is no transition from the highly developed, heavily used highway corridor to the undeveloped, lightly used wilderness landscape. Thus, the wilderness visitor may be well into the area before he feels a transition into the wilderness experience. If we were to provide a dirt spur road that was only accessible by a secondary or county road, then we could provide a transition from developed to pastoral to wilderness landscape. The person could step from his car into the wilderness experience, thus psychologically increasing the size of the area.

Second, in the case of potentially conflicting recreational activities, the best transition, or buffering effect, may be complete separation. For example, the cross-country skier and snowmobiler may enjoy the same types of terrain yet are incompatible in terms of behavior. The planner may then separate them, using separate trail head developments separated by a major topographic feature.

Succotash Syndrome. Often, because of the limited amount of land available, the planner attempts to develop every acre as activity space. The result is the placing of incompatible and conflicting uses on the same area with no experience buffer, which then lowers the quality experience and the natural aesthetic appeal of the area.

The planner should not try to provide for all activities on a single parcel of land, such as is the case in many municipal and regional parks. He should try to develop a variety of activities on a systems basis, grouping activities according to their compatibility and desirability while leaving sufficient acreage for transition and quiet space.

Public Involvement.   Today people want to be involved in the planning process. Most planners agree that the public should be involved, but then other questions arise, such as: When should they be involved? How? To what extent? There are no simple answers; in fact, this is a very controversial area of concern.

If no involvement were allowed, then the planner might tend to substitute his own biases for public input. Certainly the modern planner would not want to do so, nor involve the public superficially, nor involve the public after the plan is completed. Public involvement, then, is a matter of chronology—at what point in the planning process do we seek public involvement? Robert F. Wambach summarized the chronology of the planning process into three steps:*

1.   Establishment of objective(s) for an area.

2.   Development of alternative planning actions to meet the objectives in step 1.

3.   Evaluation of alternatives and the selection of the best alternative.

Accordingly, since we are developing recreational opportunities for the benefit of the public, they should be involved in establishing objectives, because all subsequent steps are dependent on the established objectives. However, this consideration places a burden on the planner to evaluate the recreation potential of the resource and to make the public aware of the potential and limitation of the area or site to provide certain types of recreational opportunities. The agency hired the planner to use his technical expertise in steps 2 and 3, not to substitute his values for those of the public in step 1. This has not been the case in the past; too often the agency has gone into public hearings with a completed plan which evoked criticism and polarization of attitudes—but with little positive public input.

The basic means of public involvement in a planning decision has also changed. The stolid and stifled atmosphere of the public meeting is no longer tolerated. The present-day hearing is more appropriately described as a seminar (educational output)/ workshop (public input). In the seminar,

---

*Robert F. Wambach presented the above strategy at a course seminar at the University of Montana in 1968.

the public is made aware of the resource recreation potential and limitation as well as the physical and economic constraints on certain types of developments. After an intervening time period for the individual partici-pant's digestion of information and formulation of objectives, a workshop is scheduled during which people are separated into small heterogeneous groups for discussion.

The mechanics may vary, but the philosophy is based on small group communications between people with varying interests. Theoretically, a small group is less inhibited and more willing to share ideas. With such open communications, people often find that their views are not nearly as polarized as they thought and that they share some common ideas. The summary of these inputs makes the final planning decision more acceptable to the majority of the people, although one must also realize that other inputs go into the decision, such as enabling legislation, national and agency policies, regional recreation demand studies, and coordination of development with other agencies.

One other factor must be considered: the "many public" philosophy. Not all people are interested in the same public issues; for each issue, we have a *new* public. In recreation planning, there is no "majority," since participation in any activity is generally limited to a small percentage of the potential user population. Thus, we must account for the opinions of minority user groups in the public involvement. Even on a particular issue (establishment of area objectives) where there is a solid majority of opin-ions, we should still account for minority opinions in the planning. For example, if we were developing an area plan for the Snowy Range Scenic Road corridor in southeastern Wyoming and 60 per cent of the interested public decided that the primary activities to be provided were *modern trailer camping* with interspersed activity space of certain types, would *all* campgrounds be *modern trailer parks?* No, we should also account for the needs of other styles of camping. Furthermore, in our evaluation of alternatives, we may decide that the Snowy Range Scenic Road corridor offers unique opportunities for hiking, fishing, and other activities, and that overnight camping should be moved to the fringe of the corridor. We have still provided for the desires of the public while maximizing the recreation potential of the unique corridor.

Planning Time.   Planning time is divided into physical planning time and political lag time. The physical planning time is that period that is necessary to collect and analyze data and write the final plan, whereas the political lag time is that period lasting from after the plan is completed until it is funded through the political process. This delay, which can extend for a few months to several years, should be accounted for in the planning process because cost and possibly needs will change before the plan is implemented.

This is one of the reasons for projecting visitor needs into the future and then attempting to be innovative in providing for the needs. If we do not, by the time the plan is funded it may be obsolete.

SOCIAL PLANNING CONCEPTS

Driver's Motivation-Benefit Model.   This model conceptualizes the process where the visitor behavior is an orderly movement toward personal satisfaction and benefits. The model is as follows:

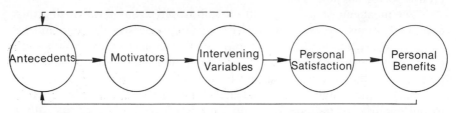

Figure 5–1   Schematic diagram of Driver's motivation-benefit model. This model was developed by B.L. Driver in his recreation research program, U.S. Forest Service, Fort Collins, Colorado.

People store life experiences subconsciously and draw upon these previous conditions or antecedents in the formation of their motivations. If they have found certain types of experiences rewarding, then they are motivated toward those in the future which leads to certain leisure behavioral patterns. This behavior can lead to some personal satisfaction and ultimately to personal benefit. However, there are intervening variables that may either block (permanently or temporarily) or facilitate the movement to personal satisfaction.

For example, the snowmobiler scores higher on the *dominance scale* than the cross-country skier.* Thus, dominance is a greater motivator to the snowmobiler. He feels a need to dominate his surroundings or other people, or both, a need which leads to a particular macro-behavior, snowmobiling. The antecedent to the dominance motivation may be loss of personal control or respect through being replaced by automation, or a domineering spouse, or some personality characteristic.

Intervening variables may either block the movement to satisfaction or facilitate the movement to satisfaction. For example, the snowmobiler may be thrown from the machine on his first attempt, or perhaps he learns to operate the machine properly through a local snowmobile club program and subsequently joins the club. His joining the club may satisfy another motivation—affiliation. This example indicates that the movement from motivation to benefit is not a simple one for one relationship; we have many motivations, based on both personality and situational factors that are closely interrelated and that cause us to pursue various courses of personal actions.

---

*Results are from an unpublished study by B.L. Driver, U.S. Forest Service, Fort Collins, Colorado.

Figure 5–2   Maslow Needs Hierarchy chart.   HIERARCHY OF NEEDS

Maslow Needs Hierarchy.*   Using the basic philosophy of the Driver model, it seems desirable to summarize basic needs or motivators for the planner. This was done by Abraham Maslow (Figure 5–2). He theorized that needs are the primary influences on an individual's behavior. When a particular need emerges, it determines the individual's behavior in terms of motivations, priorities, and action taken. Thus, motivated behavior is the result of the tension—either pleasant or unpleasant—experienced when a *need* presents itself. The goal of the behavior is the reduction of this tension or discomfort, and the behavior, itself, will be appropriate for facilitating the satisfaction of the need. Only unsatisfied needs are prime sources of motivation.

Understanding behaviors and their goals involves gaining insight into presently unsatisfied needs as depicted in the Driver model. Maslow developed a method for gaining insight by providing categories of needs in a hierarchical structure. He placed all human needs, from primitive or immature (in terms of the behaviors they foster) to civilized or mature needs, into five need categories. He believed that there is a natural process whereby individuals fulfill needs in ascending order from most immature to most mature. This progression through the need hierarchy is seen as the climbing of a ladder where the individual must have experienced secure footing on the first rung in order to experience the need to step up to the next higher rung. The awareness of the need to climb further up the ladder is a function of having fulfilled the need of managing the preceding rung, and only satisfactory fulfillment of this need will allow the individual to deal with the new need or rung. Inability or difficulty in fulfilling a lower-order need may result in an individual's maintaining immature behavior patterns or may produce a tendency to return to immature behaviors under stress or any time an individual feels a lower-order need not fulfilled to his satisfaction. The individual may also revert to behaviors which fulfill lower-order needs when the satisfaction of higher needs is temporarily blocked. That is not to say that any need is ever completely satisfied; rather, as Maslow indi-

---

*The discussion is an adaptation of the needs structure presented by A.H. Maslow. 1970. *Motivation and Personality*. 2nd Edition. New York: Harper and Row.

cates, there must be at least partial fulfillment before an indivudal can become aware of the tensions manifested by a higher-order need and have the freedom to pursue its fulfillment.

In the hierarchy, the *basic* level represents needs which reflect physiological and survival goals. At this level are such factors as shelter, clothing, food, sex, and other necessities. In a culture such as ours, where these basic needs are almost automatically met, there is not likely to be any need tension concerning the fulfillment of basic needs. However, individuals in a modern society adapt this basic level upward to include such needs as avoidance of physical discomfort, pleasant working environment, or more money for providing physical comforts.

The second level of the hierarchy consists of *safety* needs. When the individual has at least partially fulfilled the basic needs, he will experience the tensions relating to needs of security, orderliness, protective rules, and general risk avoidance. These needs are often satisfied by an adequate salary, insurance policies, a good burglar alarm system for his business, a doorman for his apartment building, and so on.

When safety needs have been met, the individual will become less preoccupied with self and will endeavor to form interpersonal relationships. The relative success of this need for *belongingness* will result in his feeling accepted and appreciated by others. Thus, the third-level needs concern family ties, friendship, and group membership.

When an individual feels secure in his relationships with others, he will probably seek to gain special status within the group. His need tension will be associated with ambition and a desire to excel. These *ego-status* needs will motivate the individual to seek out opportunities to display his competence in an effort to gain social and professional acceptance.

Because ego-status fulfillment is greatly dependent upon the ability of others to respond appropriately to the individual's efforts to perform in a superior way, they are the most difficult to fulfill satisfactorily. However, if the individual has gained satisfaction on level 4, he may be able to move up to level 5—*self-actualization*. At this level, the individual is concerned with personal growth and may fulfill this need by challenging himself to become more creative, demanding greater achievement of himself, and in general directing himself to measure up to his own criteria of personal success. Self-actualizing behaviors must include risk-taking, seeking autonomy, and developing freedom to act.

The needs levels are as apparent in leisure as they are in our work and community life. Because of the limited behavioral research, it may be difficult to correlate the various needs levels to specific recreational activities. However, the planner *may* draw some conclusions about the needs of the individual by relating the types of activities (participation patterns, level of skill development needed, and level of security/risk-taking) to the Maslow Needs Hierarchy. For example, wilderness recreation participation for the guided trail rider might properly fall between safety and belongingness, whereas the recreation participation for the hiker who just finished a 200-mile hike in the Brooks Range of Alaska might fall in the self-actualization or at least in the ego-status category. Similar judgments could be made for other types of recreationists such as the weekend inter-mediate-skilled downhill skier and the expert vacation skier who challenges the difficult mountain courses.

Activity Aggregate. To the planner, this means a specialized aggregate of activities revolving around a central activity theme.[3] Each site may offer a different combination of activities even though it may have the same central activity theme as others in the planning area. People's needs are so complex and interrelated that merely providing a major development without the proper supporting activities may not be very satisfying. For example, the planner may develop two forest campgrounds. One is water-oriented with swimming, boating, and fishing as supporting activities; the other is mountain-oriented with hiking, stream fishing, and so forth as supporting activities. Thus, while the theme is the same, each development has its own unique activity aggregate.

Recreation Carrying Capacity. Many people in various phases of re-source management have used the term "carrying capacity" to refer to the number of animals an area can sustain without detriment to existing en-vironmental conditions. Although carrying capacity is often used in refer-ence to recreation, there is no uniform definition.

Wagar states:

> Recreational carrying capacity is the level of recreational use an area can withstand while providing a sustained quality of recreation. . . . If quality is to be sustained, it is important that values not be used up faster than they are produced.[15]

This definition implies both an ecological or physical carrying capacity of a given site as well as a socio-psychological carrying capacity in terms of perceived needs or values which are to be derived from the experience. In the physical definition, there is an implication to determine that level of recreational use which can be sustained without long-term effects on the resource base—vegetation, fauna, soil, water, and air.[5] The socio-psychological definition implies a level of recreational use which would maximize personal benefits for the user population for a given type and quality of recreational experience.

The last statement is the key to the establishment of a specific carrying capacity. The recreation manager must establish management objectives for a site or area—objectives that focus on the type and quality of recrea-tional experience to be offered. Once management objectives are estab-lished, the recreational experience to be offered becomes a constant (within limits). The manager's job then becomes one of manipulating the resource, the user, or both to maximize user benefits on a sustained basis for the type and quality of recreational experience set forth in the management objectives.

In sum, recreational carrying capacity is not an absolute limit that is inherent in each area.[15] It is that level of use at which the quality of the experience remains constant for the user population. Thus, carrying capacity for a given site is dynamic and will eventually come into equilibrium with existing social and environmental conditions.

The primary inputs into the social carrying capacity, as indicated in Figure 5–3, are socio-psychological needs and environmental perception (how people react to their environment, not how the environment reacts to people). If we are able to identify the needs and visitor perception for a given recreational experience, then we can establish the type and level of use that is consistent with the management objectives.

All other factors become constraints once the primary socio-psychological inputs are identified. The ability of the resource to sustain a given level of recreational use may restrict or reduce the visitor use levels well below the social carrying capacity. On the other hand, if it is acceptable in terms of visitor perception, the planner may manipulate the resource base to sustain higher levels of use.

There are also service constraints. We may limit the type and level of use by the type and level of site and facility development, legal constraints,

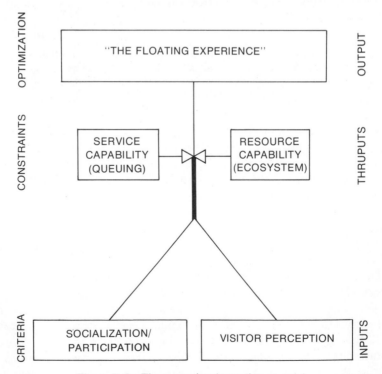

Figure 5–3   The recreational experience model.

budgeting process, and others. One problem in wilderness planning is that we have tried to increase social carrying capacity by reducing the limitations of the service component, i.e., by widening trails and decreasing gradients, improving access roads, increasing primitive development, etc.—which in reality completely alters the type of experience, increases environmental degradation, and so on. The service component, however, is one management tool that can be used to manipulate visitor use.

Supplying a Demand. In the past, some planners have taken the attitude that whatever is developed will be used. However, it is imperative that we properly allocate our limited fiscal and natural resources for recreation, using some priority system. Generally, the priority system should conform to identified *leisure needs* of the potential user population — supplying a demand.

Too often, planning projects have been monuments to the planner or have tried to offer some unique opportunities in order to *create* a demand. These sites and facilities may be used, as mentioned in the beginning; however, there is no assurance that we will offer the opportunities that will be most satisfying to the user public unless we align our planning to public *needs*. In sum, we may allocate money and space for recreation without providing for the socio-psychological needs of people.

Functionality of Design. Once the needs of the user have been identified and interpreted into specific site developments, we must ensure that the sites are functional in design, i.e., that they fit the expected normal recreational behavior.

We should project whether the site design will facilitate the expected behavior (activity participation, visitor flow patterns, environmental perception, etc.), as well as offer proper protection of the site from visitor use. One factor planners often overlook is the effect of "hidden" facilities on the satisfaction of the visitor. Poorly located and hidden facilities (those that blend with the background to the point that they are difficult to locate), such as comfort stations, water points, and access signing, may make a well-planned site very unattractive and dissatisfying to the visitor. Thus, site planning, through either improper design or "hidden" facilities, can greatly effect the satisfaction a person would otherwise derive from the experience.

RESOURCE PLANNING CONCEPTS

Naturalism and Aesthetics. The key to understanding naturalism and aesthetics is based on not whether the landscape is pristine but whether the landscape conditions (including man-made developments) are appropriate for the particular experience. The appropriateness of the large, symmetrical, clear-cut blocks in the Bitterroot Mountains in western Montana was the prime concern in the "Bitterroot Controversy." [2] The large, symmetrical blocks were not natural and consequently reduced the natural aesthetic appeal of the mountain range. Smaller, asymmetrical openings would have coincided more with natural conditions.

There are four areas of aesthetics with which planners should be concerned, regardless of the magnitude of the project:

1. *Visual Harmony.*   It is important that the recreational development be harmonious with the landscape. If it is too incongruent in its visual effects, then the site will have lost most of its natural appeal. The development should blend well with its setting, creating minimal visual disruption of the landscape. The facilities should be of appropriate materials— tastefully developed, yet not detractive from the total experience being provided.

2. *Unique Scenery.*   Unique natural scenery is extremely appealing to the visitor and should be protected for its natural aesthetics; the planner has done a good job in identifying and protecting these outstanding attractions. However, we must also understand the aesthetic appeal of the representative landscapes of a region and endeavor to protect the appeal of these landscapes. In the long run, the representative or typical landscape are the most important recreational resource because it is here that the vast majority of recreational activities take place.

3. *Visual Pollution.*   Too often we have pointed an accusing finger at the visual blight of our cities, yet we perpetuate many of these same visual problems in our recreation planning. Some examples of these are: overhead utility lines not screened by native vegetation; buildings that are inappropriate for the setting; large, gaudy signs; and sites molded by the bulldozer rather than site plans that were adapted to the natural physiographic features.

4. *Recreational Technology.*   Some people have become too infatuated with technology in recreational development. Many smaller park units have been over-developed with modular construction and inexpensive supporting facilities, leaving little undeveloped quiet space and transition space. The answers to adequately providing for the recreational needs of people do not depend on rapid development of sites using inexpensive, modular facilities (which are often expensive to maintain and have short life expectancies, besides being very unaesthetic in their appeal). Basically we must have a better understanding of human needs and not become too impatient in provisioning for these needs. There are no simple answers.

Principle of Irreversibility.   The planner must recognize that certain changes in the landscape become irreversible. Thus, once a landscape is developed, almost all other recreation land use alternatives are eliminated. The principle of irreversibility is the assessment of the resource consequences of various planning actions, using an opportunity continuum (Figure 5–4).

As we move along the continuum from resource- to activity-oriented, the opportunity of reverting the land to its original use becomes less, until we reach a point of irreversibility. Changing wilderness to backcountry and

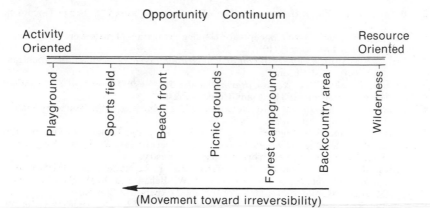

Figure 5-4 Principle of irreversibility. An assessment of planning actions based on the ability to return the land to the existing land use.

then reverting may be possible. But movement of a backcountry area to a picnic grounds may be irreversible. The point is not whether we should make the moves, but whether these are the right moves to make. Once done, most cannot be undone.

Resource Potential. Various ways of assessing resource potential will be covered in Chapter 12; however, there are two socio-psychological concerns that the planner must face. First, there is great disparity between the location of the outstanding recreation resources and the centers of population. This disparity will be even greater with reduced energy resources and mobility. More recreational developments on perhaps less spectacular sites will have to be developed nearer population centers

Second, we may have many *offsite* visitors. Many people choose certain recreational opportunities because of their local availability but would personally find other opportunities more satisfying. Thus, the resource potential of any area will not be totally realized until we have effectively eliminated the offsite visitor.

For example, many wilderness visitors choose the wilderness setting because it is the best substitute for backcountry experience. They are less than totally satisfied and may even affect the "real" wilderness visitor if for no other reason than just numbers of people. The answer to eliminating this offsite visitor is not to discourage his wilderness participation but to develop backcountry opportunities adequately and to encourage that type of participation on that area.

SELECTED READINGS

1. Beltran, E. 1962. "Use and Conservation: Two Conflicting Principles," *First World Conference On National Parks*. A.B. Adams (ed.). Washington, D.C.: U.S. Government Printing Office. pp. 35–43.

2. Bolle, A., *et al.* 1970. *A University's View of the Forest Service.* U.S. Senate Document No. 91–115.

3. Burch, W.R. 1964. "Two Concepts for Guiding Recreation Management Decisions," *Journal of Forestry,* 62(10):707–712.

4. Driver, B.L. 1970. *Elements of Outdoor Recreation Planning.* Ann Arbor, Michigan: University of Michigan.

5. Krutilla, J. (ed.). 1972. *Natural Environments: Studies in Theoretical and Applied Analysis.* Baltimore: The Johns Hopkins Press.

6. Lime, D.W. 1970. "Research for Determining Use Capacities of the Boundary Waters Canoe Area," *Naturalist,* 21(4):8–13.

7. Lime, D.W., and G.H. Stankey. 1971. "Carrying Capacity: Maintaining Outdoor Recreation Quality," *Recreation Symposium Proceedings.* Syracuse, New York: State University of New York, College of Forestry.

8. Lucas, R.C. 1971. "Natural Amenities, Outdoor Recreation, and Wilderness," *Ecology—Economics—Environment.* R.W. Behan and R.M. Weddle (eds.). Missoula, Montana: Montana Conservation Experiment Station.

9. Outdoor Recreation Resources Review Commission. 1962. *Outdoor Recreation for America.* Washington, D.C.: U.S. Government Printing Office.

10. _____. 1962. *The Quality of Outdoor Recreation: As Evidenced by User Satisfaction.* Washington, D.C.: U.S. Government Printing Office. O.R.R.R.C. Report 5.

11. Ortloff, H.S., and H.B. Raymore. 1959. *The Book of Landscape Design.* New York: M. Barrows & Company, Inc.

12. Stankey, G.H. 1971. "Wilderness: Carrying Capacity and Quality," *The Naturalist,* 22(3).

13. U.S. Forest Service. 1974. *Outdoor Recreation Research: Applying the Results.* U.S. Forest Service General Technical Report NC–9.

14. Wagar, J.A. 1964. *The Carrying Capacity of Wildlands for Recreation.* Forest Science Monograph No. 7.

15. Wagar, J.A. 1974. "Recreational Carrying Capacity Reconsidered," *Journal of Forestry,* 72(5):274–278.

PART 2

ECONOMICS OF OUTDOOR RECREATION PLANNING

This section will cover demand and methods of projection, including semantic problems. Further, the supply of recreational opportunities will be presented, and real and potential supply will be differentiated. Last, the investment considerations in public recreation will be presented, including many of the associated problems.

Thus, the application of the principles of economics is essential to proper outdoor recreation planning. Recreation participation has increased dramatically since World War II; this participation has become more vehicle oriented. At the same time, real supply has lagged in relation to participation.

All levels of government and the private sector have become involved in planning and provisioning for outdoor recreation opportunities. Millions of dollars and thousands of acres are allocated each year through the outdoor recreation planning process. Thus, if we are to allocate these resources properly, we need to understand recreation demand (and all of its ramifications), normal recreational behavior, and the resource supply necessary to provide for the estimated demand.

CHAPTER 6

DEMAND FOR OUTDOOR RECREATION

PRINCIPLES OF DEMAND

People today spend a considerable portion of their time and income participating in various forms of outdoor recreation. Facilities and services have been provided in the public sector at nominal costs. (Without this direct market mechanism, other costs have been used to project demand through related expenses of equipment, travel, and others.)

> But it is misleading to contend that economic analysis is therefore inadequate and inapplicable and that it is impossible to measure the economic worth or value of either the recreational experience as such or the recreation site.[7]

Demand Terminology. "Demand," to the economist, refers to a schedule of behavior according to which certain quantities of goods or services are demanded at various prices and have certain relationships to supply based on consumption and pricing (Figure 6–1a). The knowledge of this schedule can then be used to predict the real effects of price and quantity consumed (Figure 6–1b).

Figure 6–1a shows a simplified demand-supply situation with the market in equilibrium at a price of P and a quantity consumed of Q. On this model, an increase in demand would involve a shift of the D curve upward and to the right. A decrease in demand would mean a shift downward and to the left. An increase in supply would mean a shift of the S curve downward and to the right. A decrease in supply would require a shift upward and to the left.

When some market change takes place, price can remain at P or

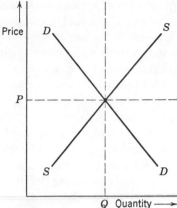

The model (6–1a)

Consumption	Price	Supply	Demand
Increases	Increases	May increase, decrease, or remain unchanged	Must increase
Increases	Remains unchanged	Must increase	Must increase
Increases	Decreases	Must increase	May increase, decrease, or remain unchanged
Remains unchanged	Increases	Must decrease	Must increase
Remains unchanged	Decreases	Must increase	Must decrease
Decreases	Increases	Must decrease	May increase, decrease, or remain unchanged
Decreases	Remains unchanged	Must decrease	Must decrease
Decreases	Decreases	May increase, decrease, or remain unchanged	Must decrease

Relationships (6–1b)

Figure 6–1   A model for demand-supply analysis.

quantity at Q only if both the supply and the demand change (Figure 6–1b). If both supply and demand increase, the quantity consumed could increase without any change in price. If demand increases while supply decreases, the price could rise without any change in the quantity consumed. If demand decreases while supply increases, price could fall without any change in the quantity consumed. In each of these cases, the new intersection of the supply curve with the demand curve would fall on one of the broken lines in Figure 6–1a.

It is much more likely that after a change in supply and demand the new intersection point will fall in one of the quadrants of Figure 6–1a, rather than on one of the broken lines. If the new intersection is in the

upper-right or lower-left quadrant, we can make certain definite conclusions about a change in demand. It would fall in the upper-right quadrant
only if demand increased and in the lower-left quadrant only if demand
decreased. When it falls in one of these quadrants, one cannot tell whether
or not the supply has changed, but one does know that there must have been
a change in demand. In order for the new intersection to be in the upper-left
quadrant, supply must have decreased. In order for it to be in the lower-
right quadrant, supply must have increased.

But why would we want to know the quantity of recreation demanded
at a given price? First, we need a standardized means for comparing the
value of recreation use with other alternative land uses. Second, this
knowledge would give a means of comparing alternative investment opportunities in recreational development. And third, an estimate of the dollar
value of the experience could be used in developing an appropriate
schedule of fees and charges.

The demand curve, as developed by Clawson and Knetsch for recreational opportunities, would appear as shown in Figure 6–2. Using this
illustration, Clawson and Knetsch stated:

> Because of the rather arbitrary nature of some of the
> estimates underlying the various demand curves, our lack of
> knowledge about how to allocate costs of trips when visits to
> national parks are combined with visits to other areas, and the
> uncertainty of the shape of the demand curve to the left of the
> observed data point, the specific curves presented in this section
> are more illustrative in character than exact in values.[7]

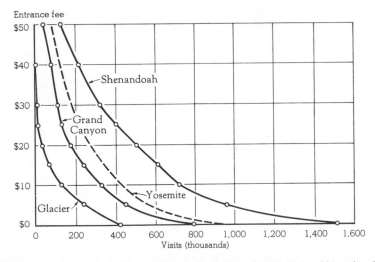

Figure 6–2 Estimated visits under various entrance fee schedules, Yosemite, Glacier,
Grand Canyon, and Shenandoah national parks (from Clawson, M., and J. L. Knetsch.
1966. *Economics of Outdoor Recreation*. Baltimore: The Johns Hopkins University Press.
p. 83).

The use of an entrance fee in the example is an attempt to develop a pricing schedule for that event. Other attempts have been made by proportioning the costs of engaging in a given opportunity if the visitor engaged in many different opportunities during his trip. Clawson and Knetsch feel that the relative position of the curves represents the relative availability to the population centers. Also, for each opportunity (and each national park should rate as a separate opportunity), there may be a satiation point or maximum level of use based on social, service, or ecological limitations.

Because of the tradition of providing recreation at or near zero costs and the lack of good costs data relative to participation, participation rates alone have been used as indicators of demand. Unfortunately, the data reflects only current participation and not demand for various recreational opportunities.[3]

METHODS OF DEMAND PROJECTION

Five basic techniques are presented for projecting the demand; a combination of techniques may be used in actually projecting demand.

Use Trends. Simple extension of past use trends for an area, or an activity within an area, can be useful to the planner, but there are also limitations. In this method, past use trends are extrapolated into the future (Figure 6–3). The primary advantage is simplicity of application. And, as indicated by Netherton,[21] where there are sufficient past data and trends are fairly constant, then the results are reasonably reliable. The rationale behind the method is that long-term trends will be the product of unknown but fundamental forces. If the trends are relatively constant, then it is safe to assume that the effects of the forces will remain somewhat constant.

The major problem is that use trends are rarely constant and predicta-

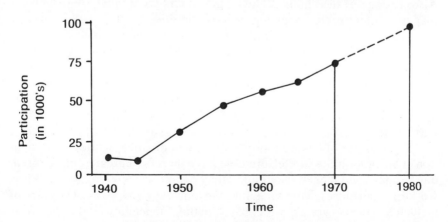

Figure 6–3   Simple extension of use trends.

ble. Thus, an understanding of the forces that shape the trends could increase the reliability of results even when there were abrupt changes.

Two notable examples of extension of trends to predict future demand were Mission 66 (National Park Service), initiated in 1956, and Operation Outdoors (National Forest Service), initiated in 1958. The principal objectives of these programs were development of new modern recreational facilities and rehabilitation of existing ones. The projected demand for various recreational opportunities was extremely low in comparison to actual demand at the end of the projection periods. Figure 6–4 shows the total recreational use projected under Operation Outdoors.[28] The problem with the projection is that we had few past use records that would reflect the coming mass vehicle-oriented recreation. In addition, planners were reluctant to follow the tremendous upswing in the curve from 1948 on; their prime reasoning was based on the slowing of the gross national product during the middle 1950s and the projected population rate of increase, which was much lower than the increase in recreation participation during the period 1948–1955. The conclusion was that participation would increase, but at a decreasing rate. However, participation spiraled because of increased mobility, discretionary income, and available leisure time.

Causal Forces. This method assumes that we know those factors that are causal agents in the formation of recreational use patterns, and that we understand their relative importance. The basic assumption is that use patterns can be correlated to causal variables, and the causal variables can themselves be projected into the future with desired accuracy.

Socioeconomic/demographic variables are often used as the causal factors to explain recreation participation, i.e., population, age, sex, income, occupation, ethnic background, leisure time, place of residence. Age has a great influence on recreational participation. In general, the older people become, the less they engage in outdoor recreation activities. At present, our age structure is changing more to the young and young adult. Also, the age of the children and stages of child and family development may also affect preferences for various activities.[2]

Income and occupation (which is closely correlated to income) affect a person's ability to pay the costs of the experience. At times of high inflation and recession, the amount of discretionary income is lower, a condition which lowers participation. Ethnic background may explain the general patterns for certain types of recreation; however, in general, racial minority groups also have limited discretionary income, which restricts their participation.

The amount of leisure time available can drastically affect participation. The larger blocks of leisure time have increased greatly: more three-day holidays and longer vacations. Many people are pressing for even less worktime and more leisure time, i.e., the four-day work week. The place of residence can also greatly affect participation, depending on the closeness of the recreation area to centers of population and on the amount of time available.

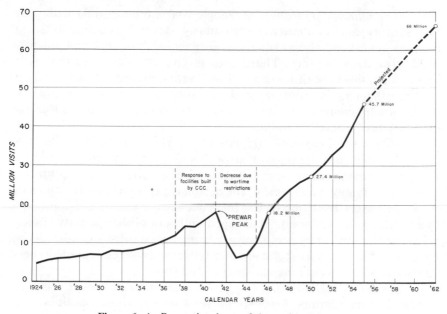

Figure 6–4 Recreational use of the national forests.

More detail could be presented; however, the point is that although socioeconomic variables may singly reflect certain types of patterns, we need to know what happens if they are taken as group or cluster. What will the cause-effect relationships be if the person is a single Caucasian woman who is an English professor with a reasonably high income? To reverse the situation, let us take another example. If I am a wilderness user, I am likely to be a professional person with reasonably high income and live in the urban environs. But just because I am a professional person with reasonably high income who lives in the urban environs does not mean that I am likely to be a wilderness user, when less than two per cent of the population actually participates.[18] As Burch suggests,[1] the mesh for separating users according to socioeconomic categories based on participation is extremely wide.

Associative Factors.   Associative factors are probably more important in explaining participation, yet are very difficult to measure. Competing *social circles of leisure* have been presented by Burch[1] as possible explanations of choosing various leisure styles. He offers three hypotheses to explain the seeking out of certain styles of leisure:

1. *Compensatory Hypothesis.*   When a person is given opportunity to avoid his regular routine, he will seek directly opposite types of recreational activities. This is a safety valve effect in that it may release a person from role overload. Or it may release a person from monotony and boredom to seek new, interesting, and challenging opportunities.

2. *Familiarity Hypothesis*. People who are concerned with comfort, security, and familiarity of surroundings develop a routine for social psychology survival. Stress situations are avoided through development of highly rigid daily routines. Thus, when given a free choice of the use of leisure time, this type of person will seek activities and facilities that will continue the familiar routines and environments. As an example, the modern trailer camper continues many of his work-maintenance routines by taking his "home" with him.

3. *Personal Community Hypothesis*. This hypothesis states that the basic social issues and psychological motivations are filtered and redirected by the important social circles with which we have contact— workmates, family, and friends. The person is exposed in early childhood to certain leisure behavior styles; the tendency then is toward continuing these styles into adulthood. Thus, apparently our leisure activity choices are shaped by individual personality traits that are basically molded during childhood. These leisure styles are then reinforced and redirected by social contact with one's workmates, spouse, and friends.

Consumer Expenditure. The gross expenditure concept identifies consumer expenditures for various recreational sites, services, and facilities, plus any costs incurred in preparation and travel, as the economic value of the occasion. The problem is that many costs that are classified as gross recreational expenditures are really normal family expenses for food, clothing, and so on, and may not represent recreational expenditures.

Thus, a refinement of the technique would be to consider only the value added to the local economy by expenditures for the recreation, the gross expenditure less the cost of providing the goods and services. This would equal the *actual* value to the local economy. The criticism of including "normal" expenses as recreational ones is still true. However, this limitation is more acceptable than merely arbitrarily assigning a dollar value to a visitor occasion, e.g., $2.00 per visitor day for reservoir use. If a person participates in more than one activity or uses more than one site, it becomes difficult to separate many of the expenditures.

Clawson and Knetsch recommend that a demand schedule be developed, based on the *added value* of participation and weighted by population density and travel distance (Table 6–1). A demand curve could then be developed from these data (Figure 6–5). Once the curve is constructed, the demand per unit price for a given level of use per 1,000 population could be interpolated. This technique probably better approximates the typical economic demand curve, even with the limitations associated with it.

Professional Judgment. Regardless of how the demand data is developed, the results must then be interpreted in relation to specific areas and the various user groups who visit the area. It is the role of the planner, based on his technical background, knowledge of the area, and specific observations on participation, to interpret regional demand analysis for the particular planning area.

TABLE 6-1 DEMAND SCHEDULE FOR RECREATION EXPERIENCE

Zone of Origin	Population of Zone	Cost/Visit	Total Visits	Visits/1000 Population
A	1,000	$1.00	600	600
B	2,000	2.00	500	250
C	4,000	4.00	300	75
D	16,000	6.00	400	25

Clawson, M., and J. L. Knetsch. 1966. *Economics of Outdoor Recreation*. Baltimore: The Johns Hopkins University Press.

PROBLEMS OF DEMAND PROJECTION

The problem with demand projections is that the categories project gross behavior—without any indication of the specific behaviors and needs associated with various activities such as camping. There are many types of camping opportunities, with variations of types and levels of development and supporting activities. Thus, merely providing a campground is no assurance that we are providing for the behavioral needs of the camper. Thus, it behooves the planner to also attempt to understand the behavioral requirements of the user.

Most of the demand projections are done at the state level in the development of the state outdoor recreation plans. There are many shortcomings in these projections.[3]

1. *Terminology.* Demand projections are not demand in the strict economic sense; they are *recreation participation surveys*. These studies measure current participation in various recreational activities and, therefore, imply discretionary behavior of people who participate in outdoor recreation. Thus, the surveys will never yield data that will fit standard economic analysis.

2. *Sampling Bias.* Many demand surveys are not based on rep-

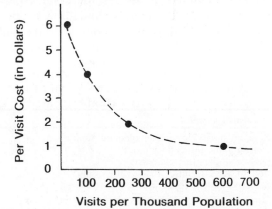

Figure 6-5 Recreation demand curve (based on the information presented in Table 6-1).

resentative sampling of the general population. Even those based on representative sampling often have uncontrolled biases. The problems are summarized in Table 6–2.

3. *Use of Interview and Questionnaires.*   As Burdge and Hendee indicate:

> Social scientists have demonstrated that personal interviews guided by a prepared schedule yield the most valid, reliable, and representative data on individual behavior, preferences, values, and beliefs.
>
> Yet, many statewide surveys are based on biased forms of data collection such as telephone interviews (certain minority groups and those upper class with unlisted numbers are missing in the sample), mail questionnaires (low rates of return and the active, middle class person is the typical respondent).[3]

Based on the preceding concerns and other lesser problems, the following suggestions are offered for the improvement of recreation participation surveys:[3]

1.   Surveys are now conducted by universities, private concerns, and state agencies. The recreation planner should utilize these organizations in data collection and analysis while maintaining supervision and control.

2.   Use patterns of the out-of-state visitor require uniform collection procedures which yield comparable data so that the information can be shared between governmental bodies. Also, there is a need for standardized reporting units for sites, facilities, visitor use, and background information.

3.   In terms of planning, the public and private sectors are interdependent and should coordinate demand data if supply of opportunities is to be efficiently met.

4.   Different kinds of activities may be interchangeable. Planners need to identify satisfying substitutes through understanding motivations and subsequent behavior if they are to provide adequately for spiraling recreational participation.

5.   Standard guidelines for conducting surveys are needed if the results are to be comparable and allow proper description of use trends.

6.   Establishment of a common data bank to share information from

TABLE 6–2   POPULATIONS SAMPLED IN TWELVE RECREATION DEMAND SURVEYS

Population Sampled	*Number*
Random statewide samples (general population)	5
Demographic projections (none)	3
On-site studies (recreationists)	2
Tourist parties (out-of-state visitors only)	1
Selective statewide samples (car owners only)	1
	12

all state surveys would facilitate research and secondary analysis (such as regional analysis). Regional analyses are important since people rarely participate in an activity based on political or administrative boundaries, or at least do not recognize these artificial boundaries in terms of their travel and recreational behavior.

DEMAND FOR SPECIFIC SITES AND FACILITIES

National and regional demand figures may be somewhat deceptive to the planner. While the demand for an activity is increasing in general, it may be decreasing on a given site. Many factors may contribute to this situation, and this is the reason the demand analysis method of professional judgment was presented. Proper regional and area planning can assist in interpreting local needs, but there will always be some unavoidable voids or duplication of facilities. Some of the factors which may cause a divergence from national and regional trends are:

1. *Discrepancy in Population Trends.* The local population trend may be different from broader trends. Some locales may be experiencing rapid growth while others are declining. Some locales may attract large numbers of people with similar interests, a situation which would reduce the array of needs identified at the regional level. Examples include the retirement village, centers of energy development (primarily blue collar workers), summer residents, winter vacationists, and so on. The number and type of leisure patterns will probably vary from one area to another. This means that the planner should be familiar with local conditions and attempt to adapt his planning strategies to those conditions.

2. *Planning Decisions as Communications.* Planning decisions can affect the demand for specific sites. The site may be in a poor location that discourages use. Or the site may not have the proper activity aggregate. Camping may be a desired activity, but the activities associated with the campground development may not fill the needs of the local camper population. Their needs may revolve around camping-boating-fishing, or some other combination of activities not available to them.

The type of vehicle circulation system and its quality can encourage or discourage certain types of use at recreational sites. The planner can use this condition to his advantage to encourage, subtly, the types of uses for which a given site was designed. If one wants to encourage small trailer or tent camping, then the road system into the campground should communicate this. A paved twenty to twenty-two-foot wide road will probably also encourage large trailer use.

The circulation pattern should be included in the area planning process because some sites may be somewhat inaccessible to the user if he cannot reach them with his vehicle. An Army Corps of Engineers reservoir project in Illinois included several modern trailer campgrounds that were difficult to use because they were only accessible by one-lane country roads.

The development of new recreational opportunities may cause tremendous increase in outdoor recreation demand. They may even cause a shift of participation from an existing site to the new site, or sites. This type of shift suggests that even though people sometimes participate in certain recreation opportunities they are not necessarily the opportunities that the people most need or desire, but often merely the best available substitutes.

3. *Physical Attributes of the Site.* The physical characteristics can affect the demand for a particular site. These characteristics may be altered somewhat through planning—screening negative visual access, minimizing physical hazards, and so on. However, basically the planner must still recognize the limitations of a given site to attract a given user population even though the demand is high for that particular experience in that particular locale.

PRESENT PARTICIPATION IN OUTDOOR RECREATION

Participation in outdoor recreation has spiraled since 1960 and is projected to increase even more in the future (Figure 6–6). The graph in Figure 6–6 indicates that the total participation in outdoor recreation use should quadruple by the year 2000. Some experts feel that recent trends in the late 1960s and early 1970s show that these projections are too low. However, this is much higher than the Outdoor Recreation Resources Review Commission (ORRRC) prediction in 1960. The planner is faced today with a shortage of planned recreational opportunities; yet this shortage should become more acute in the future.

The planner must also look at the trends in the individual activities (Figure 6–7). Greater emphasis seems to be placed on the more self-

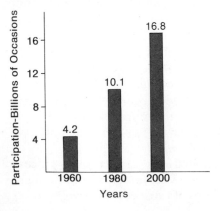

Figure 6–6 Comparison of projected participation, 1960–2000 (developed from data in U.S. Bureau of Outdoor Recreation. 1967. *Outdoor Recreation Trends.* Washington, D.C.: U.S. Government Printing Office).

Participation-Millions of Occasions

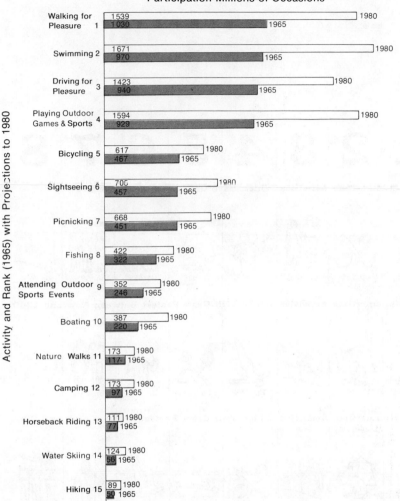

Figure 6–7 Participation in outdoor recreation activities, 1965 and 1980 (developed from data in U.S. Bureau of Outdoor Recreation. 1967. *Outdoor Recreation Trends.* Washington, D.C.: U.S. Government Printing Office).

mobile, physical activities. Interestingly, driving for pleasure dropped from first position in 1960 to third in 1965. Walking for pleasure jumped from *third to first;* and bicycling from eighth to fifth.

Possibly as important to the planner as numbers of occasions is the relative change in participation. The relative changes for the fastest growing activities are shown in Figure 6–8. The trend again seems to be toward more self-reliant, physical activities, yet in a relatively secure recreational setting. Wilderness recreation does not appear on the chart but has in-

1|2|3|4|5|6|7|8

Major Summertime Activities Which Have Grown Fastest Since 1960

| Up 105% | Up 96% | Up 82% | Up 74% | Up 62% | Up 62% | Up 59% | Up 47% |

Major Summertime Activities Which Will Grow Fastest Between Now and 1980

| Up 121% | Up 78% | Up 78% | Up 72% | Up 72% | Up 70% | Up 49% | Up 43% |

Major Summertime Activities Which Will Grow Fastest Between Now and 2000

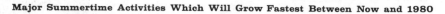

| Up 363% | Up 238% | Up 218% | Up 216% | Up 215% | Up 207% | Up 206% | Up 156% |

Figure 6–8 Expected rates of growth for the faster growing activities (from U.S. Bureau of Outdoor Recreation. 1967. *Outdoor Recreation Trends*, Washington, D.C.: U.S. Government Printing Office).

creased over 700 per cent from 1946 to 1964.[18] This projected increase from 1960 to 2000 is estimated at 859 per cent. Thus, although small in terms of total participation, wilderness recreation is perhaps the fastest growing outdoor recreation activity. Others with low total participation but increasing proportion of use should be of concern to the planner.

Using the Clawson method of categorizing recreational sites, one discovers that the activity-oriented sites, those designed for active sports and other similar activities, have the highest participation.[6] These are readily available to the user with a minimum of travel and for short periods of available leisure time. These characteristics should make them the areas of highest participation. The exact demand in terms of opportunities will vary from community to community, depending on the social and economic structure and the background of the participants.

The resource recreation opportunities receive less use, although many individual sites are heavily used and are showing rapid deterioration. There is a gap between availability and demand for the resource recreation opportunities. More planning and development are needed, but the planner should address himself to the effects on demand of energy shortage, demand for continuous participation, and reduction of discretionary income. The intermediate opportunities, balance of resource base and increased use levels, are intermediate in total demand.

We *were* the most mobile society in the history of the world but probably will never again reach the personal mobility levels of the early 1970s. However, this change should not diminish the demand for various recreational opportunities but merely reorient it to a life style of reduced mobility. This means that the planner is going to have to attempt to shift the recreational development *closer to the user population.* Even resource-oriented opportunities may be shifted closer to the user, if the planner is willing to use the typical landscape of the area. The planner must also recognize that when he does so, demand for many activities may rise rapidly because of the site's increased availability on a continuous basis.

MEASUREMENT OF PARTICIPATION RATES

In the past, participation rates have been based on limited observation and experience. In the other direction, if funds were unlimited, we could measure use directly by counting each visitor and checking the visitor's activities and length of stay. However, this is not possible because of the lack of funds, many scattered sites, and use that is not limited to the developed sites. Thus, we need to develop inexpensive and reliable means of measuring recreation participation in various types of areas and sites. The following methods of measurement are divided into developed and dispersed-use sites.

Developed Sites. Developed sites include campgrounds, picnic areas, and other sites developed for medium and high density uses. The three basic ways of measurement are self-counting, direct counting, and indirect counting systems.

1. *Self-counting Systems.* The visitor is expected to register or apply for a special permit. The results of the self-counting method are highly variable and are affected by the degree of supervision, control, maintenance of the register, and location and relative convenience of the registration/permit facility.[20] Special permits are often required for organizational camps, selected areas (such as a scientific area), open campfires, concession use, and summer homes. Certain types of use information are required when a person receives the permit; in addition, periodic reporting is required under some permits, such as the ones for organizational camps and concessions.

Individual registration may be required at campgrounds, picnic areas, visitor centers, and similar sites. The individual visitor is expected to register himself, including information on length of stay, number of people, and so on. To encourage registration, the registration facility should be conveniently located, maintained in good repair, and adequately supervised. In some instances in the past, registrations have not been picked up for extended periods, which tends to discourage proper registering. Also, in order to calibrate the registration, it will be necessary to have periodic census counts and to compare them with registrations.

2. *Direct Counting Systems.* Direct counting is done by agency personnel or mechanically recorded as the activity takes place. The problem is that counts of participants measure percent occupancy or number of visitors but they do not indicate length of stay (or rate of turnover per unit).

Census counts can be done by an attendant such as at an aerial train, parking area, or other site. If there is a full-time attendant, then rate of turnover may be obtainable. However, during peak use periods it may be difficult to obtain a complete and accurate census. Sample counts (part-time census) are possible in projecting participation rates; the problem is one of proper sampling techniques. As indicated by Marcus et al,[20] using only mid-week counts could underestimate total use; relying only on weekend counts could overestimate weekly use. The best sampling technique is probably random time sampling that can be easily statistically converted to total participation.

Direct counting can be done with continuous and time-lapse photography and with aerial photography. These are still in the developmental stage, but time-lapse photography has proven successful in describing use patterns at places such as winter sports complexes. Aerial photography can be used to count participants at various developed sites. However, the problem becomes one of sampling procedures for proper conversion of sample data, and proper directing, focusing and timing of the camera to obtain good quality photography and useful information about the specific activity.

3. *Indirect Counting Systems.* These systems must be periodically calibrated if we are to be able to estimate actual use. Calibration would require periodic sampling of total use, rate of occupancy, length of stay, and other factors.

There are two general types of indirect counting systems: traffic counters and selected services. Foot traffic counters may be installed on trails, turnstile entrances, and building entrances. If turnstiles are used, direct recording of the number of people entering the facility can be done using a mechanical recorder. In some instances, it may be more desirable to record visitor use with a pressure plate device at the entrance point. Ideally, if the facility is divided into distinct rooms, compartments, or sections, then a counter can be installed at the entrance to each section. Total use can then be separated by separate sections. Sample observation may help in understanding and interpreting the use patterns by sections. If one section is receiving little use while another is over-used, direct observation of the identified patterns may then reveal the reason. Perhaps it is a poorly designed visitor movement pattern, merely an unattractive display, or some other reason.

Indirect measuring devices are often misused by visitors who repeatedly spin the turnstile, step on the pressure plate several times, or exit through entrances. Some of the problems can be avoided by concealing the counter and making flow patterns logical and convenient.[20] As mentioned previously, calibration is necessary for converting the counts to actual visits in order to remove some of the bias of misuse, assuming that the misuse is constant over a given period.

Vehicle counters can be used on access roads, entrances to developed sites, and at any point where a distinguishable activity takes place, in order to distinguish use of each activity space/facility and general flow pattern of traffic (Figure 6–9). The most common traffic counter is the portable pneumatic machine which counts the number of axles that pass over it. Others require a 115-volt system that records counts electronically by interrupting an electrical circuit. One electromagnetic appartus is activated by the magnetic field of motors passing over it; thus, it will not count a nonmotored vehicle such as a trailer.[20]

Several problems may limit the usefulness of traffic counters:

1. Traffic direction usually cannot be recorded unless the lanes are divided or the road is one-way.

2. Nonrecreational traffic cannot be separated from recreational traffic without adequate sampling.

3. A given vehicle may be recorded several times during a single visit.

4. Vehicle counts must be converted to total participation, using sample counts of party size per vehicle.

5. Vandals may confuse, steal, or damage the counters.

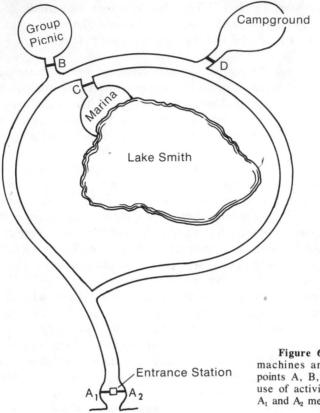

Figure 6-9 Traffic counting machines are properly placed at points A, B, C, and D to measure use of activity facilities. Positions A_1 and A_2 measure total use.

Other special problems arise when one uses pneumatic counters:

1. Axle counts must be converted to number of recreational vehicles. Trailers may activate the counter, or small cars and bikes may not, depending on the pressure used in the pneumatic system.

2. Soft or uneven surfaces may give unreliable counts; hard-surfaced roads are preferred because they allow a consistently reliable operation of the counter.

3. Ice and show may affect the operation, giving unreliable data.

Last, there are ways of measuring selected services and correlating these to total visitor use, using simple regression techniques ($y=a+bX$). Examples of possible measurements of services used by visitors include continuous or periodic recording devices on drinking water systems, solid waste, and sewage. These techniques have not been used extensively and are limited in application because, first, there must be a tested correlation between total use and the given service, and second, they do not measure length of stay or number of visits (autos, parties, individuals, etc.).

Dispersed Use Areas.   The primary means of measuring participation in dispersed use has been self-registration stations at entrance points. This is an inexpensive method but lacks reliability unless calibrated against actual use.[29] In wilderness trail registration, proper location of registration stations, the placement at the selected location, and the appropriateness of the signing will improve rates of registration.[19] However, the ultimate solution may be a mandatory permit system. Under such a system, each person would have to pick up a voluntary permit at the nearest administrative office, or a self-administered permit system could be implemented at the trail head. The success of the program would depend on convenience of operation and adequate enforcement to ensure compliance. The enforcement should include an information and education program to make people aware of the permit system and the basic need for the information (better planning, increased safety, and so forth).

Indirect methods, such as foot traffic counters, have been tried in the estimation of wilderness visitation; they yielded useful information but were inferior to trail registration in estimating use.[19]

Direct counting is generally not economically feasible even if done on a full-time or part-time basis at the entrance points. However, direct counting, using sound sampling procedures, can be used periodically (possibly every three to five years) to recalibrate the rate of registration and the related registration information.

SELECTED READINGS

1. Burch, W. R., Jr. 1969. "The Social Circles of Leisure: Competing Explanations," *Journal of Leisure Research*, 1(2):125–148.
2. Burch, W. R., Jr. 1966. "Wilderness—The Life Cycle and the Forest Recreation Choice," *Journal of Forestry*, 64(9):606–610.
3. Burdge, R., and J. Hendee. 1972. "The Demand Survey Dilemma: Assessing the Creditability of State Outdoor Recreation Plans," *Guideline*, 2(6):65–68.
4. Bureau of Outdoor Recreation. 1967. *Outdoor Recreation Trends*. Washington, D. C.: U. S. Government Printing Office.
5. Cicchetti, C. J., J. J. Seneca, and P. Davidson. 1969. *The Demand and Supply of Outdoor Recreation, an Econometric Analysis*. Washington, D. C.: U. S. Government Printing Office.
6. Clawson, M. 1959. *Methods of Measuring the Demand for and Value of Outdoor Recreation*. Resources for the Future. Reprint No. 10.
7. Clawson, M., and J. L. Knetsch. 1966. *Economics of Outdoor Recreation*. Baltimore: The Johns Hopkins University Press.
8. Cordell, H. K., B. A. James, and R. F. Griffith. 1970. *Estimating Recreation Use at Visitor Information Centers*. U. S. Forest Service Research Paper SE–69.
9. Cristy, F. T. 1970. "Elements of Mass Demand for Outdoor Recreation," *Elements of Outdoor Recreation Planning*. B. L. Driver (ed.). Ann Arbor, Michigan: University of Michigan. pp. 99–104.
10. James, G. A., and R. A. Harper. 1965. *Recreation Use of the Ocala National Forest*. U. S. Forest Service Research Paper SE–18.
11. James, G. A., and R. K. Henley. 1968. *Sampling Procedures for Estimating Mass and Dispersed Recreation Use on Large Areas*. U. S. Forest Service Research Paper SE–31.
12. James, G. A., and J. L. Rich. 1966. "Estimating Recreation Use on a Complex of Developed Sites." U. S. Forest Service Research Note SE–64.

13. James, G. A., and T. H. Ripley. 1963. *Instructions for Using Traffic Counters to Estimate Recreation Visits and Use*. U. S. Forest Service Research Paper SE–3.

14. James, G. A., N. W. Taylor, and M. L. Hopkins. 1971. "Estimating Recreational Use of a Unique Trout Stream in the Coastal Plains of South Carolina." U. S. Forest Service Research Note SE–159.

15. James, G. A., and G. L. Tyre. 1967. "Use of Water-Meter Records to Estimate Recreation Visits and Use of Developed Sites." U. S. Forest Service Research Note SE–73.

16. James, G. A., H. P. Wengle, and J. D. Griggs. 1971. *Estimating Recreational Use on Large Bodies of Water*. U. S. Forest Service Research Paper SE–79.

17. Knetsch, J. L. 1963. "Outdoor Recreation Demands and Benefits," *Land Economics*, 39(11):387–396.

18. Lucas, R. C. 1971. "Natural Amenities, Outdoor Recreation and Wilderness," *Ecology—Economics—Environment*. Missoula, Montana: Montana Forest and Conservation Experiment Station, University of Montana. pp. 131–152.

19. Lucas, R. C., H. T. Schreuder, and G. A. James. 1971. *Wilderness Use Estimation: A Pilot Test of Sampling Procedures on the Mission Mountains Primitive Area*. U. S. Forest Service Research Paper INT–109.

20. Marcus, L. F., E. M. Gould, Jr., and R. L. Bury. 1961. *Measuring Recreational Use on National Forests*. U. S. Forest Service Technical Paper SW–59.

21. Netherton, R. D. 1968. "Demand Methodology," *Proceedings of Recreation Management Institute*. College Station, Texas: Texas A&M University. pp. 11.1–11.7.

22. Outdoor Recreation Resources Review Commission. 1962. *National Participation Survey*. Washington, D. C.: U. S. Government Printing Office. O.R.R.R.C. Report No. 19.

23. _____. 1962. *Outdoor Recreation For America*. Washington, D. C.: U. S. Government Printing Office.

24. _____. 1962. *Participation in Outdoor Recreation: Factors Affecting Demand Among American Adults*. Washington, D. C.: U. S. Government Printing Office. O.R.R.R.C. Report No. 20.

25. _____. 1962. *Prospective Demand for Outdoor Recreation*. Washington, D. C.: U. S. Government Printing Office. O.R.R.R.C. Report No. 26.

26. Shaffer, E. L., Jr., and G. Meiller. 1971. "Predicting Quantitative and Qualitative Values of Recreation Participation," *The Forest Recreation Symposium Proceedings*. Syracuse, New York: The New York State University School of Forestry. pp. 5–22.

27. Trice, A. H., and S. E. Wood. "Measurement of Recreation Benefits," *Land Economics*, 34(8): 195–207.

28. U. S. Forest Service. 1957. *Operation Outdoors—Part I*. Washington, D. C.: U. S. Department of Agriculture.

29. Wenger, W. D., Jr. 1964. *A Test of Unmanned Registration Stations on Wilderness Trails: Factors Influencing Effectiveness*. U. S. Forest Service Research Paper PNW–16.

30. Wenger, W. D., Jr., and H. M. Gregerson. 1964. *The Effect of Non-Response on Representativeness of Wilderness Trail Registration Information*. U. S. Forest Service Research Paper PNW–17.

31. Wennergren, E. B., and D. B. Nielson. 1968. *A Probabalistic Approach to Estimating Demand for Outdoor Recreation*. Utah State University Agricultural Experiment Station Bulletin 478.

CHAPTER 7

SUPPLY OF OUTDOOR RECREATION OPPORTUNITIES

Supply is often viewed in relation to resources for providing various recreational activities. However, since the planner is basically attempting to provide opportunities for meaningful outdoor experiences, supply should be viewed as a program to provide for various visitor needs. Thus, the first step is to identify the needs of the user population adequately and then to provide for them in various resource settings. The selection of the appropriate resource setting is then tied to visitor needs and reflects considerations for *location and access, physical characteristics of the site, basic design considerations in proper planning for the anticipated recreational behavior,* and then finally *good administration and maintenance of the site after development.*

Supply, therefore, is a continuing process and is necessary if a given site or area is to be attractive and usable by the visitor. Furthermore, a given opportunity is not an opportunity to the visitor unless he is aware of it. Many sites and facilities are underused because they are not "informationally" accessible. If a given development is to be counted as a supply, then the total planning and management framework should include an informational program to make people aware of the various opportunities in a given area or region.

This chapter will discuss the disparity of population and supply, existing supply and supply problems, and special programs to encourage adequate supply. Finally, attention will be focused on the programs that could increase *real* supply without having to add large acreages to the existing land base.

POPULATION AND SUPPLY

Although statistically there seems to be a great supply of outdoor recreation opportunities, a great disparity exists between the location of the masses of people and the existing public lands for recreation. The disparity is indicated in *Outdoor Recreation for America:*

> Nationally, these recreation acres are located where the people are not. One-sixth is in sparsely populated Alaska. Seventy-two percent of the remainder is in the West where only 15 percent of the people live. The Northeast, where one-quarter of the people live, has only 4 percent of the recreation acreage of the 48 contiguous states. The South and North Central regions each have 30 percent of the population but have roughly 12 percent of the recreation acres in the 48 contiguous states.[11]

This disparity is illustrated in Figure 7–1. The problem of supply in relation to population becomes more acute when one realizes that the federal government manages about 84 per cent of the public recreation acres, most of which are located in the west (Figure 7–2). These large acreages may be used on a periodic or annual basis by large numbers of people and continuously by the smaller number of residents adjacent to these public lands; whereas, the vast majority of American people participate continuously on the small acreages nearby, or become more dependent on the private sector, or simply do not participate on a continuous basis. These may provide very satisfactory experiences. However, the problem is therefore not one of acres but of "effective acres."* Too often planners have identified the unique scenic and natural wonders as the major places of recreational opportunities. Thus, they have selected such acreages and developed them for general public use, sometimes to the exclusion of developing opportunities in typical landscapes close to the urban populations. If opportunities are to be continuously available, then areas nearer population centers will have to be acquired and developed. Some states and local governments have recognized this need to acquire lands nearer the service populations and have undertaken large-scale acquisition programs. This is the first step in the long-term solution to the problem of disparity. However, other innovative planning techniques can increase supply without a large increase in acreage.

Just because these acreages are acquired nearer populations does not mean that the more resource-oriented portion of the activity spectrum must be eliminated in favor of the activity-oriented developments. On the contrary, a balance of opportunities should be offered. This balance can be accomplished by the imaginative planner who seeks to offer *experiences,* rather than just resources. A garbage pile can become a ski slope; an

---

*The term "effective acres" means land and water resources that are available on a continuous basis to a given user population and managed for specific types of recreational opportunities.

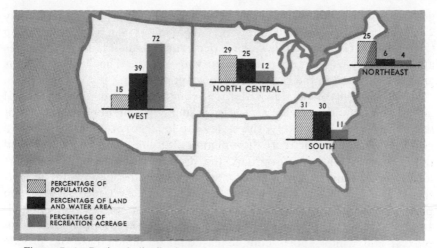

Figure 7-1 Regional distribution of population, area, and recreation acreage, 48 contiguous states, 1960. (From Outdoor Recreation Resources Review Commission. 1962. *Outdoor Recreation for America*. Washington, D.C., U.S. Government Printing Office, p. 56.)

abandoned railroad bed, a trail system; and so on. In sum, ultimately there is a limit to supply; however, the potential of a given acre may be limited only by the imagination of the planner.

LANDOWNERSHIP—THE RESOURCE BASE

Landownership is important in the planning process because it indicates the amount of acreage owned by an agency or private concern and

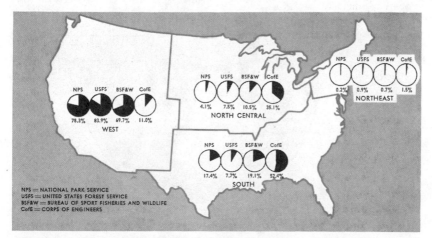

Figure 7-2 Regional distribution of federally designated nonurban outdoor recreation areas. Percentage of agency total by census region, 48 contiguous states, 1960. (From Outdoor Recreation Resources Review Commission, 1962. *Outdoor Recreation for America*. Washington, D.C., U.S. Government Printing Office, p. 57.)

general land uses for the acreage. As shown in Figure 7–3, approximately 27 per cent of the total land in the forty-eight states is in public ownership (504 million acres). Excluding the 3 per cent in Indian lands, this leaves approximately 70 per cent in the private sector. The 70 per cent is generally located in the regions of higher population.

Based on this ownership pattern, it seems appropriate for each level of government and the private sector to examine its role in provisioning for leisure services. Most likely, the states and local governments will seek a greater role in outdoor recreation planning through land acquisition and development. Where appropriate, the private sector should also offer leisure opportunities. From information based on the landownership pattern in Figure 7–3, it seems that the private sector has a large role to play in providing leisure opportunities—a role that has not been well developed. It seems that certain opportunities such as long-term camps, marina complexes, and winter sports complexes could be handled by the private sector. In some cases, all overnight accommodations might be developed by the entrepreneur, leaving the smaller, public areas for day-use types of activities.

The public recreation planner should not become provincial in planning—to attempt to provide for all opportunities on his agency's land. The success of planning will ultimately be determined through the coopera-

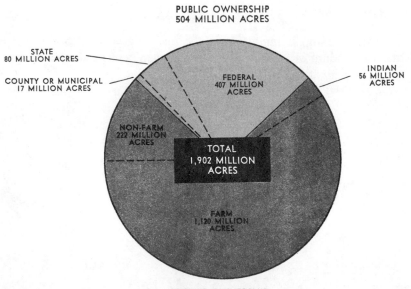

Figure 7–3 Land ownership, 48 contiguous states, 1960. (From Outdoor Recreation Resources Review Commission, 1962. *Outdoor Recreation for America*. Washington, D.C., U.S. Government Printing Office, p. 55.)

tion and coordination of all public and private recreation planning. The role each public agency or private company assumes may vary from region to region because of many social, economic, and resource factors. However, the initial factors that the planner has to contend with are landownership and population.

Acres alone cannot be use as a total measure of supply. Most of the acreage in public ownership is in large units. Only 1 per cent of the areas is over 100,000 acres, but it makes up 88 per cent of the total recreational acreage. On the other hand, over two-thirds of the areas are under 40 acres in size, but contain less than 0.1 per cent of the total acreage. Most of the large acreages are in the northwest and are isolated from the centers of population; in addition, they are not managed intensively. Consequently, supply to most people is concentrated on smaller acreages closer to the population centers. For example, the largest supply of developed recreational acres is in state ownership, 85 per cent. Of the remaining 15 per cent, local governments manage more areas than the federal government; yet, in total acreage, the federal government has 84 per cent of the land used for recreation.

SUPPLY BASED ON CLAWSON'S CLASSIFICATION SYSTEM

The supply of recreational opportunities is separated into three basic classifications. *User-oriented sites* are those developed sites that are immediately accessible to the population and that emphasize active participation, but they may also include quiet, educational, and special interest sites. Examples are neighborhood playgrounds, sport fields, and similar community facilities.

The resource-based areas are at the other end of the continuum. The recreation opportunity is developed around the natural characteristics of the landscape and may vary from forest camping to the wilderness experience. Maximum emphasis is placed on natural aesthetics while providing appropriate minimal services to allow the visitor to use and enjoy the natural landscape for various types of experiences. Thus, these types of areas are where the planner finds them, and he must develop a program that provides for the selected resource-based experiences while maintaining the integrity of the resources. Typically, those areas are located away from the large centers of population; thus, people must travel considerable distances to reach them. But this does not necessarily have to happen, if we are willing to utilize the typical landscapes.

Those areas which lie in between the two extremes on the continuum are called intermediate areas (balance between activity and resource) and frequently include state parks and forests and large urban regional parks. Here the planner can use some discretion in locating the intermediate sites. They should be relatively accessible via major transportation arteries so that they are reached by automobile and public transportation; yet, they should be a sufficient distance from major arteries to minimize the effects of sounds, sights, and traffic on the safety and recreational welfare of the visitor. In terms of effective supply, there are advantages to serving large numbers of people by providing well-placed, moderate-sized areas.

User-Oriented Areas.   In user-oriented area planning, municipal park standards have typically been applied to determine adequacy of supply. The standards are then expanded to the population base within the recommended service area. The problem with this approach is that it assumes that all populations are similar in leisure needs and that standards can be applied directly to any population.

There were approximately 1.6 million acres of city and county parks and play areas in the United States in 1970, primarily user-oriented areas. By the standard recommended by the National Recreation and Park Association, there should immediately be 0.5 million additional acres of these areas. Jensen, using the assumptions of doubling the population and quadrupling the demand for outdoor recreation, suggests that a minimum of an additional 2 million acres of user-oriented sites be added by the year 2000, bringing the total to 3.6 million acres.[9] Clawson, in 1963, predicted that by the year 2000, 5 million acres of this type of development would be needed.[4]

The major problem is that supply is focused on acres rather than needs of people. Also, many of these acres are not readily available to the user population, i.e., high density, low income locations tend to have few areas relative to the population needs. The encouraging part is that there is still land that could be acquired for user-oriented areas (including some that may need redevelopment or relandscaping). However, much of this land within and near the urban centers is extremely expensive. The question becomes, ''Are we willing to lay out the necessary capital for acquisition and development? Or are we willing to continue with ineffective supply (distribution of sites)?''

Resource-Based Areas.   Resource-based areas are developed around natural qualities of the site and offer outdoor recreational activities that emphasize these qualities. Examples of the resource-based areas are forest campgrounds, canoe trails, and wilderness areas. In sum, resource-based areas are those that are developed around existing natural resource features rather than around man-made developments.

Most resource-based areas are not high in natural productivity of the site-soil conditions. Even if attractive, they cannot supply large amounts of recreational usage without site deterioration. Consequently, much of the public land is not suitable for certain types of recreational developments, and those that are developed often have a very limited visitor capacity because the site cannot sustain heavy use.

Of the 180 million acres in the national forest system, the U. S. Forest Service has identified 14 million acres for various types of outdoor recreation. Of this amount, about 70 thousand acres have been improved for camp and picnic sites and the rest in wilderness and other roadless area opportunities. The remaining 166 million acres of national forest lands function on a limited or dispersed type of road and trail use.

The Bureau of Land Management (BLM) has 460 million acres under its jurisdiction; however, very little recreational planning and development have taken place until recent years. With greater planning, much of the BLM land could be made available for recreational use.

The National Park System probably offers the greatest supply of outdoor recreation since it provides for a great variety of opportunity (recreational, historic, and natural areas) and dedicates its land for selected recreational uses. In all, it administers almost 30 million acres of which nearly 85 per cent is in national parks and monuments.

Other resource agencies such as the Tennessee Valley Authority, the Army Corps of Engineers, and the U. S. Fish and Wildlife Service offer a considerable supply. Yet, seemingly, the level of use on the more outstanding areas is reaching crowded conditions.

In sum, resource-based areas are limited in supply because of natural productivity and their location away from population centers. The prospects for expanding the acreage having great scenic and natural qualities is limited. However, since we seem to be headed for continued energy shortages and a less mobile life style, it may behoove the planner to acquire and develop less scenic and natural areas nearer populations if we are to add to the effective and continuous supply of resource opportunities.

Intermediate Areas. Although aesthetic qualities are important, many types of intermediate areas can be created through development (man made reservoirs), landscaping (picnic areas), and other planning without having outstanding natural or scenic features.

In terms of supply, there are 3,200 state parks in the United States, a total of over 7.6 million acres. Most of these are developed to provide many day-use types of activities. Where developments are limited to day-use activities, the supply of overnight accommodations is generally on adjacent private lands.

Also, there are 12.5 million acres of state forest and 4.5 million acres of federally owned reservoirs and other resources that fall in the intermediate category. Including some city and county areas and the private sector, the acreage in this category now exceeds 25 million. Again, there is some disparity in the supply when one considers that Wyoming has more state lands for recreation than Illinois and many other high-population states.

According to Jensen

> An additional 5 million acres of these areas could be justified at the present time to fully meet public demands . . . . By the year 2000 an additional 45 million acres of intermediate areas will not be in excess of public needs.[9]

SPECIAL PROGRAMS

Special programs have been developed to encourage an adequate supply; the following are selected programs that have contributed to this end:

1. *Land and Water Conservation Fund (LAWCON).* The LAWCON Fund, established under P. L. 88–578, provides financial assistance for land acquisition by federal agencies and for planning, acquisition, and development of public outdoor recreation sites at the state and local level. The grants are usually made on a 50 per cent matching basis.

To be eligible, a state must develop a state outdoor recreation plan and have it approved by the Bureau of Outdoor Recreation. To be funded, each project must meet the priority needs identified in the plan. Because of the lack of public lands for outdoor recreation, some states, such as Illinois, have limited the program to acquisition projects only.

Approximately 60 per cent of the released funds go to state and local governments; the remaining 40 per cent, to federal agencies. Approximately 5 per cent of the monies are held in contingency for large-scale emergency projects.

The revenues for the LAWCON Fund are derived from: (1) user fees at federal areas, (2) motorboat fuel tax, (3) sale of surplus federal lands, and (4) off-shore oil leases.

2. *Recreation and Public Purposes Act of 1954.* This program, administered by the Bureau of Land Management, authorizes state and local governments and qualified nonprofit organizations to acquire designated federal lands for recreation and other purposes. Surplus public domain lands, generally small isolated tracts located adjacent to cities, and special areas are disposed of through sale or lease. The purchase price for governmental agencies is $2.50 per acre and the leasing cost is $0.25 per acre per year.

3. *Federal Water Projects Reclamation Act of 1965.* Federal water projects are developed under the authority of this act by the Bureau of Reclamation and the Army Corps of Engineers (Public Works Branch). The law states that the recreation resources of federal water projects are to be administered by nonfederal agencies. The federal government may assume up to a 50 per cent cost share for developing the recreational opportunities; the nonfederal agency must share 50 per cent of the developmental costs plus all of the operating expenses, including eventual replacement costs. In the absence of nonfederal administration, only minimal facilities for the protection of public health and safety will be provided.

Unfortunately, this is often not the boom to supply that was envisioned, because of the lack of money for administration at the local level and also the lack of interest at the federal level to ensure good planning and development of the recreational sites. In addition, many of the reservoirs are drawn down heavily for irrigation and other purposes during the prime recreation season, which tends to minimize the importance of the water for recreation.

4. *Water Quality Act of 1965.* This act is aimed at ensuring an adequate supply of suitable water for human use, including recreation. The Federal Water Pollution Control Administration administers the program, which includes monitoring water quality, coordination of water quality standards, construction of abatement facilities, and grants and research efforts.

Outdoor recreation is heavily water-oriented in many parts of the United States. If it were not for this program, the necessary water resource for recreation would continue to dwindle because of increased water pollution.

5. *National Historic Preservation Act of 1966.* P. L. 89–665 established a matching grant program, administered by the National Park Service for states and local governments, to acquire and restore property or artifacts that are of state historic significance. To be eligible, a state must develop a state historic plan that identifies properties of statewide historic significance.

6. *Wilderness Preservation Act of 1964.* This act speeded up the process of evaluating lands for inclusion in the wilderness classification. Basically, it immediately included all existing wilderness and wild areas in the system and required the U. S. Forest Service, the National Park Service, and the Bureau of Sport Fisheries and Wildlife to review existing primitive areas for possible inclusion. This requirement was later interpreted to mean all roadless areas which are presently under review.

Since the original nine million were included under the Wilderness Act, several million acres have been added and perhaps sizable acreage will be included in the near future through the roadless area review. However, agencies have been so involved in adding new acreages that they have failed to plan properly for the management of existing areas. Site deterioration and overcrowding have reduced the capacity and attractiveness of some areas, effectively reducing supply.

7. *Wild and Scenic Rivers Act of 1968.* P. L. 90–542 established a system for the preservation and management of selected rivers for their wild, scenic or recreational character or other similar values. There was a continued loss of outstanding riverways through channelization, development, pollution, change in landownership, and other factors. The intent of the program was to preserve the selected rivers for their unique values, thus ensuring a minimal stable supply of river-based recreational opportunities.

In the act, eight rivers or sections were set aside and twenty-seven others were identified for possible inclusions. Since then the list of possible inclusions has swelled to seventy-three. Also, several states have initiated their own stream preservation programs.

Many other special programs, such as the National Trails System Act of 1968 and Small Watershed Act of 1954, have contributed to an expanded supply. Without such programs, the gap between demand and supply would have widened even further than it has today.

INCREASING EFFECTIVE SUPPLY

Many factors can affect the potential supply of a given resource for recreation. However, there are several general concepts that the planner should be familiar with that could transfer potential supply to real supply, or at least stabilize existing situations.

Environmental Quality Control.   Control of environmental quality is essential if we are going to continue to offer quality recreational experiences. Some environmental considerations in maintaining the quality of the resource base and subsequently the recreational experience are:

1.   *Air Pollution.*   Air pollution can cause damage to flora and fauna, including human life. At present, there may be only isolated pockets of air pollution that may be caused by the recreationists; however, this is a real threat. The inner valley of Yosemite National Park is an example of such a pocket. Industrial, commercial, and vehicular air pollution from the larger urban complexes have at times had a great effect on more distant, undeveloped landscape.

As air pollution builds up, the quality of the outdoor experience has to be affected; as the area becomes less attractive as an outdoor recreation environment, its effectiveness in contributing to the total supply is lessened.

2.   *Water Pollution.*   Water pollution is constantly reducing the real and potential supply of outdoor recreational opportunities. Outdoor recreation tends to be heavily water-oriented; this trend seems to be escalating while the supply is being reduced and in some areas almost eliminated. Unfortunately most of the rivers near metropolitan areas are no longer fit for human use, and many are health hazards, at a time when they are most needed by the nearby populations.

Stricter water pollution abatement laws are needed, as well as adequate monitoring and enforcement. If not, water for recreation will have to be rationed to ensure a minimal supply for the using public.

3.   *Land-Use Planning.*   The lack of land-use planning or other land-use controls has contributed to a dwindling supply of recreation, particularly in the private sector. Uncontrolled second home development, lack of sewage treatment, and poorly located housing and industrial development, as well as poorly planned recreation sites and facilities, have led to the loss of the resource base.

Significant national and state land-use legislation could reduce the impact while providing for logical, orderly development, recreation or otherwise. In recreation, this legislation should insure better location of sites, better environmental planning, and hopefully a better quality experience on a sustained-yield basis.

Visitor Attitudes. Changing visitor attitudes can greatly affect the recreation supply. Basically, the behavior of the individual visitor is a reflection of his attitudes on a given subject or situation; thus, changing attitudes should cause changes in behavior.

1. *Changing Mobility.* Reduced mobility seems certain because of reduced energy resources. Also, the uncertainty, inconvenience and queuing problems (primarily scheduling) may psychologically further reduce the mobility of the visitor. Reduced mobility, real or otherwise, will reduce the supply of many outdoor opportunities and perhaps overload existing local and intermediate areas.

2. *Changing Quality of Use.* If people treat the landscape and other visitors with respect, more people can enjoy existing resources and recreational developments. If quality of use is low, fewer people can be accommodated. The planner is faced with the challenge of developing information and education programs, improved site design, and possibly special management programs (litter disposal, vandalism reduction, and so on) that would improve people's behavior.

3. *Enjoyment of the Typical Landscape.* Planners seem to have perpetuated the myth that recreational enjoyment is predicated on having a resource that is scenically, naturally, or recreationally unique. The majority of the landscape has no unique features, yet can offer many and varied types of recreational experiences. As shown previously in this chapter, most of the unique resource areas are great distances from the centers of populations and can only be used on a periodic basis. Thus, if planners are to increase supply, they must realize the potential of the typical landscape and try to capture this potential close to the user.

Management. Good management is the key to effective supply; as indicated in the beginning of the chapter, supply is a total planning/management program. The following are ways of improving or increasing the availability of a given recreational opportunity:

1. *Improved Planning and Management.* Legislative and administrative management policies and proper area and site planning can help to eliminate conflict between the users and the resource, other users, and management. Simple on-site programs such as facilities maintenance, solid waste disposal, and vegetation treatment can make a given area attractive that heretofore was unattractive to the recreationist. Unfortunately, many of the acres of supply, even those that have been developed, are ineffective because supply was not envisioned as a continuous process—a total planning and management package.

2. *Encouragement of the Private Sector.* We must become cooperative with the private sector since many of the potential resources for recreation are in the private sector. In many instances, it may be more appropriate for the private sector to assume a given role. For example,

rather than providing a transient campground on public land, it might be better developed on private land adjacent to a community where adequate services are already available.

3. *Innovativeness.* The planner should not be satisfied with traditional approaches. He should seek to fill recreational voids through innovative techniques. Recently a large midwest city hired a planning firm to develop water-based recreation, including land acquisition, within a reasonable travel distance to the city. Using a mosaic of aerial photos, the planners discovered a number of existing water areas within the city—abandoned gravel pits. These were acquired as gifts or at minimal purchase price. Reshaping of the landscape and bodies of water, plus good site planning, transformed these into desirable water-based recreation opportunities within the city and at a fraction of the original estimate of cost. Furthermore, since gravel is necessary in most urban construction, the city hired an urban land-use planning team to project the direction of the city's growth and to do feasibility studies of gravel reserves in the expansion corridors. Several reserves are being purchased, and site plans will be developed for each. As the city expands, the gravel reserves will be leased to construction companies with the stipulation that they follow a specified plan for the disposition of the overburden (soil) and location of access roads. When the gravel removal is completed, the city can do the final landscaping and facility development with the lease monies. The final product will be a large, water-based park in the newly developed residential-commercial area at *no* cost to the city. And the project removed unsightly developments left over from the early construction days, the gravel pit.

4. *Leisure Service Package (LSP).* The LSP is the innovation of the future. Since it is becoming increasingly difficult to move large numbers of people through the wildland setting with minimal disruption of the physical and social environment, the LSP will "move" the wildland setting through large numbers of people. Special settings will be developed to stimulate the five senses and offer challenge in various leisure pursuits heretofore relegated only to the wildland setting.

A person in Philadelphia may go up to the 14th floor of a public building, pay his $20, and go on a whitewater canoe trip down the Middle Fork of the Salmon River. He gets into his canoe and begins to fight the rapids while enjoying the awesome landscape shown on a continuously changing panorama. The wind blows in his face. His eyes are washed by spray. His arms ache. Two hours later he arrives at his destination. Tired! Exhausted! But satisfied! Is this possible?

Could we take a snowmobiler, blindfold and place him on a barrel bronc, throw snow in his face while he is being jostled to the tune of a snowmobile roar played on stereophonic sound, and still give him a satisfying experience? Again, is this possible? Should we? Possibly the idea seems too radical, but we should not let our past education and experiences stifle our imaginations in providing satisfying experience substitutes.

SELECTED READINGS

1. Brockman, F. C., and L. C. Merriam, Jr. 1973. *Recreational Use of Wild Lands*. New York: McGraw-Hill Book Company. Chapters 7–12.
2. Bureau of Outdoor Recreation. 1966. *Federal Focal Point on Outdoor Recreation–Related Environmental Programs*. Washington, D. C.: U. S. Government Printing Office.
3. _____. 1970. *Federal Outdoor Recreation and Recreation-Related Environmental Programs*. Washington, D. C.: U. S. Government Printing Office.
4. Clawson, M. 1963. *Land and Water for Recreation*. Chicago: Rand McNally and Company.
5. Clawson, M., and J. L. Knetsch. 1966. *Economics of Outdoor Recreation*. Baltimore: The Johns Hopkins University Press. Chapters 8–10.
6. Cooley, R. A., and G. Wandesforde-Smith (eds.). 1969. *Congress and the Environment*. Seattle: University of Washington Press.
7. Doell, C. E., and L. F. Twardzik. 1973. *Elements of Parks and Recreation Administration*. Minneapolis: Burgess Publishing Company. Chapters 4–7.
8. Everhart, W. C. 1972. *The National Park Service*. Washington, D. C.: Praeger Publishers.
9. Jensen, C. R. 1973. *Outdoor Recreation in America—Trends, Problems, and Opportunities*. Minneapolis: Burgess Publishing Company.
10. Outdoor Recreation Resources Review Commission. *List of Public Outdoor Recreation Areas—1960*. Washington, D. C.: U. S. Government Printing Office. O.R.R.R.C. Report No. 2.
11. _____. 1962. *Outdoor Recreation for America*. Washington, D. C.: U. S. Government Printing Office.
12. _____. *Public Outdoor Areas—Acreage, Use, Potential*. Washington, D. C.: U. S. Government Printing Office. O.R.R.R.C. Report No. 1.
13. _____. *Wilderness and Recreation—A Report on Resources, Values, and Problems*. Washington, D. C.: U. S. Government Printing Office. O.R.R.R.C. Report No. 3.

CHAPTER 8

COST-BENEFIT ANALYSIS: AN APPROACH TO INVESTMENT EVALUATION IN RECREATION

Cost-benefit analysis will be presented as a method of decision making in resource allocation, particularly recreation. The need for sound criteria to evaluate investment alternatives will be developed. Next, the concept and principles of cost-benefit analysis will be presented, showing the procedures and pertinent terminology. Then the problems involved in applying the concept to outdoor recreation will be discussed, emphasizing such ideas as social institutions, value-price conflict, uncertainties of predictions, and imperfection of knowledge.

The demand for most of our natural resources has increased manyfold in the last two decades. Probably the greatest increase in demand has occurred in outdoor recreation. In our national parks alone, the number of visits per year has increased from 33.2 million in 1950 to 139.7 million in 1967—a 420 per cent increase.

In accordance with this increase in demand, we must recognize that our resources are not unlimited, and that as demand increases, they become even more scarce. Scarcity is defined in terms of supply versus demand. Since the resources are scarce, one can no longer have resource combinations A, B, C, and so on; he must choose the best alternatives.

The alternatives in resource investment are not simple, straightforward calculations. They involve all possible combinations of resources at varying levels of use to meet specific objectives. Clawson and Knetsch state:

> As there are simply not unlimited quantities of all kinds of resources, decisions must be made as to how to allocate them. In some cases, the choice is between recreation and other uses. In deciding how much area is to be put into wilderness, or into national parks, or in state parks, it is important to keep in mind the cost in timber harvests forgone or in the potential hydropower sites left undeveloped. The problem of resource allocation among uses also arises. For example, each of two proposals for recreation areas may have great site value and both well might be made part of a recreation system, but priorities must be established. In these cases, there is a great deal to be gained from putting evaluations in the most useful terms possible and making investment decisions on the basis of criteria that take account of both the costs and the benefits.[2]

The tremendous increase in demand for outdoor recreation will undoubtedly mean large investments in the future, thus placing greater emphasis on the need for investment criteria. No reason is foreseen for exempting recreation investments from the principles of resource allocation. In fact, probably the greatest need in the allocation scheme is more universality in comparing *all* investment opportunities. *The greatest possible recreation opportunity should be provided relative to the supply of the resource, the desires of the people, and the limitations of capital. In the past, many groups have reasoned that there is no need for investment comparisons because all recreation is good, i.e., whatever is built will be used because the demand is high.* This is a nearer-my-god-to-thee approach which still lingers in the thoughts of some recreationists.

There is little doubt that the resources, particularly the land based ones, are becoming more scarce and that investment alternatives must be judiciously chosen. A logical way that these choices can be made to meet the given objectives is not to analyze in terms of a single project but in terms of the investment (cost) and the return (benefit) of all the various alternative projects.[4]

COST-BENEFIT CONCEPT

Competitive alternative investment opportunities for our land, labor, and capital require that choices be made. Since most of the investments in outdoor recreation are made in the public sector, the ultimate economic objective should be to maximize human welfare—the greatest good for the greatest number.[3] Cost-benefit analysis within this public framework should provide for more rational decision making and consequently should produce better investments of our resources. Even then, perfect invest-ment is but a concept, because all costs and benefits cannot be known with precision. Yet the need for making such decisions remains.

Cost-benefit analysis is really no more than a refinement of what rational people do every day when making decisions about the future. *The essential feature of cost-benefit analysis is the comparison of the cost of an investment alternative with predicted benefits.*[5] If an investment is economically worthwhile, the total benefits discounted to the present must exceed the total cost discounted to the same time. Then, the comparison of the benefits to the costs of all alternatives will *aid* in determining which investments should be undertaken.

If the analysis is to be accomplished in an organized and systematic manner, the components to be used in the investment decision should be enumerated and then measured and weighted.[6] This enumeration of com-ponents should be done in advance of the measurements and should not be adjusted after the measurements in order to fit the "analysis" to the decision.

The evaluation of costs and benefits in itself cannot make the alloca-tion decision; the analyst or planner must ultimately select the best alterna-tive, since value judgments also enter the decision. However, if the analyst goes through a systematic and logical evaluation, the investment decision will be more objective and more consistent. The process, therefore, raises our investment (resource allocation) decisions to a more sophisticated level of decision making.

Definitions.   Words employed in everyday communications often have different connotations to different people. This is often more true when one uses technical language that has not been standardized. The terminology associated with cost-benefit analysis is important to the un-derstanding of the process.

Primary costs are those costs expressed in terms of goods and services that must be foregone in order to develop and operate a given project. They include not only direct expenditures but also allowances for economic losses. Other factors involved include cost of financing and tax allowances. Only these costs should be used in the cost-benefit analysis.

Secondary costs are those costs which involve the production of secondary benefits and do not reflect the actual cost of the project. These costs are not to be used in calculating the total costs of the investment. Recreation may be a secondary benefit in a reservoir development, if the primary purpose of the development is flood control. On the other hand, recreation may be a primary benefit for a multi-purpose reservoir.

Primary benefits are those benefits which accrue to the people who make use of the goods and services provided by the project. The key is that the benefits must be directly attributable to the particular development. The theoretical value of these primary benefits is the maximum amount that the consumer is willing to pay.[5] Only this category of benefits should be used in the cost-benefit analysis, since they are the only ones which are directly attributable to the project.

Secondary benefits are those that stem indirectly from, or are induced by, the given project. Therefore, these benefits should not be used in the cost-benefit analysis.

Principles of Cost-Benefit Analysis.* Cost-benefit analysis is based on the following principles:

1. The goods and services produced from a given project have value only to the extent that there is or will be a demand for them.

2. The best alternative for supplying the desired goods and services must also be the most economical one. Thus, the cost of developing the next best alternative (which would be the most economical) establishes the upper limit of value as measured by what the public is willing to forego to develop this alternative.

3. The best alternative relative to decision making should be that project which fulfills the desired objectives and exhibits the largest benefit-to-cost ratio.

4. In order to determine the best economic point of development of the selected project, it is necessary to maximize its economic worth by increasing the amount of the investment to the point that the cost-benefit ratio is just marginal relative to the cost-benefit ratio of the next best alternative. For example, a cost-benefit analysis of alternatives A, B, and C determines the respective ratios to be 10:1, 8:1, and 6:1. Then the scale of investment in project A may be increased so long as its cost-benefit ratio does not fall below that of project B.

5. All "negative" benefits must be accounted for in the cost-benefit analysis. These values are primary costs in that they reflect recreational opportunities that are destroyed in the process of creating new opportunities. In the development of warm-water fisheries in reservoirs, we may destroy the cold-water, stream fishery. This loss is a liability of the project and, thus, should be included as a *primary cost*. Therefore, these should be included in the cost calculations of those alternatives to which they can be directly attributed.

APPLICABILITY TO INVESTMENTS IN RECREATION RESOURCES

Cost-benefit analysis as a concept is readily applicable to any investment decision. However, the word "investment" often connotes dollars spent in anticipation of a profit. If this were so, then the cost-benefit analysis could be applied only where there were market values. However,

---

*Adapted from Sewall, W. R. D., et al. 1960. "A Guide to Benefit-Cost Analysis," *Readings in Resource Management and Conservation*. Chicago: The University of Chicago Press. p. 552.

the public sector has investment decisions to make in the form of resource allocation—selecting between alternative ways of accomplishing the desired objectives. Many of the public investment decisions cannot be made using absolute values, but the decision of how much to allocate to a given resource or combination of resources must be made.

The concept of cost-benefit analysis is readily applicable to investment decisions in outdoor recreation because the land base is limited and has many competing alternative uses. Second, the recreation manager is not exempt from rational, objective decision making because of the lack of a direct pricing mechanism. Third, recreation management decisions often involve large land areas and large capital expenditures; therefore, to justify the investments, these decisions should be made as objectively and consistently as possible.

Problems in Application

Social Institutions. Nonmarketability of public outdoor recreation is a deeply rooted social institution. It affects the application of cost-benefit analysis directly because it eliminates the pricing mechanism, forcing the manager to search for other means of evaluating investment alternatives. Indirectly it manifests itself in other problems such as the ones in the succeeding sections.

Outdoor recreation as a service operates in the absence of a market mechanism for the following reasons:

1. The public prefers it that way. In fact, many accept this as part of their heritage. In many instances private enterprise has not been able to cope with this heritage philosophy. Even large private forest industrial firms have opened their lands to various forms of recreation on a gratis basis as the result of pressures of public opinion.

2. Wildland recreation experiences cannot be packaged, or mass-produced, with the goal of optimizing dollar returns. The better way of insuring maximum welfare has been to retain portions of the outdoor recreation opportunity spectrum in a nonmarket status.

3. Social externalities, or as they are commonly called, general social benefits, are directed to maximizing social welfare. The argument here is that recreation is essential to a full and well-balanced life. Those who participate in outdoor recreation tend to be better adjusted socially and better and more productive citizens; thus, the general welfare is enhanced.[2] Accordingly, everyone benefits in some way, even those who do not participate in outdoor recreation. There has been little research to test this hypothesis; therefore, many people feet that the argument is weak. However, because the argument has not been empirically tested is by no means a basis for dismissal.

4. A syndrome has developed which credits the public sector with

being quality-conscious in recreation and the private sector with being money-oriented. This quality syndrome has sometimes generated strong negative feelings toward private recreation development.

A public agency generally has greater manpower and financial capacity than a private organization, and by its control of other public services may be able to maintain a given level of recreation experience over long periods of time. Also, public development generally offers a better balance of recreational facilities and areas than could be achieved in private development. Thus, the quality in reference to the entire recreational spectrum is maintained through variety. As Burch states:

> The real issue is the careful assignment of appropriate space
> and levels of development for the different kinds of activities
> people seek—not just rule by majority.[1]

In reference to the total recreational spectrum, variety and quality of experience are sometimes overlooked in many private ventures in order to achieve maximum gains. This oversight may be necessary because the ventures require immediate returns on the investments, i.e., private developers cannot make the long-term investments that the public sector can.[2] However, in defense of private recreation, one should realize that it has not generally attempted to compete with public developments but merely to complement them by providing specialized facilities and services.

A factor that is often overlooked in the quality syndrome is that many public agencies in the process of growing become large, unwieldy clubs of bureaucracy which frequently breed mediocrity. In the case of recreation, it may be mediocrity with variety.

Value and Price.   Generally costs associated with outdoor recreation investments have been straightforward calculations which are easy to obtain, whereas many benefit values are intangible and difficult to isolate and quantify. As Clawson and Knetsch state, "[there is a] social value of natural resources used for recreation, but, in practice, it would be impossible in many cases to recapture this value."[2]

Essentially, outdoor recreation is without a direct pricing guide. However, just because the recreation experience is without a price tag does not mean that it is without value to those who participate. In many outdoor spectator sports there are fixed prices, such as admission fees, which are monetary indicators of the minimum value of the experience to the individual user. Then, why should other forms of recreation be exempted from having an estimate made on the value of the experience, even though there is no direct pricing guide?

In the preceding example, the cost of admission does not necessarily place the exact value on the particular experience, but it is the best estimate of the value of the experience to the spectator that can be expressed in monetary terms. If this rationale is true, then why couldn't the cost of opportunities that the user foregoes in order to participate in a given outdoor recreation activity, or perhaps the additional money he spends in order to participate in the activity above what he would have normally spent, be considered as an estimate of the value of the activity? Several formulations have been presented as means of evaluating outdoor recreation benefits, both on a national and a regional basis. This book will not pursue these attempts at benefit valuation.

Uncertainties of Prediction. Prediction of future events is at best hazardous even when much is known about what is being predicted. In a new professional undertaking like outdoor recreation, the task is almost impossible. Thus, the uncertainties in the cost-benefit analysis are related not only to the uncertainties of the future but also to the scanty knowledge in outdoor recreation.

This poor predictability of future events in outdoor recreation is evidenced in the failure of Mission 66 (National Park Service) and Operation Outdoors (U.S. Forest Service). Both of these programs were set up to update facilities and area developments and also to expand the construction and development phases of the programs to meet the recreation needs of *tomorrow*. The lack of total success of these two programs was directly attributable to the poor predictions of future needs. The predictions were so inadequate that by the middle 1960s the developments were further from the intended goals than when the programs were started.

This problem is not peculiar to outdoor recreation. It applies to all of our resource development programs. However, the uncertainties may be exaggerated in recreation developments. Regardless of the development, the economic analysis cannot be discarded because of the uncertainties involved. Many uncertainties will exist no matter what our level of knowledge or how decisions are made. Nevertheless, as Clawson and Knetsch state:

> An analysis of costs and benefits of alternative investments
> may help to pinpoint the nature and possible magnitude of the
> uncertainties about the future.[2]

Investment Calculations. The manner in which the costs and benefits of investments are calculated will measurably affect the cost-benefit ratio. Some agencies include secondary benefits in their calculations, a practice which creates higher than normal ratios. Others tend to overlook or omit costs or benefits, or both, that are difficult to measure.

Also, the choice of interest rates which are used to discount monies back to the present will affect the cost-benefit ratios. The difference between 3 and 5 per cent interest rates can be great in terms of total dollars, perhaps great enough to justify an investment that would not ordinarily be justified if the higher rate were used.

Imperfect Knowledge. In general, there are two areas in which we have large voids in our accumulation of knowledge about cost-benefit analysis in outdoor recreation:

1.   Very little is known about the investment opportunities in recreation. Thus, few alternatives are available from which to choose.

2.   Also, little is known about the values associated with the known investment alternatives in recreation.

In the application of cost-benefit analysis, the label "imperfect knowledge" can be applied to all phases of outdoor recreation. Outdoor recreation is a relatively new professional undertaking, and consequently, very little knowledge has been accumulated about the technical, biological, and sociological aspects. Little is known about the biological carrying capacities of outdoor recreation lands, and even less is known about the sociological, psychological, and physical needs of the users of such lands.

If so little is known about recreation lands and their potential users, then in reality the allocating of resources for recreation and choosing between alternative investments within recreation becomes an almost impossible task—a guessing game. To compensate for such shortcomings in our decision making, many assumptions have been made, many situations stereotyped, and many factors overlooked. This has not substituted for knowledge but only emphasized our shortcomings and the need for continued research.

Acceptance by Management.   Many recreation managers have been reluctant to accept the idea that outdoor recreation benefits can be quantified. The sentiment often expressed is that many values associated with outdoor recreation are intangible and can never be quantified. The phobia extends to the point where many feel that recreation is above economic analysis and that all recreation is good and necessary. However, why should all other resource investments be subject to economic evaluation and not recreation?

Even if good estimates of values are derived and many of the difficulties associated with cost-benefit analysis are removed, there will still be a need to indoctrinate the recreation manager in the value and necessity of making such an analysis. This indoctrination will probably, of necessity, begin in the university training of those who will be tomorrow's decision makers.

SUMMARY

The demand for outdoor recreation has been increasing at an increasing rate; to meet this increase in demand, there has been a gradual shift in the allocation of resources to recreation. How much of our resources should be allocated to recreation? How do you choose between alternative recreation investments? Only the resource manager can ultimately make the decision because he is the one person who has intimate knowledge of the particular operation. He must consider the resource, the user, and the capital expenditure in making his decision. However, the decision should be made as objective as possible through the use of some logical, systematic process.

Cost-benefit analysis, one of the more classical economic techniques, offers a systematic approach to decision making. The analysis in general terms involves comparing the costs and benefits of an investment to see if it is economically feasible and then comparing all possible investments to determine the best alternative.

There are many problems associated with cost-benefit analysis in resource allocation, particularly recreation. Most of the problems relate either directly or indirectly to the social institution of nonmarketability. None of the problems are impossible to overcome, but much research and education will be necessary.

What must be recognized by the manager is that cost-benefit analysis is not an automatic decision maker. All analyses must be tempered with good judgment in order for the manager to arrive at a decision. The method of analysis is then simply a means of inserting objectivity and consistency in our decision making, giving us better investments of our resources.

SELECTED READINGS

1. Burch, W. R. Jr. 1966. "Wilderness—the Life Cycle and the Forest Recreation Choice," *Journal of Forestry*, 64(9):606–610.
2. Clawson, M., and J. L. Knetsch. 1966. *Economics of Outdoor Recreation*. Baltimore: The Johns Hopkins University Press.
3. Dahl, R. A., and C. E. Lindbloom. 1953. *Politics, Economics, and Welfare*. New York: Harper and Brothers.
4. McKean, R. N. 1958. *Efficiency in Government Through Systems Analysis*. New York: John Wiley & Sons, Inc.
5. Sewall, W. R. D., J. Davis, A. D. Scott, and D. W. Ross. 1960. "A Guide to Cost-Benefit Analysis," *Readings in Resource Management and Conservation*. Chicago: The University of Chicago Press.
6. Wildland Research Center. 1962. *Wilderness Recreation: A Report On Resources, Values and Problems*. Washington, D.C.: U.S. Government Printing Office. O.R.R.R.C. Report 3.

PART 3

METHODS AND APPROACHES TO OUTDOOR RECREATION PLANNING

This part focuses on the division of planning responsibilities suggested by the planning emblem (Figure III-1). Too much of our planning has started with the smallest management unit and has then focused upward through the planning flow chart. The difficulty with this procedure is that planning is not tied to any coordinated, large-scale plan, and this ultimately causes confusion and conflict; the results are duplication, unnecessary and undesirable competition, serious conflicts between user groups, voids in leisure services, and other more subtle problems.

The logical direction is downward, focusing on successively smaller resource units to the development of the specific site plan. This type of planning ensures coordinated action in attempting to incorporate the roles

Figure III–1 The planning emblem, suggesting a logical flow pattern of outdoor regional planning—starting with broad general plans and focusing on successively smaller units down to the specific recreation site (presented by S.S. Frissell, University of Montana, Missoula, Montana).

of all agencies and organizations, public and private. Even within a particular agency, coordination is essential in proper location of site developments. Some developments require spatial separation, such as trail heads (access points) for the snowmobile and the cross-country skier. Others might require reasonably close proximity, such as a boating access and a water-oriented campground. Only a higher level plan can ensure coordination of action whether separating conflicting uses or encouraging adjacent complementary developments. Thus, each step up the emblem ladder ensures greater coordination of the next lower level of planning.

Chapter 12 develops techniques in the evaluation of the recreation-resource potential. The methods used by various agencies and their applications are discussed. Estimating the recreation potential of the resource setting is essential in predicting the suitability of the site and the ultimate success or failure of an expensive development. With scarce fiscal and physical resources, we cannot afford trial and error planning and development.

Chapter 13 attempts to put recreation in a land-use planning context. Included in this chapter is a discussion of recreation in the classical multiple-use concept of land-use planning. Also, techniques of land-use control are presented as ways of protecting scenic and recreational resources.

CHAPTER 9

DIVISION OF PLANNING RESPONSIBILITY— FEDERAL AND STATE

Each level of government must accept its responsibility in provisioning for public services, including outdoor recreation. It may provide these services directly as the managing agency or through a quasi-public, non-profit corporation, or indirectly by encouraging private enterprise to assume certain marketable services. Regardless of who offers the service, the responsible level of government should coordinate the planning or act as a catalyst in meeting the needs of the people within its sociopolitical boundaries.

Failure to assume this responsibility results in "overloading" the site developments of other levels of government, a condition called the *principle of overloading*. If one level of government does not assume its responsibility, then the people seek substitute opportunities, usually at facilities of the next higher level of government. For example, if a local government fails to meet a demand by its constituents for family picnic opportunities, then people will seek this opportunity in a nearby state park, national forest, or national park. This switch overloads facilities that were developed for state and regional needs—not as a catchall for local activities (Figure 9–1).

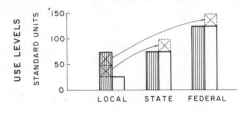

GOVERNMENTAL LEVEL

▥ DEMANDED OPPORTUNITIES

☐ SUPPLIED OPPORTUNITIES

⊠ OVERLOADING FROM OTHER LEVELS

Figure 9-1 Graphic illustration of the principle of overloading, where unsatisfied demands are shifted to other developments. It is assumed in the illustration that the state and federal governments are exactly meeting the demands of the visitor; thus, any shifting of use would overload existing developments.

NATIONWIDE PLANNING

Nationwide recreation planning is an umbrella which pulls together national leisure needs under a common roof and outlines approaches for meeting these needs. Of primary importance are the broad goals and policies that delineate leisure service programs and the roles of various levels of government in accomplishing the programs. In sum, the primary concern is *coordination* of leisure services to meet the needs of the nation, and *budgeting* of scarce resources (fiscal and physical) to accomplish priority goals.

We are presently in the throes of our first nationwide outdoor recreation plan, but this is not our first effort. In 1924 President Calvin Coolidge proclaimed:

> Our aim in this country must be to try to put the chance for out-of-doors pleasure, with all that it means, within the grasp of the rank and file of our people, the poor man as well as the rich.*

He then appointed a national committee to appraise existing conditions and to recommend courses of action where needed. The committee consisted of the Secretaries of Agriculture, Commerce, Health, the Interior, Labor, and War, and the Assistant Secretary of the Navy. The major action taken by the committee was to plan the first National Conference on Outdoor Recreation, held in Washington, D.C.; and the primary goal was to plan and direct outdoor recreation for the entire nation.

The final report, entitled *National Conference on Outdoor Recreation,* presented basic philosophies toward leisure that were emerging at the time and the cumulation of individual research efforts, though somewhat meager. But the most important part of the document was the summary and

---

*From a speech by President Coolidge on the importance of outdoor recreation, 1924.

analysis of the major national data collection surveys and projects conducted under the direction of the national conference. Unfortunately, the program was terminated after the stock market crash of 1929 because of insufficient funding.

In 1934, outdoor recreation issues were pursued by the Federal Natural Resources Board, focusing mainly on national park and related lands. Discussion was presented on population needs, available resource settings for outdoor recreation, and possible disparity between the location of the people and the location of existing opportunities. Because of the lack of funds during this time, no real effort was extended to coordinate nationwide planning, and the matter was dropped.

Recent Planning Efforts.   No further national effort emerged until well after World War II, when we began to see a tremendous increase in auto-oriented recreation. During the 1950s, demand for outdoor recreation exploded, but there was a corresponding concern for recreation resources. This concern brought about the passage of the Outdoor Recreation Resources Review Act of June 28, 1958, which established a commission of fifteen people (four from the U.S. Senate; four from the House of Representatives; and seven private citizens appointed by President Eisenhower) to direct an inventory of our nation's supply of outdoor recreation opportunities and a projection of the nationwide demand for recreation.

Twenty-seven special reports were prepared for the commission by research organizations, individual authorities, and the commission staff. The commission summarized the information and made its own recommendations to President Kennedy and the U.S. Congress on January 31, 1962, in its report, *Outdoor Recreation for America*. The report stated that the primary role of the federal government was coordinative management planning through:

1. Preservation of service areas, natural wonders, primitive areas, and historic sites of national significance.

2. Management of federal lands for the broadest possible recreation benefit consistent with other essential uses.

3. Cooperation with states through technical and financial assistance.

4. Promotion of interstate arrangements, including federal participation where necessary.

5. Assumption of vigorous, cooperative leadership in a nationwide effort.[13]

The report further recommended that a Bureau of Outdoor Recreation, Department of the Interior, be established for coordinating the nationwide effort to avoid duplication, voids, and conflicts in leisure services. One of the six major functions of the proposed bureau would be to formulate a nationwide recreation plan on the basis of state, regional, and national needs.

The recommendations received overwhelming public support, and on March 1, 1962, a Presidential message was sent to Congress announcing that a Bureau of Outdoor Recreation would be established in the Department of the Interior. On April 2, 1962, Secretary Stewart L. Udall established the Bureau, but it was not until May 28, 1963 that President Kennedy signed Public Law 88–29, the Bureau's Organic Act. Thus, we have been in the process of formal nationwide planning since then.

Although much effort and concern has gone into nationwide planning, by 1972 there was still no plan. Apparently the Bureau had completed a draft of the plan by 1966, but because of limited data and insufficient coordination, the draft was never approved. Congress further directed that a nationwide plan be submitted by 1968 and updated periodically thereafter. However, there was still no approved nationwide outdoor recreation plan five years after that target date.

In the late spring of 1972, ten national forums for citizen involvement in nationwide planning were held throughout the United States to encourage maximum public input. The culmination of this effort produced our first nationwide outdoor recreation plan in November 1973. The preliminary results were channeled into ten federal work groups:

1. Roles and Responsibilities of Public and Private Institutions

2. Urban Recreation

3. Rural Recreation

4. Quality Recreation Resource Areas

5. Resource Capacity and Recreation Use

6. Implementation and Management Techniques

7. Recreation for the Disadvantaged

8. Private Sector Contributions

9. Recreation Facility Cost Estimation

10. Federal Recreation Management Criteria and Organization

The task force organization integrated the conclusions and recommendations of the ten federal work groups into a workable plan (Figure 9–2).

The Nationwide Plan.   Although the plan is still in the infancy stage, some basic steps should be discussed. These steps, in chronological order, are:

1. Determine existing and potential supply of outdoor recreation resources, classed according to a uniform system—the B.O.R. classification system.

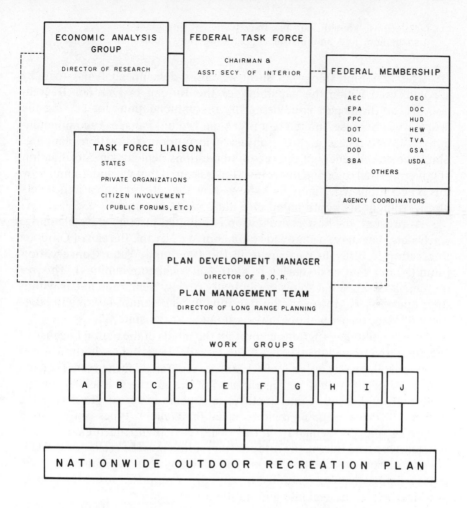

Figure 9-2 Nationwide outdoor recreation plan, task force organization.

2. Determine present and future demand for outdoor recreation opportunities. This has been done by the Bureau for various periods through the year 2000.

3. Convert demand into present and future needs for outdoor recreation resource areas, facilities, and opportunities.

4. Identify critical problems by comparing the demand to the existing and future supply. This is an important step if we are to meet the recreation needs of the public.

5. Recommend courses of action to meet the needs and resolve the critical problems, using some priority system. Recom-

mendations should be in the form of programs—
management and administration, funding, and coordination.*

The first four steps—in sum, a supply-demand analysis—can be
accomplished within the capability of the Bureau of Outdoor Recreation. The difficult part is devising the recommendations for solving the
problems of overuse, limited resources, and so on. Panacea recommendations will only cause greater confusion in outdoor recreation planning.
Since the effectiveness of the recommendations depends on coordination
of governmental roles and programs, it is essential that we understand how
this is accomplished. Figure 9–3 shows how the roles of the various levels
of government are coordinated into nationwide programs.

At present, the best coordination is effected through state planning.
Each state must have a statewide plan approved by the Bureau of Outdoor
Recreation in order to participate in the Land and Water Conservation
Fund (50 per cent cost-sharing to state and local communities). This requirement ensures that states periodically review trends and needs within
their boundaries. However, the nationwide plan cannot be a mere summary of state plans; it should give guidance to the state.

Also, umbrella programs cannot fill the needs of the nation because of
the great diversity in tastes, needs, and available resources in the various
geographical regions of the United States. Programs for the New England
area most likely would be unsuitable for the northern Rockies, or the
southeast, and so on. Consequently, it appears necessary to divide the
nation into major planning regions based on available types of recreation
resources and the demand for the resources; then, the regional office
boundaries of the Bureau of Outdoor Recreation must be realigned to focus
specifically on coordination within the planning region. Figure 9–4 indicates existing planning relationships and those proposed to ensure greater
coordination of the regional and national levels.

Incentives such as those at the state planning level could be offered to
encourage coordination of planning with the specific region. This idea is not
intended to discourage other existing or future interstate planning. This
approach is important in maintaining continuity of programs, inasmuch
as the average visitor is extremely mobile and participates irrespective of political boundaries.

Also, additional legislation is needed to ensure coordination of all
federal agencies' planning actions. At present, the Bureau of Outdoor
Recreation has only review power over federal projects relating to
recreation—from dam building to highway construction. No super-power
should hold dominion over other agencies; however, if the Bureau is to
effectively coordinate outdoor recreation at the federal level, then there
must be a review board to arbitrate differences of opinion on federal
projects—such as the suggested Federal Land-Use Planning Authority.

---

*For a detailed outline of the nationwide plan, see Part V.

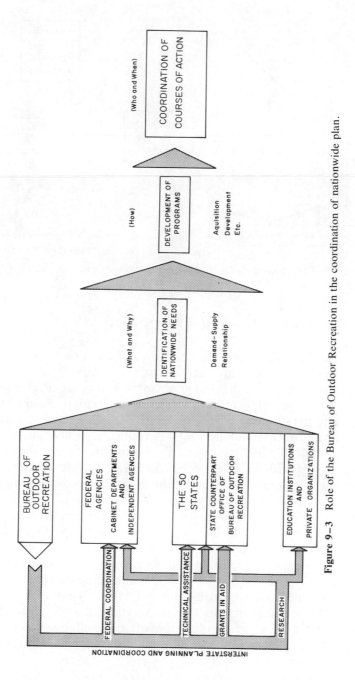

Figure 9–3   Role of the Bureau of Outdoor Recreation in the coordination of nationwide plan.

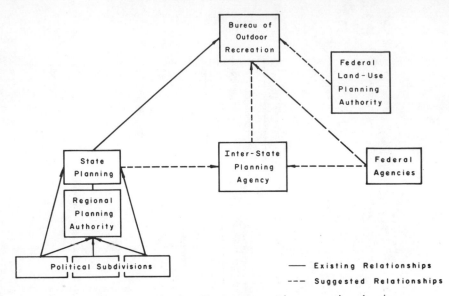

Figure 9–4   Relationships for effective state outdoor recreation planning.

STATE OUTDOOR RECREATION PLANNING

The Outdoor Recreation Resources Review Commission recommended coordinated planning throughout the nation. The commission further recommended that the best approach would be financial incentives to state and local governments for goal-oriented planning, acquisition, and development. In response to these recommendations, Congress passed the Land and Water Conservation Fund Act (Public Law 88–578) in 1964.

The LAWCON Fund was primarily a program of assistance to state and political subdivisions. Sixty per cent of the annual appropriations were allocated for this purpose. Originally the state share was apportioned as follows: two-fifths divided equally among the states and three-fifths according to population and demonstrated need. The other 40 per cent of the money was available to the U.S. Forest Service, the National Park Service, and the U.S. Wildlife Service to purchase needed recreation lands and to help offset the capital costs of public recreation, fish and wildlife, improvement of federal water developments, and similar projects.

The appropriations were to be derived from: (1) entrance and other user fees, (2) proceeds from the sale of surplus federal lands, and (3) federal motorboat fuel taxes. Later, monies from off-shore oil leases were added. The allocation of monies to the various states has increased considerably since the inception of the program.

The preparation, approval (by B.O.R.), and updating of comprehensive statewide outdoor recreation plans are prerequisites to state participation in the LAWCON Fund grant program. All states submitted their initial plans for approval by late 1966. The plans must follow a given format and can be approved by the regional director of B.O.R. for up to a five-year period. Very few of the initial plans were approved for the maximum period; however, the plans and planning process have become more sophisticated since then.

Comprehensive Statewide Plan. The state comprehensive plan is supposed to direct planning and development action on all outdoor recreation programs, both public and private. The private sector must be included because it provides greater variety and special types of services; almost 70 per cent of our potential land base for recreation is in private ownership. If we are to expand opportunities, then the private sector will have to assume a greater role in provisioning for recreation opportunities.

Where feasible, recreation planning should be an integral part of the state land-use plan, or comprehensive developmental plan. It cannot proceed as a totally separate process; it must be coordinated with urban transportation, water development, health and education, and other types of planning, since all of these types of projects affect the resource base and the leisure needs of the public. By integrating the various plans, we would be striving for optimum allocation of resources. In addition, all planning could be based on the same population, economic, and related growth data.

The characteristics of a state plan should be:

1. *Comprehensive, Encompassing All Outdoor Recreation Activities, Resources, and Programs That Are Significant Within the State.* The needs of all segments of the population—urban and rural residents, the aged, the physically handicapped, and others—should be the determinants of statewide programs. Where necessary, programs and resources should be coordinated with those of neighboring states. Finally, measures should be formulated to protect and enhance the quality of the recreation environment, natural and man-made.

2. *Focused on Significant Needs, Participation Trends, or Attendant Problems in Provisioning for Opportunities.* Broad-based policies and programs need to be designed to fulfill needs or to resolve problems. Use regulations and specific site planning are not essential parts of the plans; these are the reponsibilities of the individual agency or organization, or of private enterprise.

3. *Long-Range in Outlook on Needs, Trends, and Problems.* The plan should probe at least fifteen to thirty years into the future, reflecting creative forethought rather than merely extrapolating from present trends.

4. *Action-Oriented to Provide Input into the Decision Making Process for What, When, and Where.* Included in this characteristic is a five-year implementation program for the state as well as recommended actions for the federal and local governments and the private sector. The five-year program emphasizes continuity of effort in striving for the long-range goals but allows intermediate adjustments of programs to account for changes in trends rather than dogmatically following the 15- to 30-year projections.

5. *Flexible to Meet Changing Developmental Patterns, Social and Economic Conditions, and Environmental Impact.* Therefore, the state plan must include a method of periodic revision. For example, management policies must change to reflect changes in the recreational use of vehicles. We must not delude ourselves by constantly reflecting on our past successes; we need to look ahead and formulate policy and planning that will encourage creative problem solving—in other words, we need to plan for tomorrow's needs today.

As an example, we have been aware of snowmobile and off-road vehicle use as an expanding recreational opportunity, creating challenge and opportunity for the imaginative planner. Yet little has been done to plan for snowmobile use, except in a few states, and this lack of foresight in planning has created havoc, conflict (through polarized views), and crises.

Some essential elements that any large-scale, comprehensive outdoor recreation plan, such as the state plan, include: (1) objectives and basic authority, (2) characteristics of the planning unit, (3) inventory of recreation resources, (4) demand for recreation opportunities, (5) program recommendations, and (6) action-oriented implementation. A detailed recommended outline for a state comprehensive outdoor recreation plan is presented in Appendix C.

1. *Objectives.* Objectives should be broad enough to encompass the needs of all user groups within the state. Specific, more refined objectives should be developed for each major planning region of the state and special statewide programs such as scenic roadways, statewide trail systems, or state parks.

2. *Characteristics of the Planning Unit.* The physical and socioeconomic characteristics of the state and specific planning regions should be presented. Factors such as climate and topography, scenic and unique natural features, historical and cultural patterns, and economic development and urbanization should be surveyed and thoroughly described. In addition, a description of the resource base—timber, wildlife, watersheds, grazing, and nonrenewable resources—should be reviewed. This review is necessary to determine the potentially complementary and adverse land uses that could affect recreation planning. In sum, any factor that may influence the character and magnitude of outdoor recreation within the state should be thoroughly appraised for its possible effects on planning for statewide recreation programs.

3. *Inventory of Recreation Resources.* Of primary concern is the identification, location, size, and capacity of existing recreation opportunities, public or private, within the state. The inventory should be categorized according to the type of opportunity (modern trailer camping, wilderness, etc.) and the managing agency (State Park System, U.S. Forest Service, etc.).

Second, the inventory should cover potential recreation development areas and sites that are uniquely suited for specific opportunities, e.g., the

Oregon Trail crossing to show the role of the state in the settlement of the west, or unique geological features, or rare and endangered species that should be preserved yet interpreted to the visitor. The inventory is necessary if we are to identify where and how the opportunity spectrum can be expanded, if needed.

4. *Demand for Recreation Opportunities.*   Demand should be measured in the present and projected into the future using a minimum projection period of 15 years. The planner should attempt to correlate demand to social and economic factors that would give a more reliable basis for generalizing to the general population. Special attention should be given to factors which may directly affect demand, such as alternative opportunities, user fees, technological changes, and impact of nonresident use.

The demand analysis should recognize that the quality of the recreation environment is an important part of the recreational experience. Unusually high demand can have a deteriorating effect on the site, potentially lowering or even eliminating the quality of the recreational experience derived from the physical and social surroundings.

The last steps in initial planning include formulating recommendations and developing means of implementation. These are relative to the data and other inputs developed in the preceding steps.

Coordination of State Planning.   The first element in coordination is regionalization; appropriate regions of the state should be delineated for more detailed outdoor recreation planning. The boundaries should be coterminous with those of the state comprehensive planning regions, if they exist. Where there are no existing regions, the boundaries should be based on major changes in the physiographical features, or cultural patterns, or both, in terms of socioeconomics and cultural identification with a particular urban area or trade center.

Having identified the regions, planning can focus not only on needs but also on locational factors in terms of where the needs within the state are and how they can be met. To describe needs on a statewide basis is too abstract; there is no way to develop effective courses of action unless we know *what* is needed, *where,* and *how much.*

There is still a need for some type of organizational structure to ensure good coordination of planning and development within the state, particularly if we are to use the regionalization concept. Figure 9–5 presents a hypothetical organization chart. The governor of each state must appoint a state liason officer for state outdoor recreation planning, usually the director of the state recreation commission or department of conservation. Statewide planning is then the responsibility of the state liason officer. He is the only state official who may enter into agreements or conduct formal liason work with the Bureau of Outdoor Recreation or with the regional and local planning authorities.

Coordination of comprehensive state planning for all services is assured through representation of the outdoor recreation planning agency on the state planning coordinating board. All state agencies who have planning

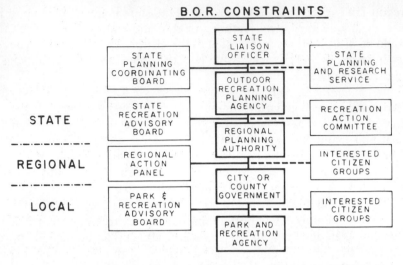

Figure 9–5   A hypothetical organizational structure in coordinating state comprehensive outdoor recreation planning.

responsibilities should be represented. All background, socioeconomic, and demographic data should be drawn from the state planning and research service. This procedure guarantees that all agencies relate their planning efforts to the same base data.

Two other advisory-coordinating groups are desirable at the state level. Through voluntary participation on the recreation action committee, the state outdoor recreation planning agency coordinates with all federal, state, and private agencies that are involved with recreation or land management. The committee's sessions are purely informational to make each agency aware of future plans and developments. This type of coordination is necessary since the state has no real jurisdiction over the federal agencies within the state.

The state outdoor recreation advisory committee would advise the planning agency of matters pertaining to statewide subsystems such as state parks, state trail systems, and others. The makeup of the committee should primarily include interested citizens from a broad geographical background.

Most states do not have comprehensive statewide planning for public services; however, a few of those that do have comprehensive statewide planning have experimented with the establishment of a regional planning authority. Because of the lack of experience factors, it is difficult to judge the success of the regionalization. However, where there are large populations competing heavily for use of limited space for recreational and other purposes, it seems a desirable concept to develop the regional planning authority to encourage maximum coordination of regional plans—coordination that may be difficult at the state level in the more heavily populated states such as California and New York. In a state like Wyoming, regionalization of authority would appear undesirable, even though planning is separated into regions for delineating needs and development of programs. It would likely prove too expensive; also, Wyomingites tend to identify statewide rather than regionally.

The regional planning authority would be responsible for data collection, supply-demand analysis, and formulation of recommendations. This information would be incorporated into the total state plan. In addition, it would serve as the clearinghouse for acquisition and development projects under the Land and Water Conservation Fund to ensure that the projects accord with the state comprehensive outdoor recreation plan. The regional authority would then make recommendations for project approval to the state agency.

Some regional authorities are requiring local governments to develop community or countywide plans through their park and recreation agencies. Then the regional authority approves them. These plans must reflect the broad-based state goals. Any project submitted after the approval of the local plan must be referenced in that plan.

Most states have not reached this level of regionalization, however. In those cases, it would be better to have an individual or section at the state level review proposals for local projects to ensure that they are in agreement with the state plan, and then have a screening committee of professionals and interested citizens select priority projects if the cost of proposals exceeds the funding limit.

SELECTED READINGS

1. Alden, H., *et al.* 1971. "What the Comprehensive Plan Does Not Do," *Proceedings 6th Annual Rocky Mountain—High Plains Park and Recreation Conference.* pp. 4–15.
2. Andersen, J. 1963. "The Bureau of Outdoor Recreation, Its Origin, Structure, Functions and Relationships to the State," *Proceedings Louisiana Outdoor Recreation Seminar.*
3. Brockman, C. G. 1959. *Recreational Use of Wildlands.* New York: McGraw-Hill Book Company.
4. Bureau of Outdoor Recreation. 1972. *America Voices Its Recreation Concerns.* Washington, D. C.: U. S. Government Printing Office.
5. ____. 1966. *Federal Focal Point in Outdoor Recreation.* Washington, D. C.: U. S. Government Printing Office.
6. ____. 1968. *Grants-in-Aid Manual.* Washington, D. C.: U. S. Government Printing Office.
7. ____. 1973. *Outdoor Recreation: A Legacy for America.* Washington, D. C.: U. S. Government Printing Office.
8. Fitch, E. M., and J. F. Shanklin. 1970. *The Bureau of Outdoor Recreation.* Washington, D.C.: Praeger Publishers.
9. Hansen, R. P. 1965. "Cooperative Interagency Relationships: Some Problems and Solutions," *Proceedings Recreation Management Institute.* pp. 1.1–1.16.
10. Koenings, R. H. 1970. "Some Broad Implications of Outdoor Recreation Planning,"

Elements of Outdoor Recreation Planning. B. L. Driver (ed.). Ann Arbor, Michigan: University of Michigan. pp. 309–310.

11. McCurdy, D. R., and L. K. Johnson. 1967. *Recommended Policies for the Development and Management of State Park Systems.* Southern Illinois University Agriculture Publication No. 26.

12. National Conference on State Parks. 1971. "State Parks," *Parks and Recreation* 8:74–80.

13. Outdoor Recreation Resources Review Commission: *Outdoor Recreation for America.* Washington, D.C., U.S. Government Printing, Office, 1962.

14. Pierce, R. L. 1970. "Statewide Outdoor Recreation Planning," *Elements of Outdoor Recreation Planning.* B. L. Driver (ed.). Ann Arbor, Michigan: University of Michigan. pp. 32–34.

15. Sargent, F. O. 1968. *Recreation Potential of Vermont.* Vermont Agriculture Experiment Station Report No. 16.

16. Sytles, F. G. 1970. "Variables Which Must Be Considered in Outdoor Recreation Planning," *Elements of Outdoor Recreation Planning.* B. L. Driver (ed.). Ann Arbor, Michigan: University of Michigan. pp. 49–60.

17. Underhill, A. H. 1970. "Hierarchy of Responsibilities in Outdoor Recreation Planning," *Elements of Outdoor Recreation Planning.* B. L. Driver (ed.). Ann Arbor, Michigan: University of Michigan. pp. 35–48.

18. Van Meter, J. R. 1970. *A Framework for Outdoor Recreation Planning in Illinois.* Illinois Department of Conservation.

CHAPTER 10

REGIONAL AND AREA PLANNING

REGIONAL PLANNING

Among the ambiguities in the planners' vocabulary is the term "region." No finely spun definition seems necessary here; a region (as the term is used in regional planning) is an area the inhabitants of which are tied together in economic, social, and sometimes governmental relationships, many of which are determined or strongly influenced by history, tradition and by natural features of the area—e.g. climate, physiography, soil types, etc. Some river basins are the archetype. Of course, very few if any regions are self-contained or self-sufficient, and their boundaries often are not lines but bands of considerable width.[21]

A region is a geographical area acquiring a concrete form and character only with respect to a given problem or situation and is greater than a single community or governmental authority. A regional plan focuses on the needs of a given region by refining national goals; coordinating action of lower levels of government; translating them into spatial, circulatory, and developmental patterns; and measuring their effect once the plan is executed.[5]

In most instances, the regional plan does not correspond in area to any single administrative unit and has no total administrative or legal sanction. The values must be derived through the cooperation of all concerned public and private agencies. Ultimately, success is dependent on total community action in the broadest sense. The best and most efficient plan should be developed regardless of political boundary. Some planners feel that many political boundaries are obsolete and should be reestablished through regional planning, because this boundary system better describes the existing socioeconomic situations.

Types of Regions. There are three major types of regions:[11]

1. *Uniform Region.* This type refers to a region that is similar in certain characteristics throughout. In recreation planning, this homogeneity may refer to the social aspects in terms of the type of participant and his expected behavior, or to the resource itself. A certain amount of homogeneity of selected variables (visitor or resource factors) is essential to a definition of reasonable regional boundaries. The Yellowstone region includes the Yellowstone National Park, and surrounding public and private lands essentially describe a somewhat homogeneous planning based on travel and participation (Figure 10–1).

2. *Nodal Region.* Society organizes itself into certain spatial patterns. The nodes of these patterns are the centers of urbanization, and the surrounding areas, which are socially and economically dependent on the urban node, circumscribe the nodal region. Many urban areas form the centers of social and economic activity for the smaller outlying communities.

3. *Metropolitan Region.* This term refers to a vast urban regional system such as those that surround the cities of New York, Chicago, Denver, and Los Angeles. It differs from the nodal region only in size and complexity. Typically it has a large urban center that is functionally central to a vast nodal region. This region comprises a hierarchy of settlements and interacting smaller nodal regions to which the metropolitan region provides specialized goods and services that the smaller centers cannot provide themselves. In addition, the metropolitan region often acts as a great market for the surplus products of the nodal regions.

Subregions. In regional outdoor recreation planning, perhaps the best approach will be to identify the five or six major regions in the United States based on social, economic, cultural, and physiographic characteristics. Those units could then be subdivided into *subregions* of urbanization, and into the surrounding areas, which would correspond to the nodal sub-regions described in the preceding paragraphs.

Standard regions and subregions can increase planning efficiency and coordination and can improve the data base at less cost if all agencies can share the same data. For example, the Yellowstone Regional Plan (Figure 10–1) would become an important subregional plan in a hypothetical Northern Rockies regional plan. Or the Chicago Metropolitan Regional Plan would become a subregional plan in a hypothetical Upper Midwest Great Lakes regional plan.

The standardization should improve the informational flow to the planning and management agencies and from them to the user. This concept is not widely accepted, so the author has chosen to use the more traditional definitions of regions given in the preceding paragraphs.

Functions of a Regional Plan. A regional plan performs four main functions:

1. *Advisory.* It provides a framework of goals rather than operative programs.

2. *Coordinative.* It attempts to rationalize and integrate a series

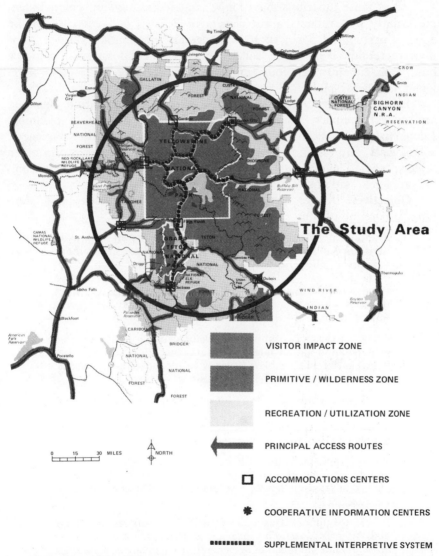

VISITOR IMPACT ZONE

PRIMITIVE / WILDERNESS ZONE

RECREATION / UTILIZATION ZONE

PRINCIPAL ACCESS ROUTES

ACCOMMODATIONS CENTERS

COOPERATIVE INFORMATION CENTERS

SUPPLEMENTAL INTERPRETIVE SYSTEM

Figure 10–1 The Yellowstone region (National Park Service. 1972. *Yellowstone Master Plan*, Yellowstone National Park, Wyoming).

of alternative actions through interagency communication and description of role responsibility for various agencies.

3. *Restrictive*. It provides a framework for positive action by identifying possible constraints and limitations and adopting restrictive policies to minimize the problems.

4. *Developmental*. It provides for the identification, location, and agency responsibility of major regional developments, including circulation patterns.

All of these functions may not be included in a given regional plan, particularly if it reflects a social service delivery system without the need of a resource base, such as a regional information service. Outdoor recreation is a social service that requires a minimal resource base. Consequently, all four functions are generally included in a regional recreation plan.

Interdisciplinary Approach. Even in regional recreation planning, an interdisciplinary approach is necessary to total planning. Economists, recreation planners, highway and construction engineers, sociologists, and others may have a role in the development of a given regional plan. The makeup of the plan will depend on the goals, technical problems, and costs involved.

Objectives. There are seven major objectives for regional planning:

1. Livability—reasonable convenience for all persons in their normal activities, including recreation and the journeys to work of those gainfully employed; sufficient open space, particularly but not only in and around dwellings, to give some sense of relaxation from the routine of work and from the constant stimulation of interpersonal contacts; the separation of incompatible land uses.

2. Efficiency—physical development in such densities of population and of land uses in its component districts that it makes for reasonable efficiency in the provision of public services and in the activities of business and industry.

3. Amenity—a setting for all land-use districts that encourages development marked by a degree of both variety and unity as well as by "character," beauty, and a sensitive and imaginative treatment of the natural site.

4. Flexibility and Choice—again, an urban structure and density pattern that allows many use districts to grow or change at least moderately without drastic disruption of adjacent areas.

5. Minimum Harm to Natural Communities of Plants and Animals—assuming changes in these communities near areas of enlarging human settlement, these changes should not be more disruptive than is unavoidable and should be estimated in advance to determine what offsetting steps could be

taken in behalf of desirable new equilibria in the near future; this consideration should extend not only to massive invasions by residential or industrial development but also to highways, areas for active recreation, dams or other interruptions of streams, disposal of human and industrial wastes, etc.; early identification and means of protecting natural areas of museum quality, both wilderness areas and other.

6. Optimum Use of Resources—an allocation of human and capital resources among the various types of public investment and between new development and redevelopment that *represents some approximation* (no one should claim more than this) to their optimum use; priorities* among the needs for urban investment at any one time that will both meet the most urgent needs first and minimize future shortages of facilities and services.

7. Public Participation—"public" here refers to nonofficials, nonprofessionals in planning; "participation" to some meaningful part in the planning process itself through regular rather than chance opportunities for criticism and voicing of preferences, either directly (whenever possible) or through acceptable representatives.[21]

AREA PLANNING

Area planning, sometimes called unit planning, focuses on areas smaller than the subregion, its main purpose to allocate space for physical development. The next step is *site planning*, where development is designed according to some spatial arrangement within the framework of the area plan. Thus, an area plan is a recreation plan for a parcel of land (and water) that is large enough to provide a variety of outdoor recreation experiences, yet small enough that the activities are potentially interacting or conflicting, or both. There is a general scenic, recreational, or historic theme for the area in order to separate it from other areas. Size is of little consequence since the emphasis is on themes such as mountains, large lakes, or historic areas; an area could vary from several hundred to thousands of acres. Generally, area plans are limited to a single ownership. A graphic layout of an area plan is shown in Figure 10–2; a complete area plan is shown in Part 5.

Reasons for Area Planning. The reasons for area planning are:

1. To make certain that each development is coordinated in an overall integrated plan.

---

*"Priorities" in the sense of a scheduling of outlays in light of the relative urgency of the needs each might help to satisfy. Of course this does not imply that the outlays would be made *seriatim;* several or many of them would usually be going ahead at any one time.

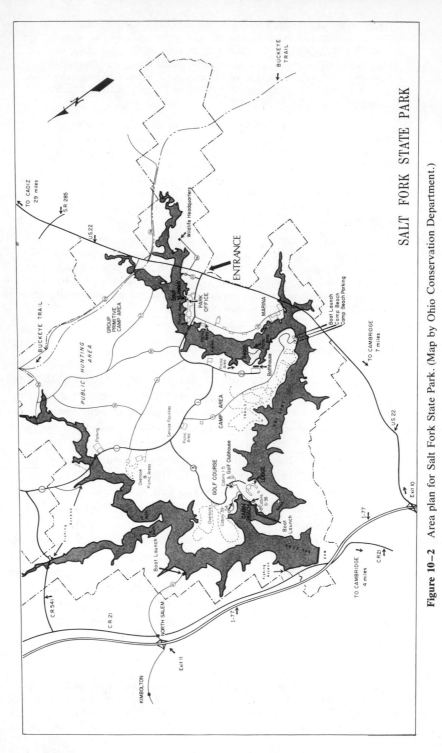

Figure 10–2   Area plan for Salt Fork State Park. (Map by Ohio Conservation Department.)

2.   To make people aware of the total program—sites, facilities, and services.

3.   To avoid duplication or overlapping of sites, facilities, and services.

4.   To serve as a guide for administrative zoning of the area for certain types of recreational uses.

5.   To ensure maximum benefit for each dollar spent in planning, development, and administration of the areas.

Steps in Area Planning.   The steps for area planning are:

1.   Project future demands for various recreational opportunities. The planner needs to project the recreational needs including types of activities, levels of use, and required services. Regional demand studies must be interpreted by the planner in relation to local conditions. For more discussion, see Chapter 6.

2.   Convert demand to spatial requirements for the particular outdoor recreation experience. There are no standards, only guidelines in terms of spatial separation of the visitor, minimal services, traffic flow patterns, and resource characteristics for a given experience. These are discussed in Part 4, *"Guidelines for Site and Facility Planning."* The type of experience, the characteristics of the resource, and the planner's perception of the user population can drastically affect the amount of space allocated to a particular development. For example, with a dense understory, one may place forest campground units close together and still maintain the needed visual privacy and aesthetics, whereas, if privacy is desired in an area of sparse understory, the units may have to be spaced much further apart.

3.   Inventory existing sites, facilities, recreational uses, and the potential for expanding these opportunities or developing new ones. Remember that certain uses have developed without planning; these are important and should be included in the inventory. The planner rarely ever deals with a totally undeveloped landscape; thus, he needs to determine what exists in the area in order to make maximum use, where possible, of existing developments. Furthermore, the resource base should be classified according to its ability to offer and sustain certain types of recreational opportunities, including specified developments, as discussed in Chapter 12. The decisions on future expansion can also be tied to the original inventory, if the resource potential was assessed in the original survey.

4.   Determine balance between demand and existing supply. It is important to compare the projected demand against existing and potential supply. The deficit in existing supply indicates the direction development should go to minimize the gap between demand and supply. It may even indicate a surplus of certain types of sites that could easily be converted to some opportunity in short supply. Once the gap is identified, it must be compared to the potential supply of the area. Some areas may have limited resource potential even though demand is high.

5.   Allocate space to selected sites, facilities, and uses in order to minimize the gap between demand and supply, realizing that certain opportunities may have to be foregone because of the limited potential of the resource base.

6.   Determine normal travel and behavioral patterns of recreationists, and then locate the selected specific sites to complement these patterns within the limits established in step 5. Place the complementing sites adjacent to one another, and separate the conflicting or competing ones. The functional relationships diagram should assist in these determinations, as discussed later in this chapter.

Layout of Plan.   A typical layout of an area plan should include:

1.   *Description of Area.*
   a.   Social attributes, including population base, economic base, social and cultural conditions, and other factors that might affect leisure life styles.
   b.   Ecological conditions, including existing land uses, sources of environmental degradation, limitations for development, and other ecological factors that may affect the quality of the resource for recreation.
   c.   Physical developments, including recreational developments, other man-made structures, and existing transportation systems.

2.   *Establishment of Broad Objectives for Planning the Area.*   The objectives should reflect the identified recreational needs of the user population and the potential of the resource to provide for these needs, and they should be broad enough to encompass a variety of opportunities under a given theme, such as back-country recreation.

3.   *Area Plan.*
   a.   Area plan map showing the types of sites and their locations. Any field working maps or diagrams should be included.
   b.   Descriptions of sites. Those sites identified in the area plan for development should be described in detail. The ultimate description should include suitability and feasibility, as discussed in Chapter 11. Each site plan could then be appended to the area plan, making the area plan a total planning package.
   c.   Description of circulation patterns and their locations, including roads, trails, and waterways. The types of anticipated circulation patterns and their best locations should be discussed, including patterns through the area and between sites, and also possible conflicts of patterns.
   d.   Functional relationships diagram. It is essential to understand the relationships between the various sites, commonly called functional relationships. These are important enough to be discussed in detail in the following portion of this chapter.

e.   Schedule of priorities for development. The needed site developments must be placed on a priority system so that development can proceed on an orderly, systematic basis.

f.   Land acquisition program. Some land acquisition may be necessary to locate developments properly or to protect certain land uses. This aspect, too, should be placed on a priority system and coordinated with the priorities for development.

g.   Reevaluation of plan. Reevaluation on a periodic basis is necessary if we are to reflect social, cultural, and environmental changes adequately and make necessary adjustments in our planning strategies. Because of budgetary and manpower problems, it is necessary to program the reevaluation on a periodic basis, generally five-year intervals.

4.   *Justifications for Planning Actions.*
   a.   Demand studies. Regional demand studies should be interpreted in relation to area needs.

   b.   Measurement of participation. Measurement of existing participation is necessary if the regional demand is to be interpreted in terms of the specific area.

   c.   On-site observation of behavior. Measurement of on-site behavior is necessary to ensure that the existing sites are meeting the behavioral needs of the visitor.

   d.   Expected behavioral patterns. Some new sites would have to be developed; others, redesigned. Thus, 4 a, b, and c should give the planner sufficient information, in addition to his own personal experience, to predict on-site behavioral patterns.

   e.   Possible management considerations. The planner should consider the effects of planning on the later management of the area, e.g., the possibility of limiting boating access in order to manage the boating experience.

   f.   Coordination with regional and subregional plans.

5.   *Limitations of Plan.*
   a.   Other pertinent social and economic data needed.

   b.   Physical and ecological limitations of the resource base. These should be explained in detail because everyone, including the public, should be aware of the limitations.

   c.   Possible ways of minimizing the limitations. The planner would have left the job undone if he did not pursue ways of minimizing the limitations associated with the planning process.

6.   *Authority for Planning.*
   a.   Statutes. The planner should include federal, state and local statutes that would affect the planning process in any way.

   b.   Administrative policies. Each agency has its own policies that must be followed. These should be continuously reviewed.

    c.   Public interest. Public interest and need should be included in establishing planning priorities.

    7.   *Appendix.* Ideally a site plan for each identified site in the area plan should be appended to the basic area plan as each site is planned. Materials and costs should also be included.

Functional Relationships. There are several steps one should go through when "fitting" the developments to an area. These are:

    1.   What types of developments are needed?

    2.   What activities are associated with the developments?

    3.   What facilities will be needed for the activities?

    4.   How do these activities and facilities depend upon or relate to one another? Also, what types of people will use the facilities?

    5.   Can these relationships function properly on the particular area? The primary relationships are the ones that are absolutely necessary in order to offer the best recreational opportunities to the various types of anticipated visitors without disruption of the experiences or site conditions.

The answers to the first three questions are the basic data for answering the last two. The answers to the first three ensure complete coverage of all planning aspects of the developments. The last two ensure proper layout and also act as evaluation criteria for the site's suitability.

The functional relationships enhance the total on-site experience by placing the complementary sites adjacent to one another and by separating the competing ones. Thus, we ensure through proper location of sites a functional area layout that facilitates movement between sites while minimizing potential conflict.

The next step is to delineate the basic behavioral patterns by user groups. Since, in water-based recreation, most people participate in an activity aggregate, separating user groups according to single activities is not desirable. The better separation, in this case, is by local (day-use) and nonresident (overnight), because each will have a different activity aggregate. At times, separation can be based on singular activities, e.g., cross-country skiing and snowmobiling.

The next step is to decide on the various types of sites to be provided within the scope of the objectives and the interrelations of the individual sites. To enhance the decision making, the strong relationships (primary ones) and weak relationships (secondary ones) should be determined. The primary relationships are those that should be fully developed in the area plan. The secondary ones are of less importance. In the following example, the primary relationships for the local user are picnicking and boating (marina); for the nonresident, camping and boating. Note that the sites on the functional relationships are situated as they would be oriented on the ground.

Because of a multiplicity of objectivies, user types, or activities, it may be desirable to develop a series of functional relationship diagrams and then attempt to integrate them on the objective, user group, or activity level. In the example, however, the integration is shown in one diagram.

Other factors can affect the decision, such as the limited potential of the resource, i.e., the lake may be too small for power boating. Or the amount of space for development may be small. Or certain socioeconomic conditions may indicate that the planner should favor a given user group. In the example about water-based recreation, imagine that the area plan is for a 285-acre parcel of public land adjacent to a lake near Minneapolis-St. Paul. Because of the high demand for water-based recreation, the ease of day-use access, and the limited space, the considerations for overnight facilities are dropped. The entire area is to be devoted to day-use activities. The planner should then encourage the private sector to develop central campgrounds within easy travel distance. He has then accomplished the total area objectives, but not all on public land.

Through the functional relationship diagram process, the planner should gain insight in:

1.   Basic behavior, according to user groups.

2.   Types of sites and subsequent facilities that would be needed in the area to meet the basic objectives.

3.   The relative importance of each site, depending on the primary or secondary relationships.

4.   The relative location of the various sites.

5.   The interrelationships that should be maintained.

The following is an example of the functional relationship diagram and the relationships depicted:

Lakeshore Area

1. *Development.*   water-based recreation area

2. *Activities.*   camping, picnicking, boating.

3. *Sites and Facilities.*   campground, picnic area, marina, and concession stand.

4. *Functional Relationships:*

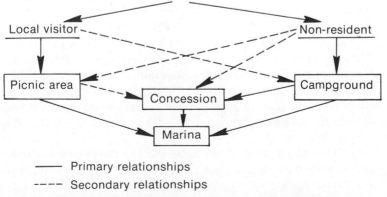

WATER-BASED RECREATION

Local visitor   Non-resident

Picnic area   Concession   Campground

Marina

—— Primary relationships

---- Secondary relationships

Figure 10–3   Diagram of functional relationships for a lakeshore area.

The diagram shows that certain relationships are readily evident and are important in the area planning. These interpretations are:

   a. Water-based recreation is important to the local visitor as well as to the nonresident.

   b. People who use the campground are generally not local people. They are definitely interested in boating (using the marina). And they should be the ones who make maximum use of the concession stand.

   c. The picnicker is the local person who is interested in the area on a day-use basis and is also interested in boating. His concession needs will probably be minimal.

   d. Campground operations should be separate from the picnic grounds. However, since the marina is the focal point of both, they should be within a reasonable distance of the boating access. Since campers are spending more time in the area and are camping as well as boating, they should have more isolation from the marina activities.

   e. The concession is more important to the camper, and thus, although generally centrally located, it should be most advantageously situated for the camper.

   f. The marina activities (boating, fishing, etc.) are the attractions for this planned development and, therefore, should receive maximum attention during the detailed site planning. In fact, each major development such as the campground, picnic area, and marina should have its own separate functional diagram to ensure proper spatial relationships of all its components. For example, a simple marina should have a boat launching area, a docking area, and a parking lot as minimum components, and these should be fitted together to ensure a logical flow pattern in the marina.

   5. *Fitting the Functional Relationships to the Area.* The relationships of facilities and developments in item 4 are the same in the diagram as one would expect to locate them on the sites. Thus, in order to fit the developments to the sites, one should have a large-scale topographic map with the ownership boundary delineated and small name cards ($\frac{1}{2} \times 2''$) with the name of each site development written on a separate card. Then, using the same general layout as developed in 4, place the card. Then, using the same general layout as developed in step 4, place the map, move the developments (cards) around until they are compatible with the topography and still maintain the proper relationships. Then, check this layout on the ground. Certain details or problems may not become evident until the ground check is made—for example, a bog that doesn't show up on the map.

If major problems arise, then move the site developments around in the same vicinity until you can select nearby alternate sites. If this is not possible, start the entire process over. Or *rethink* the type of operation you would like to have and also the functional relationships associated with the operation.

Example of an Area Plan.   Area planning is probably the most important level of planning to a given agency because it is through this process that:

1.   Park and recreation systems are planned.
2.   Space is allocated for certain uses.
3.   Commitments of money and manpower are made.
4.   Courses of action are periodically reevaluated. Thus, the area plan is necessary before site planning can begin. Each site is planned according to the guidelines and location established in the area plan. Because of this importance, a sample area plan is presented in Part 5 to show the basic framework and layout.

SELECTED READINGS

1.   Behan, R. W., and M. J. Gratzer. 1966. *Recreation At Libby Reservoir—An International Opportunity For Regional Development.* Missoula, Montana: Montana Forest and Conservation Experiment Station, University of Montana. Special Publication No.2.

2.   Bureau of Outdoor Recreation. 1968. *The Middle Missouri: A Rediscovery.* Washington, D.C.: U.S. Government Printing Office.

3.   ____. 1968. *New England Heritage: The Connecticut National Recreation Area Study.* Washington, D.C.: U.S. Government Printing Office.

4.   ____. 1967. *Outdoor Recreation Space Standards.* Washington, D.C.: U.S. Government Printing Office.

5.   Chadwick, G. F. 1971. *A Systems View of Planning: A Theory of Urban and Regional Planning.* New York: Pergamon Press.

6.   Convery, F. J. 1969. *Techniques of Regional Economic Planning.* Unpublished master's thesis. Syracuse, New York: State University of New York College of Forestry.

7.   Douglas, R. W. 1969. *Forest Recreation.* New York: Pergamon Press.

8.   Fabos, J. G. 1969. *An Interdisciplinary Approach To Regional Planning, Exchange Bibliography 74–75.* Monticello, Illinois: Council of Planning Librarians.

9.   Farness, S. S. 1966. "Resources Planning Versus Regional Planning," *Future Environments of North America.* F. F. Darling and J. P. Milton (eds.). Garden City, New York: The Natural History Press.

10.   Gunn, C. A. 1972. *Vacationscope: Designing Tourist Regions.* Austin, Texas: Bureau of Business Research, The University of Texas.

11.   McCloskey, M. C. 1971. *Planning and Regional Planning, Exchange Bibliography 174.* Monticello, Illinois: Council of Planning Librarians.

12.   National Advisory Commission on Rural Poverty. 1967. *The People Left Behind.* Washington, D.C.: U.S. Government Printing Office.

13.   National Park Service. 1963. *A Backcountry Management Plan for Sequoia and Kings Canyon National Parks.* Washington, D.C.: U.S. Department of Interior, National Park Service.

14.   ____. 1972. *Yellowstone Master Plan.* Yellowstone National Park, Wyoming: National Park Service.

15.   National Recreation and Park Association. 1970. *National Park, Recreation, and Open Space Standards.* Washington, D.C.: National Recreation and Park Association.

16.   Office of Park and Recreation Resources. 1969. *A Comprehensive Plan for Conservation and Recreation for LaSalle County Conservation District.* Champaign, Illinois: University of Illinois.

17. Perin, C. 1970. *With Man in Mind: An Interdisciplinary Prospectus for Environmental Design*. Cambridge, Massachusetts: MIT Press.

18. Sargent, F. O. 1967. *Camel's Hump Park*. Burlington, Vermont: Vermont Resources Research Center, University of Vermont.

19. _____. 1968. *How To Make A Conservation and Recreation Plan*. Burlington, Vermont: University of Vermont. Agricultural Economics Bulletin 68–6.

20. _____. 1967. *Regional Planning*. Burlington, Vermont: Vermont Resources Research Center, University of Vermont.

21. Woodbury, G. 1966. "The Role of the Regional Planner in Preserving Habitats and Scenic Values," *Future Environments of North America*. F. F. Darling and J. P. Milton (eds.). Garden City, New York: The Natural History Press.

CHAPTER 11

SITE PLANNING

Site planning is a scale graphic presentation of specific recreational site developments, including the facility components and their spatial relationships. The sites to be planned, such as ski areas, marinas, campgrounds, and others, are first identified in the area plan and then fully developed in the *site plan,* or what is called the *site development plan.*

The site plan should include:

1. A site map, which indicates the location and type of facility components of the site (such as individual units of a campground), the supporting facility components (roads, trails, signs, etc.) and service components (water point, comfort station, etc.).

2. A narrative report analyzing the potential resource base and expected behavioral patterns.

3. A general development plan, which indicates the time schedule of actions from the beginning to the completion of each development, including costs of each phase.

4. Construction plans. Construction plans should include construction methods and size and material specifications, including microlocational data (vertical and horizontal reference points). Generally, each facility construction plan, such as the water system, will be included as an appendix to the overall site plan.

SITE PLANNING PROCESS

The site planning process is: Program→ Plans → Design. Site planning has its infancy in the area plan; it is here that a basic course of action is developed. From this point, a specific program is developed for each of the identified sites, according to the access, circulatory considerations, service needs, and expected behavioral patterns. For example, an identified site development in the Black Hills of South Dakota is a central camp. Since people will stay for an extended time and will be radiating from the camp to points of interest, the camp should be somewhat centrally located to the attractions accessible to the major travel routes, and it should offer maximum services to the camper. Probably the secondary activities should be kept to a minimum, except evening activities, since people will spend most of their time at surrounding attractions.

After the program is established, the basic layout is developed to show what is needed and where. Finally, each component is designed to complement the overall program, including service, expected behavior, aesthetic appeal, and circulatory patterns.

The detailed steps in the process are:
1. *Site Selection.*
    a. Preliminary site selection (resource suitability).
    b. Final site selection (site feasibility).
2. *Site Plan.*
    a. Preliminary layout.
        (1) List of desired facilities.
        (2) Relative location of facilities.
        (3) Circulation patterns.
    b. Engineering evaluation of physical features.
    c. Coordination with adjacent sites.
3. *Site Design.*
    a. Analysis of landscape features.
    b. Fitting site program to natural landscape.
    c. Architectural design of individual facilities.
4. *Final Review.*
    a. Stake, review, and adjust.
    b. Drafting of final plan.
    c. Approval.
    d. Periodic review.

SITE SELECTION (RESOURCE SUITABILITY)

This is an important step because the resource is evaluated in terms of its potential to provide for the total site program. Since this is the preliminary site selection, it is best to develop a list of several alternative sites within the general location identified in the area plan and then to choose the best two or three sites for final site selection. This preliminary site selection generally uses a point evaluation system developed specifically for the particular opportunity and agency. Primarily, resource variables are included in the point rating to determine the suitability of the resource; however, some agencies include certain social variables if they directly affect the immediate potential of the resource, e.g., aesthetic appeal, access, and so on. An example of a rating system, *Evaluating Forest Campground Sites,* is shown in Table 11–1.

Point-Rating System. Point-rating systems for evaluating the potential of a given recreational opportunity are developed in three stages:

1. *Determining Significant Variables.* Each geographic region (its user groups and resources) and each agency philosophy may vary considerably in terms of what factors significantly affect the potential to provide a given opportunity. Research can help to identify those variables which reflect the attractiveness, the ecological limitations, and the adaptability of the site for certain uses. Experience can also assist in identifying critical variables. However, the individual agency must then select those variables pertinent to its own situation.

2. *Develop an Ordinal Scoring Method.* Once the variables are selected, a scoring method should be developed to reflect the value of each variable and subvariable. Since many variables are difficult to quantify, an ordinal scoring method (good, better, best) seems to be the most appropriate. An equal interval score can then be assigned to each subvariable. For example:

SCENIC FLOATING EXPERIENCE	
Variable	*Field Score*

I. Velocity of the water:
    a.   4–7 mph. (3 points)
    b.   <4 mph. (2 points)
    c.   >7 mph. (1 point)
II. [etc. . . .]	

3. *Verify the Representatives of the Point Rating.* Is it adequate in assessing the suitability of the site? Are the variables included in the scoring system the most appropriate? Do the scores assigned to the various factors represent their approximate values? These types of questions must be answered before the point-rating system is adopted. The only valid means of testing the system is to apply it to an existing known situation. If the planner is developing a point rating for evaluating the suitability of a parcel of land for commercial campground development in the midwest, then he should test the validity by evaluating existing successful commercial campgrounds in the same area.

Suitability Evaluation Technique. Many techniques are used for suitability evaluation, but the most common is to select, based on the professional judgment of a planner or consultant, two or three of the better sites. Where there is a limited land base for planning, this approach may have some merit. However, since many projects will affect the participation patterns of thousands of people, and a large investment of capital and natural resources will go into the projects, the planner should attempt to

Text cont. on page 148

TABLE 11-1. EVALUATING FOREST CAMPGROUND SITES

Part I: PHYSICAL FACTORS

Factor	Condition and Point Value				Sites A	Sites B
WATER						
A Size	Lake, over 200 acres 20	Lake, 50–200 acres 15	Large pond or stream 10	Small pond or stream 5	☐	☐
B Quality	Clear 20	Semi-clear 15	Turbid 10	Very turbid 5	☐	☐
C Shoreline	Sand or gravel, level 20	Sand or gravel, slight slope 15	Rocky or muddy, moderate slope 10	Rocky or muddy, steep slope 5	☐	☐
D Water depth fluctuation	Under 1 foot 20	1–2 feet 15	2.5–4.0 feet 10	Over 4 feet 5	☐	☐
E Frontage owned	Over 1,000 feet 20	500–1,000 feet 15	100–490 feet 10	Under 100 feet 5	☐	☐
F Av. dist from tent sites	Under 400 feet 20	400–600 feet 15	610–800 feet 10	Over 800 feet 5	☐	☐
RATING	EXCELLENT 120	GOOD 90	FAIR 60	POOR 30	☐	☐
TOPOGRAPHY						
A Slope	Under 10% 20	10–15% 15	16–20% 10	Over 20% 5	☐	☐
B Size of area	Over 50 acres 20	30–50 acres 15	15–29 acres 10	Under 15 acres 5	☐	☐
C Soil conditions	Smooth, well drained 20	Small rocks, moderately drained 15	Rocky, moderately drained 10	Bolders, ledge, poorly drained 5	☐	☐
RATING	EXCELLENT 60	GOOD 45	FAIR 30	POOR 15	☐	☐
POTABLE WATER						
A Distance from site	Under 100 feet 20	100–500 feet 15	510–800 feet 10	Over 800 feet 5	☐	☐
B Depth	Spring, dug well, or driven well under 50 feet 20	Driven well, 50–150 feet 15	Deep well, 160–300 feet 10	No water within reasonable depth 5	☐	☐

Factor	☐ Excellent (pts)	☐ Good (pts)	☐ Fair (pts)	☐ Poor (pts)
C Quantity	Over 20 gal./min. (20)	20–10 gal./min. (15)	9–5 gal./min. (10)	Under 5 gal./min. (5)
RATING	EXCELLENT (60)	GOOD (45)	FAIR (30)	POOR (15)
VEGETATION				
A Understory density	Under 30% cover (15)	30–50% cover (10)	51–74% (5)	75–100% (2)
B Overstory density	45–60% shade (15)	20–40% shade (10)	Under 20% shade (5)	Over 60% shade (2)
C Size of vegetation	12″ D.B.H. and over (15)	6–12″ D.B.H. (10)	Under 6″ D.B.H. (5)	Brush and saplings (2)
RATING	EXCELLENT (45)	GOOD (30)	FAIR (15)	POOR (6)
NATURAL ATTRACTIONS (Caves, waterfalls, etc.)				
A Uniqueness	Very rare (20)	Rare (10)	Fairly rare (5)	Common (2)
B Distance from site	Under 10 miles (15)	10–25 miles (10)	Over 25 miles (5)	30–50 miles (2)
RATING	EXCELLENT (35)	GOOD (25)	FAIR (15)	POOR (4)
VISTA				
A Visability	Over 10 miles (15)	5–10 miles (10)	Under 5 miles (5)	Under 1 mile (2)
B Panorama	360–180° (15)	170–90° (10)	85–45° (5)	Under 45° (2)
RATING	EXCELLENT (30)	GOOD (20)	FAIR (10)	POOR (4)
FOREST PESTS (Subjective evaluation)				
Population of objectionable insects & poisonous plants	Very low (20)	Medium (15)	Heavy (10)	Very heavy (5)
ANIMAL AND BIRD LIFE				
Abundance of wildlife	Abundant, seen often (20)	Fairly abundant, seen occasionally (15)	Very seldom seen (10)	Rarely seen (5)

Table cont. on following page

TABLE 11–1. EVALUATING FOREST CAMPGROUND SITES (continued)

CLIMATE AND MICROCLIMATE

									A	B
Air drainage	No severe thunder-storm activity	20	Occasional thunder-storm activity	15	Moderate thunder-storm activity	10	Many severe thunderstorms	5	☐	☐
TOTAL POINTS	EXCELLENT	410	GOOD	300	FAIR	190	POOR	89	☐	☐
FINAL RATING	EXCELLENT Over 350		GOOD 350–255		FAIR 250–190		POOR Under 190		☐	☐

Part II: Socioeconomic Factors

Factor	Condition and Point Value						Sites	
							A	B
LOCATION								
A Access to major highways	Under 5 miles	20	5–15 miles	10	Over 15 miles	5	☐	☐
B Distance from urban population centers	Under 150 miles	20	150–200 miles	10	Over 200 miles	5	☐	☐
C Distance from local community facilities (grocery, laundry, police, medical, amusements)	All within 20 miles	20	Half or more within 20 miles	10	Less than half within 20 miles	5	☐	☐
D Distance from historical and/or cultural center	Under 5 miles	20	5–20 miles	10	Over 20 miles	5	☐	☐
RATING	EXCELLENT	80	FAIR	40	POOR	20	☐	☐
ECONOMIC AND BUSINESS MANAGEMENT								
A Public relations and business management ability (subjective evaluation)	Excellent	20	Good	10	Poor	5	☐	☐
B Capital available for development	Over $20,000	20	$10,000–$20,000	10	Under $10,000	5	☐	☐
C Assessed value per acre	Low	15	Medium	10	High	5	☐	☐
D Local tax structure	Favorable	15	Acceptable	10	Unfavorable	5	☐	☐

Item	Description	Favorable / Excellent	Pts	Mediocre / Fair	Pts	Unfavorable / Poor	Pts	
E	Community reaction to recreationists	Favorable	15	Mediocre	10	Unfavorable	5	☐
F	Competition within 30 miles	Little or none	15	Some	10	Saturated	5	☐
G	Restrictions (town zoning, etc.)	None	15	Few	10	Many	5	☐
	RATING	EXCELLENT	115	FAIR	70	POOR	35	☐
PROPOSED CAMPGROUND FACILITIES								
A	Land available for camp sites	Over 150 sites	20	75–150 sites	10	Under 75 sites	5	☐
B	Topography suitable for both trailer and tent sites	Over 50% trailer	20	25–50% trailer	10	Under 25% trailer	5	☐
C	Soil types suitable for flush toilets and sewerage dumping station	Excellent	20	Fair	10	Poor	5	☐
D	Electricity economically possible to individual sites	Over 50% of sites	20	25–50% of sites	10	No	5	☐
E	Potable water to individual sites	Over 50% of sites	20	25–50% of sites	10	No	5	☐
F	Recreation facilities (rec. hall, horseshoes, badminton, shuffle board, playground apparatus, basketball)	Over 5 activities	20	3–5 activities	10	Under 3 activities	5	☐
G	Campground roads economically feasible	Paved or graveled, high standards	20	Dirt, good standards	10	Poor site for road	5	☐
H	Dry goods and camping needs	Fully stocked	20	Few items	10	No items	5	☐
I	Fireplace wood available	Free or service charge	15	Available, cut own	10	None available	5	☐
	RATING	EXCELLENT	175	FAIR	90	POOR	45	☐
	TOTAL POINTS	EXCELLENT	370	FAIR	200	POOR	100	☐
	FINAL RATING	**EXCELLENT Over 250**		**FAIR 150–250**		**POOR Under 150**		☐

From Allison, R. C., and R. S. Leighton. 1968. *Evaluating Forest Campground Sites*. Durham, New Hampshire: Cooperative Extension Service, University of New Hampshire, Extension Folder No. 64.

select the best sites to provide both for present and future recreation demands. Probably the best technique for this evaluation is a combination of point-rating system and landscape analysis.

"Seashore State Park, Oregon—A Hypothetical Application"

The following example was developed using an adaption of the *total site* evaluation technique described by Hills:[7]

1. *Exercise.*   Locate possible beach development site.
    Assumptions:
    a.   There is a demand for beach development.
    b.   Location is southern Oregon coast.
    c.   The primary activities are swimming, sunbathing, and boating.
2. *Analysis of the General Resource Base.*
    a.   *General site region* (1,000–4,000 square miles). This primarily involves eliminating the least desirable resource regions and then focusing on smaller resource units. Es-

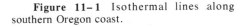

Figure 11–1 Isothermal lines along southern Oregon coast.

sentially, it is a regional landscape analysis, using small-scale topographic maps (U.S. Army maps, 1:250,000 scale) and climate and weather data. In this case, the general site region is the southern Oregon coast.

b. *Physiographic site region* (10,000–50,000 acres). The general site region is divided into several physiographic site regions, based primarily on physiographic, climatic or weather patterns. In this case, the main criterion (assumed) is an iso-thermal zone of 70° F. during the month of June (Figure 11–1).

c. *Physiographic site classes* (2,000–5,000 acres). Using aerial photos, the primary land forms of the physiographic site region should be delineated (Figure 11–2). In this exercise, the primary need at this stage of selection is a flat, somewhat well-drained land area with a sandy, stable shoreline. Note many site classes can be eliminated immediately because of the physiographic characteristics.

d. *Site types* (200–1000 acres). Physiographic site classes 1, 2, and 3 meet minimum requirements as delineated on the aerial photos. These are further divided into site types based on specific variations in vegetative types (Figure 11–3).

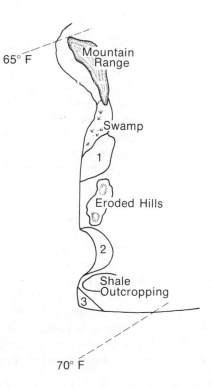

Figure 11–2   Physiographic site classes.

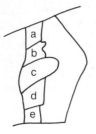

Site Class #1

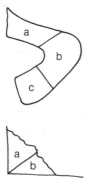

Figure 11-3 Delineation of site types using aerial photographs.

Site Class #2

Site Class #3

Changes in vegetation are easily discernible on aerial photos and generally reflect the ecological conditions of the particular site. Thus, classes 1, 2, and 3 were divided into ten site types.

The planner is now ready to go to the field for the suitability study, using a point-rating system. Up to this point, all decisions have been made in the office, using maps and aerial photos. The desirability of starting with the general site region and focusing down to the site types is that large resource areas can be quickly reviewed, thus enabling the planner to select the best potential site types for field analysis. In addition, the planner may begin the landscape analysis at any point in the process, depending on the size and variability of the geographic area.

The planner may now visit each of the identified ten site types to determine the suitability of each. In the exercise, assume that the point-rating system for beach front development is divided into a dry phase (land) and a wet phase (water), each worth 50 points, or a total of 100 points. A score of less than 30 points in either of the phases would immediately eliminate any site type from further consideration. After spending a day at each site type, the following scores were developed (Table 11-2):

TABLE 11–2   POINT RATINGS FOR THE TEN SITE TYPES

Site Type	Wet Phase 50 pts.	Dry Phase 50 pts.	Total Score	Rank
1. a.	36	40	76	(3)
b.[1]	0	0	0	
c.[2]	25	28	53	(7)
d.	31	38	69	(5)
e.	40	31	71	(4)
2. a.[2]	32	16	48	(8)
b.	42	43	85	(1)
c.	45	39	84	(2)
3. a.[2]	27	33	60	(6)
b.[2]	19	15	34	(9)

[1] Field examination indicated a swampy bottomland that did not show up on the aerial photo; thus, this one was eliminated.

[2] Four others were later eliminated because one or both of the phases failed to meet the 30-point cutoff limit.

The top ranked site types (2.b., 2.c., and 1.a.) can then be evaluated in terms of feasibility of the development, which will require an interdisciplinary study team. Several types of feasibility studies may be developed for particular circumstances. By eliminating many of the potentially undesirable sites at a minimal cost, the more expensive and detailed feasibility studies are focused only on the best potential sites.

The suitability study can begin at any point in the process described in the preceding material. If the alternatives of potential sites are limited by land ownership, area planning, or otherwise, then the process may begin at the *site type*. Ideally, the planner would begin at the highest level possible and focus downward in the site selection process.

SITE SELECTION (FEASIBILITY STUDIES)

The final step in site selection is a series of feasibility studies that focus on specific attributes of the site. These are several types of feasibility studies; some may be more important than others in a given situation. The basic types are:

1. *Recreation Experience.* Too often the needs of the potential visitor and how the site may affect the visitor are overlooked. Many natural site features can directly affect the quality of the recreational experience. Some features, such as variety, openness of canopy, weather patterns, closeness to recreational water, and others may positively affect the visitor, while others, such as insects, noxious weeds, and high pollen counts, may have negative effects. The specific study should reflect the anticipated

visitor, the contemplated development, associated secondary activities, and the specific landscape being planned.

2. *Engineering*. Engineering studies are important in determining the feasibility of placing a particular development on a given site. Some of the important concerns are:

    a. Soils stability, compactability, and limitations in terms of supporting the contemplated development and expected use patterns.

    b. Sewer and water systems. Sources of water for use in the development must be located, and rate of flow, quality, and possible effects on other uses of the water must be ascertained. The soils and underlying geology should be studied if drainage fields or evaporation ponds are to be developed. If treatment facilities are to be developed, the possible location of the facility, the type of treatment, and the side effects should be studied, including costs. Because of topography, intermediate pump stations may also be needed to ensure adequate water flow.

    c. Construction problems. The feasibility study should include potential problems with facility construction and maintenance. Construction factors to be considered include stabilization of foundations, weathering, availability of native and other construction materials, and others. Maintenance factors may include choice of materials, snow pack, periodic flooding, and so on.

    d. Roads and trails. Some estimate of costs, types of material, and problems of soil types and topographic relief is necessary. For most types of sites, there are specific requirements in terms of maximum vertical curve and slope gradients, and minimum radius of horizontal curves. Often suitable landscapes are eliminated for consideration for site development, because of steep terrain and unstable soil conditions in the projected road or trail corridors, not only within the site, but also along the potential access route to it.

3. *Site Maintenance*. The problems of vegetation management should be assessed, including visitor use effects. The vegetation may not sustain the expected levels of use without expensive site treatment programs, such as irrigation, fertilization, and other measures. Perhaps other types of ground vegetation may have to be introduced or the site designed in order to minimize the user effects (i.e., barriers, hardening of use areas, and so on.) The primary aim should be to maximize the natural aesthetics while minimizing long-term vegetative management problems.

4. *Economics*. Certain economic assessments must be made relative to:

    a. Costs of development and maintenance.

    b.   Labor market situation.

    c.   Effect on local and regional economies.

    d.   Availability of needed goods and services.

    e.   Attitudes of local populace towards proposed development.

    f.   Demands for recreational opportunities relative to supply.

    5. *Environmental Impact.*   The planner will have to project the possible environmental effects on the air, water, land, and visual resources. In the future, all public and private agencies will have to do an environmental impact analysis to determine the possible effect on the total resource base in the area.

    6. *Hazard Survey.*   A hazard survey for each potential site should determine existing hazardous conditions (from avalanches, dead trees, poisonous vegetation, dangerous waters, precipitous slopes, etc.) Once the survey is completed, the effects of the hazards should be reduced through proper location of site, site design, and management policies.

SITE PLAN

    Once the site location is determined, the planner should develop a preliminary layout to offer certain types of recreational activities. Included in the preliminary layout should be (Figure 11–4):

    1. *List of Desired Facilities, Including Supporting Facilities.*   The type of site will dictate the desired facilities and the relative location. For example, merely providing a picnic grounds is not sufficient. The site plan should reflect the style of picnicking (group vs. family) and the service needs (family destination-oriented or enroute/wayside). All supporting facilities should be listed, including sewer and water systems, parking areas, comfort stations, and concessions. Any unit equipment, such as picnic tables, fireplaces, and hardened surfaces should also be decided on.

    2. *Relative Location of Facilities.*   The facilities should be located in order to encourage normal behavioral patterns, minimize conflict and confusion, and facilitate movement within the site. Properly located comfort stations can encourage visitor use whereas poorly located ones may discourage use. Camping units that must be continually crossed to get to common facilities, such as a water point, are improperly located. This situation causes possible conflict and confusion for the visitor. Lack of information signs or poorly located signs (a supporting facility) can greatly add to the conflict and confusion.

    3. *Circulation Patterns.*   The pedestrian and vehicle circulation patterns should be developed relative to the needs of the site and the facility locations. Only those roads and trails necessary for access to and movement within the site should be developed. Unnecessary and poorly located roads or trails can be disruptive to the normal visitor use of the site. Figure

1. Facilities needed:
    a. Hardened surface for parking
    b. Utility hookups
    c. Bath house
    d. Food store/service station
    e. Access road
    f. Trails to service points
    g. Sewer and water system

2. Relative location

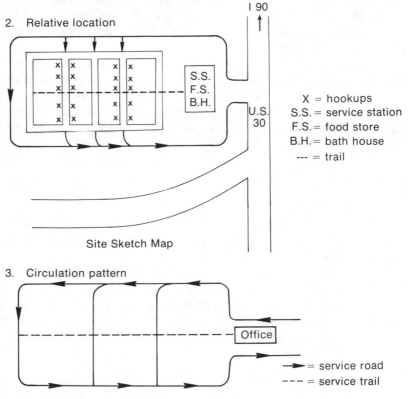

Site Sketch Map

X = hookups
S.S. = service station
F.S. = food store
B.H. = bath house
--- = trail

3. Circulation pattern

Office

→ = service road
--- = service trail

Figure 11–4   An example of a site plan (transient campground).

11–4 shows the basic layout and circulation pattern of the site plan for the transient campground. The last step is to integrate the facilities and their location with the circulation pattern. Then the planner is ready to design the site to fit the particular needs.

Site Design.   The landscape features of the site should be inventoried to determine the best microlocation for the development in terms of soil, vegetative, physiographic, and recreational characteristics. The site plan must then be fitted to the specific topographic and landscape features of the site, while maintaining the desired positions of the facilities and circulation patterns. The slope, aspect, and shape of the terrain will determine the physical constraints of the locations.

Each type of site will have its own peculiar requirements. For example, the campground should be relatively flat; the ski run, relatively steep. However, if the winter sports site caters to the local user region, the topography should conform to the needs of the beginner and intermediate skier. If it is a national site, the emphasis should be on the advanced and expert runs. The southerly aspect may be desirable to the picnicker; the northerly one, to the skier. The forest site may be desirable for the camper but not desirable for the sunbather. Also, features such as vegetative, geologic, or physiographic patterns should be considered in molding the plan to the site, since they may affect the attractiveness of the development. The point is that the way the site plan is fitted to the landscape will depend on the type of experience to be offered and the existing resource features.

Ideally, the planner should attempt to utilize the features of the landscape to enhance recreational experience, minimize site maintenance, and maintain natural aesthetics. Although fitting the development to the natural lay of the land may be more expensive and require much attention to detail, the resulting site should be more attractive, more able to handle larger visitor-use loads, and less expensive to maintain.

Site design is an important step in the total site planning process, for it is here that the plan is adapted to the site. This step allows the most innovative inputs from the planner. However, even then, the planner should conform his design to normal visitor behavior and the known limitations of the resource. These types of considerations are discussed in detail in various portions of Part 4. This step creates either the well-planned functional site or the horrendous monument to the planner with little concern for the user. The choice is yours!

SELECTED READINGS

1. Allison, R.C., and R.S. Leighton. 1968. "Evaluating Forest Campground Sites." Durham, New Hampshire: Cooperative Extension Service, University of New Hampshire. Extension Folder No. 64.
2. Bone, M.D., et al. 1965. *Site Selection and Development: Camps — Conferences — Retreats*. Philadelphia: United Church Press.
3. Bureau of Outdoor Recreation. 1967. *Outdoor Recreation for the Physically Handicapped*. Washington, D.C.: U.S. Government Printing Office.
4. Cielinski, T. J., and J. A. Wagar. 1970. "Predicting the Durability of Forest Recreation Sites in Northern Utah." U.S. Forest Service Research Note INT–117.
5. Cornwell, G. W., and C. J. Holcomb (eds.). 1966. *Guidelines to Planning, Developing, and Managing Rural Recreation Enterprises*. Blacksburg, Virginia: Virginia Polytechnic Institute. Agriculture Bulletin 301.
6. Gilchrist, M. 1971. "Strategies for Preserving Scenic Rivers: the Maryland Experience," *Landscape Architecture*, 62(1): 35–42.
7. Hills, G.A. 1967. "Approach To Environmental Resource Analysis I." *Three Approaches To Environmental Resource Analysis*. Washington, D.C.: The Conservation Foundation.
8. Jacobs, P. 1970. *Site Planning Process, Activity Allocation*. Halifax, Nova Scotia: Nova Scotia Technical College.

9.   Jubenville, A. 1971. *Self Evaluation Checklist For Outdoor Recreation Planning and Development*. Unpublished manuscript.

10.   Litton, R.B., Jr. 1968. *Forest Landscape Description and Inventories—A Basis for Land Planning and Design*. U.S. Forest Service Research Paper PSW–49.

11.   _____. 1973. *Landscape Control Points: A Procedure for Predicting and Monitoring Visual Impacts*. U.S. Forest Service Research Paper PSW–91.

12.   Mitchell, W.J. (ed.). 1972. *Environmental Design: Research and Practice*. Los Angeles: University of California at Los Angeles.

13.   Park Practice Program. 1968. *Design*. Washington, D.C.: National Recreation and Park Association and National Park Service.

14.   Public Health Service. 1968. *Environmental Health Practice in Recreational Areas, PHS No. 1195*. Washington, D.C.: U.S. Government Printing Office.

15.   Rutledge, A.J. 1971. *Anatomy of a Park*. New York: McGraw-Hill Book Company.

16.   Shaffer, E.L., and H.D. Burke. 1965. "Preferences for Outdoor Recreation Facilities in Four State Parks," *Journal of Forestry*, 63(8): 512–518.

17.   Toth, R. 1971. "Criteria in Land Planning and Design," *Landscape Architecture*, 62(1): 43–46.

18.   Van Meter, J.R. 1970. *Master Plans for Park Sites, ORPR–12*. Cooperative Extension Service, University of Illinois.

19.   Way, D.S. 1972. *Terrain Analysis: A Guide to Site Selection Using Aerial Photographic Interpretation*. Stroudsburg, Pennsylvania: Dowden, Hutchinson, and Ross, Inc.

CHAPTER 12

EVALUATION OF RECREATION RESOURCE POTENTIAL

The potential of a parcel of land for recreation is relative to the benefits that people can derive from using it. Thus, before this chapter pursues recreational land-use classifications, the recreation experience will be discussed as part of the resource potential. For example, one would not expect a person to travel through a heavily strip mined area to a campground and be surrounded by it after arriving, and still find this an *enjoyable* site.

Too often the planner has focused on the on-site experience as the total recreational experience. Yet, many other factors may directly or indirectly influence the total recreational experience. As Clawson suggests,[3] the experience is much broader and is divided into five separate phases, discussed in Chapter 1.

In evaluating an area's or region's resource potential for recreation, one should consider three factors:

1. The general character of the recreation resource setting, using a system such as Clawson's area classification.

2. The potential of the resource for certain types of recreational opportunities, as indicated in the Bureau of Outdoor Recreation classification system.

3. The specific qualities of the landscape and their possible effects on the observer.

Other factors that may affect the potential of the resource, but not discussed in this chapter, are regional transportation systems, environmental stability, and the backgrounds of the users.

157

Techniques for evaluating the potential of individual sites are discussed in Chapter 11, and the potential for specific opportunities is discussed in Part 4, Chapters 14–18.

CLAWSON'S AREA CLASSIFICATION*

Clawson's area classification divides recreation opportunities into three broad categories—*user-oriented, intermediate,* and *resource-oriented.* These identify the three parts of the continuum of recreational opportunities. In area and regional planning, it is essential to have a basis for understanding and comparing various types of opportunities. As a very general first step, this classification does just that.

User-oriented. These opportunities are characterized by outdoor sites in which supervised activities dominate and the basic landscape elements are less important. They are characterized by close proximity to the residences of the users. Such areas have only modest requirements for natural resources—small acreages which are moderately well drained and reasonably level will suffice for a playground or city park, for instance. But location of such areas is highly important; they must be near enough to where people live that they can be used in the time available—usually after school or after work, or they are unusable.

Intermediate. Intermediate outdoor recreation areas are located farther from the users' homes, but usually within a distance where they can be used readily for all-day outings—within two hours' travel distance or less, which means less than 100 miles. Within such a range, the planner normally chooses the most attractive sites. Some of these areas may be used for general outdoor recreation activities, with more emphasis being placed upon activities than upon the natural qualities of the site. For others, emphasis may shift to the site qualities, such as the forest cover with its many attractions. In the last two decades or so, particular interest has focused upon water-based recreation, and the most popular outdoor areas of the intermediate type are usually water oriented. In some instances, the water may be dominant and the surrounding area more or less incidental. Artificial water bodies—reservoirs built primarily for purposes other than recreation, or artificial lakes primarily for recreation—may serve very well for this kind of outdoor recreation.

Resource-based. A third major type of outdoor recreation area is resource-based. Here, primary emphasis is upon the natural qualities of the area, much less emphasis upon the activities, and almost none on the locational factor. One common type of such an area is the

---

* Adapted from Clawson, M. 1963. *Land and Water for Recreation.* Chicago: Rand McNally Co.

national park; here the emphasis is upon the unique natural characteristics of the area. Such areas lie usually at some distance from where most people live; hence, fairly long travel is necessary to reach them. This factor, in turn, means that they are visited primarily during vacations. Other examples of resource-based areas are outstanding historic sites and scenic wonders. Among the natural areas, the degree of access may vary greatly, from many favorite places in the popular national parks which are accessible by auto, to the more remote wilderness areas which are accessible only by horse, on foot, or by canoe.

BUREAU OF OUTDOOR RECREATION CLASSIFICATION*

The B.O.R. classification was developed in order to provide a common framework for classifying resources; it combines physical resource characteristics with expected behavioral patterns (Figure 12–1).

Class I—High Density Recreation Areas. These areas are characterized by a high degree of facility development, a condition which often requires large investment. They are usually managed exclusively for recreation purposes. Developments may include a road network, parking

---

*This section is taken from Outdoor Recreation Resources Review Commission. 1962. *Outdoor Recreation for America*. Washington, D.C.: U.S. Government Printing Office.

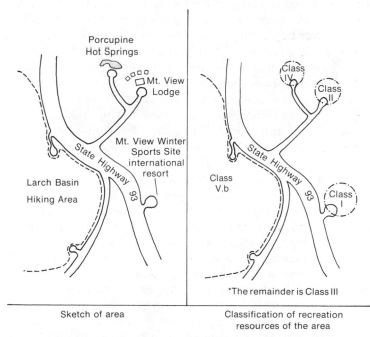

Sketch of area	Classification of recreation resources of the area

Figure 12–1   An example of the BOR classification system.

areas, bathing beaches and marinas, bathhouses, artificial lakes, playing fields, and sanitary and eating facilities. Such developments provide a wide range of activities for many people. They are particularly suited for day and weekend use. Although subject to heavy peakload pressures at certain times, they often sustain moderate use throughout the year.

These areas are generally located close to major centers of urban population, but they also occur occasionally within units such as national parks and forests, remote from population concentrations. There are no specific size criteria, and size from one area to another varies greatly.

Class I recreation areas are commonly held under municipal, county, regional, or state ownership. Many commercial resorts have similar characteristics and collectively provide a significant portion of Class I opportunities.

Class II—General Outdoor Recreation Areas. These areas provide a wider range of opportunities than Class I sites and usually involve more extensive, less crowded use. Their special feature is the ability through development of facilities to sustain a large and varied amount of activity, such as camping, picnicking, fishing, water sports, nature walks, and outdoor games. They are found under both private and public ownership and accommodate a major share of all outdoor recreation. Included are portions of public parks and forests, public and commercial camping sites, picnic grounds, trailer parks, ski areas, resorts, streams, lakes, coastal areas, and hunting preserves. These areas range in size from several acres to large tracts of land and are popular for day, weekend, and vacation use.

Class II areas encompass a wide variety of physical resources that have been or can be developed and managed to provide a diversity of recreation experiences. One of their distinctive characteristics is that they are always equipped with some man-made facilities, which may vary from the simple to the elaborate. Campgrounds, for example, may have only the barest necessities for sanitation and fire control, or they may have ample and carefully planned facilities such as cabins, hot and cold running water, laundry equipment, and stores. There may be a museum and a small library. Entertainment may be furnished. There may be playing fields for children and sometimes for adults.

Trailer parks may have the same conveniences as those on the outskirts of a city. Ski areas may have permanent tows and buildings that provide rest and refreshment. At lakes, reservoirs, and seashores, there may be well-equipped marinas, which provide not only boats but gear for fishing, skindiving, and water skiing. Hunting preserves may provide lodges for their members and guests. Dude ranches and luxury hotels may provide more than the comforts of home.

The wide variety of activities and facilities characteristic of general outdoor recreation areas (Class II) requires that management objectives be stated in very broad terms. Many factors, particularly the nature of the resources and the prospective demand, must be taken into consideration in determining for what purposes these areas will be used and how intensively they will be developed.

Public areas in this class should be managed to provide a wide range of outdoor opportunities in a relatively natural setting. The principle of activity zoning should be utilized within Class II areas to reduce conflicts among recreation activities, such as between swimming and motorboating, or between camping and field sports. Facilities and services should be dispersed to maximize use of the entire area.

Class III—Natural Environment Areas.   Resources in this class represent a transition type between general (Class II) and primitive (Class V) areas. The primary recreation management objective should be to provide for traditional recreation experiences in the out-of-doors, commonly in conjunction with other resource uses. It should encourage users to enjoy the resource "as is," in a natural environment where man has to fend largely for himself.

Class III areas occur throughout the country and in terms of acreage constitute the largest class in both public and private ownership. They commonly support grazing, lumbering, or mining in addition to recreation. Also, many areas in national and state parks are managed exclusively for recreation purposes that involve primarily enjoyment of the natural environment. Despite this limited use, the types of outdoor recreation experiences provided qualify them for inclusion in Class III.

There are no size criteria for areas in this class, which may include an entire ranger district in a national forest or a similar area in a national park or privately owned timberlands. Many areas suitable in part for assignment to this class, such as portions of the Allagash country of northern Maine and cutover areas in the northern Lake States, have been repeatedly logged, but their general natural characteristics remain somewhat unchanged. This in part distinguishes them from Class II resources. Public lands of this category often adjoin unique natural (Class IV) and primitive (Class V) areas in national and state parks and forests, as is the case in places like Grand Teton National Park and the Superior National Forest.

Typical recreation activities are hiking, hunting, fishing, camping, picnicking, canoeing, and sightseeing. In contrast to Class II areas, planning and development in Class III areas should emphasize the natural environment rather than the provision of man-made facilities. Developments on Class III sites should include provision of access roads, trails, and basic but not elaborate improvements necessary for camping and related activities. Comparable types of development on private lands should be encouraged.

Many extensive areas of land, both in public and private ownership, are capable of providing recreation opportunities of this type in harmony with other uses. The only special measures necessary are for fire control, safety, and the prevention of vandalism. For example, some areas might be temporarily closed to the public during periods of extreme fire hazard, or public use of logging roads might be stopped while logging operations are in progress.

Class IV—Unique Natural Areas.   This class consists of individual areas of remarkable natural wonder, high scenic splendor, or scientific importance. More than one such area may be included in a single large administrative unit such as a national park or forest. The preservation of these resources in their natural condition is the primary management objective. Adequate access for the enjoyment and education of the public should be provided wherever consistent with the primary objective.

The scenic sites and features included in this class are limited in number and are irreplaceable. They range from large areas within Yosemite Valley and the Grand Canyon to smaller areas such as Old Faithful in Yellowstone National Park; Old Man of the Mountain, New Hampshire; the Bristle Cone Pine Area in the Inyo National Forest, California; and parts of Cape Cod.

The size of unique natural areas (Class IV) will depend upon the physical features of the central attraction. In general, the areas should be of sufficient size to ensure an appropriate atmosphere and to protect the unique characteristics. They will often occupy only part of a national or state park or forest or other sizable administrative unit. Under some circumstances, the "line of vision" concept should be used in determining the desirable size of areas in this class. That is, inappropriate developments are not visible from within a Class IV site. Extensive natural landscapes are not usually considered Class IV areas.

In recent years, parts of many unique natural areas have been subjected to extremely heavy use that will tend to increase. If the quality of these resources is to be maintained under such pressures, stringent management regulations will be required. The kinds and amount of use that the areas can sustain are limited, and there is a critical point beyond which further use brings about deterioration. This point will vary from one site to another, but in all cases the recreation activities that can be permitted must be measured in terms of the preservation of the particular area and education of the user, rather than in terms of public demands.

Through limitation of the kinds of recreation activity permitted, the amount of appropriate uses might be expanded significantly. For example, by excluding food and lodging facilities from the immediate vicinity of the central attraction, the manager can reduce undesirable and damaging crowding, and all activity can be focused upon enjoying the outstanding natural features. This management policy would permit a larger number of people to benefit from the values for which the resource was initially selected and dedicated.

Class V—Primitive Areas.   The essential characteristics of these areas are that the natural environment has not been disturbed by commercial utilization and that they are without mechanized transportation. Their natural, wild, and undeveloped characteristics distinguish them from all other recreation resources included in this system of classification. They may or may not possess the unique quality characteristic of Class IV areas. Size is a limiting factor only to the extent that the area must be large enough and so located in order to give the user the feeling that he is enjoying a "wilderness experience"—a sense of being far removed from the sights and sounds of civilization. The size will vary with different physical and biological conditions and will be determined in part by the characteristics of adjacent land. Size will also vary in different parts of the country because of past land-use patterns.

Class V.a. lands are those with the general characteristics described in the preceding material, but which have not been designated under the Wilderness Act of 1964. They are known as "defacto wilderness." Class V.b. lands are those areas designated as wilderness under the Wilderness Act, and are commonly called "institutionalized wilderness." The areas may vary in terms of management, level of primitive development, and types of experiences offered. However, the essential ingredients are the roadless condition, lack of past disruptive land uses, and the opportunity for "perceived" solitude, away from man-made development.

Class VI—Historic and Cultural Sites. These are sites, associated with the history, tradition, or cultural heritage of the nation, that are of sufficient significance to merit their preservation. Many are already under the jurisdiction of the National Park Service, state and local agencies, and private organizations. They are of local, regional, and national importance. Examples are The Hermitage, Mount Vernon, the Civil War battle areas, the historic Indian dwellings in Mesa Verde National Park, and the Picture Rocks in Michigan.

Although these resources do not provide outdoor recreation opportunities in the usual sense, they are closely associated with vacation travel and hence are included in this classification system. The primary management objectives should be to effect such restoration as may be necessary, to protect them from deterioration, and to interpret their significance to the public. Suitable access and prevention of overuse are equally essential.

A Comparison of B.O.R. Classes

High density recreation areas (Class I) are usually, though not necessarily, located near urban centers. They may provide facilities for all kinds of recreation appropriate to the terrain, to the location, and to the accommodation of large numbers of visitors. The "mass" use of the area is its most distinguishing characteristic.

General outdoor recreation areas (Class II) utilize natural resources for the specific recreation activities for which they are particularly suited, irrespective of location. Generally, they are readily accessible and are equipped with a wide variety of man-made facilities, which may vary from

the simple to the elaborate. Although use is often heavy, it seldom has the "mass" feature characteristic of Class I. Because of the localized nature of the activities, Class II areas may often occur as enclaves in Class III and very rarely in Class IV.
Class IV.

Natural environment areas (Class III) are usually large compared with Class I and Class II areas, and recreation activities include those which are feasible in a natural environment with few or no man-made facilities. Scattered rather than concentrated use is normal. Utilization of resources for economic purposes is common but not essential.

Class IV areas are unique in their scenic splendor, natural wonder, or scientific importance. Accessibility is important, but recreation activities are strictly limited to those which will not result in any lessening of the area's unique value.

Primitive areas (Class V) are open only to such developments and such uses as will not interfere with their undisturbed and primitive character.

Class VI areas are set aside and managed in order to make their cultural and historic values available to as many people as possible without deterioration.

A noteworthy feature of the classification system is the difference in the availability of the several classes for various recreation activities. Camping, for example, is possible in Classes I, II, III, and V, although rather rarely in Class I. Hunting is a typical activity in Class III and Class V areas, except in national parks and monuments. Motoring for pleasure is common through Class III areas, but it is impossible through Class V areas.

One of the prime virtues of the B.O.R. classification system is that it makes possible the logical and beneficial adjustment of the entire range of recreation activities to the entire range of available areas. When physical conditions permit the classification of a given area in more than one class, the classification which promises the optimum combination of values in the long run should be selected.

LANDSCAPE ANALYSIS*

The landscape has a great effect on the recreationist; consequently, the planner should recognize this effect in terms of the potential of the resource for various recreational opportunities. Although it is difficult to totally quantify visual perception, certain variables are known to affect how people perceive the landscape. The basic model is: Visual Perception = Background of Observer + Environmental Conditions + Landscape Characteristics + Observer-Landscape Relationships. The background of

---

*This section is based on Litton, R.B., Jr. 1968. *Forest Landscape Description and Inventories*. U. S. Forest Service PSW-49.

the observer and the environmental conditions under which the observation takes place are not generally manipulatable in an outdoor setting. The observer-landscape relationships (distance, observer position, and sequence) are important because they affect the observer and are directly manipulatable, since people travel in established patterns over road, trail, and other transportation systems. The landscape characteristics (form, spatial definition, and light) are indirectly manipulatable through corridor selection for the transportation system; certain landscape elements can be emphasized by making them visually accessible from the corridor.

Observer-Landscape Relationships. 1. *Distance.* Ideally we should have some balance in the landscape in terms of the observer's distance from the landscape. Certain types of recreationists, such as the cross-country hiker and the boater, can select scenes and viewing distances. However, most people move from one scene to another on an established trail or road system. Consequently, we should consider viewing distances when establishing the travel system.

A standard approach is to designate distance-zones by the terms "near-viewing," "intermediate," and "far-viewing." In describing landscape distance zones, it is easier to use absolute distance (Table 12–1).

Near-viewing gives maximum perception of size and detail, without distortion. In addition, it is easy to describe in relation to the observer's position. Here the observer receives the greatest sensory experience of sight, sound, smell, and touch, and becomes personally involved with the physical setting.

Far-viewing is generally reduced to an outline shape, basic color pattern, and loss of detail. The open sky often gives this zone a sense of spaciousness. And if rolling hills or mountains show in this zone, there is a greater vertical and horizontal perception of spaciousness.

The intermediate zone is the linkage between the near and far zones and tends to dominate the view. It is the transition that gives both detail and generalizations. Here the observer sees the emergence of shapes and patterns, drainages, vegetative types, unique geological features, and so on. Man-made postures are more apparent here in their effects on the visual harmony of the landscapes. Thus, the planner should give careful attention to the effects of development on the landscape in the intermediate zone.

2. *Observer Position.* Observer position is the vertical location of

TABLE 12–1 LANDSCAPE DISTANCE ZONES

Zones	Boundary of Zone (Miles)	
	Near	Far
Near-viewing	0	¼–½
Intermediate	¼–½	3–5
Far-viewing	3–5	∞

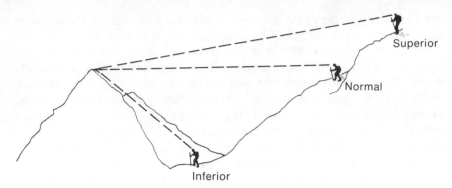

Figure 12–2   The three observer positions.

the person relative to the object being viewed. (Figure 12–2). The three positions are normal (at same level), inferior (below the object observed), and superior (above the object).

The observer assumes the normal position when the dominating elements of the landscape are on a level line of sight from the observer. Since the intermediate zone tends to dominate, the dominating elements should generally be in this zone.

The superior position, the observer above the observed object, tends to be the least restrictive in screening; opportunities exist for maximum viewing, even distant viewing, and for orientation to the total landscape. This position creates a sense of detachment from the observed landscape and a sequential climax for the observer moving from a lower to an intermediate, to a higher (superior) position. To some people, the attainment of the superior position may be as important as the view itself. This position may be used to allow people to utilize an area visually without having to visit it. In addition, it can give the recreationist a sense of achievement and greater freedom of choice in determining his own travel pattern through orientation to the total landscape.

The inferior position occurs when the observer is below the surrounding landscape, essentially enclosed by the landscape. This position tends to be the most restrictive to viewing, allowing mostly near-viewing. The most restrictive would be formed by enclosed steep topography such as a steep, narrow canyon. The position may be used to mask negative landscape elements, to create a feeling of greater distance by obscuring the terminus of the trip, and to direct attention to foreground detail such as particular rock strata, wildflower displays, and others.

3. *Sequence of Visual Experiences.*   The progressive interplay of forms, distances, lighting, and observer position can enhance the visitor's appreciation of the variety and complexity of the landscape. The sequence of views of a given landscape can make the experience more interesting and

personally rewarding, even to a mixture of observer types. This characteristic should be considered in any road or trail layout.

4. *The Indirect Factors.* The factors of form, spatial definition, and light can be manipulated by the location of the road, trail, or individual site. We may not change their absolute measurement in terms of size, space, and so on; however, we can change the visual perception through locational patterns of sites and facilities.

    a.   Form. This term refers primarily to topographic form with convex elements of the geomorphic base such as mountain, hill, cliff, etc. Contrast is necessary to distinguish form, and contrast may result from size, isolation, or surface variations. Isolation, such as a butte in the middle of a flat prairie, will provide a major contrast in topography. A series of buttes, one towering much higher than the others, will also provide contrast. Or the variation in vegetation on the north and south aspects may give great contrast. By means of the contrast we can distinguish form, and contrast can be enhanced by properly locating the viewing point.

    b.   Spatial definition. This term refers to a concave configuration created by topographic or vegetative features. Specific features include valleys, cirques, gorges, meadows, etc., and appear as limited or bounded space. These give us a sense of depth perception, or a reference by which we can judge the size of space, vertically and horizontally. The maximum spatial definition of the landscape can be obtained when the observer is in the bottom of the enclosure (concave space) and close to an enclosing wall. There are four sources of variation:

       (1) Wall height to floor size. The higher the walls and the smaller the floor, the greater the spatial definition.

       (2) The nature of the enclosing walls and floor. The sheer rock wall with flat, grassy floor will have greater spatial definition than the forested wall with an undulating floor.

       (3) The configuration of the floor as it intersects the wall. A small, elliptical floor, such as a meadow, will be more easily discernible than a large valley having secondary configuration patterns, such as a dendritic drainage pattern.

       (4) Differences in absolute size. Landscapes may vary in scale yet be similar in the pattern of enclosure. Scale is more easily discernible in a well-founded space (good spatial definition). Where the walls and floors have irregular or diffuse boundaries, scale from the observer's standpoint becomes less well-defined. Regardless of the other effects, probably the most important need for good spatial definition is to provide a visual yardstick for the

observer to put all elements in perspective with one
another and with the total landscape.

    c.   Light. Light conditions will vary considerably during the day
and between seasons. These changes should be considered
when one attempts to emphasize or mask a given portion of
the landscape.

Color of the landscape is expressed as *hue* (the quality of the color,
such as blue, green, red) and *value* (the tonal quality of the color between
light and dark). The variation in hues gives greater clarity to the landscape,
particularly where strong hues are contrasted, such as where a dandelion
meadow intercepts the brilliant blue of a mountain lake, or where the
bright yellows of the aspen leaves contrast with the deep green of the surrounding spruce forest.

Color value generally predominates over hue in most landscapes,
particularly in more distant viewing. Thus, general patterns of color values
arise:

1. The sky is lighter than the earth.
2. Grasslands are lighter than forests.
3. Soil is lighter than vegetation.
4. Disturbed soil is generally lighter than undisturbed soil.
5. Hardwoods are lighter than conifers.
6. Flat lighting diminishes color value differences.

Distance, because of the scattering of the light rays, tends to cause
more distant objects to have a more blue or gray color. And the color value
diminishes toward a uniformity or lack of contrast.

The direction of light can also affect visual perception. The directions
are described as backlight (facing into light), frontlight (facing away from),
and sidelight (from either side).

In terms of the availability of direct sunlight, north has the least; south,
the most. Thus, north slopes tend to be more obscured by shade and
shadows than south slopes. The east and west slopes have similar availability but during opposite times of the day.

Backlighting tends to obscure detail and create visual impairment at
the extremes, facing into the sunrise or sunset. In frontlighting, shadows
tend to be shorter, shading falls away from the observer, and more surface
tends to be in direct sunlight. Thus, there is less contrast and more uniformity of the landscape, creating a less interesting scene because of the
reduced variation. Sidelighting, on the other hand, gives greater contrast
and a greater sense of the scene's three-dimensionality.

Types of Landscapes.   For a given physiographic province, there is a
continuum of recreational landscapes, often with no clear boundaries between them. At times, because of natural changes (fire, rockslides, etc.) or
man-made changes, the transition may be very abrupt—an intrusion on the
landscape's continuity and visual harmony. Even with the problems of

boundary identification or intrusions, Litton[9] identified four basic types of landscapes:

1. *Panoramic Landscape.*   Panoramic landscape is one with a 360° view limited by the continuous line of the horizon, such as one might find on a flat, continuous surface like a large body of water. On land the panorama is often limited to 180° or less because of change in landscape composition, limits of peripheral vision, or natural side screening. The basic dimension is horizontal, with little feeling of boundary or visual restriction. This landscape gives the greatest feeling of distance and openness, with no single, dominant feature.

2. *Feature Landscape.*   This is a landscape that is visually dominated by a singular or closely related group of features, natural or man-made. There is a great diversity in the types of dominant features, scale (relative to other items around it), configuration (shape), orientation (vertical or horizontal), and position relative to the observer and other potentially dominant elements. All of these variables must be considered when the planner attempts to feature a given element for the observer. If too many elements are featured, the dominance the planner hopes to present

Figure 12–3 Panoramic landscape, superior position, Emphasis on intermediate viewing zone—Snowy Range, Wyoming (photograph by Tom Buchanan).

Figure 12-4   Feature landscape, dominant cone form, massive scale, superior position
—Mt. Hood, Oregon (photograph by Elaine Eastman).

may be obscured. Similar shapes, orientation, and other factors may confuse the observer. Also, objects in the near-viewing zone may appear larger
than the high mountain peak in distant-viewing zone—the item the planner
might have wanted to emphasize in the landscape.

   3.   *Enclosed Landscape.*   This landscape type is created by vertical
sides enclosing a base plane. The vertical sides in a natural landscape are
formed by either vegetation or topographic features, and the base generally
approaches a horizontal plane. The water's edge forms a conspicuous
junction of the vertical walls (vegetation or steep topography) and the
horizontal base (flat water). The enclosure is then created by well-defined
limits of space; if the base (body of water, meadow, etc.) is enlarged to the
point that the vertical walls become insignificant or even invisible, then the
feeling of enclosure is lost. And the landscape then approaches the
panoramic type.

   4.   *Focal Landscape.*   This type of landscape is structured by a
series of parallel lines, or aligned objects, which converge or tend to
converge on a focal point within the landscape. According to Litton:[9]

> Both point convergence and feature terminus may occur
> with or without side enclosures; that is, either may be overlaid on

an open panoramic landscape or can occur as corridors on a flat plane. Portal or self-enclosure compositions can occur only in the context of enclosed landscape. . . . A stream course or a road tangent are the most likely places to look for the focal landscape. Perhaps the most commanding or effective focal composition occurs when a landscape feature is present as a visual terminus.

5. *Secondary Landscape Types.*   These may be a part of the basic landscape types, are smaller in scale, and generally have more detail because of their closeness to the observer:

    a. Canopied landscape. Vegetative canopies tend to limit viewing and are relatively small scale. Thus, the landscape is easily seen and observed by the pedestrian; but the vehicle operator, because of his closeness, speed of travel, and focus on the detail of the road, is not able to grasp the detail. However, if he were in an open panorama, he might be able to detect the primary landscape patterns without detail.

    Roads within a canopied situation present the closest contact that many auto visitors have with the out-of-doors. These rapidly moving observers can sense three sources of contrast in the canopied landscape: changes in general vegetation

Figure 12–5   Enclosed landscape, water base, large scale—southern Ontario (photograph by Tom Buchanan).

Figure 12–6 Focal landscape, self enclosure, large scale—Encampment River, Wyoming (photograph by Tom Buchanan).

types, marked changes in size, class and condition of vegetation, and spatial definition of the canopied enclosure. There are three basic canopied postures: the broad open corridors of major highways; the medium closure corridors of secondary, moderate-speed roads; and the small corridors or completely enclosed vegetative tunnels on slow-speed, minimally improved roads.

We can give a feeling to the motorist of contact with the natural landscape by bringing the edge of the road to the forested edge, and minimizing or lowering road cuts and fills. On the other hand, we can create a feeling of detachment by separating the road from the forest edge and increasing cuts and fills. We can also increase vegetative contrast by running roads or portions thereof somewhat perpendicular to the

Figure 12-7 Canopied landscape, Aspen type, over forest road—Medicine Bow National Forest, Wyoming (photograph by William R. Eastman III).

major topographic features, since changes in topography generally reflect changes in vegetation. As Litton states:[9]

Transferring the characteristics of the slower-speed road to high speed roads has little chance to succeed. Lane division and use of broad median areas can help maintain contact with forest stands. But we should recognize that each road type imparts a different scenic quality to the stand—more light or less; more enclosure or less; more closeness or less. One is not better than the other. Each offers a difference which should be retained for variety and contrast.

b. Detail landscape. A detail landscape is part of a basic landscape that focuses on specific detail close to the observer. The detail requires a slow pace from the pedestrian and a desire to seek out the natural, artistic amenities in the detail. The pat-

Figure 12–8   Detail landscape, conical shape, spring mushrooms (photograph by Elaine Eastman).

terns, the forms, and the symbolism the observer perceives can offer personal satisfaction. They may be unique, symbolic, or merely reflective of the total landscape composition. The detail may be composed of plants, rock deposits, water, and other features; however, the skillful location of the observer position in terms of background, lighting, and changing weather can focus attention on the specific detail while creating a sense of changing landscape detail brought about by minute changes in light, weather, and other conditions. Thus, the observer may want to return again and again to receive the full continuum of visual opportunities from the specific detail landscape. Also, this type of landscape can be used as a relief and transition from one observer position to another in a given basic landscape, or between basic landscapes. This situation is similar to using a foreground detail (and dialogue) as a transition scene in a play while the larger background scene is changed.

c.   Ephemeral landscape. The ephemeral landscape depends on temporal or transitory effects that may last a few seconds or perhaps several days. Five types of influences give ephemeral effects to the landscape: atmospheric conditions, projected and reflected images, displacement, signs, and animal presence. Atmospheric conditions are the most extensive effects and are formed by cloud and fog formation, precipitation, changing light, and wind motion.

Projected and reflected images are secondary images created by light shadows or reflections on water. Reflections are more conspicuous than shadows because they reflect a mirror image of the real form, although the color may be somewhat darker. Under suitable conditions, the secondary image can be complete and can enhance recognition of objects.

Signs are indications of former life or occupancy by animals or plants. Animal tracks, bird nests, spider webs, tree snags, feathers, or bubbles from feeding fishes indicate that animals were recently present. Animal presence is a transitory influence on the landscape, generally in the near-viewing zone. Signs and animal presence are generally subtle secondary landscapes available mostly to the pedestrian.

Although impossible to control, the ephemeral landscape is important and is extremely motivating to many observers as

Figure 12–9 Ephemeral landscape, low cumulus cloud cover, open prairie (photograph by William R. Eastman III).

they seek out the subtle transitory landscape elements. Timing is often important, and the observer should be made aware of timing in the appreciation of these elements.

Scenery Analysis—An Application

Although it is difficult to quantify landscape values properly in terms of visual perception, many agencies have developed point rating methods for evaluating scenic potential for a given recreational experience. An example of this type of evaluation was the system devised by Sargent.[15] He subjectively developed point values for various positive and negative elements of the landscape and then applied this system to three different locations.

This type of approach is often necessary when the research is insufficient to isolate and quantify the most significant elements. However, the planner should strive for more objective approaches such as the one devised by Shafer,[16] in which various elements of the two-dimensional landscape on photos were used to predict the elements that affected landscape perception. The basic model could be used to select vistas, road and trail location, and so on; however, there are some limitations, such as scale, only two dimensions, and variability of the observer and observation conditions.

Litton[9] offers an analytical approach to landscape inventories without specific quantification. He attempts, through deductive reasoning, to apply the concepts and principles of landscape analysis, as previously presented in this chapter. He attempts to lead the planner, by example, through landscape perception analysis and subsequent management prescriptions. This type of approach is workable if the planner has sufficient understanding and practical experience in evaluating the scenic elements and their possible effects on the observer.

ENVIRONMENTAL RESOURCE ANALYSIS— THE OVERLAY METHOD

Lewis and McHarg have developed resource analysis techniques that involve inventorying specific resource values, identifying each value on a separate overlay, and then superimposing these to create a composite overlay.[8,12] From this technique (Figure 12–10) one can easily determine the type and locations of important land-use values, including recreation. In addition, one can determine points of possible conflict from incompatible uses as well as the better locations for future development in terms of quality recreational experiences and the natural ability of the resource to sustain that type of use.

This type of approach requires a team effort to identify properly the desired social values, their location and significance, and also the natural values of the resource, the natural processes to our life support systems, including aesthetics. Herein lies the main problem—choosing the values to

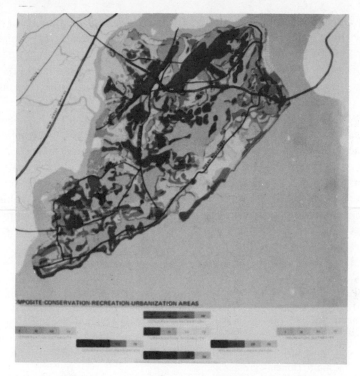

Figure 12-10 Composite overlay of values used in planning (overlay by McHarg, I.L. 1969. *Design With Nature*. Garden City, N.Y.: The Natural History Press. p. 114).

be studied. If the proper ones are not chosen, then the wrong conclusions are drawn. If too many are selected, then the cost of data collection and analysis soars.

Once the values are identified, the chief planner must insist on a field evaluation of each value, including the capabilties and limitations of the resource to sustain the use. Also, certain judgments will have to be made about the compatibility of land uses. Once this process is completed, each value is placed on an overlay and then the composite overlay is made (Figure 12-10).

This composite is intended as a simplification of the overlay technique in evaluating the resource base for recreation and other land uses. McHarg's thesis in his process is that natural values should determine the selection of planning alternatives.[13] He assigns very little value to human and cultural processes. Lewis stresses both social and natural values. In his work, he found that most values lie in corridors, particularly along the natural or man-made ribbons—rivers, roads, and other features. Many values are also clustered at nodes within the ribbons.

If the overlay technique is to be effective and efficient, then a team effort is necessary to identify both social and natural values properly. Furthermore, some priority system for these values must be developed so that planning decisions can be made. In terms of recreation, the recreational experience must be considered first—What are people seeking? What is their basic behavior? And how does a given physical setting or activity satisfy identified needs? The resource must then be evaluated in terms of ability to sustain this use over time. If it cannot sustain this use, then the program should be altered to reduce use or to shift it to another area.

However, to make a decision purely on the program's effects on the resource base precludes consideration of human or social values. To make this kind of decision ensures that certain planning actions will take place, but none of these actions may satisfy human needs. The irony of the situation is that none of these factors take on value except as people identify them as values. For the planner to say that only natural values are important is to supplant the value system of the total society with his own personal values.

SELECTED READINGS

1. Alexander, C., and S. I. Chermayeff. 1964. *Notes on the Synthesis of Form.* Cambridge, Massachusetts: Harvard University Press.
2. Arnheim, R. 1954. *Art and Visual Perception, A Psychology of the Creative Eye.* Berkeley, California: University of California Press.
3. Clawson, M. 1963. *Land and Water for Recreation.* Chicago: Rand McNally Co.
4. Clawson, M., and J. L. Knetsch. 1966. *Economics of Outdoor Recreation.* Baltimore: The Johns Hopkins Press.
5. Dansereau, P. 1966. "Ecological Impact and Human Ecology," *Future Environments of North America.* Garden City, N. Y.: The Natural History Press. pp. 425–462.
6. Herrington, R. B., and S. R. Tocher. 1967. *Aerial Photo Techniques for a Recreation Inventory of Mountain Lakes and Streams.* U. S. Forest Service Research Paper INT–37.
7. Leopold, L. 1969. *Quantitative Comparison of Some Aesthetic Factors Among Rivers.* Geologic Survey Circular 620.
8. Lewis, P. H. 1964. "Quality Corridors for Wisconsin," *Landscape Architecture Quarterly.* 54:100–107.
9. Litton, R. B., Jr. 1968. *Forest Landscape Description and Inventories.* U. S. Forest Service Research Paper PWS–49.
10. Litton, R. B., Jr., and R. H. Twiss. 1967. "The Forest Landscape: Some Elements of Visual Analysis," *Proceedings, Society of American Foresters.* pp. 212–214.
11. Lowenthal, D. (ed). 1967. *Environmental Perception and Behavior.* Chicago: University of Chicago. Geography Research Paper No. 109.
12. McHarg, I. L. 1969. *Design With Nature.* Garden City, N. Y.: The Natural History Press.
13. _____. 1966. "Ecological Determinism," *Future Environments of North America.* F. F. Darling and J. P. Milton (eds.). Garden City, N. Y.: The Natural History Press.
14. Outdoor Recreation Resources Review Commission. 1962. *Outdoor Recreation for America.* Washington, D.C.: U.S. Government Printing Office.
15. Sargent, F.O. 1967. *Scenery Classification.* Report No. 18. Burlington, Vermont: Vermont Resources Research Center, University of Vermont.
16. Shafer, E. L., Jr., J. E. Hamilton, Jr., and E. A. Schmidt. 1969. "Natural Landscape Preferences: A Predictive Model," *Journal of Leisure Research,* 1(1): 1–20.
17. Simonds, J. O. 1961. *Landscape Architecture.* New York: F. W. Dodge Corp.
18. Thiel, P. 1961. "A Sequence-Experience Notation for Architectural and Urban Spaces," *The Town Planning Review,* 32(1): 33–52.
19. Woodbury, C. 1966. "The Role of the Regional Planner in Preserving Habitats and Scenic Values," *Future Environments of North America.* F. F. Darling and J. P. Milton (eds.). Garden City, N. Y.: The Natural History Press.

CHAPTER 13

RECREATION IN LAND-USE PLANNING

THE PROBLEM

More and more people are trying to overcome the mistakes of our past treatment of the landscape, and are struggling to maintain a quality livable environment and to reconstruct those landscapes that have been previously scarred. As Jensen states:

> With respect to nature, archeologists and historians have found that civilizations pass through four stages. In the first stage man battles nature for his survival. He attempts to cope with nature and conquer it. In the second stage man cooperates with nature in an effort to become domesticated, and nature helps him to produce the goods that he needs. After he has first coped with nature, then learned to cooperate with it and use it to his advantage, he enters the third stage, that of exploiting nature by overharvesting her resources and overusing her goods. After recognizing his error and the futility of his approach, man enters the fourth stage, that of rehabilitating nature, attempting to heal the wounds he has caused. The divisions between these four stages are not clearcut, and at a particular time a society may not be at the same stage with respect to all kinds of natural resources. We Americans have seemingly passed through the first and second stages, and for the most part we have been in the third stage for quite some time. We are now, let us hope, surging into the fourth stage. In many respects we have overharvested and overused our natural resources, and we are still doing so. But at least some of our wiser leaders have recognized this fact and are attempting to lead us into the fourth stage, that of rehabilitating the overused resources. Extensive exploitation of natural resources results in ugliness and certain kinds of pollution which seriously detract from the lives of people.

> If the historians were asked to pass final judgment on our nation at this particular juncture of history, they might well conclude that in terms of the energy of the American people, in terms of our technological skill, in terms of the scope of our science, we have reached a pinnacle of material success. Certainly in terms of wealth and what we call progress, we have achieved a level of prosperity no other society or civilization has ever achieved. But simultaneously we have failed to create an overall environment worthy of our wealth and power. We have failed to build handsome cities and to create an environment of order and dignity. Some noteworthy leaders of the world have referred to the large American cities as "catastrophies of continental proportions." As land stewards and builders of cities, we have experienced a large degree of failure, and we will continue to experience such failure unless we lay down new guidelines for growth and shake off the dead dogmas of the past.[12]

Along with the search for a pleasing environment must come a recognition of our past mistakes and a firm dedication to improve the situation. We have not only ravaged the terrestrial landscape but also polluted our air and water, to the point that they are often no longer desirable space for living or, in some cases, suitable for mere existence.

The problem has been myopic planning for short-run economic benefits without considering all of the costs involved—loss of natural aesthetics, loss of open space, and loss of a healthful environment. All of these costs must be paid if we are to rehabilitate our environs.

The greatest cause of the problem has been a perception of the landscape as infinite; as one oasis ran dry, we moved to the next. Only recently have we begun to realize that there are no more oases; we must live with the existing, finite resource base.

Even in outdoor recreation, the recreational experience has deteriorated for many participants. Population increase has caused overloading of existing facilities. In addition, the quality of recreational use has seemingly been reduced, causing a tremendous aesthetic and environmental impact. Mechanized recreation has reduced the *psychological size* of a given area through increased speed of travel, thus limiting the amount of perceived open space. This condition in turn creates the feeling of increased crowding. Furthermore, mechanized recreation has had a tremendous environmental impact—increased noise levels, site deterioration, and air and water pollution.

Most of the deterioration has occurred because of the lack of comprehensive planning in allocating and managing our resources for recreation and other land uses. What is needed for the comprehensive planning to proceed is a "community" ethic that places the value of the intact landscape (the community in which we live) above the short-run economic gains that may be derived from that landscape.

There is a need in recreation planning to balance leisure needs with the ability of the landscape to support them. Indications are that many people are pushing aside the recreation vehicle for more self-mobile, self-reliant types of activities. People are seemingly recognizing the limits of recreation space and are attempting to seek leisure satisfactions in the total recreational experience, including a more leisured travel. With reduced mobility, some people are looking at the nearby landscape and are taking action to maintain it. In sum, people are finally realizing that if we are to maintain quality in our leisure experiences, we must protect the finite landscape. We are rapidly running out of landscapes to ravage, plunder, and litter during our leisure time, only to move on to new landscapes.

Environmental education in schools, communities, and agencies has helped make people aware of the consequences of their actions, whether the action be siting of an industrial plant or engaging in an outdoor recreation activity. Thus, people have become more aware of new air and water pollution standards and the need to moderate our activities through land-use planning.

LAND-USE PLANNING

Land-use planning as a goal and a process is not well defined. Too often it is viewed as planning for a single use, such as timbering or recreation, or selected uses, such as recreation, timber, watershed, grazing, and wildlife. On the other hand, some planners see land-use planning as strictly an urban process where space is allocated for urban growth, including subsystems such as transportation, industrial development, and marketing.[1]

Some people perceive land-use planning as based strictly on biological principles. Ovington[15] foresees the process correlating to ecosystem boundaries so that energy flows are not disrupted. Leopold[13] feels that durability of the land, in terms of the ability to absorb punishment and still remain productive or stable, should be a prime criteria. Others, such as Chapin,[1] see land-use planning as a means of balancing social needs with the potential limitations of the environment.

Basically we need to establish the definition and goal for land-use planning before we can establish criteria or process. In sum, land-use planning is a means of systematically anticipating and achieving adjustment of the physical and biological environment consistent with social and economic trends and sound principles of ecology and aesthetics. The basic goal is to ensure proper allocation of space for all land uses in order to maximize the needed flow of goods and services to the population while minimizing the conflict between subsystems (production of specific goods and services) and the effect on the environmental base on which they are dependent.

Thus, all of the opening descriptions are included under the umbrella of *land-use planning*. It is a coordination of land uses to meet growing human needs while minimizing the environmental impact by selecting the land that is most durable for a given use. However, we must put this process in some historical context, in terms of existing urbanization, industrial development, utility and transportation systems, leisure service systems, and so on, and also in the context of political framework, in terms of existing political boundaries, the decision making process, and pressure group politics.

Senator Henry M. Jackson proposed in 1970 that land-use legislation is essential to the orderly growth of America; yet his proposed legislation only focuses on industrial, conservation, and recreation programs. If we are to have effective land-use controls, we must enumerate the various subsystems, the limitation of resource base to sustain a given subsystem, and the needs of the population in terms of goods and services, including quality of life needs such as clean air and water, natural aesthetics, and human dignity. In a democratic society, the choice in land uses for a given parcel of land should not be dictatorial. However, the choices or alternatives may be limited because of the limitations of the resource to provide a given use, the durability of the resource to sustain that kind of use, and restrictions for development. This way, an individual developer should be able to evaluate a given land-use alternative economically, based on having to develop within certain restrictions including such factors as air or water pollution abatement, soil erosion control, maintenance of aesthetics, and others. On a national or regional basis, the balance of the flow of goods and services to meet population needs can be accomplished by the way certain systems (such as transportation and utility systems) are laid out and by monetary incentives to public and private agencies.

The Highway Trust Fund and the Land and Water for Conservation Fund are monetary ways of ensuring, at the state level, well-planned and coordinated action in highway development and park development, respectively. These and other systems should be coordinated under a nationwide land-use plan to ensure minimum conflict and maximum coordination of action. In essence, the basic authority on allocation of space for a given system should be a nationwide land-use plan. The following systems should as a minimum be coordinated within the plan:

1. Transportation and Utility.
2. Residential and Municipal Development.
3. Park, Recreation, Open Space, and Conservation.
4. Industrial Development.
5. Agriculture and Renewable Resources.
6. Energy and Nonrenewable Resources.

The binder for the six systems, legal and institutional factors, is extremely complex and often confusing and conflicting. Thus, a complete appraisal and updating of our laws, legal systems, and existing government and administrative institutions are necessary for well-conceived land-use plans.

Economics as a Determinant.   The economic explanation of existing land use patterns begins with forces extending well beyond the immediate or local land use pattern and involves the structure and relationship of the regional economy and even the nation as a whole. Certain types of land uses that are tied to resource productivity are only appropriately developed wherever the resource is located. The "cash-grain" belt of the midwest, the national parks, the wilderness areas, and the like are tied to a unique land resource; thus, these patterns of land use are related very closely to the total national economy, even though they may also be important regionally.

Other patterns of land use relate strictly to the regional economy. Local economies and their land-use patterns reflect both local conditions and their tie to the regional economy and its land-use pattern. This tie is just as important for the winter sports complex or sawmill as it is for the agriculture business or industrial development. Thus, it is necessary that the location and spatial development of recreation developments be coordinated to transportation and utility systems, processing, marketing, and other services. No one community or municipality is self-sufficient; each contributes to and is dependent upon the regional economy.

Implicit in this idea is that local and regional forces interact to shape land-use patterns. Local land uses are generally tied to the capability of the specific land to produce certain goods and services desired throughout the region. Thus, the land only takes on increased value as these goods and services are demanded. Ideally, in a regional economy, there would be sufficient diversity of land uses to produce all the needed goods and services. But no region is self-sufficient; thus interdependency of regions balances the needed flow of goods and services.

The local pattern of land use may evolve from an economy based on a year-round recreational and tourism program. The primary force may be the unique resource base, such as that around Jackson, Wyoming. The attendant land-use patterns mirror the primary forces; motels, hotels, winter sports sites, scenic roads, dedicated open space, summer home developments, and other similar land uses come into existence, reflecting the central theme of recreation and tourism. Other goods and services more appropriately produced in other locales in the region would be supplied to Jackson through the regional economy. In turn, Jackson would supply some of the desired recreation and tourism to the region.

On a regional level, certain unique land-use patterns develop to perform certain functions not possible at the local level. Regional industrial developments, distributorships, marketing mechanisms, and transportation systems ensure an adequate flow of goods and services. Locating an industrial development in an urban center of the region may attract transportation companies for moving the goods, regional distributorships for selling the goods, residential and municipal service developments for the expanded resident population, and other land uses related to this regional development.

Land uses, their location, and attendant problems are accounted for in the market place. According to Chapin:

> Here users of land bid for sites in accordance with what will maximize their profits and minimize their costs. Land users in retail business and services tend to bid for space at the highest prices, and land best suited for these activities shows the highest value. For this type of use the revenue component in the above formulation of land value is based on the volume of sales expected at alternative sites, and the cost component is based on the costs of doing business to obtain these sales at these sites. Similarly, for industrial users, the revenue component is based on product sales potentials at different competing sites, and the cost component is based on costs of production at those sites. For households the revenue component is based on the dollar value placed on benefits anticipated from alternative sites, with costs being measured in terms of commuting expenses, taxes, improvement costs, and so on at each such alternative site.[1]

Through land-use planning, the restrictions placed on developing the land for certain types of uses would be identified. The developer can then include all of the associated costs in his economic evaluation of the development.

Culture as a Determinant.   Probably no other determinant has had a greater effect on the existing land-use patterns than *cultural* patterns. Early pioneers viewed the wild land as hostile and forbidding, something that was to be "overcome," and worked to produce needed food and shelter. With only primitive means, they carved farming land out of the landscape. When the soil became worn out, the farmers moved on to tame new lands. These types of attitudes have persisted; land has been viewed as limitless and having great resilience to man's abuse. Thus, people have ravaged the landscape with strip mines, junkyards, and other unattractive and environmentally degrading land uses.

Historically, urban and municipal development occurred along waterways, the early American highways. Thus, these land uses are located in highly productive but very sensitive lands, in terms of low stability and periodic flooding. Other historical land-use patterns have evolved in agriculture, forestry, mining, and other similar significant land-use patterns. Too often these have developed on areas that are perhaps unsuitable for the use or environmentally unstable; yet these uses persist with minimum controls.

Timbering has become an accepted land use in many northern Rocky Mountain areas. Yet, many of the areas are unsuitable because of shallow soils and steep topography. The foothill country is generally more stable and productive but is not managed for forest products, as most of it is private ownership. The problem is that much land relegated to more contemporary land uses such as conservation, wildlife management, and outdoor recreation has low productivity, less stability, and low durability in terms of intensive human use.

All of these uses stem from historical patterns which have molded particular land uses. The planner must then realize that many existing land uses have deep cultural and historical roots and are not likely to change rapidly. Consequently, future planning of any type, including outdoor recreation, must accept much of the existing patterns of land use.

Social Behavior as a Determinant.   It is important to understand human behavior and values as they influence land-use patterns, if we are to develop land-use plans adequately. It would be presumptuous of the author to attempt to present the complex and dynamic factors relating to human behavior and the development of various land uses. However, certain behaviors should be discussed:

1.   *Human Needs.*   Land use patterns as an aggregate of individual and group actions reflect human behavior as activated by needs or motivators. The individual and group actions in the past have mainly occurred without the umbrella effect of land-use planning and regulatory controls. Consequently, many actions have lacked coordination, and at times they have been incompatible and ineffective in meeting the needs of the people.

2.   *Human Values.*   Social values play an important role in establishing the various land-use patterns. They may be latent or conscious values and may relate to specific societal systems, such as economic, aesthetic, social, and political. Generally mass values, those held by a majority of people, affect area and regional land-use planning so that the desired products and services are available to the public. Group values, those held by special interest groups, generally have an effect on specific local land-use concerns. Mass values are more stable than group values; however, even these may change over time. Certain mass values on recreational land uses, such as manifested in the Wilderness Act and the Wild and Scenic Rivers Act, have only recently become accepted. The application of these statutes in particular locales is affected by group values.

3.   *Social Forces.*   Certain social forces have affected the way man has chosen to locate himself spatially on the earth. Places of work tend to dominate these forces to the point that many choose to locate themselves where their specific skills are most needed. Other forces of concern are quality of environment, convenience of obtaining desired goods and services, availability of recreation opportunities, and others.

Public Opinion as a Determinant.   Public opinion, as a cognitive, oral expression of public values, is important in the planning process. The difficulty in using public opinion is in measuring it and incorporating it into the decision making process, particularly if the decision relates not only to local needs, but also to regional and national needs. However, this difficulty does not mean that we should forego public opinion in planning.

Also, general welfare considerations, in terms of public interest, need to be accounted for. Quality of life has become very important to people, and they have begun to seek more pleasing aesthetic and healthful environments and a better planned physical environment.

Environmental Factors as a Determinant. It is important that we understand the natural environment and the effects of various land uses on it if we are to maintain necessary life support systems, quality of life, and products and services derived from the land. Specific factors are:

1. *Potential of the Land.* Ascertaining the potential of the land to produce various products and services is essential to proper land-use planning. We must allocate land for the most productive use or combination of uses; otherwise, we will have a very inefficient system. The other problem is that many lands have historically been allocated to inefficient uses. For example, many urban areas are located on highly productive lands that would be more suitable for high crop production.

2. *Durability of the Land.* The ability of the land to sustain the various uses and still remain stable and productive is important if we are to sustain the land uses in perpetuity. In land-use planning, the durability is assessed along with the constraints associated with development. Then any developmental planning like those in recreation must overcome the constraints associated with the land forms.

3. *Natural Aesthetics.* Natural aesthetics, in terms of existing visual environment, have become important to people. Certain types of land uses have tremendous effects on natural aesthetics. Ideally, the visual effects of any land use are considered in land-use planning. Each use is made as compatible as possible with the task of maintaining natural aesthetics, although the planner realizes that certain uses will cause some visual disruptions. Attention to the visual concerns is imperative if we are to maintain a pleasing and livable environment.

LAND-USE CONTROLS

There are three major types of controls: legal, environmental, and administrative. All of these are important in any type of planning; however, the emphasis in this section will be on controls that are important to the outdoor recreation planner as land-use controls.

Legal Controls. The legal controls are:

1. *Zoning.* According to Whyte:

> Broadly speaking, the community applies the police power to see to it that people do not use land in a way that injures the public welfare. . . .
> In principle, zoning is invoked to protect the public's health, safety, morals, and general welfare, and under this rubric there would appear to be no limit to the forms of beneficent land control we could with invention contrive. In practice, zoning has so far been used principally for the protection of property interests.[18]

The major problem with zoning is that it has been primarily negative to prevent people from developing certain uses, rather than positive to suggest the better locations for various land uses. Second, it has often been very arbitrary in application. Any industrialist or businessman who wanted to put in a development in a nonindustrial or nonbusiness zone could easily obtain a zoning variance based on the economic good that it would bring the community. Too often the variance was against the wishes of the residents but was granted in the name of community needs.

2. *Fee Simple Acquisition.*   When we acquire a parcel of land with all the rights of land ownership, the type of acquisition is called *fee simple.* The best way to establish total land control is through fee simple purchase. The problem with this method is that the public must have the money to purchase the lands. Generally, the need is greatest for purchasing park and open space where the land values are highest. Thus, the fee simple purchase, although perhaps the proper device, may not be the best one because of economics.

More monies, literally millions of dollars, have become available through state revenue sharing, the Land and Water Conservation Fund, HUD Open Space and Urban Beautification programs, and others. Unfortunately, the price of land has soared at an even greater rate. In the urban areas, the increased cost of open space has nearly tripled that of other nearby lands. Thus, while monies have increased, the ability to preserve open space and park and recreation lands through fee simple purchase has decreased.

A possible solution to the problem was offered by Whyte:

> One solution is a revolving fund. The legislature provides
> the agency with an initial stake for making tactical purchases of
> land in advance of need. Later, when the legislature makes
> regular appropriations for the projects involved, money covering ·
> the cost of the purchases already made will be credited to the
> fund, thus replenishing it for additional advance work. The ad
> vantages are many. It helps the agency beat out speculators for
> land it knows it is going to have to buy eventually. It also gives its
> negotiators much greater latitude in dealing with the land market.
> Often it is best to wait until a property comes onto the market.
> Then the owner wants to sell, perhaps urgently. If the negotiator
> can take advantage of such situations as they come up, he will do
> far better than if he has to force the market later, and on a lot of
> properties all at once. By the advance buying, he will also have
> spared the public from having to pay extra for any additional
> building that may have been done on the properties.[18]

Other techniques of fee simple acquisition which offer some possibilities to the planner are:

    a.   Life estate. In this you may purchase land with its fee simple rights with the stipulation that the existing owner, and rarely the first generation beyond the immediate owner, may live out his normal life on the property. There are two economic advantages to this arrangement: the acquisition costs are generally less because you allow him continual use of the land, and the costs may be spread over a period of years. The advantage to the planner is that he can maintain the existing compatible land use until such time as the public receives the land in fee simple ownership. Thus, it is really a combination of fee simple and negative easement.

b.   Gift. Most public agencies have not actively pursued a program of gifts or endowments. Some cities have been very successful in acquiring real property through that type of program. However, one obstacle to this type of program is that many park and recreation agencies cannot be a receivership; the gift must go to the general receivership of the local, state, or federal government. Thus, the wording of the gift is important to ensure that the property is maintained in the specified land use. Furthermore, some levels of governments are forbidden from selling land once it has been accepted. Thus, an agency could not accept a parcel of property with the idea of trading or selling and then acquiring another property more suitable to needs of the community or area. If it could do this, the agency could reduce the capital costs of land acquisition. Some have found it convenient to establish a private, nonprofit foundation in conjunction with the agency to act as a receivership without the agency legal constraints.

c.   Lease. The lease has been recognized by some federal programs as a legitimate form of land control if the length of the lease is at least equal to the expected life of the contemplated development (buildings and other facilities). The problem is that if the land is needed now, it will be even more important in the future. Most likely the cost of acquisition after the lease period would be prohibitive. Thus, this tends not to be a good alternative.

d.   Condemnation. Condemnation, or eminent domain, is the legal right of a government to take private land for public purposes with just compensation to the private owner. It is rarely used, except in extreme problem cases. Even though the land is taken in the name of public need, the method seemingly compromises the rights of the private landowner and often creates ill will and distrust for the total park, recreation, or open space program. This problem could lead to a neutralization of the effects of the program if the local people do not support the condemnation. Sometimes these aggravations are harbored for years. A word of caution in the application of eminent domain—be sure that the total program is desirable, that the particular property is needed, and that eminent domain is the last alternative for fee simple acquisition. Be sure of your actions, and act as objectively as possible.

3.   *Less Than Fee Simple.*   We may wish to acquire less than fee simple rights. For a given purpose, we may only need one right or more, not

the whole package. We may buy these in the form of an easement. When we buy these rights, they may be in the form of positive or negative easements.

Positive easement is the one with which we are most familiar. We acquire the right to do something with part of another's property. We may buy a right of way for an access road to public land, a bicycle trail through a neighborhood, a utility corridor to a public camp, and so on.

In the negative easement, we are not buying the right to use but the right of the present owner to change the land from a given land use. This method is used to preserve a given landscape. The exact conditions of what can or cannot be done must be stated in the easement. Typically, these have been conservation or scenic easements.

In the scenic easement, we may want to preserve a given land use along a parkway, such as a nonmechanized farm, a stand of trees, a rustic home nestled in the valley. Or we may want to preclude any obtrusive developments, such as billboards or housing developments. In essence, we pay the landowner not to do these things. In the conservation easement, we buy up certain rights for conservation purposes. It may be to save the potholes on the prairie, to protect an endangered species, or to ensure adequate winter range for the bighorn sheep.

The easement is a useful tool for controlling certain land uses at a cost much less than fee simple acquisition. In addition, there are only minimal management and administrative costs in the management of the easement. However, it does have its limitations. Some people have considered it as a means for sweeping control of whole regions. In this context, a public agency would acquire easements for all the open land, not merely to keep it open but to stage development; step by step, certain easements would be relinquished so that development would be encouraged to go where the area or regional plan indicated it would be best located.

The problem in this case is that the easement is being used dogmatically to dictate total land-use patterns. It was never intended for that; land-use planning, as stated previously, is an attempt to allocate land wisely through democratic principles to provide necessary goods and services while protecting the common societal values of aesthetics, life support systems, and so on. Easements were only intended to be applied to specific locales under specific conditions.

Environmental Controls.   Indirect control of land-use change is obtained through environmental impact analysis. Any significant change in land uses must be evaluated in relation to its impact on the total ecosystem—land, water, air, and visual effects. These types of studies will ultimately be required of all developments, public and private. Most recreational site developments have the potential for significant environmental impact. Consequently, the planner should be able to justify the need for the development, the location chosen, and the specific site design. Also, its relationships and effects on other land uses should be assessed.

Administrative Controls.   The best administrative control is systems planning to ensure a balance of goods and services from any administrative unit, relative to the potential of the land and needs of the region and the nation. In this, the administrator zones according to the ability of the land to produce the various goods and services, and then attempts to produce the goods and services on those lands that are most suitable. He must realize that there will always be problems in balancing the flow of goods and services because of scarcity of the resource, changing demand, conflicting land uses, and lack of means to stabilize uses (mining claims, private holdings, and so on).

SELECTED READINGS

1. Chapin, F.S., Jr. 1965. *Urban Land Use Planning*. (2nd edition) Urbana, Illinois: University of Illinois Press.
2. Ciracy-Wanthrup, S. von. 1968. *Resource Conservation: Economics and Policies*. Berkeley, California: University of California Agriculture Experiment Station.
3. Clawson, M. (ed.) 1973. *Modernizing Urban Land Policy*. Baltimore: The Johns Hopkins University Press.
4. Cooley, R.A., and G. Wandesforde-Smith (eds.) 1969. *Congress and the Environment*. Seattle: University of Washington Press.
5. Courteny, J.H. 1967. "Land-Use Planning and Classification," *Proceedings of the Recreation Management Institute*. College Station, Texas: Texas A&M University.
6. Darling, F.F. and J.P. Milton. (eds.) 1966. *Future Environments of North America*. Garden City, New York: The Natural History Press.
7. Delafons, J. 1969. *Land-Use Controls in the United States* (2nd edition). Cambridge, Massachusetts: The MIT Press.
8. Donner, P. 1972. *Land Reform and Economic Development*. Baltimore: Penguin Books, Inc.
9. Ewald, W.R., Jr. 1968. *Environment and Change: The Next Fifty Years*. Bloomington, Indiana: Indiana University Press.
10. Foss, P.O. 1970. *Public Land Policy, Proceedings of the Western Resources Conference*. Boulder, Colorado: Colorado Associated University Press.
11. Graham, E.H. 1944. *Natural Principles of Land Use*. New York: Oxford University Press.
12. Jensen, C.R. 1973. *Outdoor Recreation in America: Trends, Problems, and Opportunities*. Minneapolis: Burgess Publishing Company.
13. Leopold, A.S. 1966. "Adaptability of Animals to Habitat Change," *Future Environments of North America*. F.F. Darling and J.P. Milton (eds.). Garden City, New York.: The Natural History Press.
14. McClellan, G.S. 1971. *Land Use in the United States*. New York: The H.W. Wilson Company. The Reference Shelf Volume 43, No. 2.
15. Ovington, J.D. 1966. "Experimental Ecology and Habitat Conservation," *Future Environments of North America*. F.F. Darling and J.P. Milton (eds.). Garden City, New York: The Natural History Press.
16. Reilly, W.K. (ed.) 1973. *The Use of Land: A Citizen's Policy Guide to Urban Growth*. New York: Thomas V. Crowell Company.
17. Shepard, P., and D. McKinley. 1969. *The Subversive Science: Essays Toward An Ecology of Man*. Boston: Houghton-Mifflin Co.
18. Whyte, W.H. 1970. *The Last Landscape*. Garden City, New York: Doubleday, Inc. (Anchor Books).

PART 4

GUIDELINES FOR SITE AND FACILITY PLANNING

This part focuses the elements of planning on specific types of outdoor recreation sites. Ultimately the success or failure in the views of the visitor will depend on how the particular development and travel patterns are designed. The average visitor finds it difficult to conceptualize area and regional planning and the need for them. He is more concerned about his specific needs in specific situations.

We may do an extremely good job in area and regional planning—to the point of identifying needs and the proper developments and locations to satisfy these needs. But if we do a poor job of developing specific sites and their accompanying facilities, then the entire effort is lost. The tangible development is the barometer of success in outdoor recreation planning. If developments are not used, or if improper types of uses are encouraged, or if conflicts are precipitated, then we have failed.

In this section, each major type of recreation site is discussed, including terminology, planning and design considerations, spatial factors, references, and sample layouts. The chapters in this section focus on the specific facility components of the various types of developments. Subjects include roads and trails that determine travel patterns within a particular site; the type and amount of visitation; and the components of the recreation site, such as the picnic table, comfort station, and others.

CHAPTER 14

CAMPGROUND PLANNING

Good campground planning is essential if we are to meet the expanding needs of the camper. Participation in camping activities is increasing at a phenomenal rate. Modern trailer camping is increasing; however, there is a trend to the more primitive forms of camping, both auto and hike-in. Thus, the participation figures in Figure 14–1 can only indicate the importance of camping. In terms of planning, we need to understand that not all people seek the same type of camping experience. Some prefer modern trailer camping; others, primitive walk-in camping. In other words, a variety of camping experiences are needed to satisfy the total camper population.

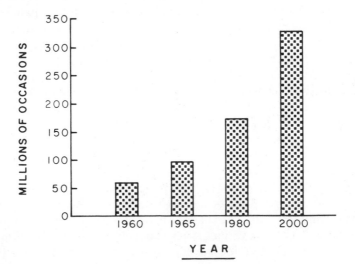

Figure 14–1 Camping participation, by millions of occasions (Bureau of Outdoor Recreation).

Figure 14–2 A family camping experience. (Photograph by South Dakota Department of Highways.)

What is quality to one may be undesirable to another. What is aesthetic to one may be a ravaged hillside to another. Thus, a single campground and its surrounding environment may be satisfying only to a given portion of the camping spectrum. However, what is needed is a realistic approach that encompasses *types of campgrounds* for specific camping experiences and *levels of development* within the various types. This approach would allow the camper maximum choice in selecting the opportunity that best fits his camping style.

ELEMENTS OF CAMPGROUND DEVELOPMENT

Types of Campgrounds. Styles of camping have changed rapidly since the turn of the century, from horse-oriented to auto-oriented, to recreational vehicle camps. However, the planner must remember two factors: first, there is no rule by majority. Campgrounds must be developed to meet the varied needs of the camper population. And second, the primary purpose of the campground is to create a total environment (physical, social and psychological) that provides satisfactory experiences to the visitor. An additional consideration is the ability of a site to sustain the planned use with minimum disruption and degradation of the total environment. Therefore, a campground classification system must be oriented to the needs of the visitor; but the application of the system depends on the particular environmental factors prevalent in a particular locale. A modification of Wagar's classification can be used for the basic orientation toward campground planning and development, as shown in Table 14–1.[25]

1. *Transient Campground.* The transient campground emphasizes minimal development for the accommodation of the overnight visitor. Services such as a bath house, dump station, grocery store, service station, and restaurant may be desirable to meet the needs of the transient camper. In this situation, the camper is seeking those services to prepare him for the next day's travel, yet ensure a safe, comfortable evening's rest.

Very little attention, public or private, has been given to the transient camp, yet there is a very real need for it. In the west during the summer, most interstate highway rest stations are inundated with overnight campers, particularly from those with modern recreation vehicles. The stops are convenient substitutes even though they are not designed or managed as transient camps. This situation points out the need and generally the

TABLE 14–1　CAMPGROUND CLASSIFICATIONS BASED ON VISITOR-USE PATTERNS

Class	Description of Visitor-Use Patterns
1. Transient or traveler	Designed for the overnight visitor; emphasis on specific service needs such as bath house and laundry; little consideration of activities or programs or maintenance of natural aesthetics.
2. Central	Designed to offer maximum service; however, the visitor uses this camp as his headquarters to radiate out to points of interest within the area.
3. Long-term	Designed to offer maximum service and leisure programs on extended visits; introverted in that the campground and immediate environs are the focal point or activity center.
4. Forest	Designed to accent the natural landscape, yet provide minimum service facilities for the convenience of the visitor; often coordinated as a satellite development to a central camp.
5. Peak load	Designed as overflow camp to handle peak load use; minimum facilities to handle temporary peak use fluctuations.
6. Back-country	Designed for the hike-in visitor; minimal primitive facilities to protect the environment.
7. Wilderness	Recognition of environmental factors that tend to attract the wilderness visitor; planning is on manipulation of visitor use to protect the integrity of the experience and the resource setting; no developed facilities.

desirable locational and developmental criteria. However, the question is: Should this be a public agency or private enterprise responsibility?

The question of responsibility is certainly debatable, but the important issues in terms of visitor satisfaction are the location and development of the camp and the services to be offered. Logically the camp should be located adjacent to heavily-used travel routes, especially routes like our interstate highways. It should be located at access nodes along these routes. If a person had to travel away from the major route for overnight accommodations, he would most likely choose to continue along the intended route in search of substitute accommodations because of the possible time lost and the lack of travel and camping accommodations away from the main flow of traffic.

Because of the concentrated use of the site and the lack of emphasis on natural aesthetics, the surface should be hardened through graveling or paving with consideration given to ease of access and closeness to service facilities. Some landscaping around the periphery will help to maintain general attractiveness. Since it is vehicular-oriented, most of the camp units should be developed for the modern trailer/camper, thus eliminating the need for much of the standard unit equipment such as picnic tables, fireplaces, and so on. These, however, may be necessary for the tent transient.

Several restaurant-service centers in the midwest have developed adjacent transient campgrounds. Space per unit is kept to a minimum, sometimes as little as 22-foot centers between the pull-through camping spurs. This keeps development costs (and resulting fees) to a minimum while providing services close to the camping unit.

2. *Central Campground.* Central camps have become more popular and more necessary with the increased mobility of the camper population. In the past, the philosophy has been to build campgrounds adjacent to visitor attractions; a person camped, visited the attraction, and then moved on to the next.

The modern camping visitor seems to prefer to have a site where he can set up his "home" and visit those attractions within a day's driving distance without being burdened with moving his camp and locating at a vacant campsite elsewhere. This arrangement gives maximum freedom from the mundane aspects of camping and larger blocks of time for participating in day-use activities away from camp. This type of camp is especially important where there are national and regional visitor attractions which would dictate the daily mobility of the camper.

Since the primary purpose of the central camp is to provide a place of accommodation and service while the visitor enjoys nearby points of interest, the planning emphasis should be on services and related facilities such as bath houses, laundry, utility hookups, camper store, and other developments desired for comfort and convenience.

A secondary goal is to maintain the elements of the natural landscape to protect the site and to offer the visitor an aesthetically pleasing environment. However, those portions of the site that receive intensive use will require hardening through paving and other measures. The intermediate-use portions of the camp will require intensive cultural treatments such as irrigation, thinning, and fertilizing in order to sustain that level of use with minimum destruction of the setting's character. The remaining portions are protected by natural barriers or through road and trail layouts with physical or vegetative barriers strategically located to confine travel to the designed routes. Using this concept and the concept of cluster development, we can maximize available open space and activity areas (Figure 14–3).

Cluster development is an important concept in planning central and long-term camps. By concentrating developments on smaller acreages with variation in types and levels of developments and services, we can offer desirable camping while maintaining maximum open space and the aesthetics of the immediate and surrounding landscape.

3. *Long-term Camp.* This type of campground is designed to accommodate visitors for extended periods of time. It is necessary to separate the long-term camper from the short-term camper; goals and service needs are quite different.

The long-term camper becomes somewhat agitated at excess traffic and noise and having to put up with overflow camping on a nightly basis. On the other hand, the short-termer is upset that all conveniently located campgrounds are completely occupied by long-termers. Really it becomes a matter of placement to capture the type of desired experience without attracting undesirable uses.

The emphasis at the long-term camp is on the enjoyment of camping and activities closely associated with the campground setting, such as fishing, short hikes, and others. The camp is the center of activity. Since people spend most of their time within the campground, the heavily used portions of the site will have to be hardened to withstand the heavy impact, and desirable secondary activities should be developed. The recreation vehicle is generally the primary camping accommodation; this, coupled with the need for certain services and facilities because of the extended stay, requires intensive development, maximum service, and continuous supervision. Consequently, because of the high development cost per visitor accommodation, public agencies have been reluctant to develop long-term camps. Usually these camps are developed as private enterprises, the using campers paying the entire cost. However, if the public agency develops a long-term camp, it should be located where it will have the least environmental impact, including visual impact; where it will be least expensive in development and maintenance costs; and where it will not monopolize the *best* recreation areas.

Since the responsibility has been assumed by private enterprise, maximizing the attractiveness of the development can be accomplished by combining the central camp and the long-term camp. Both have many facilities and services in common with a general demand for maximum

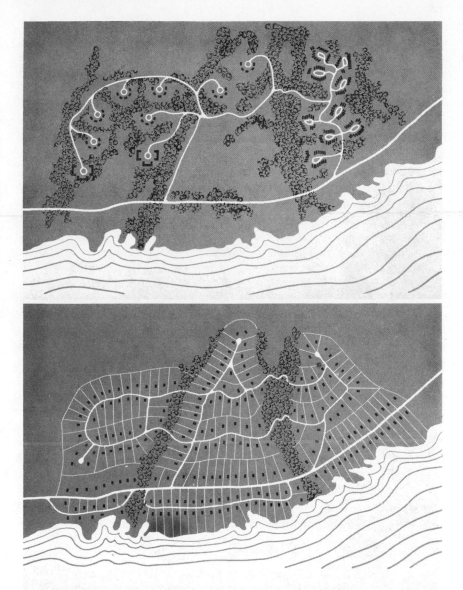

Figure 14–3 Cluster development in a water-oriented central camp. (From Citizen's Committee for the Outdoor Recreation Resources Review Commission Report, 1964. *Action for Outdoor Recreation in America.* Washington, D.C., p. 20.)

convenience. One type of camper radiates out to points of interest, and the other centers his activities near the campground. Maintaining both styles of camping becomes a matter of separating them. If a sufficiently good job is done in the campground layout, the central camper may be attracted for a more extended stay after he has visited the points of interest around the area.

4. *Forest Camp.* The forest camp is primarily family-oriented, with emphasis on natural aesthetics and privacy through screening with native plant material. The typical unit will be single-family size with some variation to allow multi-family camping. These are commonly called *primitive auto campgrounds.*

The planning is based on maintaining the natural landscape while offering reasonable auto access and site protection. Minimal facility development, including access roads, parking spurs, individual campsite equipment, comfort stations and water points, is offered. The architectural emphasis is on the natural and rustic appearance of the facilities. Typically the spacing between the heavy impact zone of the camping units has been limited to a minimum of one hundred feet. Probably the spacing is not nearly as important as maintaining the native plant material for screening between units. The spatial separation keeps these intermediate zones from destructive recreational impact. With more sophistication in vegetative cultural techniques (e.g., fertilizing, irrigation, etc.), spacing may be reduced considerably as long as noise levels remain acceptable.

Forest camps are used by some vacationers as a central or long-term camp, particularly if desired bathing, laundry, and store facilities are close by. The determinants in this type of relationship include reduced expense, the desire for more natural surroundings, the desire for greater separation from other camping units, and the urge for more primitive, tent-style camping.

5. *Peak Load Camp.* This type of campground, commonly called an *overflow camp,* is designed to accommodate, for short periods, large numbers of visitors who are unable to be accommodated within the existing developed campgrounds. It would not be economically justifiable to develop sufficient camps to handle the maximum camping impact which occurs two or three weekends per year—notably on the Fourth of July and Labor Day. The excess facilities would go unused the rest of the year.

Optimum planning would smooth out peak use to encourage a more uniform visitation rate. However, barring the unforeseen, the peak visitation periods will remain as American institutions. Therefore, the only rational solution is to designate an area for overflow camping and restrict the overflow to that site. In doing so, you can offer the camper minimum services and facilities that would not be available if he camped anywhere else. In addition, this arrangement gives environmental protection to the area by confining visitor use, waste disposal, and sanitation to a place where they can be managed.

Site selection is important in that these areas should have stable, well-drained soils with maximum ground cover. Where possible, the more hardy grasses should be encouraged because they offer a pleasing location for any style of camping without restricting visitor movement. If necessary, primitive roads may be developed using minimal gravel surfacing. Some large trees are desirable for the aesthetics and shading, but not to the point that the ground cover is affected by shading.

Site selection in terms of location is also important in encouraging overflow camping. The site should be located near the regular camp it is to serve but should not be located nearer to the particular local attraction. Furthermore, the site should be easy to seal off from access during nonpeak periods in order to encourage use of the developed sites, since the overflow site is only minimally adapted to sustain camper use.

Minimal facilities include a few strategically located toilets, a potable source of water, and possibly portable fire rings. Depending on the frequency of use, the toilets may be permanent pit toilets or portable. However, unless an existing developed water supply is adjacent to the overflow camp, it would probably be more desirable to dispense water from a water trailer on a scheduled basis.

Peak load campgrounds serve the overflow use from the forest and central campgrounds. Other types of use such as group camping, transient camping, and camping with out-sized vehicles should be discouraged because they establish precedents of use on sites that were not designed to sustain them.

6. *Back-country Camp.*   Back-country camps are those that are located in a roadless area and offer minimum primitive facility development to accommodate the hiker, horseman, or boater. On specially designed trail systems, these camps may accommodate the trail bike or snowmobile enthusiast. By developing the back-country camp, the planner can accommodate increased visitor use with minimal destruction of the site and minimal costs of maintenance and protection.

Although what is perceived as desirable development will vary with the type of visitor, primitive facilities may include rustic tent pads, half-log picnic tables, rock fire rings, pit toilets, and potable water supply—plus horse facilities, if needed. In some instances, rustic lean-tos have been favored over the open rustic tent pad, particularly where rains or snows occur frequently during the primary-use seasons.

This type of camp is not to be confused with the wilderness camp within designated wilderness areas. Wilderness camps are temporary and carried by the camper from place to place. In the past, the land manager has used primitive development to protect worn-out sites without regard to attracting increased use or effect on maintaining the pristine environment. However, the Wilderness Act of 1964 specifically forbids permanent de-development within the designated wilderness areas.

7. *Wilderness Camp.*   The wilderness camp is presented not as a development but as an activity that must be planned. Since no development or manipulation of the site is allowed, this type of camping becomes a matter of recognizing potential camping locations, and of managing visitor use to protect the site. Use can be dispersed or limited through permits, rest and rotation of sites and information programs. However, in the initial planning, we should determine where the most attractive camping areas are and attempt to avoid concentrations of people on sensitive and unstable locales through judicious location of trail systems—while trying to main-

tain a quality wilderness recreation experience. Thus, the planning tool is the trail, its character and location, since almost 99 percent of the wilderness users travel by trail.

LEVELS OF DEVELOPMENT

The preceding classification is a uni-dimensional scale that separates camping into broad-based activity categories. This is desirable in campground planning since it distinguishes basic camping subcultures. However, we should recognize that there are variations even within these classes or subcultures, and we should attempt to identify these variations and plan our campgrounds accordingly. This type of planning would give a vertical dimension to the existing horizontal planning spectrum (Figure 14–4).

Many agencies have stereotyped the developmental planning for forest and central camps to the point that one can readily predict what the next camp will look like. This uniformity ensures that all developments will meet some minimum standard and can be easily designed by the nonprofessional planner. The problem is that often these developments do not fulfill the needs of the potential camping subculture and consequently go unused. Many camping units in a forest campground may go unused while informal, overflow camping takes place around it. The campground apparently does not meet the social needs of the camper even though it is located in a desirable environmental setting.

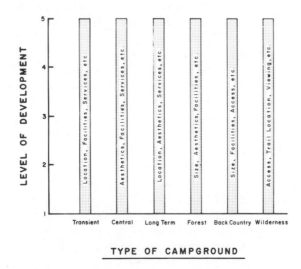

TYPE OF CAMPGROUND

Figure 14–4   Campground development—a two-dimensional planning scale.

As an example, if there were variations in the level of development of the forest camp, people might find a camping unit suitable for them. In terms of economics, the variations can be designed into a single campground by varying the levels of development of different segments, or loops, of the campground. If properly done, such a campground can be just as attractive to the multi-family or small group as to the single-family unit, without eliminating either.

Factors in the levels of development include:

1. *Physical Attributes of Site.* The physical attributes certainly dictate locational patterns in terms of facility placement, particularly if we try to maintain the naturalness of the landscape. These natural attributes will vary from site to site. The imaginative planner will try to use these strong attributes to maximize the recreational potential of the site by varying the development to fit the landscape. The unimaginative planner will attempt to do the same by molding the site characteristics to meet the specifications of the plans. The latter becomes more costly to develop and maintain while the natural amenities of the place, which may have been a major reason for the original site selection, are severely modified or lost.

2. *Size (Spatial Allocation).* Not only can we vary the size of the campground in terms of total number of units, but we can also vary the space allocated to each individual unit. The multi-family camping unit is an example of this principle while it still maintains the rustic, forest camp setting. In this case, there is a need for a larger, high-impact area around the campsite and perhaps a greater buffer area between units. Standards in terms of size and distance between units are not the answer; what is needed is local planning that accounts for the variation in camper needs, the resource capability, and the particular lay of the land.

3. *Facilities and Services.* Within a given camp type, the size, number, type, and location of facilities and services are important considerations. In terms of meeting the minimal daily maintenance needs of the camper, the desired facilities will vary greatly according to the camper's individual background, interests, and previous experiences, all of which tend to mold the anticipations of the camper.

A recent trend has been to cater to the needs of the modern trailer camper, a condition that tends to increase and modernize the available facilities. These facilities may become heavily used, but if we do not offer variety (alternatives within a particular style of camping), we may eliminate those who prefer a more rustic, natural setting.

4. *Access.* Access is important in making opportunities available to the visitor. It can be the camper's best friend and worst enemy. Variation in access will encourage or discourage certain types of camping. Minimum access will discourage modern trailer camping and encourage tent and truck camping; but if the planner is trying to encourage tent and truck camping, a wide, hard-surfaced road with long parking spurs will encourage competing uses that cannot be handled in a single campground. Thus,

variation will have to be accomplished by providing separate campgrounds or major camping loops.

5. *Secondary Activities.* Not all participants seek the same activity aggregate. Some people prefer fishing and boating; others, hiking and climbing. Some activities complement the more modern camp, while others complement a more rustic setting. Rather than stereotyping secondary activity needs, one should try to capture those that best fit the physical attributes of the site, always keeping in mind the needs of the user population. If a natural lake is present, the activity themes should focus on it. If there is a mountain, focus on that. The variety, then, comes from the mix of activity opportunities within and between sites.

CAMPGROUND DESIGN

Basic Layout Designs

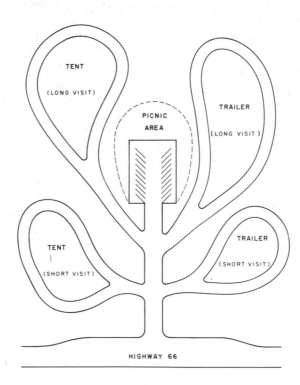

MULTI-LOOP CAMPGROUND

Figure 14–5 Multi-loop campground (multi-purpose—long-term, central, etc.).

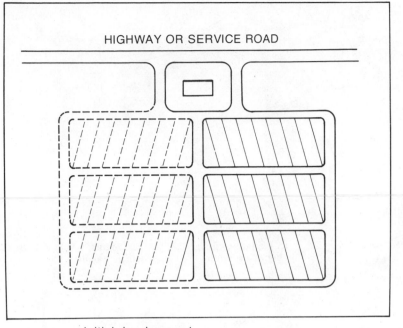

HIGHWAY OR SERVICE ROAD

— initial development
--- future expansion

Figure 14–6 Transient camp.

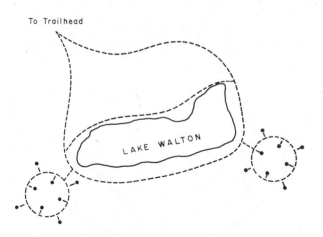

To Trailhead

LAKE WALTON

Figure 14–7 Back-country camp.

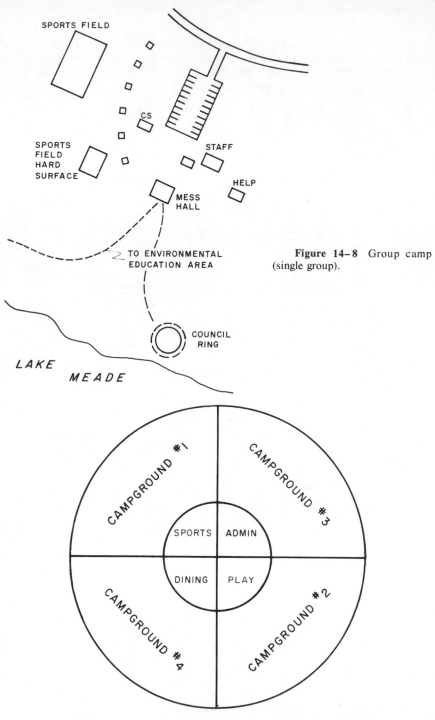

Figure 14–8 Group camp (single group).

Figure 14–9 Group camp (conceptual design, multi-group).

Design of the Campground Unit

The basic elements in a campground design are the road system, the unit equipment, and supporting facilities. Three types of roads are involved in the campground design—access roads, service roads (the internal road network), and parking spurs. Access and service roads depend on the type

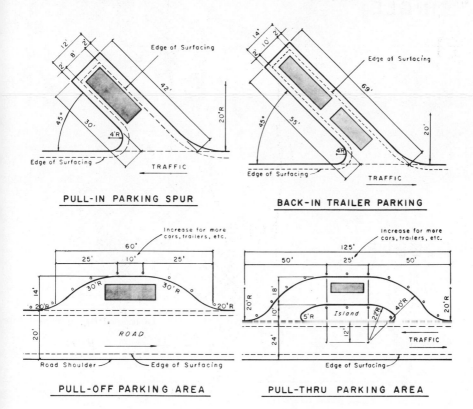

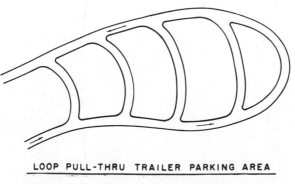

Figure 14–10 Types of campground parking spurs.

SINGLE

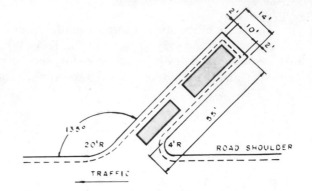

DOUBLE

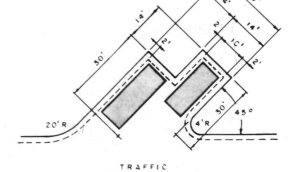

SPLIT

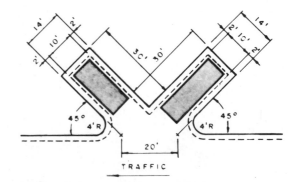

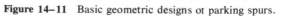

Figure 14–11 Basic geometric designs of parking spurs.

of camping to be encouraged. However, it should be noted that service roads are generally single-lane, one-way loops, where feasible. The design of parking spurs (part of the unit design) is quite flexible, depending on the type of vehicle, the lay of the land, and the desired traffic patterns (Figures 14–10 and 14–11).[22]

The unit equipment consists of a table, a tent pad, a fireplace, a garbage can, and a hardened area around the equipment. The unit layout should be closely oriented to the parking spur. The determination of where to locate each piece of equipment is based on shading, prevailing winds, micro-topography, and natural screening material. The table is the first item to be located. It is placed close to the spur for ease of moving food and cooking equipment to and from the vehicle and is oriented to maximum shading around the middle of the day. The secondary consideration is a relatively level spot that minimizes the need for leveling.

Next, the fireplace is located reasonably close to the table but down wind in order to reduce the problem of smoke blowing around the table. This should be the most distant item from the parking spur, as indicated in Figure 14–12.

Sand is a well-drained soil that is easily maintained and offers a relatively smooth surface for the tent. All vegetation (and also reachable

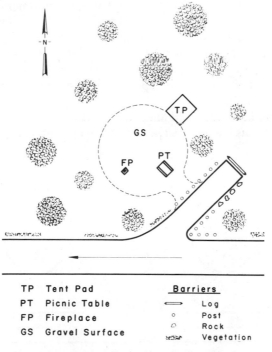

TP	Tent Pad	**Barriers**	
PT	Picnic Table	⇌	Log
FP	Fireplace	∘	Post
GS	Gravel Surface	⌒	Rock
		〜	Vegetation

Figure 14–12   A typical campground unit layout.

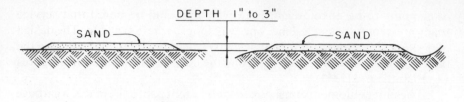

PROFILE – SMOOTH   PROFILE – ROLLING

Figure 14–13 Typical profiles of tent pads.

overhanging branches) is removed within the unit area, and the ground area is graveled, except the tent pad, which is made of sand. A profile of the tent pad is shown in Figure 14–13.

The garbage can should be conveniently located but away from the camping unit proper. If it is located in the unit, it becomes a nuisance to the camper and is too far away for efficient garbage collection. If it is located along the service road, the visitor may not properly dispose of his garbage or the road appears as "garbage can alley." A more ideal situation is depicted in Figure 14–14.

The attention given to the placement of unit equipment is essential to ensure good utilization of the individual unit. All other things being equal, the placement will determine the desirability of the camping unit. Unfortunately this type of detail is often turned over to the technician or bulldozer operator with no pertinent layout instructions and no supervision. Thus, the placement of unit equipment appears to be the simplest but weakest link in the planning chain.

Supporting facilities include comfort stations, bath houses, roadside barriers, wood bins, water systems, and sewage disposal systems.

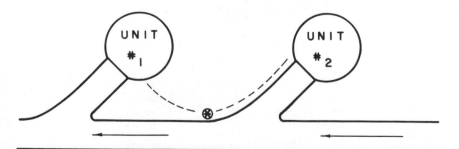

Figure 14–14 Convenient and efficient location of garbage collection points.

COMMON WEAKNESSES IN CAMPGROUND PLANNING
AND DESIGN*

1. *General.*
   a. Confusing or poor entrance and information signs.
   b. No tent spaces.
   c. No segregation of types of campers, or campers and other users.
   d. Thinning of trees—too much or too little.
   e. Incomplete construction.
2. *Location.*
   a. Campground.
      (1) Unstable soil (shallow soil, alluvial fan,etc.).
      (2) Poorly drained soil (high water table).
      (3) Steep slope (excessive cut and fill).
      (4) Unstable vegetation.
      (5) Flood hazard.
      (6) Inaccessible.
   b. Camp unit.
      (1) Single-family only.
      (2) Too steep (or too much cut and fill).
      (3) Too close together.
      (4) Lack of screening vegetation.
3. *Traffic Patterns.*
   a. Auto traffic.
      (1) Inadequate access and interior roads.
      (2) Two-way roads.
      (3) Funneling of other traffic, which increases traffic flow through camp.
      (4) No visitor parking.
      (5) Road barriers—too many or too few, and generally too close to road.
      (6) Inadequate parking spurs.
         (a) Too narrow or too short.
         (b) Too steep an angle.
         (c) Excessive cut and fill.
         (d) Not level.
4. *Fireplaces.*
   a. Improper location.
      (1) Poor orientation to table.
      (2) Poor orientation to prevailing wind.
   b. Not surfaced around use area.
   c. Firehole over 9 inches deep.

---

*Taken from an unpublished list by S. S. Frissell, University of Montana.

    d. Grate too low to ground for cooking.

    e. Nonstandard grate.

    f. Poor concrete (use only heat resistant).

5. *Tables*.

    a. Site not leveled.

    b. Site not surfaced (reduces dust and erosion).

    c. Poor local lumber.

    d. Poor treatment of wood.

    e. Poor staining.

    f. Inadequate fastening of top.

    g. Tops and benches not level.

    h. Nonrust hardware not used.

    i. Poor concrete bases.

    j. Inadequate footing of bases.

6. *Toilets*.

    a. Interior.

        (1) No coat hooks.

        (2) Poor door spring.

        (3) No interior door latch.

        (4) No seat lid or stop for lid.

        (5) Poor paint job.

        (6) Inadequate natural lighting.

        (7) Too little space.

        (8) No toilet paper.

    b. Building.

        (1) Home-made door.

        (2) Poor ventilation.

        (3) Not tight or flyproof.

        (4) Not clearly marked "Men" or "Women."

        (5) No screening panel in front of door.

    c. Pit.

        (1) Inadequate in size (should be 60 cubic feet or more).

        (2) Not properly cribbed or should be waterproof vault.

        (3) Excavation not cleaned up.

        (4) Not properly vented.

    d. General.

        (1) Toilet hidden and hard to find.

        (2) Poor trail to toilet.

        (3) Not centrally located.

GROUP CAMPING—A SPECIAL CASE

Group camps are sites developed to serve organizational camping with the capability of offering recreational, social, and educational programs as well as meals, lodging, and comfort facilities. Earlier group camps were operated as a recreational business for "fun and profit"; however, much of the group camping today is sponsored by nonprofit youth organizations. It is not the intent of this book to cover the entire subject of group camping—development, programming, management, counseling, supervision. However, an outdoor recreation planner should be familiar with the needs of the camper, appropriate types of facilities, and appropriate types of activity developments.[3] Many of these topics are discussed elsewhere but may take on special connotations when applied to a group camp situation.

Locational Aspects.   Privacy but reasonable access is essential. Privacy, in terms of eliminating the effects of outside influences, creates a feeling of harmony and togetherness for the group. It gives greater freedom of movement and security for the individual group member and his property. In addition, this criterion decreases safety problems from traffic and other outside influences.

However, the camp must be accessible by automobiles and large trucks. This allows easy access for the camper but should not encourage visitation by others. Also, it is necessary to get large trucks with supplies and groceries into the administrative area. The most desirable situation for such a camp is to be located near a secondary hard surface road which is connected to a main highway. There is less traffic but there is easy access even during the winter months. Geographically, the camp should be located where the aggregate travel distance for the service area is minimal.

There should be only one access road which should terminate at the central parking area. A service road should lead from the parking lot to the administrative area of the camp. Barriers, natural or man-made, should limit traffic movement to the designated roads. For safety and ease of movement, no roads should bisect the property.

Characteristics of the Land.   The setting should offer opportunities for outdoor living, educational experiences, living accommodations, and activity areas. Thus, a variety of topography (rolling, flat, flood plain, and so on) and eco-units (forest, meadows, streams, lakes, and so on) are desirable for offering diversified camp programs.

The minimum recommended standard is one acre per camper, with 100 to 125 campers per week plus required staff as an economic minimum. Thus, the minimum acreage would be 100 to 125 acres if adjacent lands are available for programming.[21] If all of the programming is done within the grounds, the desired acreage should be tripled.

One constraint on the desired variability of the land is the need for flat, stable, and well-drained areas for the camp proper (including living area, administrative area, maintenance shops, and activity space).

Developmental Needs.   There are four areas of special developmental needs beyond the obvious administrative buildings (headquarters, maintenance, and dining hall-auditorium) and camper accommodations (cabins, shower house, and assembly area) these are utilities, health and safety facilities, recreation activity space, and outdoor education sites and facilities. The specific needs are outlined below:

1. *Utilities and Communications.*
   a. Adequate water supply and treatment.
   b. Adequate sewage disposal to meet federal, state, and county standards.
   c. Gas and/or electrical service.
   d. Communications.
      (1) Telephone service.
      (2) Mail service.
      (3) Adequate connecting road system.
      (4) Coordination with local law enforcement.
2. *Health and Safety.*
   a. Adequate plumbing to meet governmental codes.
   b. Adequate wiring to meet governmental and insurance codes.
   c. Adequate fire-fighting equipment.
   d. Safe swimming area with adequate water quality controls.
   e. Thorough hazard survey (sheer cliffs, swamps, swift waterways, poisonous plants, etc.) and hazard reduction.
3. *Recreation Activity Space.*
   a. Sports fields.
      (1) Adequate open space.
      (2) Flat terrain.
   b. Developed team sport facilities (volleyball, badminton, etc.).
   c. Aquatic area.
      (1) Swimming.
      (2) Boating.
      (3) Fishing.
4. *Outdoor Education Areas.*
   a. Primitive camping area.
   b. Education developments.
      (1) Nature center.
      (2) Nature interpretative trails (flora, fauna, geology, historic or archeological features).
   c. Campfire rings for programs.
   d. Special environmental education sites (terrestrial or aquatic ecosystem, rare or endangered species, special habitats, etc.).

SELECTED READINGS

1. Beardsley, W. 1967. "Cost Implications of Camper and Campground Characteristics." U.S. Forest Service Research Note RM–86.
2. Bond, R.S., and G.J. Ouelette. 1968. *Characteristics of Campers in Massachusetts* Massachusetts Agriculture Experiment Station Publication No. 572.

3. Bone, M.D., *et al.* 1965. *Site Selection and Development—Camps, Conferences, Retreats*. Philadelphia: United Church Press.
4. Burch, W.R., Jr. 1966. "Wilderness—the Life Cycle and the Forest Recreational Choice," Journal of Forestry, 64 (9): 606–610.
5. Burch, W.R., Jr., and W.D. Wenger, Jr. 1967. *The Social Characteristics of Participants in Three Styles of Family Camping*. U.S. Forest Service Research Paper PNW–48.
6. Cole, G.L., and B.T. Wilkins. 1971. "The Camper," *Recreation Symposium Proceedings*. Syracuse, New York: State University of New York School of Forestry.
7. Family Camping Federation. 1968. *Family Camping Kit*. Martinsville, Indiana: American Camping Association.
8. Hendee, J.C., and F.L. Campbell. 1969. "Social Aspects of Outdoor Recreation—the Developed Campground," *Trends in Parks and Recreation*, 10:13–16.
9. Hutchins, B.W., and J.R. Van Meter. 1969. *Guidelines for Developing Private Campgrounds*. Illinois Agriculture Extension Publication ORPR–8.
10. Jubenville, A. 1973. "Quasi-Wilderness," *Parks and Recreation*, 3:38. pp. 43–48.
11. LaPage, W.F. 1968. *The Role of Customer Satisfaction in Managing Commercial Campgrounds*. U.S. Forest Service Research Paper NE–105.
12. _____. 1967. *Camper Characteristics Differ At Public and Commercial Campgrounds in New England*. U.S. Forest Service Research Paper NE–59.
13. _____. 1967. *Successful Private Campgrounds—A Study of Factors That Influence Length and Frequency of Camper Visits*. U.S. Forest Service Research Paper NE–58.
14. LaPage, W.F., and C.P. Regain. 1972. "Campground Marketing—The Impulse Camper." U.S. Forest Service Research Note NE–150.
15. Mobile Home Manufacturers Association. 1965. *Mobile Homes Park Planning Kit*. Chicago: Mobile Home Manufacturing Association.
16. Orr, H.R. 1967. "Analytical Approach to Design," *Park Maintenance*, 20 (2):34–37.
17. Park Practice Program. 1972. *Design*. Washington, D.C.: National Recreation and Park Association and National Park Service.
18. Recreation Vehicle Institute. 1970. *Vehicle Parks . . . A Profitable Investment*. Des Plaines, Illinois: Recreation Vehicle Institute.
19. Reiman, L.C. 1957. "Campsite Selection, Layout and Development," *Recreation*, 3:23–26.
20. Shafer, E.L., Jr. 1969. *The Average Camper Who Doesn't Exist*. U.S. Forest Service Research Paper NE–142.
21. Solomon, J.H. 1959. *Camp Site Development*. New York: Girl Scouts of America.
22. U.S. Forest Service. 1962. *Working Drawings of Basic Facilities Campground Development*. U.S. Department of Agriculture Information Bulletin No. 264.
23. U.S. Public Health Service. 1966. *Environmental Health Guide for Travel Trailer Parking Areas*. Washington, D.C.: U.S. Government Printing Office.
24. U.S. Public Health Service. 1966. *Environmental Health Practice in Recreation Areas—A Guide to the Planning, Design, Operation, and Maintenance of Recreation Areas*. Washington, D.C.: U.S. Government Printing Office.
25. Wagar, J.A. 1963. *Campgrounds for Many Tastes*. U.S. Forest Service Research Paper INT–6.

CHAPTER 15

PICNIC AREAS

Picnicking has long been accepted as a public recreational activity. One of the first types of outdoor recreation facilities in the public domain was the *picnic area*. It has been pictured as the picnic basket and blanket activity. In reality, however, most picnicking takes place at developed facilities, even though much picnicking does occur on a broadcast basis at undeveloped sites.

Although some planners would prefer to allow people to picnic just anywhere, there are some very good reasons for developing facilities. According to Douglass,[4]

> Developed facilities not only add to the convenience, safety, and enjoyment of the users but they also serve to keep the people grouped together in places designed to accommodate them. This centralizes wear, reduces soil and water pollution, consolidates the rubbish, and facilitates cleanup and maintenance.

Forested areas that have had proper predevelopment thinnings to allow sunlight to reach the forest floor are generally excellent picnic areas. They have sufficient shade, aesthetics, privacy, and site stability to provide a pleasant, stable site for the day-use activity of picnicking. These forested sites may be within or close to the urban environs or distant wildland settings. However, cabana-type shelters for individual picnic units in open, grassy areas can offer similar qualities by blending with the landscape tone, color, and configuration. Unfortunately, too often the equipment salesman makes the decision on the cabana-type picnic shelter—the pink, yellow, and blue one that even a chameleon would have difficulty blending with.

Most of the picnic areas in the United States are located close to urban areas since picnicking is a day-use activity. In fact, some urban areas have commercial picnic areas with several hundred picnic units. One such picnic

214

area is located near Chicago; it was recently expanded to 330 units. When a person goes picnicking there, he buys a given amount of time to use a unit; the normal daily turnover rate for the summer weekends is 2.3 groups or families per unit per day. Regardless of location, most picnic use comes from within a thirty-mile radius of the facility. Even in the northern Rocky Mountain region, the use is local, either from residents or tourists who are camping or staying at a commercial overnight accommodation.

There are three basic types of picnic areas: family, group, and enroute. Each of these plays a distinctive role in providing a quality picnicking experience:

1. *Family Picnic Area.* Designed primarily for the family.
2. *Group Picnic Area.* Designed for the group or organizational picnic outing.
3. *Enroute Picnic Area.* Designed primarily for the family along its travel route.

FAMILY PICNIC AREA

This is the most common type of picnic area. The use is destination-oriented, with picnicking the primary activity that the user seeks; or it is done in conjunction with other activities, such as boating, hiking, and so on.

In terms of basic on-site behavior, family picnicking is generally a more passive type of outdoor recreation where the group seeks privacy, relaxation, and sharing of previous experiences, including the events of the day. It may be the primary, planned activity or a culmination of a complete day of activities; in both cases, the pace of activity around the picnic unit is more leisurely than if the picnicking is a secondary activity of merely eating a noon meal. If it is a secondary activity engaged in between active types of experiences, the pace is more hurried so that the participants can quickly return to other activities. This situation will depend on the particular activity aggregate available and the type of expected visitor. Furthermore, the planner should realize that many of the units will be used in the early evening hours for socializing and light cooking while the visitors enjoy the aesthetics of a campfire.

Planning and Design. An important consideration in planning picnic areas is to facilitate normal behavioral patterns, rather than to disrupt behavior, as planners have often done in the past. For this reason, there is a need for more baseline studies to describe behavior under various environmental stimuli. This need applies to all outdoor recreation activities. There are ''unwritten rules'' on how to family picnic, just as there are written rules for sports games. The planner needs to know what these rules are and what variability is associated with them so that he may properly plan and design sites to meet the expected behavior. Research is not going

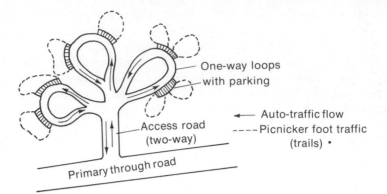

One-way loops
with parking

Auto-traffic flow
---- Picnicker foot traffic
(trails) •

Access road
(two-way)

Primary through road

Figure 15–1   Circulation pattern for a family picnic area.

to provide these data immediately. Thus, the planner should develop his observation skills so that he can better describe behavior in his own location.

The circulation pattern should be considered first after the site has been selected (Fig. 15–1). The circulation pattern should be coordinated with the area or site complex circulation system. Family picnicking, group picnicking, and forest camping are generally not compatible and should be separated through a well designed area or site complex circulation system. The access to the family picnic site should be a terminal road off the main circulation pattern in order to segregate and minimize traffic flows. The entire layout should be located so that the user does not have to cross traffic flows to participate in other day-use activities around the picnic area. Ideally, the picnic access road is divided into several one-way loop roads that lead to parking lots. This measure provides a clustering of picnic units around the parking lot, which minimizes traffic on any one loop and offers a quiet, private, and pleasing experience that can be molded to the specific behavior patterns of the visitor. If necessary, a hardened service road of about one lane in width, closed to private vehicles but used as a trail for maintenance of the individual units, can be developed within the site. The necessitating factors for such a trail include the size of the picnic site, the level of uses, and the amount of site maintenance.

The central parking lot on the one-way loop should facilitate safe movement into the picnic area, control total usage, control vegetation damage, and be as unobtrusive as possible. This means that the picnic area and parking lot should be located around the outer portion of the loop to minimize safety problems and to maximize the possible open space associated with the development. The number of parking spaces should be approximately 1.25 to 1.50 times the number of units, a proportion that allows some multi-family picnicking at single units. To have many extra parking spaces may encourage other incompatible day uses, or picnicking where there are insufficient specific unit facilities either for the enjoyment of the visitor or the protection of the resource.

Unfortunately, there is a potential for heavy resource damages to the site if vehicles are not confined to the hardened road and parking lot. Thus, it becomes necessary to develop identifiable but unobtrusive barriers to subtly discourage driving or parking off the hardened surface. Ideally, the surfaces are gravel or asphalt, depending on the expected level of use. Angle parking allows efficient use of space, with approximately 300 square feet of surface area per parking stall.

Narrow vegetated strips may be left as visual barriers between the parking lot and picnic site to maintain aesthetics, minimize noise, and give a greater feeling of spaciousness. Or, for the more open terrain, artificial barriers can be created with soil mounds. However, these should not be simple geometric forms but something that appears natural to the landscape. This type of barrier should be stabilized with appropriate vegetation to sustain heavy use by children and to appear natural (Figure 15–2).

The service components of the picnic site are the access trail, comfort station, water point, and solid waste containers. Access trails into the picnic area from the parking lot should be in the form of short loops so that most of the units are within 250 feet of the parking area and not more than a 400-foot walk via the trails.[2] Trails are necessary to direct people to the picnic units in order to minimize disruption to other picnickers and to control user effects on the site. Where evening use is expected, the trails should be well marked.

The U. S. Public Health Service recommends that a water point should be within 150 feet of each unit. As Douglass indicates,[4]

> however, the distance can be stretched to approximately 200 feet in less heavily used areas. All faucets should be self-closing and non-threaded to conserve water. Exceptions to this faucet design should be made where strategically placed outlets are designated for fire suppression purposes.

Comfort stations can be located as far as 500 feet from the units; however, they should never be located close enough for the odor to be offensive. Wherever use is heavy, flush toilets should be installed to handle the heavy sewage disposal problem. Flush toilets require adequate water pressure and favorable water supply. The location of the comfort station

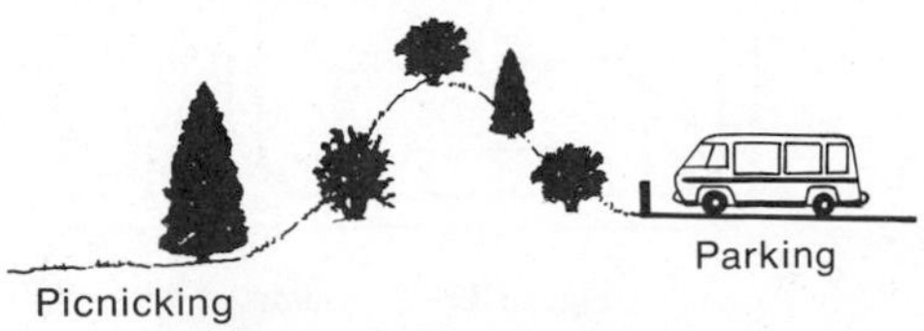

Figure 15–2 Visual barrier from the picnic site to the parking area.

Picnicking

Parking

should be along the trail, centrally located to the service radius but oriented more towards the parking lot. Solid waste containers should be centrally located to a small group of family units in order to encourage use of the container, but sufficiently far away to minimize odor and other negative effects.

The number of units to be developed in any one picnic site will vary depending on the demand for picnicking, the turnover rate per unit, and the potential of the resource. Density varies from five to fifty units per acre. Fifteen units per acre is considered the most favorable density. In terms of space utilization, approximately 30 to 40 per cent of the site should be developed (roads, parking, unit and supporting facilities). The remainder is left for screening, noise buffering, and aesthetics. Commercial family picnic sites should have a minimum of one hundred units with a favorable daily turnover rate of 2.0 or more.

The following are some typical layouts for the family picnic sites:

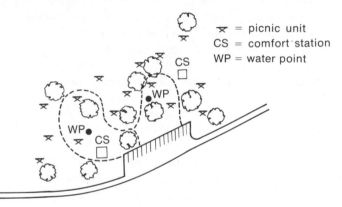

Figure 15–3   Simple layout for picnic area.

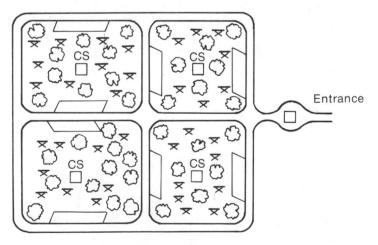

Figure 15–4   Complex high-density layout for picnic area.

Unit and Equipment. The picnic unit is approximately 400 square feet in size, centrally located around the picnic table. Ideally it is oriented to provide the unit with maximum shade from approximately 11:00 A.M. to 3:00 P.M. during the summer months. The unit equipment includes the table, a fireplace or grill, and the hardened surface around the table. The table should be centrally located in the hardened area, and the fireplace should be down wind from the table (Fig. 15–5). The common facilities of comfort station, water point, and solid waste containers are located outside the unit.

The unit normally handles from three to eight people; thus, the table should be large enough for eight people. The table, including attached seats, should be made of durable material and secured in the area hardened for heavy use. If people were allowed to move the table to other locations, uncontrolled deterioration of the site and also theft of tables might occur.

The molded concrete table design combines durability, aesthetics, and securability (Fig. 15–6). Durability is provided by concrete end supports, which are molded from rough, knotty lumber and tinted to give them a natural appearance. The planks may be of pressure-treated or untreated lumber. The treated ones are more expensive but last longer. They should be removable, using hidden bolts, so that the planks can be removed and retreated during the nonuse season. The removal and storage of the planks may be necessary in areas of heavy snow pack or vandalism. Prestressed concrete planks are being used by some agencies to overcome the problems of maintenance.

Elaborate fireplaces are not as important as they once were; however, some type of fireplace or grill is still necessary. Many people prefer a grill mounted on a post for charcoal cooking, although others prefer a ground-level grill which can double as a fireplace for an evening fire. Today, many

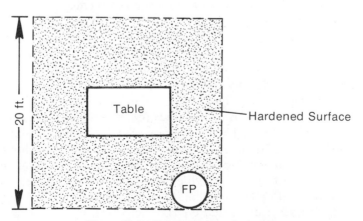

Figure 15–5 Unit layout, vertical view.

Figure 15–6   Picnic table design with built-in tie down. (Photograph by Alan Jubenville.)

people bring their own portable charcoal grills; others need only a fire ring for an aesthetic evening fire and not for cooking. An inverted end of a thirty-inch sewer pipe makes an inexpensive fire ring but lacks aesthetic appeal. In sum, a combination of types of fireplaces, depending on the expected needs of the visitor, is ideal for a given picnic site.

Variety of Opportunity.   There are several ways to vary the design of the family picnic area, to offer a varied experience:

1. *Clustering of Tables.*   Tables grouped in clusters of two or three may offer a picnic unit for the small group or multi-family picnicking. When the tables are clustered, only one fireplace is necessary.

2. *Number of Units.*   The number of units and their density can be varied to change the perception of privacy, quietness, and crowding.

3. *Type of Travel.*   The picnic area can be vehicle-, hiking-, or boat-oriented. Most of them are designed for the vehicle; a few have been developed for the boater. However, with the increase in hiking and the seeking of more self-reliant activities away from the vehicle, there is opportunity to develop hike-in picnic sites. These could be developed in conjunction with other dispersed types of activities.

ENROUTE PICNIC GROUNDS

With increased travel, there has been an increase in demand for wayside facilities for the traveler to relax and prepare a meal while enroute to his destination. The enroute picnic grounds are a variation of the family picnic area which offers a picnicking opportunity to the traveler. These have also been called wayside or roadside rest stops. In the past, these have typically been small, one- or two-unit developments. However, today, these picnic grounds along the major highways, particularly the interstate system, are large, modern developments.

The necessary facilities are picnic tables, toilet facilities, and drinking water at a safe, convenient location along the route. Fireplaces are not necessary because of the rapid rate of turnover. However, because of the heavy use, flush toilets should be installed.

Figure 15-7 Layout of an enroute picnic grounds. (Photograph by Wyoming Highway Department.)

GROUP PICNIC AREAS

Group picnicking is a popular day-use activity for organized groups. Its importance is increasing, but the activity should be provided on a site separate from the family picnicker, because the on-site participation is distinctly different. Behavior is primarily socialization and "active" activity participation. Much enthusiasm and noise is generated through this behavior.

By providing a separate picnic area for organizational groups, possible conflict with the family picnicker is reduced. Also, each group picnic unit should be afforded privacy, and the heavy use contained in a location designed to sustain that use. With separate sites for the group picnicker, the units can be reserved in advance to minimize scheduling problems and overloading of facilities. Maintenance and solid waste disposal can then be coordinated with the schedule.

Planning and Design.   The group picnic area should be designed for large group participation. The exact size should reflect the needs in the area; however, the recommended minimum size is twenty-five people. The site development, including the free play area, should not utilize more than 60 per cent of the site. A sufficient vegetated area should be left to maintain aesthetics and to separate units.

There is much conjecture on the proper location of group picnic areas. Some planners feel that the access road should pass the family picnic area before reaching the group site in order to minimize nonscheduled use in the group area. Others feel that the group site should be reached first because this location immediately eliminates heavy traffic through the rest of the recreation area, and it allows easy access during evening hours. If this type of development is part of a waterfront site complex, its location is determined by the location of the marina and surrounding cluster of day-use activities. The marina is placed at the most suitable site first. Then the other related activities—family picnicking, concession, swimming, and so on—are clustered around the marina. Group picnicking is spatially separated from the cluster to maintain the integrity of the organizational group participation and to minimize conflict with other users. I am not suggesting that the group picnic area should be put on the least desirable site, but that, in this case, other locational factors are more important.

Each unit should have its own separate parking lot and access road to minimize traffic control problems. The access road will ordinarily be relatively short and enter the main park road at right angles. The road and parking area should have barriers to reduce damage from heavy vehicle use. A controlled vehicle trail to the picnic shelter, using some type of locked but removable barrier, may be desirable to allow equipment and food to be moved to the shelter.

A typical layout follows:

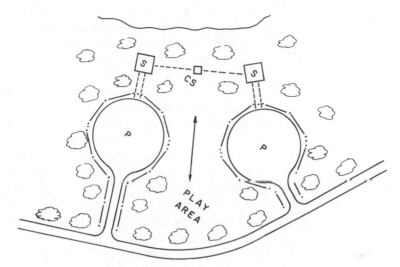

Figure 15–8 Group picnic area design.

Figure 15–9 The picnic shelter. (Photograph by Alan Jubenville.)

The Unit and Equipment.   The unit equipment consists of a parking lot, picnic shelter, comfort station, water point, and open play space. The picnic shelter is the central facility which serves both as artificial shading and protection from the wind and rain. The shelter should be designed for an average-size group, usually twenty-five to fifty persons. It should blend with the immediate landscape. Natural materials are desirable if they are available. The floor should be concrete for durability and easy cleaning, and the ground immediately around the floor (approximately three to four feet) should be graveled to sustain heavy use. If overflow picnicking is anticipated (larger groups than the unit is designed for), the graveled apron around the shelter should be increased and movable tables placed on the apron when necessary. Tie downs for the tables will minimize movement and theft.

The comfort station should be reasonably accessible to the shelter; however, the water point should be at the shelter, both for convenience and clean up. The open play area, approximately 200 feet square, allows for games, sports, and other types of socialization.

SELECTED READINGS

1.   Backman, E. E. 1967. *Recreation Facilities*. U.S. Forest Service Publication (unnumbered).

2.   Burke, H.D. 1964. "Picnic-Table Use Depends Upon Distance From Parking Area," *Journal of Forestry,* 62(10):753.

3.   Cox, L.D. 1940. *The Design and Development of Picnic Grounds*. Syracuse, New York: New York State University, College of Forestry. Bulletin Vol. 13, No. 3–C.

4.   Douglass, R.W. 1969. *Forest Recreation*. New York: Pergamon Press.

5.   National Recreation and Park Association. 1964. *Picnic Site Survey*. Washington, D.C.: National Recreation and Park Association, Management Aid Series No. 4.

6.   Pennsylvania Bureau of State Parks. 1969. *State Park Planning Guidelines*. Harrisburg, Pennsylvania: Department of Forests and Waters.

7.   Ripley, T.H. 1962. *Recreation Impact on Southern Appalachian Campgrounds and Picnic Sites*. U.S. Forest Service Research Paper SE–153.

8.   Stott, C.C. 1967. *Evaluating Water Based Recreation Facilities and Areas*. Washington, D.C.: National Recreation and Park Association. Management Aid Series No. 70.

9.   U.S. Public Health Service. 1965. *Environmental Health Practice in Recreation Areas*. Washington, D.C.: U. S. Government Printing Office. P.H.S. Publication No. 1195.

CHAPTER 16

WATER-BASED RECREATION SITE COMPLEXES

Water-based recreation site complexes include a variety of site developments, from marinas and beaches to picnic areas and campgrounds. The plan for the site complex can be viewed as a comprehensive mini-area plan because it often involves many close and interrelated sites on a relatively small area. Consequently, it is called a *site complex* that would have its origin in the comprehensive area plan. It also has many characteristics of the area plan, including a primary circulation pattern, functional relationships, and a coordination of site programs.

Because of the high degree to which the sites are interrelated, there is a need for specialized planning to facilitate normal behaviors while minimizing conflicts between the various users. The effectiveness of any recreational development depends on good management, and good management can only be accomplished through proper initial planning and design of the individual sites and location of the sites relative to each other. For example, it would be impossible to eliminate swimming-boating conflicts through good management if the boats leaving the marina had to pass through the surface water used by the swimmers. Without adequate planning, boats may be launched at dangerous places, boats may be occupying the same space as swimmers, shoreline damage may occur from recreation use, and so on, all of which may cause conflict, confusion, and loss of satisfaction for the water-based recreationist.

BASIC PLANNING CONCEPT

In developing a water-based complex, it is important to understand that each complex will have a certain *activity aggregate*. The central themes, however, should be the primary water-related activities such as boating, swimming, and fishing. In planning, the site developments to support the water-related activities should be located first on the better sites along the shoreline (Fig. 16–1). The other site developments, such as family picnic areas and forest campgrounds, should then be clustered around the water-based developments.

Day-use activities such as picnicking and nature study should be located relatively close to complement each other. Overnight facilities should be located for easy access to water-based activities, yet sufficiently separated from each other to maintain privacy and quietness. A layout design of a total water-based site complex is shown in Figure 16–2.

A variety of water-based activities (e.g. power-boating, nonpower-boating, fishing, boat camping, boat picnicking, swimming and so on) may be provided. Most of the specific waterfront developments, other than the secondary ones of picnicking, camping, trail systems, and so on, are included under the categories of marinas, beaches, and stream-based developments. However, before proceeding with the planning process of the site complex, the planner must determine the needed site developments and their relationships—much the same as in area planning (Chapter 10). Once the sites and facilities have been determined, the water and surrounding shoreline should be zoned according to its best use and the specific activities to be provided (Fig. 16–3).

MARINA DEVELOPMENTS

Marina developments may vary from relatively simple (access road, parking, boat ramp, and sanitary facilities) to extremely complex sites

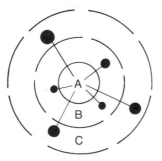
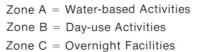

Zone A = Water-based Activities
Zone B = Day-use Activities
Zone C = Overnight Facilities

Figure 16–1 Concentric planning zones showing clustering of developments around water-based activities.

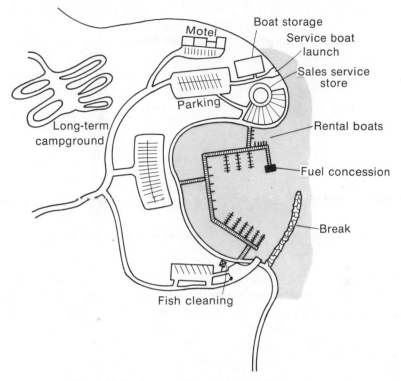

Figure 16–2   Layout of a water-based site complex.

(several interrelated sites, including concessions). The type of marina chosen should be based on levels of use, need, and the willingness of the public to pay.

Site Selection.   For the more complex marina developments, site selection is very important. The basic considerations are:

1.   Close to population or seasonal visitor-use center.

2.   Accessible by main road artery to move boats easily into the site, and close to main routes so the site can be easily reached by the traveler.

3.   Sufficient water in the marina basin for development and boat maneuvering.

4.   Sufficient water depth and surface to allow for all desired activities.

5.   Natural protection from winds, storms, and flooding.

6.   Stable shoreline conditions.

7.   Good southerly exposure for warmth and sunlight.

8.   Good quality of water with the potential to maintain that quality.

9.   Aesthetic qualities of surrounding landscape.

10.   Lack of hazardous or unsafe conditions.

11.   Reasonable fluctuation in water levels.

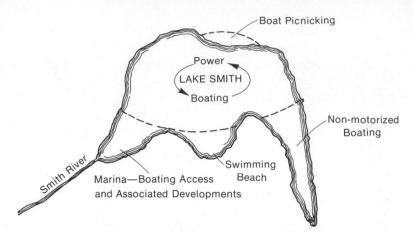

Figure 16–3 Zoning for water-based recreational activities.

Fluctuation in water level is extremely critical, particularly during the peak use season. Consequently, many water supply and irrigation reservoirs are not suitable for marina development.

Site selection to allow use of the more isolated bodies of water is not as critical in terms of social needs, particularly if limited access is the primary goal. Certain resource considerations, items 3 through 11 of the preceding list, however, should be included in the site selection.

Basic Designs.   The basic design for a complete site complex should include proper circulation patterns to minimize conflict and confusion, should enhance the social interest of the visitor, and should provide necessary supporting services.

The circulation pattern would include:
1.   Access roads to the site complex.
2.   Separation of the various user groups via the road system.
3.   Boaters are the first user group to be separated.
4.   Sufficient parking and access trails.
5.   Proper informational and safety control signs.

Possible social interests may include:
1.   Toilet and shower facilities.
2.   Restaurant/store operations.
3.   Motels and hotels.
4.   Clubhouse.
5.   Picnicking.
6.   Camping.

The supporting service facilities may include:
1.   Slips and moorings for the boats.
2.   Service center, repair and sales shop.
3.   Boat launching equipment.

4. Boat storage facilities.
5. Sewage disposal and water point for boaters.
6. Fire fighting equipment.

The circulation pattern, social interests, and supporting service facilities are integrated into the design of the marina. Figures 16–4 and 16–5 show a simple layout and a somewhat complex layout, respectively.

Water fluctuations can affect the design. If there is more than a four-foot fluctuation in water levels, the boat dock should be a floating structure rather than static. Figure 16–6 is an example of a dock that fluctuates with the tidal conditions. The dock is supported by floats and actually rides on the water; it can be anchored by pilings, yet be free to move with water fluctuations.

Individual Marina and Related Facilities. Several categories of marina and related facilities are discussed below:

1. *Access and Vistas.* The access road into the water-based complex should be wide enough to handle a large volume of two-way vehicle-trailer traffic. Ideally, the recreationist is given a scenic view of the water and the complex at a vista along the access route. The vista gives him a preview of the complex and the opportunities available; he can then choose

Figure 16–4 Simple roadside marina. (Photograph by South Dakota Department of Highways.)

Figure 16–5 Complete marina layout—Yankton Boat Basin. (Photograph by U.S. Army Corps of Engineers, Omaha, Nebraska.)

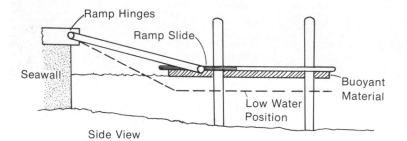

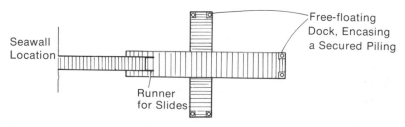

Figure 16–6 Floating dock structure.

the sites he wants to visit. Many people may just want to enjoy the aesthetics of the waterscape and then leave; a vista allows them to do so in minimum conflict with other recreationists. After the vista, the boating traffic should be segregated first and directed into the marina. This measure eliminates the large-volume, less maneuverable car-boat trailer traffic. Each separate site has its own terminal access road off the main access route.

2. *Parking and Circulation.*   Each of the sites should have a separate parking lot, and the marina should provide separate parking for each subactivity—boat launch, docking, and service area. The parking lot for the boat launch should be designed to accommodate about 1.5 vehicles times the average number of boats, to allow some multi-family boating, some spectators, and some overflow use during peak periods of boating. Indiscriminate parking, which may cause loss of vegetation and subsequent erosion, is not tolerable along the waterfront. If the boating is primarily engaged in by those who keep their boats docked at the marina, then the necessary parking can be reduced by 50 per cent or more.

Where the boater is using the launch, parking should be designed to accommodate the vehicle and the boat trailer. For the day user, pull-through parking stalls may be more convenient. If some visitors will be spending several days, special trailer parking may be desirable because the individual visitor may wish to use his vehicle for other purposes during his stay.

The better parking design in terms of convenience and efficiency is the 45-degree diagonal stall—allocating approximately 300 square feet of gross space per vehicle. For the vehicle-trailer combination, approximately 600 square feet of gross space should be allocated, space which would include the stalls, road lanes, barriers, and interior beautification.

For total circulation, trails or walkways should connect the individual sites and the other activity space in the marina. No trail should cross a road; thus, the planner will have to use some innovative road crossings such as tunnels or depressed roads with overhead walks. The heavy traffic use and potential circulation problems would be in the marina proper and primarily around the boat launch site. Specific launch design features will be discussed later; however, one should realize that the circulation pattern in the boat launch is normally counterclockwise to minimize traffic congestion.

3. *Boat Launch.*   A boat launch consists of a terminal service road, a ramp, and a maneuvering space (Figure 16–7). The terminal service road should be two lanes wide and connected to the parking area. Where the terminal road connects the ramp, a maneuvering area is enlarged for turning and backing the boat trailer.

The Bureau of Outdoor Recreation recommends twelve-foot-wide ramps for single vehicle launching. A twenty-foot-wide ramp should handle dual launching. The length should be short enough to minimize backing difficulties but long enough to launch and retrieve boats during low

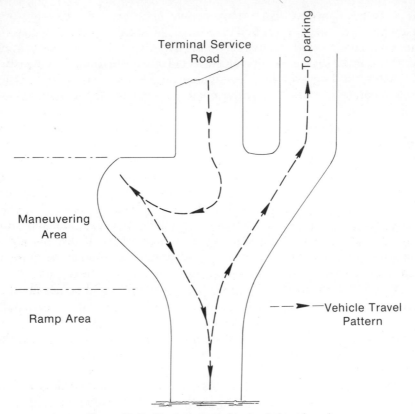

Figure 16-7 Vertical view of a simple boat launch.

water. The ramp gradient will vary from 10 to 12 per cent, with a maximum of 14 per cent (Fig. 16–8). The approach to the ramp may be somewhat steeper, if necessary. The ideal surface is a rough concrete. Never use asphalt, because it creates a continuous oil slick. A rock-sand mixture may be a stable enough surface for low use sites; or surplus steel runway planking may be more desirable if ground conditions are loose, sandy, or washy.

The upper ramp, including the approach, can have a higher gradient than the ramp proper. The steeper lower ramp will allow boats to be launched during low water, yet the pulling vehicle remains on the 10 to 14 per cent gradient and is still able to climb the ramp easily. Approximately two feet is the minimum water depth needed to launch the smaller boats. Because of terrain, the upper ramp may not be necessary; however, wherever the maneuvering area begins for the driver to turn around and back down the ramp, the surface should be relatively level if at all possible. The turn around space tends to be the greatest bottleneck to the efficient operation of the total boat launch.

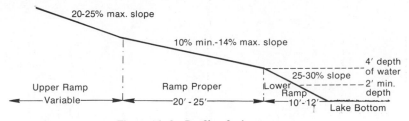

Figure 16–8 Profile of a boat ramp.

Other types of launching may be desirable under specific conditions. The hoist launch, in heavy use areas, can increase efficiency, sometimes as much as a 500 per cent increase over the simple vehicle boat launch. An abutment, or seawall, is necessary to move traffic to the water's edge for unloading, using the hoist. The vehicle with trailer is stopped parallel to the edge, the straps from the hoist are secured around the boat, and then it is lifted off the trailer and into the water. The vehicle continues to the parking area.

The hoist launch may be desirable where bottom conditions and water depth necessitate some dredging. An abutment can be built adjacent to the channel. This procedure reduces the amount of dredging and the total space needed for the operation.

A monorail may be more appropriate where the vehicle backing distance is great or where much of the launching is from a storage facility. This type of launch, too, is more efficient than the vehicle launch. However, both hoist and monorail require constant manning, supervision, and maintenance—all of which are expensive operating costs. The two types would probably only be economically feasible at a large private or concession operation.

One other possibility exists for increasing efficiency without using the mechanical launch. A series of single ramps connecting a perpendicular two-lane, but one-way, service road offers some possibilities (Figure 16–9). The boater drives through in the left lane, stops just beyond the first empty ramp, slowly pulls over into the right lane to begin backing. Once the boat is off the trailer, the boater pulls back into the right lane and leaves by the left lane when traffic is clear.

This design causes two problems. The boater must have a partner to shuttle the boat immediately from the small courtesy dock to a larger one out of the ramp area. This way, each ramp remains open for continued use, and pedestrians and vehicular traffic are not mixed. Also, the vehicles must be stopped at some point prior to the first ramp to minimize traffic congestion at the critical points, yet the ramps should be visible from the stopping point. This operation requires some traffic management to make it work.

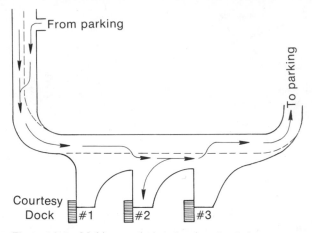

Figure 16–9   Multi-ramp design showing circulation pattern.

BEACH DEVELOPMENTS

Only beach developments around natural or man-made bodies of water are discussed here. These include ponds, lakes, reservoirs, rivers, and oceans. These types of developments are becoming more popular, particularly in the warmer climates nearer population centers. Beach recreation is often a primary activity in an activity aggregate that may include camping, picnicking, boating, and walking for pleasure.

Site Selection.   There are six major considerations in selecting a site for a beach development:

1.   It should be close to a permanent or transient seasonal population center to justify the expense; this is particularly true for a commercial development. Some limited facilities may be developed at less heavily used sites; however, the agency must remember that certain legal and moral responsibilities go with these types of developments.

2.   The site should be easily accessible to the major through routes. If access to the immediate site is not available, the costs of the development of those roads must be included in the financial decision-making.

3.   Climatic conditions are important in the site selections. The minimum water temperature should be in the upper 60s during the swimming season. This range requires continuous warm, sunny conditions, even before the swimming season, to warm the water sufficiently and to attract the swimmer and the sunbather. Also, the area should be free of seasonal storms that would effectively reduce the use season.

4.   After development, both existing and projected water qualities should be analyzed. The bacteriological quality should be less than 100 coliform per 100 ml. of water; however, each state may vary in its require-

ment.[12] Other potential pollutants such as industrial wastes, mine drainage, siltation, and agricultural wastes should be checked.

The swimmer will add to the bacterial count; thus, the planner should attempt to account for this factor in his site selection. Streams and rivers are continuously flowing but should have a minimum flow rate of 500 gallons per user day in order to prevent bacterial accumulation from the swimmer.[12] For standing bodies of water, the problem of bacterial buildup is acute. The larger ones may have sufficient surface water movement and mixing of water with the right wind conditions and natural water movement to at least partially cleanse themselves. For the smaller bodies of water, there does not appear to be any immediate solution.

5.   Certain land and water features should meet some minimum suitability criteria:

Land Phase

a.   Slope of beach. The slope should be between 2 and 10 per cent; 5 per cent is the most ideal figure.
b.   Material of beach. The surface should be at least a twelve-inch layer of sand or mixture of sand and pea gravel. Rocks, woody material or other similar materials are undesirable.
c.   Area of beach. The Bureau of Outdoor Recreation recommends 75 square feet of beach per swimmer day.[2] Approximately the 20 to 30 feet nearest the water's edge should be designated as a *circulation area*. It is here that the swimmer moves into and out of the water, and that most visitors move laterally along the beach. The next 50 to 150 feet comprise the general use zone for sunbathing, formal play, and sightseeing.
d.   Nuisances. A general survey of the site should show locations of any noxious weeds, sharp rocks, and other potential nuisances or hazards to the beach user.
e.   Aesthetics. Aesthetics of the landform, vegetation, and so on, including the color of the sand, is important if the beach is to be attractive. The more typical landscape with some variation in topography and vegetation should be sufficiently attractive.

Water Phase

a.   Slope of bottom. The better slope condition is 7 per cent, variable from 5 to 10 per cent, with a gentle, uniform slope to a depth of six feet.
b.   Material of bottom. The bottom should also be of coarse sand or sand and pea gravel to a twelve-inch depth. Remember that mud bottoms will have to be stabilized with a crushed rock base and then overlaid with coarse gravel before the sand bottom can be stabilized.
c.   Water nuisances. Noxious water plants and animals and

sharp rocks should be identified and eliminated. Also, hazardous water conditions should be checked. These problems can severely reduce satisfaction to the swimmer, or even eliminate the site from consideration.

d. Aesthetics. The color and odor of the water and the condition of the shoreline can affect how people perceive the total landscape.

e. Protection from the wind and water currents is necessary to provide a safe and desirable swimming experience.

6. The total site should be oriented to the sun for maximum warmth, sunbathing, and cheerfulness. However, some shade, natural or manmade, may be adjacent to or a part of the general use portion of the beach.

Site Layout. The planner must realize that many activities actually take place on the beach, including varying levels of participation in a given activity. In order to maintain orderliness, both in terms of safety and participation, the first step is to zone the beach, including the water, for certain types of uses (Figure 16–10).

In the service zone, the primary planning concerns are the access road, parking, and trails to the beach. Special facilities which may be located in this zone, particularly at the interface between this zone and the general use zone, are the bathhouse, comfort station, small organized play fields, small family picnic areas, and any concessions, such as food service.

The primary provisions in the general use zone are for activity space— small open play areas, open space for sunbathing, and sightseeing. Minimum development is desirable in order to maintain natural appeal. Special facilities may include fire rings for evening bonfires; however, they should be located near the service zone and away from the main foot traffic.

The circulation zone should have only one facility, the lifeguard sta-

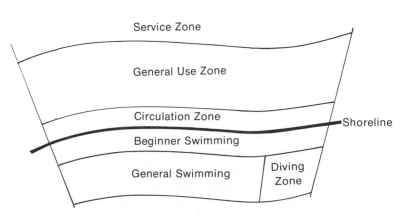

Figure 16–10 Schematic diagram showing the zones of beach use.

tion or crow's-nest. It should be located so that the lifeguard will have an uninterrupted view of the swimming zones.

The swimming zones should be separated by ropes with floats, anchored to hold them in place. The beginning swimming and wading zone is generally three and a half feet in depth or less. The general swimming zone extends from there to about the seven-foot depth. It may be desirable to provide a diving platform in the outer reaches of the general swimming zone. The depth in the immediate vicinity of the diving platform should be at least nine to ten feet. Be sure that tidal changes do not create too shallow diving depths. If use is heavy in the general swimming zone, an additional floating platform should be developed at the edges of the zone for lifeguarding. A total layout is shown in Figure 16–11.

Supporting Facilities 1. *Parking Areas.* If the beach is large, several parking areas may be desirable to disperse use. Each parking stall should be 300 square feet, and for the smaller beaches, the parking area should be designed to handle fifty to a hundred vehicles. For the larger beaches, where people accept higher density use and turnover rates are high, the parking lot should be more centrally located and enlarged to accommodate several hundred vehicles. This measure may consolidate needed services and reduce acquisition and development costs. The trails leading from the parking area to the beach should be paved or hardened with a non-heat-absorbent material.

2. *Bathhouses.* These are necessary for clothes changing, and because of their exposure to increased weathering and susceptibility to mildew and odor accumulation, it is necessary to choose a hearty material such as rock or concrete and to develop a good air circulation-ventilation system. The basic fixture recommendations are one shower and one lavatory per one hundred fifty people. No specific designs are shown; however, the building should facilitate movement within, including changing clothes, showering, and so on. The exterior appearance should be as unobtrusive as possible; it should not be a "main" attraction.

3. *Comfort Station.* Ideally, the comfort station should have one toilet and one urinal per seventy-five male visitors and one toilet per fifty female visitors.[12] It should be located in the central bathhouse in order to centralize facilities, reduce initial costs, and reduce required maintenance. Where there are several parking areas to disperse use, a suitable comfort station should be at each location. A water fountain with faucet should be located near the comfort station. However, it should never be located inside a building, because such a location would increase the amount of unnecessary traffic in the building, maintenance problems, and humidity accumulation.

Refuse containers should be conveniently located at the access trail to the beach, at the bathhouse/comfort station, and at the rear of the lifeguard station.

4. *Concession.* Certain concessions may be desirable, such as a

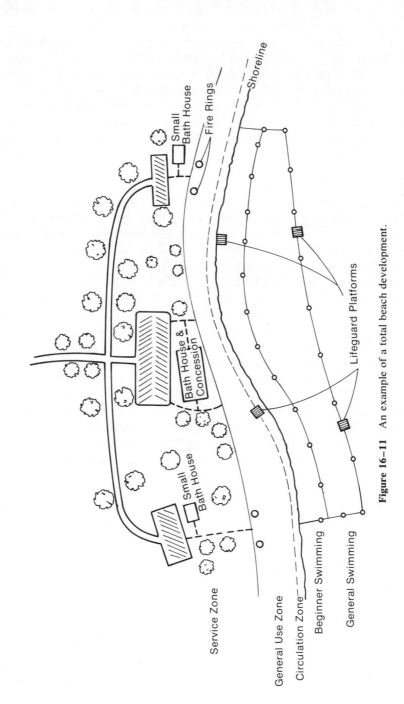

Figure 16–11   An example of a total beach development.

restaurant, an equipment rental facility, and a supply store. The bathhouse and comfort station could be housed in the concession complex.

Extensive Water-Based Developments

Extensive type of developments are greatly needed along streams, rivers, and lakes. The necessary developments should include parking lots, trail systems, foot bridges, comfort stations, and possibly back-country camps. Discussion on planning these types of developments is generally included in Chapter 18, "Wilderness, Backcountry and Other Roadless Areas."

SELECTED READINGS

1. Bureau of Outdoor Recreation. 1967. *Outdoor Recreation Space Standards*. Washington, D.C.: U. S. Government Printing Office.
2. _____. 1970. *The Potomac – A Model Estuary*. Washington, D.C.: Department of the Interior.
3. _____. 1966. *Water-Oriented Outdoor Recreation: Lake Erie Basin*. Ann Arbor, Michigan: Lake Central Region, Bureau of Outdoor Recreation.
4. Dorning, F.E. 1965. "Multiple-Purpose Reclamation Projects Provide Public Recreation," *Proceedings of the Society of American Foresters*.
5. Fogg, G.E. 1974. *Park Planning Guidelines*. Washington, D.C.: National Recreation and Park Association.
6. Knetsch, J.L. 1974. *Outdoor Recreation and Water Resources Planning*. Washington, D.C.: American Geophysical Union. Water Resource Monograph 3.
7. National Recreation and Park Association. 1967. *Design*. Park Practice Program. Washington, D.C.; National Recreation and Park Association and National Park Service.
8. _____. *Management Aid Series*. Washington, D.C.: National Recreation and Park Association
   a. Bulletin No. 8. "Small Lake Management Manual and Survey."
   b. Bulletin No. 44. "Lake Zoning for Recreation."
   c. Bulletin No. 51. "Public Beaches."
   d. Bulletin No. 54. "Marinas."
   e. Bulletin No. 70. "Evaluating Water Based Recreation Facilities and Areas."
9. Outdoor Recreation Resources Review Commission. 1962. *Water for Recreation — Values and Opportunities*. Washington, D.C.: U.S. Government Printing Office. O.R.R.R.C. Study Report No. 10.
10. Palmer, E.Z. 1960. *Recreational Aspects of Three Nebraska Lakes*. Lincoln, Nebraska: Bureau of Business Research, University of Nebraska. Community Study No. 3.
11. Pennsylvania Bureau of State Parks. 1969. *State Park Planning Guidelines*. Harrisburg, Pennsylvania: Department of Forests and Waters.
12. U.S. Public Health Service. 1965. *Environmental Health Practice in Recreation Areas*. Washington, D.C.: U.S. Government Printing Office. P.H.S. Publication No. 1195.

CHAPTER 17

WINTER SPORTS SITE COMPLEXES

As far back as 1856 "Snowshoe" Thompson carried 40 pounds of mail through the California mountains on skis. Other snowbound mailmen were soon making their appointed rounds on skis, and for the fun of it, holding races. Legend has it they skimmed the snow at 80 miles an hour (60 miles an hour is considered near tops in competition). In the 1880's Norwegian families brought skiing to the Midwest. The Lake Placid Club started skiing early in this century, followed by the Dartmouth Outing Club in 1910 and the Williams Outing Club in 1916. One of Uncle Sam's Forest Rangers in 1930 made the first ski ascent of Mount Baker and described the ride down as the finest of his life. The mountain's lower slopes are now one of the most popular National Forest ski areas.[19]

Skiing as a major commercial recreation enterprise began during the 1930s with the development of resorts in New England, Minnesota, and Idaho. Use has continued to grow since then; more and more Americans are turning to winter sports, including skiing. The great surge in participation occurred during the late 1950s and early 1960s — skier visits in the west tripled from 1.4 million in 1955 to 4.3 million in 1963.[6] Attendance increased in the lake states nearly 20 per cent per year from 1960 to 1967.[11]

Participation has continued to increase in our affluent society. The number of ski areas has also increased drastically, and many have expanded their facilities. The larger areas are most popular, accounting for nearly 60 per cent of the total visits.[6] The average skier must travel a considerable distance to ski, even to small ski developments. This situation creates some question about the future. Will inflation, the energy shortage, and changing leisure values affect skiing participation? And what effect will these trends have on newly planned sites or on the operation of existing ones? The future of skiing will be affected by:

    1.   Spiraling costs of participation.

2. Amount of travel time to site.
3. Size of area.
4. Location close to urban populations.
5. Improved safety conditions.
6. Greater promotional efforts.

The exact future is difficult to project, but the success of any winter sports site appears to derive from how well it responds to the preceding concerns.

SKIING

Site Selection

The site selection process is important and should include social and economic variables as well as resource variables. However, this chapter will focus mainly on the resource variables, including terrain, weather, and landscape.

Figure 17–1 A typical winter sports site complex, Treasure Mountain Lodge. (Photograph by Bureau of Reclamation, U. S. Department of the Interior.)

Terrain Features. First, the topography should be analyzed in terms of its appropriateness for the type of proposed development. As shown in Table 17–1, the distribution of the types of slopes will vary according to the skier population that they attract.

The figures represent typical layouts, so the percentage of area may vary according to the type of skier population that uses the area. Even in national attractions, a certain portion of the area should be devoted to beginner slopes, to encourage the novice skier.

There should also be a description of the ecological-physiographic attributes of the site, including:

1. *Landscape Features.* Landscape features (bowl, broad ridge, flat bottom, side hill, undulating, etc.) will affect the location of ski runs, as indicated in Table 17–1, whereas others are more desirable in the flatter base areas. Negative features such as gullies, rock outcroppings, and natural chutes should also be identified, because they may reduce the feasibility of using a given location for winter sports development.

2. *Ecology.* The vegetative types should be mapped according to the dominant species, stocking and condition of vegetation, and characteristics of the soils. This procedure can assist in projecting possible effects of such measures as clear cutting and thinning of the vegetation. In addition, the cost factors for vegetation manipulation, soil stabilization, and maintenance of aesthetics can be more realistically assessed.

The effects of development on other land uses and values in the area should be determined. The potential development may be located on critical big game winter ranges, migration routes, or unique natural features — values which society may want to perpetuate. Heavy vegetation removal may change water runoff and water quality downstream, or cause other effects. Consequently, any future winter sports development should be evaluated not only in terms of its on-site effects, but in terms of the total ecological system.

TABLE 17–1　CLASSIFICATION OF SKI SLOPES BY TYPE OF WINTER SPORTS DEVELOPMENT

Description of Slopes			Percentage of Area by Type of Development			Range of Vertical Rise		
Type of Slope	Gradient	Minimum Width	Local	Regional	National	Local	Regional	National
Practice	12–20%	As wide as long	one per area minimum					
Beginner	15–25	200′	30%	15%	15%	500–	1500–	2500–
Intermediate	25–40	150	50	55	40	2000′	2500′	3500′
Advanced	40–50	100	20	20	25			
Expert	55–80	60	—	10	20			

3. *Aspect.*   Aspect is important in maintaining proper cold temperatures and maximizing shading. The critical part of the day tends to be 11:00 A.M. to 3:00 P.M.; thus, north and northeast aspects are better suited for maintaining good snow conditions, except for the extreme cold conditions of high altitudes or far north latitudes. In those conditions, aspects giving warmer temperatures may be more desirable if skiing is to take place.

East aspects are usually good because they do not face the sun during the critical afternoon period. West aspects may be usable if they have intervening topography or vegetation to the west to shade the runs. South and southeast aspects may be acceptable on less steep terrain at higher elevations. The problem is that the concentration of solar energy on the slope causes rapid deterioration of the snow, suncrusting, and possible overnight icing. The southwest aspect should be completely avoided.

4. *Size of Slope Area.*   The slope area should be large enough to support the immediate development and possible future expansion, as previously shown in Table 17–1.

5. *Land Ownership.*   The maintenance of desirable land use patterns is important, but this may create the need for a large land acquisition program. The fee-simple ownership or long-term lease of the area is essential before substantial investment should be made. Also, scenic easements may be necessary to minimize visual impact from other future development near the location.

Snow Conditions and Hazards.   The length of the quality skiing season is the primary concern. The snow conditions for the season are a product of snowfall, air temperature, relative humidity, wind, sun, and terrain. Snowfall is the first factor to be considered, including total amount, timing, and frequency. The total snowfall should be high, with reliable early snow in November and December. Spring snow depths are generally no problem except in the more southern portions of the snow belt. The other factors—air temperature, humidity, wind, sun, and terrain—affect the quality of the snow by drying, melting, and drifting the snow crystals.

A complete avalanche survey should be made. More sophisticated methods of avalanche forecasting are now available so that certain kinds of avalanche problems can be managed; however, base area facilities and on-slope developments should be located out of the avalanche corridor. If the hazards are too great or will effectively reduce the skiing season, one should consider an alternate site.

Access.   The immediate access should be evaluated for physical, engineering, aesthetic, and economic problems. Questions to be asked are:

1. Will a new access route need to be constructed? Old route reconstructed?

2. Will additional land need to be purchased?

3. What are the technical engineering problems?

4. What are the total costs?

5. What will the road development do to roadside aesthetics?

Access is further compounded by winter road maintenance problems such as steep road gradients, ice conditions, avalanches, blowing and drifting snow, and the high costs of snow removal programs.

Beyond the immediate location, accessibility should also be considered in terms of convenience to major highway systems, railroads, air terminals, and other local and regional transportation systems. The degree of access needed to the various regional transportation systems will depend on the level of attraction—local, regional, and national.

Base Area Needs.   The base area is generally highly developed to meet certain needs of the visitor. If the size is not sufficient for immediate development plus expansion, then the planner should consider a different location or rethink the needs. The array of possible facilities includes parking, shelters, administrative and maintenance buildings, lodges, first aid station, lower lift termini, and ski storage, as well as water, sewer, and utility systems.

Also, because of the potential for greater environmental impact in the base area, the planner should prepare an appraisal of the potential impacts and attempt to minimize their negative effects. Secondary developments such as second home developments can also have a tremendous impact.

Skier Capacity.   The planner should determine the skier capacity in order to predict total use and possible incomes from the operation. A formula for determining daily capacity is:

$$\text{Daily capacity} = \frac{\text{(Vertical rise)} \times \text{(Hourly capacity—No. of people)} \times \text{(Hours of operation)} \times \text{(0.82 Loading efficiency)}}{\text{Vertical feet per skier day}}$$

Average vertical feet per skier day is:

1.	Low intermediate	6,000 feet
2.	Intermediate	7,500 feet
3.	Advanced	9,000 feet
4.	Expert	10,500 feet

The vertical rise and the hourly capacity are for a given lift and runs associated with that lift. The loading efficiency generally averages 0.82.[6] This figure will be considerably less for the smaller sites. The daily capacities for all lifts are then added, as well as spectator use, to obtain the total daily capacity for the ski development.

Skier Population.   The potential market should be separated according to time/distance travel patterns (Figure 17–2). Within each of these zones, the planner should evaluate:

1. *Urban/Nonurban Population Trends*.   Skiers tend to have an urban rather than rural background. Yet only a little more than one per cent of the total population actually skis.

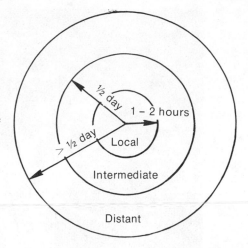

Figure 17–2 Travel zones by time periods for the potential skier market.

2. *Age/Sex Distribution.*   Age distribution is important because skiers tend to be younger people. And males generally outnumber females as much as two to one.

3. *Income Trends.*   Skiers tend to have much higher than average incomes. Skiing is an expensive individual sport; the average daily expenditure in 1965 was $20.54. [6]

4. *Educational/Occupational Groupings.*   Skiers tend to be professional people with higher levels of education, or children from those types of families. Blue collar workers generally do not ski. This tendency often does not reflect family economics but merely variation in leisure taste patterns for many blue and white collar workers.

5. *Transportation Systems.*   The types of transportation systems, intervening physiography, and winter travel conditions should be surveyed. The planner should ensure that each major transportation system operates year-round with minimal delays because of weather conditions. Eventually everyone must reach the development by a road system. Are these roads adequately maintained in the winter? Certain high mountain passes may be closed, which may shift travel into the more distant zones.

6. *Competition.*   One should also evaluate the market competition in terms of travel, skiing opportunity, services, efficiency of operation, and financial success.

Site Design

The design should include the entire site complex, including the ski slopes, the base area, the secondary winter activities, and the access corridor. As shown in Figure 17–3, the focal point is the lodge/shelter area; people radiate out to the activity areas and return. The activities should be

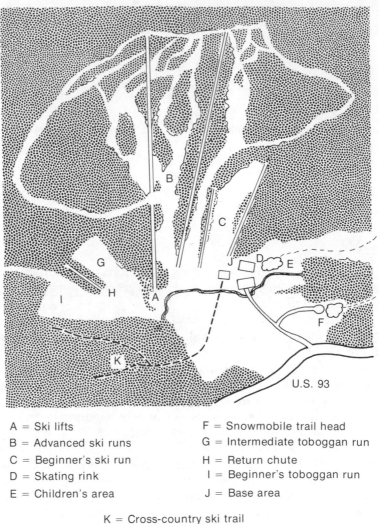

A = Ski lifts   F = Snowmobile trail head

B = Advanced ski runs   G = Intermediate toboggan run

C = Beginner's ski run   H = Return chute

D = Skating rink   I = Beginner's toboggan run

E = Children's area   J = Base area

K = Cross-country ski trail

Figure 17–3   A site plan for a total winter sports site complex.

separated, yet each should be easily accessible from the base area for the convenience and safety of the user. Alpine skiing is the main activity that justifies intensive development. Other important winter activities to be offered may include cross-country skiing, snowmobiling, ice skating, tobogganing, and snowshoeing. Special instruction and group tours may help to promote the understanding and enjoyment of these activities.

    The overall site complex plan should be to medium scale (approximately $1'' = 200'-300'$) with ten-foot contour intervals. Larger intervals may not adequately show the topographic relief. The base area plan should be large-scale to show the scale size of each facility and its location. Two-to five-foot contours should be sufficient to locate each facility properly. The construction plans should be appended for each major facility.

Design of Ski Slopes. The slopes should meet the gradient requirements outlined earlier, plus the following specifications:

1. *Locate Parallel to Fall Line (Perpendicular to Contour).* This direction is easier to ski, will have a greater capacity for skiing, and requires less snow maintenance. If you do not locate parallel to the fall line, then you are developing side hill runs which create narrow rutted trails on the lower side.

Side hill runs cause
narrow rutted trails

2. *Offer Variation in Gradient.* On a given slope, offer variations in the gradient and visual experiences to make it interesting and challenging for the skiers. Monotonous terrain may be okay for the beginner because he is concentrating on technique.

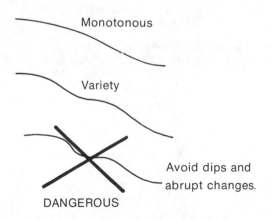

Monotonous

Variety

DANGEROUS

Avoid dips and
abrupt changes.

3. *Widen Steeper Portion of Runs.* Particularly on the intermediate runs, you must widen the steeper portions so the skiers will not wear out snow by sideslipping. In addition, this measure will make it easier on the skier who is not used to the steeper gradients.

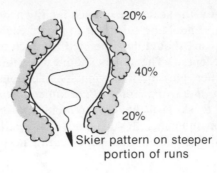

20%

40%

20%

Skier pattern on steeper
portion of runs

4. *Separate Runs and Lifts*.   Do not terminate advanced runs in the beginner area. Invasion by the advanced skiers may cause a considerable drop in participation by the novice skier.

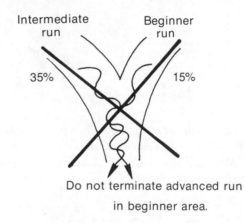

Intermediate
run

Beginner
run

35%

15%

Do not terminate advanced run

in beginner area.

Also, lifts should be separated from runs to maximize safety and minimize conflict. Any training area should be separated from all other ski runs.

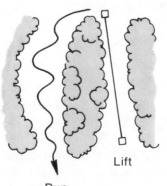

Lift

Run

Separate lifts from runs.

The upper and lower lift termini should be separated from the head of the ski run and the runout, respectively. The lift terminus should be a flat, well-marked area for easy mounting and dismounting from the lift.

5. *Increase Shade and Wind Control.* There should be an above average amount of shade on the ski runs. Shading from the south side is critical, particularly for those runs that are oriented in an east-west direction.

Increased shading

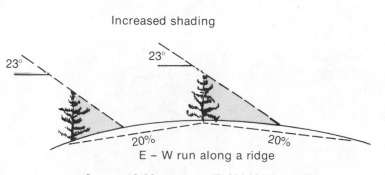

E – W run along a ridge

Sun at 12:00 noon at 47° N latitude, 11/23

Trees may be more important for wind control. Certain types of trees tend to be highly susceptible to windthrow; also, certain types of topography, and cutting patterns increase the possibility of windthrow. Saddles and ridge tops generally have more windthrow. Runs facing into the wind, particularly on the steeper gradients, are more susceptible. Also, leaving small patches and narrow strips, having straight cutting boundaries with right angle corners, or leaving indentations in boundaries will drastically increase the possibility of windthrow.

Forest margins along ski runs which are cut perpendicular to the prevailing wind act as a wind barrier, provided the width of the run is not large. The effect of a 50 per cent density barrier, such as a stand of trees, will give maximum reduction of wind force at three times the height of the barrier.

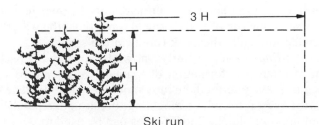

Ski run

Maximum reduction of wind

6. *Feather the Cutting Boundary.*   By feathering the boundary of a run (carefully reducing stocking of the overstory trees to 10 to 40 per cent), one can improve aesthetics by eliminating the unnatural appearance of the cutting boundary. Also, this maintains good powder snow conditions longer for the powder hound. However, during the latter part of the season, the snow depth will tend to be lower around these trees because of radiation absorption by the trees. Those types of forest stands that are highly susceptible to windthrow should not be feathered along the margins.

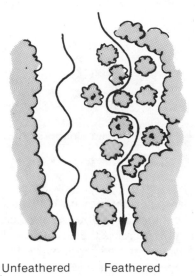

Unfeathered   Feathered

7. *Groom All Ski Runs.*   Grooming (removal of natural obstacles on ski runs) will provide safer skiing and a longer season. A groomed run may be skiable with four to six inches of packed base, whereas a comparable run on an ungroomed one may require eighteen inches of snow to cover the rocks, stumps, and so on. Groomed slopes are particularly susceptible to erosion; thus, immediate soil protection is necessary until the new ground cover is established. Water bars are necessary to divert the runoff during the revegetation. One-foot-wide water bars at two per cent gradient and twenty-five-foot intervals should be sufficient on the intermediate slopes. Remember that spring runoff is the critical time; thus, the water diversion should be made to handle the peak runoff in the spring.

8. *Snow Maintenance.*   Early snowfalls should be packed after each storm to retard the formation of "sugar" snow and to slow early melting. Beginner and intermediate runs should be packed after each storm throughout the season to reduce moguling, break up ice patches, reduce melting, and improve skiing. Snow fences can be used to control drifting and increase snow in bare areas. However, one may have to also manage

the use of the slopes by closing off runs with marginal snow, concentrating use in packed runs, and flagging hazards.

9. *Moguling.* Slopes around 25 per cent gradient or higher will mogul with heavy use. Skiers may move several tons of snow per day down the runs. A concave slope will not mogul as fast as a flat or convex one. On the flat or convex slopes over 25 per cent, wider runs and lighter use will reduce moguling, but it cannot be eliminated without maintenance.

Continued heavy use without maintenance increases the size of the moguls until the low spots reach the ground surface. If these are not filled and packed, each new snow is quickly worn out in the same spots. For slopes under 45 per cent, moguling can be controlled with vehicular equipment such as a small dozer with drag or rollers. Over 45 per cent, the maintenance must be done with nonmechanized equipment.

Base Area Design.   The base facilities are primarily for the skier and include:

1. *Easy Winter Access.*   There should be easy access from the major highway systems leading to the area.

2. *Parking.*   The average is about a hundred cars per acre (less where snow removal is limited).

3. *Administrative Buildings, Including Maintenance.*   Approximately one acre should be sufficient for a local winter sports site, three acres for regional sites, and five or more acres for national attractions.

4. *Service Shelter.*   The shelter should offer the basic services, including food service, warming lounge, equipment rental, and visitor information. One should figure about one acre for these services at a local site, three acres at a regional site, and five acres at national attractions.

5. *Lodge and Other Overnight Accommodations.* Up to ten to fifteen acres may be necessary at regional sites and a minimum of a hundred acres at national ones.

6. *Ski Patrol and First Aid Shelter.*   For local sites, this facility may be located in the service shelter. It may require as much as a half-acre for the other sites.

7. *Lower Lift Terminus.*   Approximately one acre of relatively flat terrain is needed for each terminus.

8. *Sewer System.*   Because of the large number of people who use the sites during concentrated periods of time, winter conditions, and sensitivity of the environment where most sites are located, sophisticated and expensive sewage treatment is necessary. Sewerage systems should be designed to fit total base area needs and should conform to federal, state, and local health and environmental protection regulations.

9. *Water Supply.*   Approximately five to ten gallons per person per day use are needed, depending on services, comfort facilities, and average length of day use. As much as forty gallons per person may be necessary for overnight use.

All of the base area facilities should be properly located in relation to the ski slopes, to facilitate movement between base area and slopes while minimizing possible conflict between the various types of skiing and other activities. Avalanche zones and other hazards, no matter how small, should be avoided in the base area. Also, sufficient land should be secured in the initial planning to allow for future expansion. The land may not be available in the future or it may be prohibitively expensive.

1. *Traffic Flow.* A traffic flow chart should be developed to integrate the vehicle entrance traffic, base area traffic, and activity patterns (Figure 17–4). The diagram in Figure 17–4 is schematic to show the main traffic flows. For vehicle access traffic, one should include the following:

a. Traffic flow and safety signs.
b. Unloading zone.
c. Separate parking for day guests, lodge guests, and service people.
d. Special parking for buses.
e. Maintenance of landscape aesthetics.
f. Expansion of parking (future).

For traffic flow in the base area proper, one should include the following:

a. Commercial loading zone and ramp.
b. Walkways (heated, covered, or maintained).
c. Separate location for each service (food, equipment, lounge, etc.) with well-integrated foot traffic from the vehicle access zone to and through the base area zone, to the activity zone.
d. First aid shelter located and designed for ease of access to the activity zone and vehicle access zone, including a service road to the shelter.

The following should be considered in the traffic flow in the activity areas:

a. Packed trails to skate pond, children's area, free play, and cross-country skiing trail head.
b. Special road into edge of activity zone with developed trail head facilities for the snowmobiler.
c. Packed trails to ski jumps, practice and instructional slopes, and toboggan runs.
d. Separation of beginners and other skiers as they move to lower lift termini.
e. Established lift line patterns.
f. Ski racks at interface of base area and activity zones.

2. *Parking.* Parking is an important consideration in the design of the base area. There are three types of parking: field, strip, and compartment (Figure 17–5). Field parking is inexpensive in that the ground is allowed to freeze and snow is then removed to form an open parking lot. However, during warming periods the surface may thaw, creating muddy conditions which deter use during that time. Furthermore, this type may

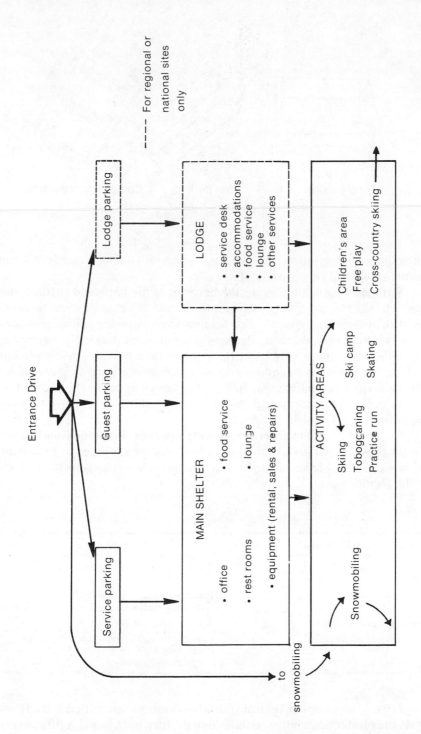

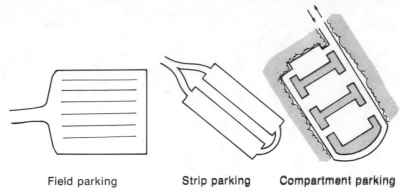

Field parking   Strip parking   Compartment parking

Figure 17-5   Three types of parking.

cause loss of vegetation and erosion, which in turn will accelerate the maintenance and repair costs of the site.

Strip parking is a better design because of the hardened surface, the ability to shift traffic during snow removal, and the ease of snow removal because of the narrow width. For field parking, large area plowing makes snow removal very difficult. Perhaps compartment parking is better because there are more options in terms of snow removal, yet convenient parking for guests is maintained. You can regulate parking patterns by closing certain compartments. Also, it is a convenience to the guest to be able to detect open parking spaces easily without having to drive through the entire lot, as in field parking.

3. *Shading.*   Shading is important; however, maximum shade is not always the rule. All parts of the total site should be surveyed to determine the amount of shade and sunlight. The general shade requirements of each of the facilities are:

Amount of Sunlight/Shading	*Facilities*
Maximum shade	Toboggan runs, open skating, and ski jumps.
Maximum sunlight	Parking areas, spectator facilities, sun lounges, walkways, and picture windows.
More than average shade	Ski runs and tow lifts.
More than average sunlight	Central shelter, administrative buildings, and lodges or other overnight accommodations.

Lifts.   Most uphill ski transportation systems are called *lifts*. However, the proper descriptive terminology is "lifts and tows." A lift actually "lifts" the skier from the terminus and moves him up slope without any surface contact. A tow is a device for moving the skier up the slope by towing him along the surface.

Uphill transportation capacity should correspond with downhill and base area capacity. If not, long waiting lines may be common at the lower termini. Skiers tend to avoid winter sites that have long waiting lines. The planner should recognize that the rated capacity of most uphill systems is higher than the operating capacity; the average efficiency is 0.82.[6] Efficiency is generally higher for the larger sites because of increased maintenance, better qualified maintenance personnel, and more and better qualified lift personnel.

The following are the advantages and disadvantages of the various lifts and tows:

1. *T-Bars*. The T-bar is moderate in cost with a variable speed capability. The inverted "U" frame at the towers allows considerable ski tracking. There are no unloading problems if the unloading spot is groomed. Slopes up to 60 to 70 per cent can be negotiated, but the steeper the grade, the faster the tow must operate.

The disadvantages of this type of tow are many. It is tiring to ride over three to four thousand feet on the tow because it must follow the fall line and a smooth tow track must be maintained. Because of this, the tow cannot be used in the summer or during poor snow conditions. Finally, the upper and lower termini must be relatively large and flat for ease of loading and unloading.

2. *Poma Tow*. It is less expensive and easier to ride while having advantages similar to the T-bar's. Also, it is less disruptive of landscape aesthetics than the T-bar. It has the same disadvantages. Neither operate well on windy slopes, and neither should cross runs or trails.

3. *Chair Lift*. Chair lifts are suitable for longer rides, up to six or seven thousand feet. They do not have to follow the fall line and can cross ski runs and trails or avalanche paths. Because of these characteristics, the lift can operate during the summer and during marginal snow conditions.

Probably the greatest disadvantages are the higher cost and the lack of comfort on windy slopes. Also, this type of lift is more disruptive to the natural landscape. Other factors to be considered are that the distance above the terrain should not exceed 25 feet, and that it is desirable for the entire lift line to be visible to the operator. Double chair lifts should be favored over a single chair because of the minimal additional costs for doubling the capacity.

The gondola lift (two- to four-passenger cabin) is much the same as an enclosed double chair lift. It has a lower hourly capacity and much higher costs. Thus, it is rarely used.

4. *Aerial Tramway*. The tramway can overcome most of the disadvantages of other lifts. It is comfortable to ride over long distances and can traverse greater elevation and terrain differences. The only disadvantage is the high cost of construction and operation. There must be a high rate of use year-round to justify the tramway.

OTHER WINTER SPORTS ACTIVITIES

The remaining portion of the chapter will briefly focus on some of the planning aspects of other winter sports activities. These are not meant to be portrayed as secondary activities. Each activity is extremely important and should be considered in any total winter sports program. Planned and developed individually, these activities and associated facilities take on immense proportions. However, when developed on a smaller scale for a commercial clientele at a winter sports site, these activities generally attract fewer people than alpine skiing does.

Snowmobiling.   Snowmobiling includes both trail and nontrail types. Our discussion will be related to trail head facilities and trail planning only. Nontrail snowmobiling is difficult to plan and manage except on a large zone basis.

1. *Trail Heads.*   Traffic to the trail head should be separated from the main traffic pattern in order to maintain safety and minimize conflict at the departure point. Facilities at the trail head include the following as a minimum: parking lot, loading ramp, comfort station, and warm-up area (Figure 17–6). The parking area should be adequate to accommodate vehicles with trailers. One other facility, a warming hut, may be desirable but expensive and prone to vandalism. Ideally the trail head is a multiseason development, including perhaps a trail head for trail bikes, a parking area for a group picnic grounds, or an overflow campground. The loading ramp could be constructed of packed snow and should be periodically refurbished by packing new snow.

2. *Trails.*   There are three types of trails: warm-up area (minimum of five acres), maze (minimum of forty acres), and cross-country. The warm-up area is used to check the operation of the machine. The maze is simply a high-density, meandering trail system but without any crossing of trails. It is used as a beginner's or instructional trail.

Existing roads and trails that are not maintained in the winter will make good cross-country trails. However, the emphasis should be on the variety of the snowmobiling terrain with varied intermediate zone viewing.

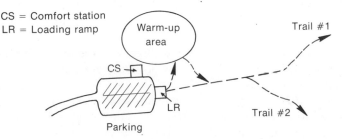

Figure 17–6   Typical snowmobile trail head layout.

Scenic vistas could be established along the route. This may require developing new connecting trails and new loop trails to produce a continuous one-way travel experience, rather than having people retrace their route. Each trail should be well marked and periodically packed to improve the surface for the convenience and safety of the visitor. Artificial retaining barriers such as drift fences should be used to contain traffic to the trail in open areas.

Depending on snow depths, the overhanging vegetation should be cleared to a minimum of eight to ten feet for safety. The maximum sustained gradient should not exceed 8 to 10 per cent, or 20 to 25 per cent for short distances. The trails should vary in length, from five to twenty-five miles or more. If possible, for trails of twenty-five miles or more, or a major trail system, one should develop a series of trail heads to disperse use and to encourage certain types of experiences—individual, family, organizational, and racing—on certain trails, or portions thereof.

Several types of resource features should be avoided:

1.   Lake and stream crossings, except by building up the ice and periodically checking the conditions.

2.   Avalanche hazard areas.

3.   Cliffs and other steep terrain.

4.   Thermal pool areas.

5.   Road crossings on maintained roads.

6.   Areas of wildlife concentrations.

7.   Zones for cross-country ski use.

More information is needed on the effects of snowmobiling on the small mammal population, changes in vegetation, and changes in snow melt because of snow compaction before we can do a total job of planning. Also, we need to know the effects of snowmobiles in terms of mechanical damage to vegetation.

Cross-Country Skiing.   Many of the same planning guidelines for the snowmobiler are applicable to the cross-country skier. However, some differences in terms of perception and behavior should be considered in planning trail heads and trails. Only minimum trail head facilities are needed—a plowed, flat area for parking and a comfort station. Perhaps a narrow meandering trail through dense vegetation (canopied landscape) as one leaves the trail head should discourage all but the cross-country skier. Once he leaves the trail head, his travel posture is slow and contemplative. If the ratio of typical speeds for the snowmobiler and cross-country skier is 10 to 1 (20 m.p.h. to 2 m.p.h.), the efficiency of the speed ratio might be 20 to 1 because of the cross-country skier's periodic stops to catch his breath, enjoy the scenery, and share the experience with fellow skiers. Although panoramic viewing is a desirable landscape along the trail, emphasis should also be placed on primary and secondary landscapes in the intermediate and near-viewing zones. Enclosed, canopied, and detail landscapes may be very appealing to the skier. However, to be continuously exposed to a

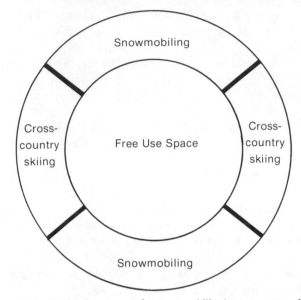

Figure 17–7   Zoning large areas for snowmobiling/cross-country skiing.

single landscape would create a monotonous visual experience. The slower pace also encourages other activities such as sightseeing, photography, winter nature study, and group discussions.

Even without attempting to describe basic underlying motivations of the behavior, the planner should at least recognize the inherent differences in the behavior of the snowmobiler and the cross-country skier and attempt to plan for these differences. The first step should probably be to zone an area under the area plan, realizing that the only identifiable difference is travel and related behavior (Figure 17–7). By starting from separate trail heads and using natural barriers to separate the snowmobiler and cross-country skier, one has effectively zoned as in Figure 17–7 without actually designating a particular location for a single use.

The zones for snowmobiling and cross-country skiing should have well-defined topographic boundaries to separate them physically, visually, and aurally. The free use space is open to use by both, yet, because each will enter from a different point, the traffic should be well-dispersed. The typical day-user skier will travel less than five miles in a day and return to his point of origin. Thus, if there is an opportunity for some open, distant viewing, the ski trails could lead to the interface with the free use space so that the skier can visually utilize it without having to occupy it. The snowmobiler may wish actually to use the space. Variation in topography and vegetation is desirable generally to mask such movements from the observer visually utilizing the same area.

Tobogganing.   Much diversity of opinion exists about what constitutes a good toboggan run. Thus, the following is presented as a typical classification for a neighborhood toboggan slope area:

TABLE 17-2   TOBOGGAN HILL CLASSIFICATION

Type of Slope	Minimum Length of Run (Feet)	Slope Area (Percent)	Gradient (Percent)
Tot	50–75	10%	<15%
Beginner	150	40	15–25
Intermediate	300	40	25–40
Expert	300	10	>40

All beginner and intermediate runs should be straight, at least 150 feet wide, well-groomed and sodded so they are usable during marginal snow conditions. Expert runs may be narrower but longer with longer runout aprons. Each run should be steeper at the top and shallower at the bottom. The return chute to the top of the hill should be at least twenty-five feet wide; ideally there are separate return chutes for the tot and the beginner. Also, there should be a minimum of one return chute per two runs, regardless of the type of slope; and vegetative strips should separate runs from return chutes.

On small toboggan hills, the east, west, and north aspects could be devoted to different types of runs and the south aspect reserved as access to the top, providing snow conditions are adequate. This type of hill does not ordinarily require vegetation to separate the runs; however, it requires constant supervision. Approximately one to five acres are necessary for the smaller hills; for the larger ones, the number and types of runs that are appropriate will dictate size. The top of the hill, or wherever the starting point is, should be relatively flat and large enough to accommodate a number of people. A typical layout is shown in Figure 17-8.

The toboggan runs at a winter sports site complex should be easily accessible from the base area but separated from the ski runs and lifts. One beginner and one intermediate run is a minimum.

Ice Skating.   This discussion will pertain to natural ice, open conditions. A pond or small lake may offer excellent skating if there are extended periods of cold weather. The surface should be shaded from direct sunlight, with a minimum ice depth of eight inches. Some people recommend less ice depth where there are low visitor use and uniformity of ice conditions.

Where there is no body of water, open areas can be flooded to create a skating surface. The ground can be flooded in stages, using sideboards to contain the water. Or existing hard surface areas may be used if proper coverings are used prior to flooding. The minimum facilities are a flooded area with side boards, warming hut, and small equipment concession. The height of the side boards should be about twice the thickness of the ice to prevent surface rippling by wind during the initial freezing. Also, the sides should be screened to minimize direct solar radiation to the ice and wind chill to the skater. The surface should be maintained during the early morning hours by lightly watering the surface. In general, this is the coldest part of the day, with minimal wind.

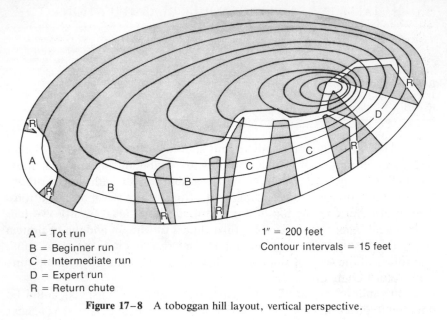

A = Tot run
B = Beginner run
C = Intermediate run
D = Expert run
R = Return chute

1″ = 200 feet
Contour intervals = 15 feet

Figure 17–8   A toboggan hill layout, vertical perspective.

Natural ice on ponds and lakes can be increased or surface improved by induced flooding. The snow should be pushed back from a portion of the lake's surface; then a hole should be cut through the ice outside of the cleared area. A hose pumping system should be used to pump the super-cooled water onto the cleared surface. Depth would be built up in thin layers, the mounded snow acting as sideboards.

At the winter complex, the skating surface should be near the main shelter and separated from other activities. A lighted area will encourage night skating as a welcome change of pace to the rigors of skiing during the day.

SELECTED READINGS

1.   Bureau of Outdoor Recreation. 1970. *International Snowmobile Congress Proceedings*. Ann Arbor, Michigan.
2.   Caskey, G.B., and D.G. Wright. 1966. *Coasting and Tobogganing Facilities*. Washington, D.C.: National Recreation and Park Association. Management Aids Bulletin No. 62.
3.   Chubb, M. 1971. *Proceedings of the 1971 Snowmobile and Off the Road Vehicle Research Symposium*. East Lansing, Michigan: Recreation Research and Planning Unit, Michigan State University. Technical Report No. 8.
4.   Gaylor, E.L., and C.C. Rombold. 1964. *Handbook for Ski Slope Development*. Washington, D.C.: National Recreation and Park Association. Management Aids Bulletin No. 36.
5.   Gunn, C.A. 1958. *Planning Winter Sports Areas*. East Lansing, Michigan: Michigan State University. Cooperative Extension Service Circular R–306.

6. Herrington, R.B. 1967. *Skiing Trends and Opportunities in the Western States*. U.S. Forest Service Research Paper INT-34.

7. Hill, G.A. 1970. "A Look Beyond New York's Snowmobiling Statute," *Conservation Circular* (of New York State College of Agriculture, Cornell University), 9(1): 1-5.

8. Horney, R.L. 1970. *Snowmobiling*. National Recreation and Park Association. Management Aids Bulletin No. 89.

9. International Snowmobile Industry Association. 1969. "Snowmobile Trails: Basic Recommendations." Unnumbered Circular.

10. James, G.I. 1968. *Pilot Test of Sampling Procedures for Estimating Recreation Use on Winter-Sports Sites*. U.S. Forest Service Research Paper SE-42.

11. Leuscher, W.A. 1970. *Skiing in the Great Lakes States: The Industry and Skier*. U.S. Forest Service Research Paper NC-46.

12. Minnesota Department of Conservation. 1970. *Minnesota Snowmobile Survey*. St. Paul, Minnesota: Minnesota Department of Conservation.

13. Natural and Historic Resources Branch. 1965. *Winter Recreation and the National Parks: A Management Policy and a Development Program*. Ottawa, Ontario: Canadian Department of Northern Affairs and National Resources.

14. Rombold, C.C. 1964. *Natural Ice Skating Surfaces*. Washington, D.C.: National Recreation and Park Association. Management Aids Bulletin No. 37.

15. Rombold, C.C., and R.E. Owens. 1964. *Artificial Ice Skating Facilities*. Washington, D.C.: National Recreation and Park Association. Management Aids Bulletin No. 38.

16. Soil Conservation Service. 1958. *Snow Survey Safety Guide*. Washington, D.C.: U.S. Government Printing Office. Agriculture Handbook No. 137.

17. _____. 1967. *Snow Survey Sampling Guide*. Washington, D.C.: U.S. Government Printing Office. Agriculture Handbook No. 169.

18. U.S. Forest Service. 1972. *Planning Consideration for Winter Sports Resort Development*. Rocky Mountain Region, U.S. Forest Service.

19. _____. 1964. *Skiing*. Washington, D.C.: U.S. Government Printing Office. Forest Service Pamphlet 525.

20. _____. 1968. *Snow Avalanches: A Handbook of Forecasting and Control Measures*. Washington, D.C.: U.S. Government Printing Office. Agriculture Handbook No. 194.

21. Vollmer Associates. 1963. *Belleayre Mountain Ski Center: Feasibility Study of Expanded Facilities for Year Round Use*. New York, New York: Vollmer Associates.

22. West Virginia, State of. 1968. *Summary of Skiing in West Virginia: Feasibility Study of Year-Round Resort Potential of Four Selected Sites*. Charleston, West Virginia: West Virginia State Planning Office.

23. Wisconsin, State of. 1965. *Skiing, Major Winter Component of Wisconsin's Year-Round Resorts*. Madison, Wisconsin: Wisconsin Department of Natural Resources.

CHAPTER 18

WILDERNESS, BACKCOUNTRY, AND OTHER ROADLESS AREAS

Wilderness and other similar trail recreational experiences are probably our fastest growing form of outdoor recreation. From 1946 to 1964, use increased sevenfold, while the amount of area has increased only slightly.[14] Use has increased even faster since 1964; some popular locales within many wilderness areas are experiencing overuse and deterioration of the site and the recreational experience.

HISTORY OF THE WILDERNESS MOVEMENT

Aldo Leopold, called the "wilderness prophet," was one of the first to express the need for wilderness areas. He warned the public that the wilderness was not inexhaustible and that unless they acted as public interest groups to ensure proper legislation, the real wilderness would be lost.

In 1926 the regional offices of the U.S. Forest Service were requested to inventory possible National Forest wilderness areas. These regional surveys served as the basis for the Secretary of Agriculture's Regulation L–20, issued in 1929. This regulation authorized the establishment of "primitive areas" and set up the basic policies under which these areas were to be managed. However, it did not give permanence to these areas

Figure 18-1 Mt. Moran; wilderness zone in Grand Teton National Park. (Photo by Alan Jubenville)

inasmuch as the philosophy underlying the basic policies was "in primitive areas, as elsewhere in the National Forests, the principle of highest use will prevail." In fact, Regulation L–20 appeared to have deeply rooted utilitarian undertones indicative of the era.

Shortly after the establishment of Regulation L–20, Robert Marshall, a young advocate of wilderness preservation, defined what he thought to be a true wilderness and suggested that a study should be made to determine the roadless recreational needs of the country and to establish a system of such opportunities.

Concern over the perpetuity of the primitive areas established under Regulation L–20 prompted Marshall to urge the development of new federal regulations which would provide greater protection for wilderness-type areas. This protection was later provided by regulations U–1, U–2, and U–3, which were adopted by the U.S. Forest Service in 1939. The classification and reclassification of areas under those regulations was a slow and difficult process—a process which was interrupted by World War II. However, these regulations were later to become the basis of the federal legislation on wilderness preservation.

During the 1950s, many people became interested in wilderness preservation. Public interest, aroused by the Wilderness Society, Sierra Club, and other special interest groups, resulted in several wilderness bills being offered to Congress. The first of these bills was proposed in 1956. The fight for this legislation was arduous and time-consuming. Finally, in 1964, this fight climaxed in the passing of the Wilderness Act (P.L. 88–577).

This brief history brings the problem to that point in time at which wilderness-type areas are allocated and protected by federal legislation under the Wilderness Act. Significant during this period is an increasing awareness of the sociological and psychological attributes of wilderness recreation. The basic philosophy underlying the Act is "to secure for the American people of present and future generations the benefits of an enduring resource of wilderness." [24] This phrase indicates three important aspects of the current wilderness philosophy: (1) use, (2) perpetuity, and (3) recognition of the wilderness as a resource.

The greatest problem since the Wilderness Act has been a lack of interest from the agencies in planning and management of the wilderness experience. Some people have suggested that the lack of planning for each area has been a result of the infatuation with developing a total system. If this charge were true, agencies would at least be attempting to develop a variety of roadless recreation experiences to balance the system.

USE AND CAPACITY

Three factors should be considered: type of user (background and perceptions), quality of use (types and effects of depreciative behavior), and carrying capacity (integrity of the social and physical aspects of the experience).

Type of User. There are different types of roadless area users. Some are seeking solitude in a vast, pristine environment, whereas others may seek simple respite from the automobile and the highly developed landscape in a small, primitively developed, roadless landscape. Thus, the type of user (based on the type of experience he is seeking), his relative participation, his resident location, and travel norms should be considered in apportioning roadless landscapes for various recreational experiences.

The types of users will vary somewhat for a given type of roadless experience. These variations should be accounted for in the planning process in order to provide the appropriate experience, minimize conflict, and protect the resource. These variations may include mode of travel, size of party, length of stay, activity participation, and travel behavior. [11]

Quality of Use. Quality of use is a variable that is important but difficult to control through site planning. Filtering and separating users through the experience buffer and certain types of pychological barriers may increase quality of use relative to the experience being offered. De-

Figure 18–2 Fishing Lake Ervin in Colorado. Fishing is a primary wilderness activity. (Photograph by Colorado Game, Fish, and Parks Department.)

preciative behavior is not simply contained by separating people according to the types of recreational experiences they are seeking; however, it may reduce the problem, or make it easier to manage. Education and law enforcement can also reduce depreciative behavior, but these are primarily management programs.

Carrying Capacity.   The definition of carrying capacity is based on the traditional definition presented in Chapter 5. A more advanced theory presented by Frissel and Stankey[5] suggests that there are limits of acceptable change and that we should plan and manage the roadless areas within these limits. These limits must be established both for the ecological and sociological qualities of the area. The theory recognizes the inevitability of change wherever recreational use occurs and seeks to establish constraints on the definition of these acceptable changes. A primary constraint is the management objective in terms of the recreational opportunity for the particular roadless area. Within that context, there are four discrete points along the continuum of roadless recreation opportunities: quasi-wilderness, wildland, backcountry, and wilderness.

TYPES OF ROADLESS RECREATION EXPERIENCES

The following are a series of continuums to describe in general terms the four roadless recreation opportunities:

TABLE 18–1 QUALITIES THAT DESCRIBE THE FOUR
BASIC TYPES OF ROADLESS OPPORTUNITIES

		Roadless Opportunities			
Qualities of Roadless Areas	Direction	Quasi-Wilderness	Wildland	Backcountry	Wilderness
Level of use	Decreasing				
Opportunity for solitude	Increasing				
Size of area	Increasing				
Access	Decreasing				
Level of development	Decreasing				
Mode of travel	More primitive				
Character of landscape	More primitive				

In the past, an individual may have sought a wilderness experience as a best substitute, yet he may have been more satisfied in a general wildland setting. Types of roadless experiences other than wilderness have not been well developed, or have been informationally unavailable to the user.

Quasi-Wilderness. The quasi-wilderness hiking experience is probably one of the most difficult recreational activities to define. The definition of the experience will vary from region to region, according to the socioeconomic and cultural background and previous experiences of the user. While an exacting definition seems impossible, there are some general descriptions that most people will agree with, such as: (1) roadless, (2) opportunity for privacy, (3) free of motorized traffic, (4) primitive development, (5) reasonable trail access, (6) relatively close to the population, and (7) protection of the character of the landscape. A pristine environment and vast acreages of land are not included as important facets of the quasi-wilderness experience. Thus, the opportunities need not be limited to particular geographical regions of the United States.

The idea is to offer trail opportunities beyond the high density, developed recreational site. We have viewed wilderness as a singular opportunity, yet it appears to be a perceptual phenomenon or a frame of mind. To some, this opportunity may be a reclaimed railroad bed screened by evergreen plantings; to others, a one hundred-acre stand of timber with a well-planned trail system and primitive developments such as pit toilets and fireplaces. A hike-in campground about a half-mile from the road might be another type of quasi-wilderness experience. A person, regardless of age, can enjoy this roadless experience as a respite from the highly developed landscape and the automobile by having his camping equipment "delivered." Perhaps a person dressed as a mountain man delivers and returns camping equipment to a predetermined tent site on a twice-a-day schedule, using a small burro pack train. Paramount to his notion of quasi-wilderness is the acceptance of some site modification, including hardening the site through facility development as long as the developments are minimal and blend with the landscape.

If we judiciously search for those remnants of undeveloped open space, we may be able to provide quasi-wilderness experiences within the urban landscape. Or through our infatuation with recreational technology, we may completely eliminate or severely restrict an important segment of the recreational user population—the hiker.

Wildland. "Wildland" is a term used to describe relatively undeveloped lands in the nonurban landscape which have at least partially maintained their wild character. The Bureau of Outdoor Recreation's class III lands, natural environment, generally correspond to the wildland classification, but only for those roadless portions that are dedicated to carefully controlled development and limited vehicular use (Fig. 18–3).

These lands are most likely larger, more wild, and more isolated than the quasi-wilderness. The trails offer more of a challenge to the user and more opportunity for privacy. Less emphasis is placed on development, yet primitive development is a prime consideration. Perhaps if the area is wild in character but not large in size, the primitive development may be eliminated or restricted to certain zones.

The type of primitive development is generally limited to hike-in campsites, trails, and skiing. Administrative facilities and horse-use facilities may also be desirable. Vehicle use should be limited to special access corridors for off-road vehicles and designated trails for trail-bikes. These areas, in contrast to backcountry and wilderness areas, are more temporal, or the trail use is limited to a specific corridor where other less compatible land uses occupy essentially the same land base.

Backcountry. Lands and waters which are roadless, have maintained their wild, pristine character, and are large enough to provide a feeling of solitude by separation and dispersal of visitors qualify as backcountry areas. Generally, the difference between backcountry and wilderness is that backcountry management allows minimal primitive development to accommodate the visitor and for administrative purposes and other types of resource manipulations, such as encouraging more natural horsefeed, bridging unsafe water crossings, establishing emergency telephone systems and managing human waste disposal. There is still a tremendous variation in the types of experiences: pioneer areas, hiking areas, horse-use areas, and so on.

Historically, the term "backcountry" has been an administrative designation. Because of lack of concern for this type of roadless experience, most roadless areas suitable for backcountry recreation have been slowly reduced in size as other land uses invaded the areas. Thus, although not intended, most of the present backcountry areas are much smaller than wilderness areas.

This type of area needs to be recognized, planned, and managed if planners are to provide a balance in roadless experiences. Without this balance, they will create more impact on the existing wilderness resources, which will degrade the environment, the wilderness experience, and offer a less than satisfying experience to those who are seeking only minimal solitude and primitive development for their convenience.

Wilderness.   According to the Wilderness Act of 1964, wilderness is defined as:

> A wilderness, in contrast with those areas where man and his own works dominate the landscape, is hereby recognized as an area where the earth and its community of life are untrammeled by man, where man himself is a visitor who does not remain. An area of wilderness is further defined to mean in this Act an area of undeveloped Federal land retaining its primeval character and influence, without permanent improvements or human habitation, which is protected and managed so as to preserve its natural conditions and which (1) generally appears to have been affected primarily by the forces of nature, with the imprint of man's work substantially unnoticeable; (2) has outstanding opportunities for solitude or a primitive and unconfined type of recreation; (3) has at least five thousand acres of land or is of sufficient size as to make practicable its preservation and use in an unimpaired condition; and (4) may also contain ecological, geological, or other features of scientific, educational, scenic, or historical value.[24]

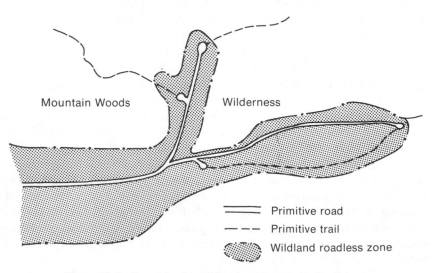

Mountain Woods   Wilderness

———— Primitive road
— — — Primitive trail
🌫️ Wildland roadless zone

Figure 18–3   Example of a wildland roadless recreational zone.

Thus, wilderness is a pristine environment that is managed for solitude and unconfined types of recreation, and where permanent site development is not allowed. The management is strictly visitor management—to manipulate visitor use to protect the integrity of the resource and the primitive recreational experience. The only allowable development is the trail head and the trail system. Thus, the planning tool is the trail, its character and location, since most wilderness travel is by trail.

Even in wilderness recreation, there is an opportunity to offer a varied experience. The first step is to zone by levels of trail development, as in the Grand Teton National Park Master Plan (Figure 18–4). People can seek out the level of wilderness use that is most satisfying. The small number of trails and the more primitive character of those trails tends to segregate use based on people's perception of a wilderness experience. Furthermore, this segregation should ensure that the ultimate in wilderness experience (maximum solitude) will remain a viable recreational opportunity. However, when certain people are psychologically forced out of the wilderness, other less challenging roadless opportunities should be made available.

Trail Planning and Primitive Development

The access road to the trail head should give a transition to the roadless experience—an experience buffer. Ideally, the transition goes from high density travel route to medium density and then to low density, nonhardened surface, terminal access road with very minimal development leading to the trail head.

Trail Heads. The trail head should be at a flat, well-drained location at the road terminus. A small loop with angle parking at the road terminus will facilitate vehicular traffic movement. Minimal trail head facilities should include parking, rustic parking barrier, registration station, comfort station, and the beginning of the trail system. If horse use is to be encouraged, then a loading ramp, small holding corral, and truck parking will be necessary. Also, a stream should be nearby to be used in watering the livestock.

Types of Trails. There are three types of trails:

1. *Primary Trails.* Primary trails are those that are continuous through routes that originate at the trail head. These are primarily for directing people through an area while promoting a certain type of experience. Ideally the primary trails are located in the most stable environs, yet they give the visitor a variety of visual and physical experiences as he passes along the trail. This type of trail should never pass through a point of visitor concentration.

2. *Secondary Trails.* These are shorter and used to connect pri-

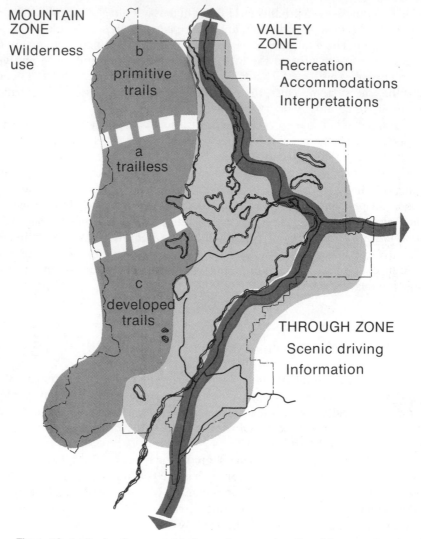

MOUNTAIN ZONE

Wilderness use

b primitive trails

a trailless

c developed trails

VALLEY ZONE

Recreation
Accommodations
Interpretations

THROUGH ZONE

Scenic driving
Information

Figure 18-4 Zoning for recreational experiences, primarily wilderness. (Developed from Department of the Interior, National Park Service.)

mary trails, or are smaller, secondary branchings of primary trails. They encourage movement between two primary trails or facilitate dispersal of use through secondary branching (Figure 18–5). They may originate at a trail head if the purpose is to facilitate movement to the primary trail.

3. *Spur Trails.* These are trails that lead from primary or secondary trails to points of visitor interests—overlooks, campsites, or day-use activity space. These are usually very short, varying from a few yards to as

much as one-half mile or more. This length should reduce social encounters along the trail by moving people off the trail when they stop to enjoy a particular attraction. Also, it reduces social encounters at points of interest (an overlook, a mountain meadow, a mountain lake, etc.) by moving through traffic away from these. However, the attractions should be made visually accessible from the primary trail, if for nothing more than a fleeting glance through intervening vegetation. Otherwise, curiosity about what is at the end of the spur may become an attraction in itself.

Character of the Trail.   Since most people travel in roadless areas via trails, the character of the trail is important because it connotes the type of experience being offered. It is impossible to establish standards for wilderness and other types of trails in roadless areas. However, by defining what is not appropriate, one should have a greater sense of what is important in trail design. Why should trail standards be the same in the wilderness as those used in the quasi-wilderness, or elsewhere? Shouldn't there be different standards that are more aligned with the setting and the particular experience? If one looks at the question from a negative perspective, wilderness trails should not be six feet wide with a five per cent gradient and cleared of all obstacles to visitor travel, as many of them are! Narrow, winding trails with steeper gradient changes would be more appropriate. Uncertainties, risks, and physical obstacles are a part of the wilderness game, but the basic safety of the visitor cannot be overlooked. General statements for other types of roadless experiences could be formulated, depending on the particular circumstances involved.

Location of the Trail.   Trails should be oriented to road access because people travel to the area in their personal vehicles. As one leaves the trail head, the route should follow a course that immediately masks the trall head or other developments. These developments may reappear in the

Secondary connecting trails
▬▬▬▬ Primary trails
───── Secondary trails
● Trail heads
─ ─ ─ ─ Roadless boundary

Between primary trails   Trail heads to primary trail

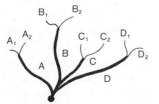

Dichotomous secondary
 branching, dendritic configuration

Continuous linear secondary
 branching, dendritic configuration

distant viewing zone; however, if they are small enough and blend with the landscape, they should not appear as incongruent elements.

Once into the area, the trail should be located to give a variety of visual experiences, as discussed in Chapter 12. All of the life zones should be visually accessible along the trail not only because of the variation in landscape, but also to give the visitor an appreciation and possible understanding of the complexity and interrelationships of the various ecological communities. Also, the trail corridor should be chosen to give a variation in gradient in order to present a physical challenge commensurate with the recreational experience. If possible, a panoramic view of the area or some major portion along the first part of the trail may give better orientation and a greater choice of travel alternatives to the visitors.

The time/distance factors of travel must be considered in the actual trail layout. If people are seeking to travel long distances and stay long periods of time, the location of the trail system should reflect this behavior. However, a system that is designed that way but receives mainly short distance, week-end use, may prove very dissatisfying. In sum, the location of a trail system reflects the time/distance travel behavior of the visitor so that there is minimal disruption of the normal travel behavioral patterns.

Also, the ecological durability of the area for recreational use should be surveyed to determine the potentially stable corridors for the trails. Each potential corridor, or segments thereof, should be appraised for its scenic qualities and access to points of visitor interests. This way, one can integrate resource and social concerns to determine the best locations of trails. Even then, there may be a need for some minor changes to avoid small unstable locales (landslides, erosion problems, and so on) and ecologically sensitive eco-units (meadows, rare flora or fauna, or shoreline around high mountain lakes).

Trail Systems.   Historically there has been no trail system planning. Most of the existing trails in roadless areas are early access trails for fire patrolling, with possibly some rerouting at critical points. These trails may have facilitated fire fighting; however, they have often tended to create undesirable travel patterns and to increase visitor contact, site deterioration, and conflict between foot, horse, and trail bike users.

In planning, one must examine the specific *purposes* of a trail system for a roadless area, using the following general categories:

1. *Facilitate Movement Within the Roadless Area.*   The type and character of the trail may vary considerably; nevertheless, when the planner puts in a trail, the basic intention is to facilitate movement along a ribbon to points of visitor interest. Furthermore, the idea is to facilitate movement through the area and allow a return to the trail head with a minimum of route retracing, taking into account the normal travel patterns of the various types of visitors. If the planner does not account for normal travel patterns, he may create similar problems, as with the older fire trails.

For example, if much of the use is from day users along the fringe of the roadless area, then the trail system should include more trails of a shorter length, perhaps one-way loops to minimize contact.

2. *Enhance the Appropriate Experience of the User.* The use of the trail should be part of the total recreational experience. The amount of use, the types of users, and the quality and variety of scenery encountered along the trail should affect the quality of experience one receives. These factors can be somewhat controlled in the planning process by the type, character, and location of the trail, as discussed earlier in this chapter.

3. *Separate Incompatible Trail Uses.* The planner must recognize potential incompatible trail use: large versus small parties; horse versus foot use; motorized versus nonmotorized; wilderness purist versus non-purist; and so on. The first step is to recognize the potential incompatibility and second, to design a trail system that minimizes the conflict or improves the managment of such conflicts.

4. *Protect the Resource Base.* The quality of the resource base is important and should be maintained. A survey of the various vegetation types should be made, along with an assessment of the ability of these types to sustain certain kinds of recreational use. The less stable areas should then be bypassed and perhaps made visually accessible to the trail user. It becomes a difficult situation to manage if the trail leads to or through places that are highly sensitive to recreational use or are environmentally unstable.

Within the context of the preceding purposes, there are three main types of trail systems:

1. *Singular Trail System.* Singular trails are those that are designed for a single type of trail use or an acceptable mix of uses. Where the types of users and use patterns are compatible, a singular trail system may be sufficient, particularly if use is low. Most existing trail systems are in this category and are consequently difficult to manage, since there are only minimal means of separating uses, reducing visitor contact, and so on.

2. *Dual Trail System.* The dual trail system has separate trails for the primary user groups. This way, the planner can separate the primary user groups and develop separate resource and visitor management programs. Most likely this method creates a tremendous ecological and visual impact that may be unnecessary.

3. *Combination Trail System.* If the planner has a sufficient inventory of the resource and visitor behavior patterns, he should be able to develop a trail system that is a combination of singular and dual systems. It should be a primarily singular system but with segments of a dual system at critical points. For example, the East Fork of the Bitterroot Trail in the Anaconda-Pintlar Wilderness receives heavy day use hiking for the first two miles. This segment also receives heavy through horse use. Since the horse user is merely passing through the area, a second trail that bypasses

the first two miles and then connects to the main East Fork Trail would possibly eliminate conflict, enhance the experience, and improve the management of the trail use. The same approach could be used where resource deterioration might occur.

There are three trail system configurations:

1. *Linear*.   A linear configuration is one that has all separate primary trails and no secondary trails, except an occasional connecting one. Each primary trail starts from a separate trail head and returns to that point. It may be continuous, such as a circular route, or a discontinuous one that leads to a given point.

 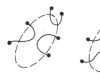 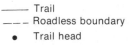

Linear, continuous,
one trail head

Linear, continuous,
two trail heads

Linear, discontinuous

The discontinuous linear trail may be used where intervening topography may limit access to a narrow corridor. Or it may be used where the amount of visitor use is not important, there is limited stable soil conditions for developing trails, and the travel distance to the point of interest is reasonably short. One other possible application is in a large roadless area where the emphasis is on recreational activities away from the trail. This is commonly called "zone use," as opposed to the typical trail use (activities participated along or near the trail). The linear trail allows people to move into the area and then disperse off the trail into a given zone or zones, rather than moving through zones that are already occupied.

The continuous type with one trail head is appropriate for small watersheds, to move people through the area, to give them a range of visual and physical experiences, and to minimize visitor contact by appropriate one-way trail zoning. The continuous type with two trail heads is more appropriate where the headwaters of two small elongated watersheds are contiguous. The trail leads from trail head A up watershed A and over the divide to watershed B and returns to trail head B.

2. *Trellis*.   The trellis pattern is a main through route (primary trail) with secondary trails leading to or from the primary trail. This pattern is typical of areas that have major topographic features such as a backbone of a mountain or elongated river system along which the primary trail is oriented. For small areas, a trellis pattern with secondary trails leading to points of interest may create more of an illusion of size and privacy, provided people do not mind medium levels of use on the primary trail.

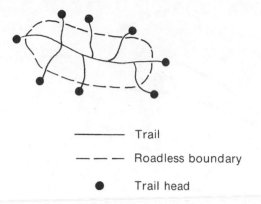

——————— Trail

— — — — Roadless boundary

●   Trail head

For a large area, the trellis pattern may work well if the users are seeking to travel into the interior of the area and spend considerable time. If people are going to travel only short distances and stay short periods of time on the secondary trails, then according to the criterion of behavior, these are linear trails, as previously discussed. And they should have been designed as linear trails. The new configuration would be a trellis trail system having a few secondary trails leading to the primary through route, and several separate linear trails.

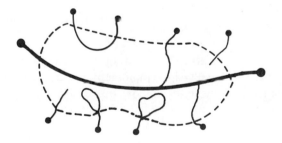

Combination of trellis and linear patterns

3. *Dendritic*. The dendritic pattern is somewhat fan-shaped, a pattern in which several major trails essentially have a common point of origin. This is typically used where you have limited access into a major watershed; the trail leads upstream and then branches into several primary trails. One or two of the trails may extend, through the limited access points across the watershed divide, to connect other trails in the next watershed.

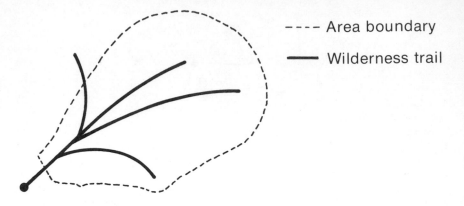

Dendritic pattern

The dendritic pattern is a good way of dispersing use rather than concentrating on a single through route. It can provide better utilization of space while maintaining reasonable privacy for the user. Also, this pattern leaves more options open to the manager in terms of visitor and resource management. One can use a rest and rotation system on the trails to allow natural rejuvenation of the various points of visitor concentration. Or one can separate and disperse potentially conflicting uses, such as horse use and hiking, and still make the watershed available to both of them.

MANAGEMENT BY DESIGN

The planning concepts presented in this chapter should help to minimize the face-to-face visitor management, a minimization that is necessary to maintain the integrity of the roadless experience and the ecology of the area. The following list is a summary of those concepts:

1. *Total Roadless System.* A variety of roadless experiences is necessary to offer the visitor a choice in selecting the one that is most satisfying to him. This choice should help to disperse use voluntarily and thus reduce social and ecological impact.

2. *Information System.* Wilderness areas have received much national and regional attention, whereas many intermediate roadless opportunities, where they have been developed, have not been well advertised. Consequently, many wilderness areas have become overused and the intermediate areas, lightly used. In fact, many people have chosen less than satisfying experiences because of the informational voids. If a variety of opportunities is to be offered, the potential user population should be made aware of them so its members may choose the most appropriate experience to meet their needs.

3. *Area Planning.*   Roadless planning should be incorporated into the *recreational area planning,* as discussed in Chapter 10. All land uses in the area can have an effect on each other; consequently, the area plan should attempt to coordinate uses and minimize possible conflict. For example, an auto campground developed at the trail head to a roadless area may cause an unnecessary and undesirable increase in use of the trail system and greater impact on the resource than would ordinarily be expected. Furthermore, this type of development may disrupt the transition from intensive development to the roadless experience. Thus, all development should be properly located through the area planning process, or conflict and confusion may occur.

4. *Boundary Location.*   One of the primary management problems is improperly located boundaries. If the boundaries are not properly located, it is difficult to maintain the ecological integrity of the area, reduce visual intrusions, and manage vehicular use. The boundaries should generally follow the hydrographic divide to maintain an easily identifiable and easily managed boundary—to protect the resource, minimize visual intrusions, and manage off-road vehicle use. However, it may be more ideal to include total life zones as they encircle a major topographic feature, rather than to disrupt them along a single hydrographic boundary. This procedure will ensure protection of the contiguous watersheds in a single topographic unit (Figure 18–6).

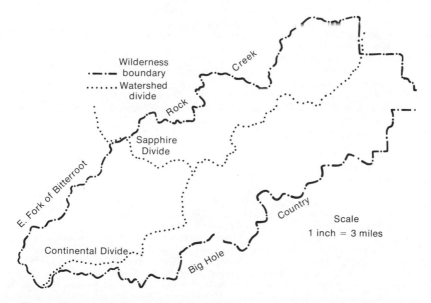

Figure 18–6 The Anaconda-Pintlar Wilderness, a roadless area. The boundary encircles the major physiographic units.

Figure 18–6, the Anaconda-Pintlar Wilderness, is an example of a boundary that encircles the major physiographic unit, the Pintlar Range at its intersection with the Sapphire Range. The three major watersheds are protected from their headwaters downstream to the foothills' physiographic province. The boundary is then located along the hydrographic boundaries of the secondary streams at the point where they enter the main drainage basins.

5. *Types and Location of Facilities.* The trail is the focal point of management; as shown in the previous parts of this chapter, the character, location, distance, and geometric design of the trails can assist in dispersal of use—directing use to the more stable areas, reducing visitor contact, and separating potentially conflicting use, while providing an interesting and varied experience for the individual.

One of the common problems of managing roadless areas has been eliminating the motorized visitor. Appropriate location of the boundary can minimize the problem, and appropriate trail design can effectively eliminate it. Natural obstacles such as rock outcroppings, dense timber, or steep topography can be used effectively to eliminate the off-road vehicle user. Perhaps a steep trail with sharp switchbacks can cause the trail biker to reassess his motives and choose a less difficult trail opportunity.

SELECTED READINGS

1. Brandborg, S. M. 1968. "The Wilderness Law and the National Park Service." The Wilderness Society (unpublished manuscript).
2. Burch, W. R., Jr. 1966. "Wilderness—The Life Cycle and Forest Recreational Choice," *Journal of Forestry,* 64(9): 606–610.
3. Burke, H. D. 1969. "Wilderness Engenders New Management Traditions," *The Living Wilderness,* 3:9–13.
4. Cowan, I.M. 1968. *Wilderness—Concept, Function, and Management.* VIII Horace M. Albright Conservation Lectureship. Berkeley, California: School of Forestry and Conservation, University of California.
5. Frissell, S. S., Jr., and G. H. Stankey. 1972. "Wilderness Environmental Quality: Search for Social and Ecological Harmony," *Proceedings of the Society of American Foresters.* pp. 170–183.
6. Gould, E. M., Jr. 1975. "Wilderness: What Are the Opportunities," *Journal of Forestry,* 73(1): 8–11.
7. Hendee, J. C., W. R. Catton, Jr., L. D. Marlow, and C. F. Brockman. 1968. *Wilderness Users of the Pacific Northwest: Their Characteristics, Values, and Management Preferences.* U. S. Forest Service Research Paper PNW–61.
8. Hendee, J. C. , and R. W. Harris. 1970. "Foresters' Perception of Wilderness User Attitudes and Preferences," *Journal of Forestry,* 68(12): 759–762.
9. Hendee, J. C., and R. C. Lucas. 1973. "Mandatory Wilderness Permits: A Necessary Management Tool," *Journal of Forestry,* 71(4): 206–209.
10. Jubenville, A. 1971. "A Test of Differences Between Wilderness Recreation Party Leaders and Party Members," *Journal of Leisure Research,* 3(2): 116–119.
11. ———— . 1970. "Travel Patterns of Wilderness Users in the Anaconda-Pintlar Wilderness." University of Montana (unpublished Ph. D. dissertation).
12. Koehler, B. N. 1972. "An Evaluation of Wilderness Potential of Sixteen Areas in the Medicine Bow National Forest." University of Wyoming (unpublished master's thesis).
13. Lucas, R. C., 1971. "Hikers and Other Trail Users," *Recreation Symposium Proceed-*

       ings. W. T. Doolittle and R. E. Getty (eds.). Syracuse, New York: U. S. Forest
       Service.

14. _____ . 1971. "Natural Amenities, Outdoor Recreation and Wilderness," *Ecology, Economics, Environment*. R. W. Behan and R. M. Weddle (eds.). Missoula, Montana: Montana Forest and Conservation Experiment Station, University of Montana.

15. _____ . 1973. "Wilderness: A Management Framework," *Journal of Soil and Water Conservation*, 28(4): 150–154.

16. Mills, A.U. 1968. "Back Country and the Hand of Man." Region 1, U. S. Forest Service (unpublished manuscript).

17. Montana Wilderness Association. 1970. "Wilderness Guidelines—An Aid for Citizens in the Evaluation of Wilderness," Montana Wilderness Association.

18. National Park Service. 1972. *Master Plan: Grand Teton National Park, Wyoming*.

19. Outdoor Recreation Resources Review Commission. 1962. *Wilderness and Recreation: A Report On Resources, Values, and Problems*. O.R.R.R.C. Report No. 3 Washington, D. C.: U. S. Government Printing Office.

20. Snyder, A. P. 1966. "Wilderness Management—A Growing Challenge," *Journal of Forestry*, 64(7): 441–446.

21. Spurr, S. H. 1966. *Wilderness Management*. VI Horace M. Albright Conservation Lectureship. Berkeley, California: School of Forestry and Conservation, University of California.

22. Stankey, G. H. 1971. "Myths in Wilderness Decision-Making," *Journal of Soil and Water Conservation*, 26(5): 183–188.

23. _____ . 1973. *Visitor Perception of Wilderness Recreation Carrying Capacity*. U. S. Forest Service Research Paper INT–142.

24. U. S. Congress. 1964. "Wilderness Act, P.L. 88–577."

25. U. S. Forest Service. 1970. *Beyond Road's End: Wilderness*. Wilderness Workshop, Region 1, U. S. Forest Service.

26. _____ . 1968. *Management Direction: Wilderness And Primary Recreation Zones*. Pacific Northwest Region, U. S. Forest Service.

27. Wagar, J. A. 1964. *The Carrying Capacity of Wild Lands for Recreation*. Forest Science Monograph No. 7.

28. Wenger, W. D., Jr. 1964. *A Test of Unmanned Registration Stations on Wilderness: Factors Influencing Effectiveness*. U. S. Forest Service Research Paper PNW–16.

29. Wilen, H. G. 1974. "Wilderness Redefined," *American Forests*, 80(5): 16–19.

PART 5

PLANNING INFORMATION PORTFOLIO

This part of the book is a collection of planning material to give the reader greater insight into the planning process at all levels of government and the private sector. This anthology is important because it attempts to bridge theory, principles, and concepts of outdoor recreation planning to real situations.

It is desirable for the student and the working professional to relate to the experience of others, to test their own "wings" at planning, and where necessary to tear down old theories and concepts and rebuild them. Most people respond to new situations and new ideas if they have something real and concrete to grasp. Hopefully these selections will provide the concreteness and stimulation to plan for the future, using the ideas and information developed in the preceding parts and tempering them with good judgment and imagination.

The selections cover the basic levels of planning, from nationwide to state, to area and site planning. A suitability/feasibility study form is included, as well as an attitude-interest-behavior questionnaire used for assessing leisure needs.

SELECTION A

DETAILED OUTLINE OF THE NATIONWIDE OUTDOOR RECREATION PLAN*

I. INTRODUCTION
    A. Recreation in America. (Brief statement on the expanding interest in the use of leisure over the last decade.)

        1. The rationale for recreation.
            a. What it does for people.
            b. Recreation as a public good.
        2. Recreation boom of the 1960s and prospect for the 1970s.
        3. Changing recreation patterns in the United States.
        4. Recreation as a creative public program.
        5. Recreation as a major partner in resource management.
        6. Recreation as a shaper of land use.

    B. Why a Nationwide Plan for Outdoor Recreation?

        1. Need for a centralized evaluation of recreation, with focus on its problems and a forecast of the future—a national overview.
        2. Need for a framework from which a coordinated effort at problem solving can emanate.

---

*This selection has been derived from a mimeographed planning outline by Bureau of Outdoor Recreation.

    3.   Need for a communication mechanism.

    4.   A basis for the policy-goal-setting process.

    5.   Framework within which federal programs will be developed and managed.

    6.   Guidance to states, their political subdivisions, private organizations, groups, enterprises, and individuals.

C.   Background and Authority for the Plan.

    1.   Outdoor Recreation Resources Review Commission.

    2.   Pertinent sections of Public Law 88–29.

    3.   Other federal laws requiring conformance with plan.

D.   Nature of the Plan.

    1.   Plan theme

        a.   Provision of recreation opportunities and services (areas, facilities, and programs) to people.

        b.   Recreation as a shaper of land use.

        c.   Both services and recreation land use to be discussed in terms of central cities, suburbs and fringe, small cities, countryside, and special recreation resource areas.

    2.   Plan approach.

        a.   Use of the problem/solution technique, with focus on a number of selected problem areas.

        b.   Ranking of alternative solutions by priority in terms of cost effectiveness where feasible.

        c.   The Bureau of Outdoor Recreation will consult with other federal agencies, states, and their political subdivisions, and with representatives of conservation and recreation groups and the private sector concerning their views on recreation problems and programs.

    3.   Definition and scope.

        a.   Definition—"Outdoor recreation" includes active and passive leisure-time activities which normally occur out-of-doors, whether in urban, rural, man-made, or natural environments. The activities are of a pleasurable nature, excluding work and life- or home-support activities.

        b.   Scope.

            (1)   The scope of the plan will be broad but not exhaustive, embracing a diversity of programs and needs.

            (2)   The plan will cover the roles and responsibilities of the several levels of government as well as the contributions which private profit and nonprofit

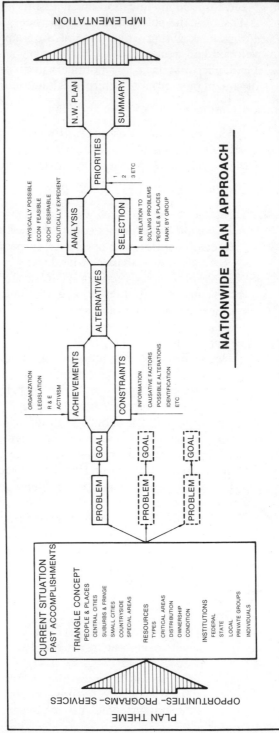

NATIONWIDE PLAN APPROACH

recreation and socially oriented interests can make to meeting outdoor recreation needs.

(3) The plan will identify and assess the impact of outdoor recreation on individuals, society, and the environment.

(4) The plan will identify methods and actions necessary to optimize the use of recreation resources as a means of achieving effective and full creative use of available recreation time out-of-doors. It will also identify means of protecting and enhancing recreation resources.

(5) The plan will deal with environments as they relate to leisure-time recreation activities.

(6) A major thrust of the plan will be directed toward the provision of recreation opportunities close to where people live and work.

E. Highlights. (Brief statement of across-the-board findings and conclusions that should be highlighted; acts as a bridge to what follows.)

II. SUMMARY OF FINDINGS AND ALTERNATIVE SOLUTIONS TO PROBLEMS

The role and responsibilities of the federal, state, and local governments and private groups and individuals will be summarized as they relate to basic findings, in respect to each of the following areas:

A. General.

B. Central Cities.

C. Suburbs and Fringe.

D. Small Cities.

E. Countryside.

F. Special Recreation Resource Impact Areas.

III. BACKGROUND

A. Accomplishments to Date. (Brief discussion of benchmark events by general, federal, state, local, and private groups and individuals over the past ten years, such as but not limited to:)

1. Outdoor Recreation Resources Review Commission and the establishment of the Bureau of Outdoor Recreation.

    2. Land and Water Conservation Fund.
    3. Special legislation, e.g., rivers, trails, etc.
    4. President's "Legacy of Parks" program.
    5. HUD open space program.
    6. Recreation support program.
    7. New Jersey green acres program.
    8. Walt Disney World.

B. Man and His Recreation Environment: The Current Situation.

    1. The triangular relationship—a recreation overview of the nation as a system of people, resources, and institutions:
       a. As components of demand-supply relationship in outdoor recreation.
       b. The ways in which institutions use resources to provide opportunities for people.

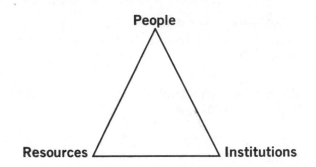

    2. People: the basis for action—describe by geographical settings (central cities, suburbs and fringe, small cities, and countryside). This section will describe briefly the general composition of the nation's population in the context of its bearing on the types of recreation services provided and its effect upon outdoor recreation participation:
       a. Socioeconomic characteristics: numbers, location, distribution, income, age, sex, education, and migration patterns.
       b. Attitudes and aptitudes.
       c. Mobility and other factors.
    3. Recreation resources: the places for action—graphically displayed and described in relation to central city, suburbs and fringe, small cities, and countryside. This section will include maps and a brief discussion of existing and potential outdoor recreation lands, waters, and facilities. Existing and potential outdoor recreation resources will be discussed in terms of capacity, location in relation

to people, access, constraints on utilization, fragility, quality, and availability.

    a. What are the resources?

      (1) General types of recreation resources.

      (2) Areas of critical concern.

    b. Distribution.

    c. Ownership.

    d. Use pressures.

    e. Resource condition.

4. Man's institutions: organizations for action—the framework within which recreation opportunities are provided. This section will include a discussion of the programs, program levels, operations, and ownership relating to existing recreation lands, waters, and facilities provided by government agencies and the private sector. Subjects covered will include: acquisition, technical assistance, grants, development, planning, programs, operations, maintenance, and credit.

    a. Institutional factors—economics, transportation, development patterns and their relationship to recreation.

    b. Federal responsibilities—programs and services.

    c. State responsibilities—programs and services.

    d. Political subdivisions of the state—programs and services.

    e. Private sector—programs and services.

      (1) Private enterprise.

      (2) Quasi-public and public groups and organizations (nonprofit).

      (3) Citizen action groups.

      (4) Families and individuals.

IV. ECONOMIC ANALYSIS

A. The Demand for Outdoor Recreation.

  1. Definitions of Outdoor Recreation.

    a. Demand = needs with no mention of price.

      (1) Assumptions of definition (implicit and explicit).

      (2) Pros and cons of definition.

    b. Economic definition (demand functions and curves).

      (1) Assumptions of definition (implict and explicit).

      (2) Pros and cons of definition.

      (3) Examples of demand functions.

        (a) Market demand function (i.e., demand

over geographic region for a particular activity).
    (b)   Site demand function (i.e., demand for a particular recreation facility).
    (c)   Demand functions by season, weekend, etc.
  c.   Difference between definitions *a* and *b*.
    (1)   Implication of budget or income constraint.
    (2)   Resource allocation implications.
2. Formulation of structure of market demand functions.
  a.   Major formulations used in past (ORRRC, Cichetti, Kalter, etc.).
    (1)   Assumptions of formulations.
    (2)   Pros and cons of formulations.
  b.   Formulation of demand function to be used in NWP.
    (1)   Assumptions of formulation (implicit and explicit).
    (2)   Pros and cons of formulation.
3. Estimation of parameters of current market demand functions.
  a.   Assumptions of methods.
  b.   Pros and cons of methods.
  c.   Data used in estimation, including assumptions and implications of data used.
  d.   Level of detail of demand estimates.
    (1)   Pros and cons of estimating.
        (a)   By activity (fishing, swimming, etc.)
        (b)   By groups of activities.
        (c)   By facilities (tennis courts, swimming pools, etc.).
        (d)   By groups of facilities (water, winter, etc.).
        (e)   By geographic region.
    (2)   Level of detail to be used in NWP estimates. (by geographic region) including reasons for level of detail.
  e.   Results of estimation of current demand functions, including comparison of results with results of other studies.
4. Site demand functions.
  a.   Previous use of site demand functions (Clawson, etc.).
  b.   Uses of site demand functions for policy purposes (especially for local policy).
    (1)   Rationing via price mechanism.
    (2)   Measurement of benefits.
    (3)   Revenue generation.

        (4) Financing operating and maintenance costs of one site with revenues generated from another site.

    c. Estimation of site demand functions.

        (1) Specific examples of site demand functions, where data allows estimation.

        (2) Apply the concepts of A.4.b.(1) through A.4.b.(4) to the specific examples.

B.   The Supply of Outdoor Recreation.

    1. Definition of supply.

       a. Number of facilities, acres, capacity, etc., and the pros and cons of each

       b. Definitions used in other studies (ORRRC, etc.).

       c. Definitions used in NWP studies.

        (1) Pros and cons of definition.

        (2) Discuss "quality" as a factor in supply.

    2. Estimation of existing supply in geographic regions.

       a. By activity or activity groups.

        (1) Percent government (federal, state, local).

        (2) Percent private.

       b. By facility or facility groups.

        (1) Percent government.

        (2) Percent private.

C.   Projections of Demand and Supply.

    1. Projection of demand.

       a. Methods of projection used in other studies (brief discussion).

       b. Methodology used to project demand in NWP.

        (1) Assumptions (implicit and explicit) of methodology.

        (2) Pros and cons of methodology used.

       c. Results of forecasts by geographic regions.

        (1) By activity or activity grouping.

        (2) By facility or facility grouping.

       d. Limitations and confidence intervals of forecasts.

    2. Projection of supply by geographic regions.

       a. By private sector.

        (1) Capital expenditures.

           (a) By activity and/or activity group.

           (b) By facility and/or facility group.

        (2) Operation and maintenance expenditures.

           (a) By activity and/or activity group.

           (b) By facility and/or facility group.

        (3)   Projected supply in units of capacity.
           (a)   By activity and/or activity group.
           (b)   By facility and/or facility group.

  b. By state and local government.
        (1)   Capital expenditures.
           (a)   By activity and/or activity group.
           (b)   By facility and/or facility group.
        (2)   Operation and maintenance expenditures.
           (a)   By activity and/or activity group.
           (b)   By facility and/or facility group.
        (3)   Projected supply in units of capacity.
           (a)   By activity and/or activity group.
           (b)   By facility and/or facility group.

  c. By federal government.
        (1)   Capital expenditures.
           (a)   By activity and/or activity group.
           (b)   By facility and/or facility group.
        (2)   Operation and maintenance expenditures.
           (a)   By activity and/or activity group.
           (b)   By facility and/or facility group.
        (3)   Projected supply in units or capacity.
           (a)   By activity and/or activity group.
           (b)   By facility and/or facility group.

  d. Total supply by geographic region.
        (1)   Capital expenditures.
           (a)   By activity and/or activity group.
           (b)   By facility and/or facility group.
        (2)   Operation and maintenance expenditures.
           (a)   By activity and/or activity group.
           (b)   By facility and/or facility group.
        (3)   Projected supply (in units of capacity), based on C.2.a.(3), C.2.b.(3), and C.2.c.(3).
           (a)   By activity and/or activity group.
           (b)   By facility and/or facility group.

  e. Limitations and confidence levels of supply projections, including implications of limitations and confidence levels.

D. Benefit/Cost Analysis.

  1. Calculate benefits from projected market demand functions.
      a. Alternative methods used to calculate benefits.
        (1)   Assumptions behind alternative methods.
        (2)   Pros and cons of alternative methods.
      b. Method of benefit calculation to be used in NWP.

      (1) By activity or activity group.

      (2) By geographic region.

  2. Calculate costs per unit of capacity.

    a. Capital costs per unit of capacity.

      (1) By type of facility.

      (2) For range of capacities.

    b. Operating costs per unit of capacity.

      (1) By type of facility.

      (2) For range of capacities.

  3. Calculation of net benefits (benefits minus costs). Net benefits will be calculated under various assumptions about the levels of economic and policy variables.

V.   CONCLUSIONS AND GENERAL PROBLEMS

Based upon the preceding assessment of people, resources, and institutions, major conclusions will be drawn and problems in meeting outdoor recreation needs will be defined. The problems will come under the following geographic areas:

A.   General.

B.   Central Cities.

C.   Suburbs and Fringe.

D.   Small Cities.

E.   Countryside.

F.   Special Recreation Resource Impact Areas.

VI.   GOALS

A.   Concepts of Goals. (A positive statement of action related to the delivery of recreation services and to recreation land use which should be considered in alleviating the problem previously defined, to provide a framework from which the recommendations of the nationwide plan will emerge.)

B.   Goal Discussion.

  1. Specific statement of each goal categorized in relation to a major problem identified in V.A.

  2. Discussion of goal in relation to:

    a. People and places.

      (1) Central city.

(2)   Suburbs and fringe.
(3)   Small cities.
(4)   Countryside.
  b.   Recreation resources.
    (1)   Special impact areas.
    (2)   Other.
  c.   Delivery of services.
  d.   Institutions.
    (1)   Federal.
    (2)   State.
    (3)   Local.
    (4)   Private.
    (5)   Citizen.

3.   Current and prospective accomplishments in relation to goal attainment by federal, state, and local governments and private groups and individuals through:
  a.   Organization/management.
  b.   Legislation.
  c.   Research.
  d.   Education.
  e.   Activism.

4.   Problems related to goal attainment (may be more than one per goal).
  a.   Statement of problem.
  b.   Background information.
  c.   Causative factors.
  d.   Isolation of factors subject to alteration.
  e.   Identification of constraints.
  f.   Alternative solutions to individual problems.

C.   Discussion of Relative Importance of Goals.

VII.   ANALYSIS OF ALTERNATIVES

A.   Scope. (Discuss selection process.)
  1.   Physically possible.
  2.   Economically feasible.
  3.   Socially desirable.
  4.   Politically expedient.

B.   Discuss Alternatives Identified in VI.B.3 and B.4 in Relation to Solving Problems and Achieving Goals. (Include the consequences and ramifications, including cost and effectiveness, where feasible, of each and analysis of compatibility with alternatives for other problem solutions.)

    C.   Group Alternatives by Priority. (Under the following relation to federal, state, local, private, and citizen:)
1. General (including international).
2. Central city.
3. Suburbs.
4. Small city.
5. Countryside.

    D.   Rank Priorities. (From priorities identified by institution in VII.C., establish comprehensive order in terms of overall importance. Assignment of responsibility will be explicit in each item.)

VIII.   NEEDS FOR FURTHER STUDY

Discussion of the kinds of analyses which need to be made. Examples may include:

    A.   Public Costs and Aggregate Value of Outdoor Recreation Resources, Areas, Facilities, and Programs.

    B.   On site Participation Observation.

    C.   Behavioral Studies. (Why do people recreate the way they do?)

    D.   Timing of Facility Provision.

    F.   Leisure Time Available for Recreation. (Measured in relation to total free time—workweek, holidays, etc., are factors to be considered.)

IX.   APPENDICES

    A.   Forum Summaries.

    B.   Economic Analysis.

SELECTION B

OUTLINE OF STATE OUTDOOR RECREATION PLAN*

Plan Requirements. The mandatory requirements for a state outdoor recreation plan are set forth in the following material. They have been arranged in a sequence and general format which the state may wish to use as a general guide.

A. *Introduction.*

(1) Statement of objectives and scope of plan.

(2) Citation of legal authority for the state to participate in the Land and Water Conservation Fund program.

(3) Designation of state agency responsible for preparation and maintenance of the state outdoor recreation plan.

(4) Certification that the plan is the state's official comprehensive outdoor recreation plan.

(5) Statement of manner in which the plan will be maintained and, as necessary, amended.

This section of the plan should establish the broad interest of state government in the provision of outdoor recreation opportunities for its citizens. The principal areas of concern to which the plan is directed should be set forth and the legal status of the plan described. The manner in which the plan will be maintained, amended, and used as a guide to state programs and activities should be stated.

---

*This material is taken from *Outdoor Recreation Grant-in-Aid Manual*. 1968. Chap. 2.

In addition, the procedures established by the state to coordinate outdoor recreation planning with that directed to related functions should be described. Cooperative arrangements among state agencies and, at the regional level, with appropriate regional and local agencies, for the common use of planning resources (funds, personnel, facilities, services, etc.) should be set forth.

B.   *Summary of Findings, Policies, and Recommendations.*

(1)   Statement of major policies and standards that will guide the state's programs and activities in outdoor recreation and environmental quality.

(2)   Recommendations for state programs, legislation, financing, coordinating mechanisms, and other actions required to implement the plan.

(3)   Recommendations regarding the respective roles of the federal government, the local units of government, and the private sector in meeting outdoor recreation and environmental quality requirements within the state.

This section should set forth the general commitment of state government to the satisfaction of outdoor recreation needs and to the preservation and enhancement of the quality of the environment. The anticipated or recommended relationship of federal, local, and private efforts in outdoor recreation and environmental quality should be generally described.

C.   *State Characteristics.*   General description of those factors, such as climate, topography, scenic resources, wildlife, history, population composition, and urbanization, which influence the character and magnitude of outdoor recreation activity within the state.

The objective of this section should be to present an overview of the physical and social characteristics of the state, highlighting those factors that relate to outdoor recreation and environmental quality.

D.   *Outdoor Recreation Inventory.*

(1)   Identification of governmental agencies (federal, state, and local) that administer significant recreation resources or programs and a statement regarding levels of responsibility and significance in meeting demands for outdoor recreation opportunities.

(2)   Aggregate listing, by planning regions and by administering jurisdiction (state, federal, and local), of lands and waters presently dedicated to outdoor recreation, including the design capacity of the areas. (States are encouraged to utilize the Bureau of Outdoor Recreation Classification System or to design an alternate system which facilitates the analysis of supply data.)

(3)   Summary evaluation of the potential of existing public lands and waters for additional development without impairment of scenic, recreational, ecological or other values.

(4)   Identification, by planning regions, of private lands and waters which presently provide significant outdoor recreation opportunities or represent an important potential for this purpose. This category might

include private forest lands, water impoundments, or shoreline. Future use and availability of these areas for recreation purposes should be analyzed.

(5) Identification of all sites within the state included in the National Register of Historic Places, areas eligible for the National Register of Natural Landmarks, areas eligible for the Register of National Historic Landmarks, as well as other areas and facilities of statewide historic significance.

(6) Identification of routes which offer significant potential for development as elements of a nationwide trail system, including:

   (a) extended routes having recreation use potential of national significance, which may be recommended for designation by Congress as National Trails;

   (b) routes within areas now under public ownership or administration in or reasonably accessible to urban areas, which will provide a variety of outdoor recreation use and which may be designated by appropriate federal agencies as part of the nationwide system;

   (c) routes of state and local significance which may be established by state and local interests on lands owned or administered by states or in or near urban areas, and which may be designated by the Secretary of the Interior as part of the nationwide system.

(7) Identification of rivers, streams, or portions thereof and related adjacent lands, which offer significant potential for conservation as elements of a nationwide system of wild or scenic rivers including:

   (a) rivers or portions thereof, and related adjacent lands having recreation and similar values of national significance, which may be recommended for designation by Congress as National Wild or scenic River Areas; and

   (b) rivers or portions thereof, and related adjacent lands having recreation and similar values of state or local significance, which may be established as wild or scenic river areas by state or local interests and which may be designated as part of the nationwide system by the Secretary of the Interior.

The inventory should represent a relatively complete catalog of the location, size, and capacity of those areas in public and private ownership which are significant in terms of providing outdoor recreation opportunities. As part of its inventory, the state should assess lands and waters whose future development presents special problems or opportunities and which should be preserved or restored in a natural state for recreational use. These might include floodplains, sharply-sloping topography, areas of poor soils, marsh and tidal areas, mined-over lands, ground water recharge areas, etc.

E.   *Demand for Outdoor Recreation Opportunities.*   Identification of existing and projected demand by major types of outdoor recreation activity. Projections must extend over at least a fifteen-year period into the future.

(1) The objectives of the demand analysis should be to secure an approximate measure of the present and projected demand for opportunities to participate in major categories of outdoor recreation, with particular emphasis on those types of activities and levels of satisfaction which fall within the responsibility and capability of the various levels of government. The projection of future demand should not be predicated solely upon present patterns of outdoor recreation use. Since present use is controlled largely by the character, amount, and location of existing recreation resources, it is not necessarily an indication of future demand. Demand studies undertaken as part of the state outdoor recreation plan should include consideration of the effect of the following factors on present and future participation rates:

    (a) socioeconomic factors, such as age, sex, family composition, and disposable income;

    (b) alternative arrangements in the availability and use of recreation resources and types of recreation activities;

    (c) user fees and charges;

    (d) technological advances, education, interpretation, and promotion; and

    (e) impact of nonresident use on recreation areas and resources. (This is particularly important when recreation areas are located in proximity to population concentrations in other states and thus are subject to continuous and intensive use by out-of-state visitors.)

(2) Demand analysis should also include recognition that the quality of the environment, while not always susceptible to quantitative measurement, is an important component of the outdoor recreation experience. Therefore, criteria should be developed to assess scenic areas, wilderness areas, scenic waterways and highways, and historical and cultural sites which are related to the quality of the environment and the enhancement of the outdoor recreation experience.

F.   *Policies, Standards, and Recommendations.*

(1) Statement of the appropriate role of the public and private sectors in meeting outdoor recreation needs; and in assuring the future quality of the environment, including:

    (a) designation of those types of outdoor recreation opportunities and aspects of environmental quality which have been determined to be the primary responsibility of state government, and the general level of demand which will be met through state programs;

    (b) statement of the goals, policies, and standards which will guide state programs and actions;

    (c) identification of specific state actions, such as legislation, new programs, financing, and allocation of federal assistance funds which are required to meet deficiencies;

    (d) designation of those types of outdoor recreation activities and aspects of environmental quality which have been determined to be the appropriate responsibility of the federal government, local units of government, and the private sector; and

(e)   recommendations regarding the level of demand to be met by other levels of government and the private sector; specific actions required to meet the level of demand, and the manner in which state government will participate, e.g., legislation, financial support, technical assistance, coordination of interagency planning, etc.

(2)   State of existing and future requirements by planning region (projected over at least a fifteen-year period into the future) for outdoor recreation lands, waters, and facilities, including:

(a)   land, water, and facility requirements related to types of outdoor recreation activities; and

(b)   requirements related to the quality of the environment.

(3)   Identification of special problems and opportunities, including recommendations for state, private, and intergovernmental actions directed to these concerns.

This section of the plan should represent the conclusions of the analysis of the entire range of factors, including supply and demand, which influence the provision of outdoor recreation opportunities within the state. The objective of this section should be to determine the types of outdoor recreation opportunities which will be provided and the general level of demand to be met; to translate activity demands into requirements for land, water, facilities, and programs; and to set forth the policies, guidelines, and specific actions which will be undertaken to meet the agreed-upon level of demand over the period of the plan.

The determination of deficiencies will necessarily involve the development and application of standards to convert activity demands into land, water, and facility requirements. The standards adopted by the state should be set forth explicitly in this section of the plan. They should reflect the acceptable level for provision of outdoor recreation opportunities to the public. Standards adopted by the state should also consider realistically the financial capability of public agencies to meet deficiencies in accordance with the standards adopted.

Consistent with the central coordination and leadership role of state government, explicit responsibilities and recommended actions should be set forth in terms of the involvement of the federal government, local units of government, and the private sector.

As a basis for the preparation of the implementation program, requirements must be identified, insofar as possible, in terms of land, water, and facilities by planning region. (The use of the Bureau of Outdoor Recreation Classification System is encouraged, but, in any case, the classification system used to express requirements should be consistent with that used in other sections of the plan.)

G.   *Implementation Program.*   Identification of state actions proposed to effectuate the policies and recommendations of the plan, including:

(1)   A detailed description of those actions which are proposed to be under-
      taken within the first five-year plan period. Actions should cover the
      entire range of measures by which the state proposes to influence the
      provision of outdoor recreation opportunities and the quality of the
      environment, including legislation, planning, technical and financial
      assistance, research and education, direct programs, intergovernmental
      coordination, etc.

(2)   A schedule of acquisition and development, with cost estimates, pro-
      posed to be undertaken within the first five-year plan period, arranged
      by planning region, unit of government, and fiscal year. This section
      must be updated annually and extended one additional year as each
      year's program is completed. It must include:

      (a)   acquisition and development proposals of the federal government
            which have a significant relation to the satisfaction of outdoor
            recreation deficiencies identified in the plan. (The state may wish
            to indicate its assessment of the priority of actions proposed and
            to elaborate its position on the timing, scale, and other aspects
            of the federal proposals);

      (b)   all acquisition and development proposals of state government
            which have a significant relation to the satisfaction of outdoor
            recreation deficiencies identified in the plan; and

      (c)   those acquisition and development proposals of local units of
            government which have a significant relation to the satisfaction
            of outdoor recreation deficiencies identified in the plan *and* which
            will be assisted by state government, either through direct state
            funding or through the allocation of the Land and Water Con-
            servation Fund assistance made available to the state.

The implementation program should provide information and direction for the orderly and coordinated execution of the plan. The program
must be related logically to results of the analysis completed as part of the
planning process and specifically correlated with the sections of the plan
which identify demands and deficiencies.

The acquisition and development schedule should represent the best
estimates the state can make of the magnitude, cost, and priority of outdoor
recreation actions that are planned in the succeeding five-year period.
Because of the requirements for annual updating, it is suggested that the
schedule be prepared as a separate plan document.

For advanced planning purposes, the state may not consider it necessary or desirable to identify proposed acquisitions and developments in
terms of specific geographic locations. The degree of detail set forth in the
schedule of acquisition and development will be dependent on capital
budgeting procedures utilized in each state. However, proposed acquisitions and developments should be identified by planning regions. Proposed
acquisition and development may be identified by general classes of recreation use or recreational resources, or both. The Bureau recognizes that
anticipated sources of financing will be estimates and therefore do not

constitute a commitment on the part of the state legislature or other governing bodies.

H.   *Appendix.*   Background studies, detailed demand and supply data, descriptions of methodology and other separate but related documents may be submitted as appendices to the state plan. A complete list of such documents should appear in the table of contents of the plan.

SELECTION C

REPORT ON THE MASTER PLAN: PARIS LANDING TENNESSEE STATE PARK

The following (excerpted) report was prepared under the auspices of the Tennessee Department of Conservation by Barge, Waggoner and Sumner, Incorporated, Nashville, Tennessee, and Miller, Wihry and Brooks, Louisville, Kentucky.

LIST OF PLANS AND CHARTS

TABLE OF CONTENTS

PURPOSE AND OBJECTIVES

Major expansion plans have been announced for Paris Landing State Park by the Tennessee Department of Conservation.

Since the impoundment of Kentucky Reservoir in 1944, the site at the west side of U. S. Highway 79 in Henry County, Tennessee, has been recognized as an area with considerable park potential. Contributing factors include the gently rolling terrain, natural harbors and a focal point of highways, making the area accessible from Paris, Clarksville, Memphis, Nashville and other cities.

Recognizing the unique advantages of the area for state park development, lease arrangements were worked out between the State and the Tennessee Valley Authority in 1945 and an attractive and popular water-oriented recreation area has been developed. While to date a boat dock, inn and swimming areas have been the principal features, an immediate development program anticipates a marina, inn expansion, family cabins, air strip, 18 hole golf course and camping facilities. Land is being acquired for the purpose and additional land will be available from the Tennessee Valley Authority.

The expansion program is being made possible with financial aid through State Bond Issues, and matching funds from the Bureau of Outdoor Recreation as well as State and Federal matching funds for recreational airports.

Impetus to the program is provided by the fact that facilities in the park could only partially meet the demands of park visitors and commencement of development of TVA's Land Between the Lakes Recreation Area immediately across Kentucky Eeservoir. This major park area, estimated to attract millions annually to outdoor-type activities, needs the support of more resort-type recreation areas in the region.

It is recognized that objectives for expansion and development plus any requests for Federal funds or land should be supported by a Master Plan. Therefore, consulting firms offering services in planning, landscape design, engineering and architecture were charged by the state with the responsibility of making specific recommendations in a master development plan and program. Purposes of the plan as presented herein are as follows:

(1) Study the feasibility of preliminary proposals for park expansion or alteration, recommending specific areas to be acquired for this purpose.

(2) Make projections on demand including the number, characteristics and needs of the people in the service area looking primarily toward the territory within a 25 mile radius; secondarily to the limits of a broader area extending 50 miles or a driving time of one hour; and finally to the needs of the traveler from the remainder of Tennessee and outside the state's borders.

(3) Translate the projected visitations according to interest and purpose into specific recreational facilities.

(4) Propose the location, type and size of additions or new improvements in a master design program based on an analysis of the site and adequacy of existing facilities.

(5) Recommend a development schedule complete with cost estimates for construction and operation.

AERIAL VIEW
PARIS LANDING PARK SITE

SUMMARY OF RECOMMENDATIONS

Studies related to the service area, access to the park and an analysis of the site itself in terms of its suitability for expansion or development to meet outdoor recreational needs show that major park expansion is feasible as well as desirable. It would provide the people of West and Middle Tennessee and visitors to the area with a complete park facility making maximum use of natural and historical features in accordance with the Department of Conservation's objectives for the provision of state parks. The following general recommendations are made to the Department in its program for park acquisition and development.

(1) Complete the acquisition program already commenced in order to consolidate lands totaling 827 acres at the park site on both sides of U. S. Route 79 on the west side of the reservoir.

(2) Relocate the main park entrance to a two-way separated drive extending from a new rotary intersection on State Route 76 (U. S. 79) to the lodge and picnic areas. Close the existing north park entrance and permit access to that side from a central control point on the south by way of a new overhead bridge crossing the main highway.

(3) Expand facilities at the boat dock in order to have a first-class marina. The marina would have a floating service building, excursion boat dock and fishing pier, a fish cleaning station and adequate launching area. Main harbor improvement plans call for 430 slips, 130 of which are covered and 200 of which will be housed in a dry storage building. The remaining 100 slips will be primarily for transient use. Long-range plans call for return to the park of the land around the north harbor previously leased by the TVA to the State (but subsequently returned to TVA) for development into a second marina, to be used to a large extent for sailing.

(4) Construct a 3900-foot airstrip following an old highway cut on the west side of the park by the Tennessee Aeronautics Commission in cooperation with the U. S. Federal Aviation Agency. Thirty "fly-in" camp sites would be provided.

(5) Provide a greatly expanded lodge including a conference center, with auditorium, meeting rooms, private dining, 140 more units with supporting swimming pool, tennis courts and transient boat dock.

(6) Add a cabin complex to be located across the estuary from the lodge with 40 rental units.

(7) Further develop the resort potential of the park by the construction of an 18 hole championship golf course, pro-shop and lighted nine-hole par three course.

(8) Picnic areas would be greatly expanded, providing for a total of 400 units in four locations, all in attractive locations near the water and easily accessible from drives and parking areas.

(9) Camping areas would be improved with 218 sites to be provided to meet special needs such as highway tourists, water front and fly-in use. Normal tent and trailer camping needs in the area will be adequately met in the Land Between the Lakes Recreation Area.

(10) The Master Plan anticipates that a park theme will be ultimately developed playing upon something unique to the area and providing a central interest feature and activity appealing to large numbers of family groups drawn to the area by Land Between the Lakes. Because of the large number of early Indian sites in the vicinity of the park, an interpretive center with the theme "Indians of

SIGN AT PARK ENTRANCE

the Tennessee Region" is proposed. Along with the center, there will be an outdoor exhibit with replicas of an Indian village, Indian agriculture, pottery making display, and tool and weapon making display. An amphitheater is included for outdoor lectures or drama. In addition, acquisition of three outlying, but related, sites are proposed to be acquired and developed in Henry, Stewart and Humphreys Counties, two of which are "Temple Mound" sites and one of which is an outstanding, but little-known, Indian Flint Quarry. It is recommended that 420 acres be acquired at these historical sites.

(11) Provide complete park service facilities including maintenance areas, superintendent's and rangers' residences, public water and sanitary service facilities.

THE PARK AND ITS SETTING

Paris Landing State Park, established in 1945 on land leased to the Tennessee Department of Conservation by the Tennessee Valley Authority, is one of the outstanding parks in the state system. Situated on the western shore of Kentucky Reservoir, the park's lodging, boating, fishing, picnicking, swimming and camping facilities were used by one-third million visitors during 1967.

Paris Landing is located almost half way between Dover and Paris in Henry County, Tennessee. It is only five miles south of the Kentucky state line and 25 miles upstream from Kentucky Dam. Nashville is 86 miles to the east and Memphis is 144 miles southwest.

The park occupies an attractive site of over 200 acres characterized by wooded slopes leading gently to the water's edge. Its accessible location at the U. S. Highway 79 crossing of the reservoir near the south entrance to Land Between the Lakes, a major national recreation center under development by TVA, provides Paris Landing with one of the most strategic locations in the park system.

Heavy demands on existing facilities, plus the evident need for additional improvements to satisfy the requirements of the people in the surrounding service area and the increasing number of tourists to the general area, have led the Department of Conservation to plan for major expansion. Largely because of the new Barkley impoundment and Tennessee Valley Authority's Land Between the Lakes 170,000 acre recreation area, the region will

experience a large influx of recreation-oriented visitors over the next 10 to 20 years. TVA has estimated that 8,000,000 visitors will come to the park by 1974 with over twice this many in the general area. Since the Land Between the Lakes Recreation Area will offer only outdoor pursuits such as camping, hiking, hunting, nature study and water sports, surrounding parks including Paris Landing might offer supporting facilities such as lodging and restaurant facilities, plus additional sports such as golf. The Park Division of the Department is in the process of acquiring 377 acres from private owners and approximately 330 additional acres from the Tennessee Valley Authority.

Existing Facilities: Present facilities include a 63-unit inn which is a rambling exposed beam lodge of contemporary but rustic design. This facility was opened in 1953, and expanded in 1958 to its present capacity. Extensive use of glass and redwood relate the structure to the expansive out-of-doors including an impressive view of the lake. All rooms are sound-proof and air-conditioned. The main dining room will accommodate 150 people; and private rooms, 250 people. Both inn and dining room are open year-round.

AERIAL VIEW OF INN

The park has an outstanding boat dock with 104 slips, only a small number of which are covered. The picnic area with 80 tables is located near the park entrance along the reservoir shoreline. Camping facilities are very limited with 100 unit spaces now available. In addition, the park offers a variety of other activities including tennis, archery, croquet, shuffleboard, badminton, horseshoe pitching, play fields and playground equipment for small children.

According to the Department of Conservation's monthly activity reports for the 1966-67 fiscal year, the following principal activity and income figures are shown:

Lodge	Participation	Income
Inn	18,936	$64,970
Restaurant	NA	72,301
Gift Shop and Concessions	NA	10,888
Boating and Fishing	48,921	16,198
Camping	14,826	4,617
Picnicking	87,771	—
Swimming	29,732	77,535
Other		
		$246,509

Physical Characteristics: Physiographically, the site is located in the East Gulf Coastal Plain. Geological formations of this province consist of loose, unconsolidated sand, clay and gravel. The Highland Rim section of the Interior Low Plateau province lies across the Tennessee River, and a few outcrops of cherty limestone prevalent on the Rim show in the park area. Loess, a mantle of windblown silt, up to six or seven feet thick in some parts of the county covers most of the park area.

The terrain is highly diversified with relief ranging from undulating to hilly or steep. Streams in the area have a comparatively steep gradient into the Reservoir. The ridge tops are well-rounded and suitable to many types of park uses.

Soils: Soils in the area are derived from three sources: the silt and clay materials of the coastal plain; the thin mantle of windblown loess; and the cherty, light textured soils from the Fort Payne formations that cover the western Highland Rim.

THE LODGE GUEST POOL

Along the stream bottoms are the Hieman and Beechy silt loams which are poorly drained bottomlands subject to flood. They consist of loessal and coastal plain materials washed from the uplands. The Freeland silt loams found on stream terraces, notably in the vicinity of the park lodge, are also alluvium-type and moderately well-drained, yellowish-brown, strongly acid and low in organic material and plant nutrients.

The higher elevations of the ridges are characterized by either the Dulac or Bodine-Ruston associations. The Dulac soils are moderately well-drained and consist of a layer of loessal or windblown silt over coastal plain material. They are also very acid and low in fertility. A strong silt pan contributes to slow subsurface drainage. The Bodine series, covering about one-fourth of the park area, or about the same as the Dulac soils, covers many of the ridge slopes. They are weathered from the cherty limestone formations and are probably least desirable from an agricultural standpoint since they are not only rocky but strongly acid and low in organic material.

Climate: The climate of this part of Tennessee is humidcontinental. It has moderate winters characterized by short, erratic cold spells, hot summers and a well distributed mean annual precipitation of 50 inches. Mean minimum temperature in January, the coldest month, is 30°F. and the mean maximum in July is 91°F. Extremes reach as high as 100°F. or as low as 0°F.

U. S. Weather Bureau records on precipitation and temperatures are available at the Paris Station:

PRECIPITATION AND MEAN TEMPERATURE
PARIS LANDING STATE PARK*

	Precipitation in inches	Temperature °F.
December	4.26	40.5
January	5.96	38.5
February	4.68	41.9
Winter	14.90	40.3
March	5.21	48.9
April	4.08	59.1
May	4.05	67.5
Spring	13.34	58.5
June	4.02	75.2
July	3.94	79.3
August	3.11	73.8
Summer	11.07	73.1
September	2.91	71.5
October	2.77	63.7
November	4.33	43.1
Fall	10.01	60.1
Annual	49.32	59.2

* Source: U. S. Weather Bureau Data from Paris Station for period through 1960. Published in Decennial Census of United States.

Plant Ecology: The native vegetation is classified as an Oak-Hickory forest and is composed of these tree species:

Predominant:

Bitternut hickory	Carya cordiformis
Snagbark hickory	Carya ovata
White oak	Quercus alba
Red oak	Quercus rubra
Black oak	Quercus velutina

Other Components:

Pignut hickory	Carya glabra
Black hickory	Carya texana
Mockernut hickory	Carya tomentosa
Green ash	Fraxinus americana
Black walnut	Juglans nigra
Black cherry	Prunus serotina
Chestnut oak	Quercus muhlenbergii
Spanish oak	Quercus falcata
Swamp oak	Quercus lyrata
Blackjack oak	Quercus marilandica
Shumard's oak	Quercus shumardii
Post oak	Quercus stellata
Basswood	Tilia americana
American elm	Ulmus americana

In addition to these tree species, grasses have been planted in some of the cleared areas of the undeveloped, recently purchased areas of the park. There are some regions that have been cultivated in the past and are now eroding quite badly. There is a ground cover of lichens over much of this eroded section which will eventually allow grasses to develop and control the erosion.

Camping facilities should be constructed on minimum slope, provided with a gravel base, covered with sand, and in turn with a thick Bermuda grass sod.

PARK POOL COMPLETED IN 1967

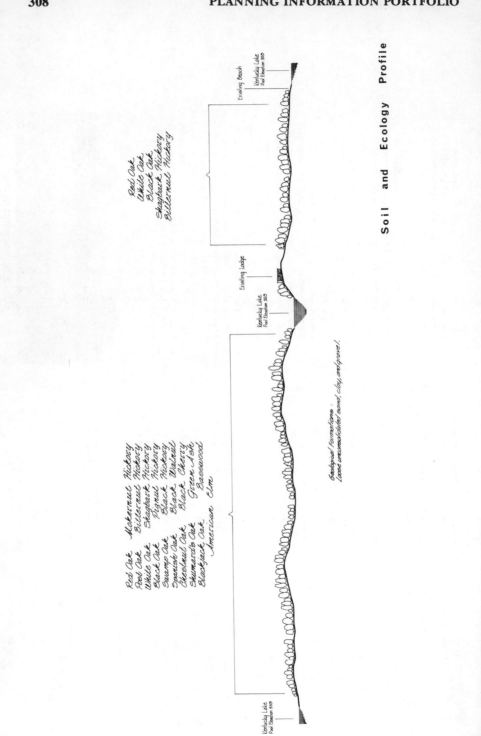

Soil and Ecology Profile

Picnic areas are difficult to provide on limited space due to the large amount of use they receive. In the most heavily used picnic areas asphalt or other cover should be considered, extending over all but areas around the trees (4-5 feet radius). This could not only prevent erosion but would provide for easier cleaning.

The golf course should be designed in such a way as to avoid placing fairways running parallel to a valley. By placing fairways across a valley, the area which is crossing the water course can be underlain with culverts, covered with a base, and finally with a thick Bermuda grass sod.

AREA FACTORS

History: The region surrounding Paris Landing Park was occupied by a range of Indian cultures extending from the very earliest known Ice-age hunters to the Chickasaws, who lived there at the time of the coming of the white man. An unusual number of outstanding sites in the vicinity have been discovered, marking points of habitation of all principal early groups.

Nomadic hunters of the Old Stone Age (Paleolithic era) who were a part of the first migration from Siberia over a plain connecting two continents reached this vicinity according to carbon-dating and fluted spear points found in Humphreys, Montgomery, Dickson and Weakley Counties. Very little is known of this group except that they lived in North America during the period between 9,000 and 25,000 years ago and hunted prehistoric animals.

During the Archaic Era (which is the Mesolithic or Inter-mediate Stone Age) a later wave of prehistoric peoples migrated from the northern forests of Asia after the ice cap had retreated. There is evidence that these people ate plant foods, nuts, seeds, small game and a seemingly inexhaustible supply of shellfish. They had a more settled existence and lived in fairly substantial structures. There is evidence that this group resided about 6,000 years ago in what is now Tennessee. The basic way of the archaic life is characterized by the "Eva" settlement along Cypress Creek about 25 miles south of Paris Landing. This is one of the outstandingly known settlements of the time and existed about 5200 B.C. Archaeological investigations have revealed burials and heaps of decomposed trash and discarded mussel shells. These early people remained in the Tennessee River area and, with the arrival of

more advanced groups from the north, learned to make grooved axes, polished stone ornaments, stone pipes and pottery. This more advanced culture of the archaic people is called the "Big Sandy Phase" because of findings on the Big Sandy River settlements (immediately south of Paris Landing) dated about 1000 B.C.

The early Woodland Indians (Neolithic or New Stone Age peoples) who occupied eastern North America during the period from about 5000 B.C. until 1000 A.D. have also been placed in the vicinity. This group introduced the domestication of plants and animals, thus emancipating man from the uncertainties of wild food supplies. They used corn, or maize, brought in from Middle America. The Woodland Indians are also known as the Burial Mound Builders and are related to more advanced cultures found in Guatemala and Mexico. The most advanced and best known of this group are probably the Hopewells of the Ohio Valley. The Harmon Creek Indian settlements near Paris Landing Park in Benton County were very permanent and diggings have indicated burials in baskets. There is also a ceremonial center described as spectacular in Stewart County occupying a big ridge extending into the Tennessee River flood plain.

One of the most impressive examples of the work of the next culture in Eastern North America, the Temple Mound Builders (or Mississippian culture), is also located in this area. These temple mounds are located near the headwaters of the Obion

OLD FIELDS AND SECOND GROWTH FOREST IN THE PARK AREA

River in Henry County. The temple is described as having a spacious plaza 1,000 feet long and 500 feet wide flanked by small mounds. The largest structure is a big earthwork approached by a broad ramp leading to the summit. Its great bulk represents six stages of construction, each succeeding addition increasing in dimension. Excavations have revealed that the ceremonial center at the Obion River site was established early in the Temple Mound period by a people still living in the Stone Ages, with no knowledge of metalurgy. This group of people evidenced some very distinctive pottery, had the use of corn and beans and many varieties of pumpkins, squash and sweet potatoes. There were no domestic animals except dogs. Pinson Mound near Jackson and Chucalissa Indian Village near Memphis are also permanent works of peoples of this same period.

The Duck River Indians of Humphreys County, about 30 miles south of Paris Landing, are a subgroup that are especially known for what has been called the most extraordinary flint work ever done by man. Flint objects in the area have been found to represent sun disks, turtles and other items. Many pieces of spearhead 17 to 28 inches long have been found. An outstanding location for flint quarries, from which the Duck River pieces were made, is located in Stewart County, to the east of Paris Landing.*

The Indians lived generally along the stream terraces facing the Tennessee River and had what is considered to have been a fairly advanced culture. Numerous relics including bits of pottery, stone tools and weapons, as well as stone images are still being found, particularly at times when the Reservoir is brought to unusually low elevations where its wash has exposed materials beneath the surface.

At the time of the first exploration of the white man, the territory was claimed by the Chickasaw and Cherokee Indian tribes which had very sparsely settled the western parts of Tennessee and Kentucky. There is little evidence that these groups lived in the area and, in actuality, the Federal Indian census of 1825 revealed only 1000 in all of West Tennessee.

In 1818 Andrew Jackson and Isaac Shelby, representing the U. S. Government, entered into the Treaty of Old Town with four chiefs acquiring all the parts of Tennessee and Kentucky west of the Tennessee River under the condition that the Indians would receive $20,000 a year for 15 consecutive years. A further stipu-lation was that the Chickasaws reserve a four square mile site containing a salt spring near the mouth of the Big Sandy River some three miles south of Paris Landing. This land, too, was soon lost to the white man, and by 1900 a resort on the site known as "Sulphur Well" flourished there.

* Tribes that Slumber, Indians of the Tennessee Region, Thomas M. N. Lewis and Madeline Kneburg. Published by the University of Tennessee Press, 1958.

Lands in Henry County in the vicinity of Paris Landing were claimed by Stewart County residents immediately upon its opening in 1819. Settlement of the entire county was rapid and by 1830 most of the land had been taken up. Prior to the War Between the States, Paris Landing was established as a boat docking site for supplies moving into Paris. The place originally known as "Gray's Ferry" was the principal crossing for many miles in both directions.

Henry County was established by the General Assembly of Tennessee on November 7, 1821 and the same year a commission was formed to select the site of the County Seat. Fifty acres were selected. The land was plotted and 104 lots sold with income going toward the construction of a log court house. The town was incorporated in 1823, being the first municipal charter issued in West Tennessee.

The principal historical significance of the park site relates to its position on the Tennessee River, a main supply route for the Federal armies during the War Between the States. General U. S. Grant was in command of the Union Forces, and on February 2, 1862, set out from Cairo, Illinois with 16,000 troops and a flotilla of metal-clad gun boats to split Tennessee. He reached Fort Henry, which is about six miles downstream and across the river from Paris Landing and on the 6th of February opened attack. The fort, manned by 2,600 men under General Tilghman, was indefensible in the face of such odds and surrendered after most of the men were moved to Fort Donelson. With the fall of both these forts, the main supply route for the defense of the Middle South became very difficult.

In late 1864, General Nathan Bedford Forrest had cut the railroad in back of Sherman's army and determined to disrupt the river supply line including the depots at Johnsonville where goods were trans-shipped by railroad to Nashville. Forrest ordered General Abraham's brigade to blockade the river in the vicinity of the mouth of the Big Sandy. Batteries were placed at Paris Landing and five miles downstream at old Confederate Fort Heiman. Orders were given not to disturb any transports or gunboats until they had passed between the batteries. As a result, several gun boats, transports and barges were destroyed or captured. General Forrest and his troops then moved with some of the boats to a position across the river from New Johnsonville, which was destroyed.*

After the war and into the early 1900's, most of the property

* Gunboats and Cavalry, published by Nathan Bedford Forrest Trail Committee, Memphis, Tennessee.

FLINT CEREMONIAL OBJECTS MADE BY DUCK RIVER INDIANS (MACE-LIKE FORMS, SYMBOLIC TURTLES AND SUN DISKS)

at Paris Landing including the dock facilities, a large mercantile store and a saw mill belonged to Dr. A. J. Weldon. In addition, there were perhaps a dozen houses in the settlement. The area often flooded and the large wooden home occupied by Dr. Weldon burned. Some of the settlement, including Dr. Weldon's "hill house" away from the flood land area, was on the high ground at the location of the present park.

The first bridge across the river was constructed about 1917 and was later elevated with the impoundment of Kentucky Reservoir. In 1944, the entire flood plain, at this point reaching a width of two miles, was inundated in what at the time was the largest man-made lake in the world. Subsequent events including the establishment of Paris Landing State Park on land leased and deeded to the State by the Tennessee Valley Authority in 1945 have been largely water-oriented.

Surrounding Land Use: Recreational uses in the area surrounding the park are quite varied, but trend most generally toward a water-oriented resort type. Because of the slopes and poor quality of the soil, there has been little farming in the immediate area since inundation of the river and creek bottoms. Only 54 percent of the land in the two immediate counties is in farms with most of the remainder largely in timber tracts. Farmsteads are fairly large and increasing in size, generally averaging 140 acres in Henry County and 151 acres in Stewart. At the same time land values on farms are relatively low with the average worth being $78 per acre in 1959.

The principal crops are corn and hay which are mostly fed to livestock on the farms. Cattle and hogs are particularly important in the farm economy, especially in central and western Henry County. Money crops such as cotton, tobacco, vegetables and soybeans which are very significant in many other Tennessee counties are not produced in large quantity here, although tobacco is found on many farms.

Immediately across the lake is the Land Between the Lakes Recreation Area with 188 square miles. Across the Big Sandy embayment on the long peninsula separating the main body of the Reservoir from the Big Sandy, about half of the land area (some

20 square miles) is taken up by the Tennessee National Wildlife Refuge and the Nicky Brothers Wildlife Management Area which is operated by the Tennessee Game and Fish Commission. On the west side of the Kentucky Reservoir most of the immediate shoreline is occupied by wildlife management units, public access areas or commercial docks and resorts.

Within four miles of Paris Landing Park, there are 12 commercial docks, most of which include some additional recreational and lodging facilities. Ten of these are on the west side. Most of the developments are of poor quality and very limited in what they are able to offer. In addition, there are four camps occupied by organizations such as church and scout groups. Commercial uses such as restaurants, tourist courts, small stores and service stations are scattered without plan or pattern along Highway 79.

Many private homes and camps have been established along the lakefront. Subdivision activity has been especially high in the area, and hundreds of lots have been put on the market in recent years. While many of the lots have been sold, there is little evidence of building and, in fact, a relatively high percentage has become tax delinquent. Improvements serving the lots in the way of standard streets and utilities are almost totally lacking while layout, including lot size and pattern, falls far below minimum standards of good design.

The prevailing pattern of poor quality resort and dock facilities, uncontrolled commercial development along the highway, and poor quality residential development in the vicinity seriously threaten the State's investment. Measures should be taken by county officials in the way of subdivision regulations, zoning and building controls to assure more orderly development of surrounding uses. With such an objective in view the State might well consider withholding development funds for parks in counties that have shown little or no interest in assuring a compatible environment.

Henry County has a Planning Commission established for the purpose of developing an overall plan and exercising and recommending controls for the area, but this body has been almost altogether inactive for many years. Stewart County has never had a planning commission until recently and presently anticipates the development of a comprehensive plan, focusing to some extent on the Cumberland City and Dover areas as well as Highway 79 and the south entrance to Land Between the Lakes. Both Henry and Stewart Counties should become more active in giving direction to land use development, particular in resort and park areas since the existence of these facilities depends on their attractiveness and ability to offer recreational and related services in an orderly and convenient atmosphere.

Population And Economy: The immediate service area of the park includes eight counties containing a population estimated in 1965 to be 191,515. This includes all of the section of the state within 50 miles or one hour's driving time plus Calloway County, Kentucky.

The major service area of the park, however, is not merely limited to surrounding counties, but extends over a radius of hundreds of miles including such urban centers as Memphis, Nashville, Evansville, Paducah and even St. Louis and Chicago. Present use of existing park facilities, especially the lodge, already indicates a great bulk of visitors from outside the area. With the development of the Land Between the Lakes Recreation Area, the proportion of visitors drawn to the area and stopping at Paris Landing and other resorts will increase.

The 1965 population of Henry County was estimated at 21,306, having shown a steady decline from nearly 24,000 since 1950. Stewart County, with a population of 8,438, has also shown a net decrease during the past 15 years. The same trend has occurred in most other counties except Montgomery with its sizable urban center of Clarksville and the Fort Campbell Military Base. Throughout the eight counties, the population is expected to increase by over six percent during the five years between 1965 and 1970, and by almost 12 percent during the following 10 years to 1980. This projected trend, in accordance with the accompanying table, shows an increase approaching the national average by 1980 when the immediate service area is estimated to have over 224,000 people. Clarksville and Montgomery County are expected to lead other counties in the increase and will have an estimated 89,213 people by 1980.

Population trends and projections reflect a strong rural out-migration which will be more than offset by normal births-over-deaths plus increased industrialization in urban centers and New Johnsonville.

While local usage of the park facilities will remain high, increasing numbers of tourists are expected from the much broader service area, including five states. This position is taken based on current use of the park's lodge, camping facilities and the vast market area of the Land Between the Lakes Recreation Area. These states, including Illinois, Indiana and Missouri, as well as Tennessee and Kentucky, are expected to keep pace with the National growth trends.

PAST, CURRENT AND PROJECTED POPULATION FOR PARIS LANDING STATE PARK SERVICE AREA *

Immediate Area	1950	1960	1965	1970**	1980**
Henry County	23,838	22,275	21,306	20,218	17,705
Stewart County	9,175	7,851	8,438	9,088	10,480
Calloway County, Kentucky	20,147	20,972	21,398	21,829	22,721
Montgomery County	44,186	55,645	63,178	72,059	89,213
Weakley County	27,962	24,227	24,526	25,057	26,981
Carroll County	26,553	23,476	24,536	25,341	26,828
Benton County	11,495	10,662	11,054	11,098	11,700
Humphreys County	11,030	11,511	11,313	11,307	11,640
Houston County	5,318	4,794	5,766	6,647	8,346
Total	179,704	181,413	191,515	202,644	225,614

* *Source:* 1950 and 1960 figures from U. S. Census of Population. 1965 Estimate from Population and Personal Income Estimates for Tennessee Counties, Bureau of Business and Economic Research, University of Tennessee.

** 1970 and 1980 Projections for Tennessee Counties from State Planning Office, Tennessee Department of Finance and Administration, Unpublished Data.

The accompanying table indicates lower-than-average per capita income in the counties within the immediate service area. It may be seen that higher incomes will prevail in the future in keeping with State and National averages.

Studies by the Federal Outdoor Recreation Resources Review Commission in 1962 indicate that with higher incomes the participation in active recreational pursuits will increase. Sightseeing, family outings and camping trips, golf and boating are activities desired more and more as the population reaches middle and upper income range.

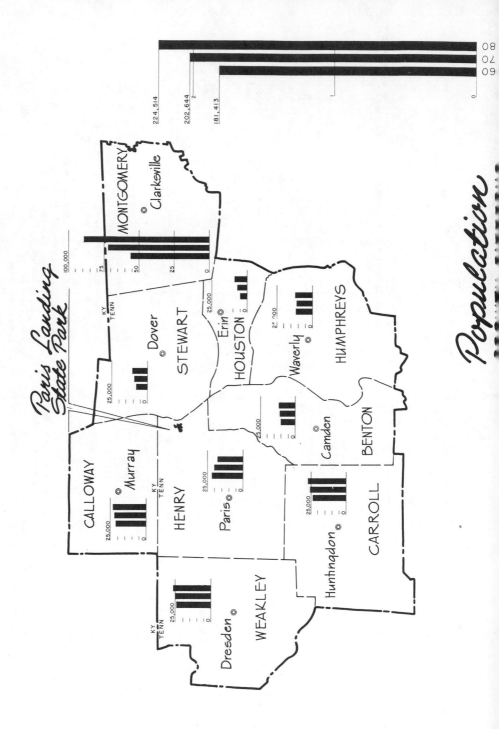

POPULATION PROJECTION
STATES IN GREATER SERVICE AREA FOR PARIS LANDING STATE PARK

State	1950	1960	1965	1966	1970	1975	1980
Tennessee	3,291,718	3,567,089	3,850,000	3,883,000	4,069,000	4,287,000	4,547,000
Kentucky	2,944,806	3,038,156	3,175,000	3,183,000	3,281,000	3,402,000	3,551,000
Illinois	8,712,176	10,081,158	10,641,000	10,722,000	11,225,000	12,059,000	13,051,000
Indiana	3,934,224	4,662,498	4,893,000	4,918,000	5,155,000	5,542,000	5,991,000
Missouri	3,954,653	4,319,813	4,492,000	4,508,000	4,573,000	4,824,000	5,133,000
Mississippi	2,178,914	2,178,141	2,309,000	2,327,000	2,483,000	2,629,000	2,801,000
Alabama	3,061,743	3,266,740	3,486,000	3,517,000	3,656,000	3,923,000	4,230,000
Total for Greater Service Area	28,078,234	27,846,855	32,844,000	33,058,000	34,442,000	36,666,000	39,304,000
United States	150,697,361	179,323,175	193,795,000	95,857,000	208,249,000	225,123,000	244,566,000

Source: Population Estimate, February 7, 1966, U. S. Department of Commerce.

PER CAPITA INCOME STATES IN GREATER SERVICE AREA FOR PARIS LANDING STATE PARK

State	1950	1960	1963	1970	1975	1980
Tennessee	995	1,604	1,806	2,243	2,560	2,920
Kentucky	958	1,602	1,814	2,246	2,624	3,060
Illinois	1,920	2,751	2,986	3,387	3,752	4,150
Indiana	1,612	2,283	2,513	2,905	3,279	3,700
Missouri	1,449	2,299	2,551	2,986	3,374	3,630
Alabama	867	1,525	1,676	2,114	2,475	2,750
Mississippi	729	1,219	1,407	1,791	2,117	2,370
United States	1,491	2,313	2,479	3,005	3,405	3,750

Source: 1950 Data from U. S. Census.
1960-1975 National Planning Association
Report No. 65-11, October, 1965
1980 Figures are mathematical extensions

The economy of the two immediate counties is among the most varied in the rural counties of the State. It is characterized by a declining agricultural base, recently located manufacturing enterprises and a small but very promising recreation industry.

Principal industries and their employment according to data compiled by the Tennessee Division of Industrial Development are as follows:

PRINCIPAL INDUSTRIES
HENRY AND STEWART COUNTIES, TENNESSEE*

PARIS

Industry	Year Established	Employment
Bowling Green Rubber Co.	1947	40
Clippard Instrument Co.	1955	160
Dreshu, Inc. (shoes)	1961	190
Golden Peacock, Inc. (cosmetics)	1917	150
Kentucky-Tenn. Clay Co. (mining)	1927	55
Mitchum Co. (drugs)	1913	135
Paris Mfg. Co. (carburetors)	1949	556
Salant & Salant. Inc.	1934	450
H. C. Spinks, Inc. (clay mining)	1918	152

PURYEAR

Laird Brick Co.	1960	31

DOVER

Ely & Walker (men's slacks)	1962	225
Natcor Store Fronts	1954	60

* Source: 1966 Director of Tennessee Industries. Staff Division of Industrial Development.

PAST AND PROJECTED PER CAPITAL PERSONAL INCOME FOR IMMEDIATE SERVICE AREA OF PARIS LANDING STATE PARK *

Immediate Area	1962	1970	1975 (1962 Dollars)	1980
Henry County	1,584	1,959	2,346	3,809
Stewart County	1,147	1,739	2,219	2,831
Calloway County, Ky.	2,252	2,500	2,900	3,300
Montgomery County	1,862	2,166	2,433	2,732
Weakley County	1,529	1,968	2,385	2,888
Carroll County	1,173	1,533	1,792	2,093
Benton County	1,217	1,694	2,070	2,527
Humphreys County	1,770	2,496	3,126	3,913
Houston County	1,039	1,672	2,065	2,550
Average for Service Area	1,508	1,970	2,370	2,850
Tennessee	1,694	2,243	2,560	2,920

* Source: Population and Personal Income Estimates for Tennessee Counties, Bureau of Business and Economic Research, University of Tennessee, May, 1964. 1960 Data projected for Calloway County. 1980 Projection based on 1970-75 increase.

CENTRAL BUSINESS DISTRICT, PARIS, TENNESSEE

EMPLOYMENT BY INDUSTRY GROUP IN COUNTIES ADJACENT TO PARIS LANDING STATE PARK *

| | Counties | | |
Industry Group	Henry	Stewart	Total
Agriculture	1,319	574	1,893
Forestry, Fisheries and Mining	175	39	214
Construction	454	268	722
Manufacturing	2,042	408	2,450
Transportation and Utilities	536	111	647
Wholesale and Retail	1,359	353	1,712
Education	366	192	558
Services and Misc.	1,761	440	2,201
Total	8,012	2,385	10,397

* Source: 1960 Federal Census of Population.

Access And Travel Pattern: Present access to the park is by way of U. S. Highway No. 79 which connects Bowling Green and Louisville with Memphis and cities to the South. State Route 119 provides secondary access from Kentucky and carries visitors from Murray and southbound travelers cutting off from U. S. Route 641. The entrances to the park are on both sides of Highway 79 immediately adjacent to its intersection with Route 119. The accompanying table gives further information concerning amount and type of traffic on these routes:

TRAFFIC COUNTS ON U. S. HIGHWAY 79 AT PARIS LANDING STATE PARK *

Route	Average Daily Traffic	Percent Automobiles	Percent Out-of-State
U. S. 79 east of entrance	1,320	69	47
U. S. 79 west of entrance	1,600	64	34

* Total counts according to Tennessee State Highway Department, 1965. Percent for passengers and out-of-state vehicles taken from Tennessee State Highway Department, August, 1964, counts.

The counts indicate a relatively low total volume but a high percentage of out-of-state cars. This same travel pattern is substantiated by special counts made of cars entering and leaving the park by State Highway Department survey in 1965 as follows:

VEHICLES ENTERING AND LEAVING PARIS LANDING STATE PARK *

Vehicle Type	Average Daily Traffic	Percent of Total ADT	Percent Out-of-State
Passenger Cars	235	85.8	38.3
Car/tent Trailer	5	1.8	60.0
Car/house or Travel Trailer	2	0.7	100.0
Pickup or Panel Truck	22	8.0	0.0
Pickup/camper	1	0.4	100.0
Pickup or Panel Truck/Trailer	0	0.0	0.0
Trucks (misc.)	9	3.3	0.0
Camper Buses	0	0.0	0.0
Buses (misc.)	0	0.0	0.0
Total	274	100.0	35.0

* Traffic counts taken from Tennessee Department of Highways study made August 4, 1965, between 7:00 a.m. and 3:00 p.m. at the main entrance to Paris Landing State Park on U. S. Highway 79.

While preparing the state's comprehensive outdoor recreation plan, a survey of State and Federal areas was made to determine the source of recreation-oriented visitations to Tennessee. This information, indicating that in 1964 organized recreation areas in West Tennessee received almost on-third of their visitors from outside the state, is significant in determining the number and type of visitations to the proposed park.

The source of origin by state is shown on the accompanying table.

State Route 76 (U. S. 79) through Paris Landing State Park and across Kentucky Reservoir

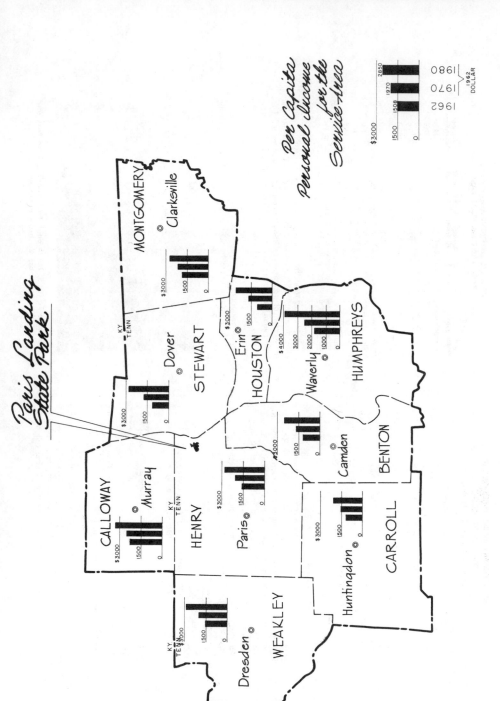

Per Capita Personal Income for the Service Area

STATE OF ORIGIN TO RECREATION-ORIENTED VISITORS TO TENNESSEE, 1964 *

Percentage of Visitors Coming from Each Market Area State to:

State	All Sections of State	West Tenn.	Middle Tenn.	East Tenn.
Tennessee	63.1%	66.7%	73.1%	57.6%
North Carolina	5.4	0.5	1.6	8.3
Kentucky	5.2	7.3	6.9	3.9
Alabama	2.8	1.8	2.5	3.1
Ohio	2.7	1.8	1.7	3.4
Illinois	2.7	5.0	2.7	2.1
Georgia	2.6	0.6	1.4	3.7
Indiana	2.0	3.1	1.6	1.9
Florida	1.9	0.7	1.5	2.4
Virginia	1.6	0.4	0.8	2.3
South Carolina	1.4	0.2	0.3	2.2
Michigan	1.2	1.1	0.7	1.5
Missouri	1.0	2.6	0.6	0.8
Mississippi	0.8	1.2	0.6	0.8
Texas	0.7	1.3	0.7	0.6
Arkansas	0.6	1.7	0.5	0.3
Louisiana	0.4	0.6	0.4	0.3
Wisconsin	0.3	0.2	0.3	0.4
All Others	3.6	3.2	2.1	4.4
Total	100.0%	100.0%	100.0%	100.0%

* Source: Planning for Outdoor Recreation, The Tennessee Planner, The Tennessee State Planning Commission, Spring, 1966.

The table of source of visitors to specific sites in the area gives further indication of out-of-state usage to be expected.

The actual source of visitation has been checked by state or origin of vehicles by address of lodge occupants. This information, including data for the month of August, 1966, reveals the following:

Address	No. of Registrants
Tennessee	257
Memphis	209
Remainder West Tennessee	74
Nashville	138
Remainder Middle Tennessee	37
East Tennessee	9
Indiana	17
Illinois	15
Missouri	37
Kentucky	27

Alabama	25
Ohio	23
Mississippi	21
Other	64
Total	746

SOURCES OF VISITORS TO PARIS LANDING AND SELECTED FACILITIES IN VICINITY *

(percentage by State)

	Paris Landing	Kentucky Dam	New Johnsonville Steam Plant
Alabama	—	.4	2.3
Mississippi	1.8	.6	1.3
Kentucky	2.3	39.4	3.1
Missouri	2.7	8.3	3.1
Tennessee	37.6	5.6	79.1
Illinois	26.3	18.9	1.7
Indiana	3.3	12.0	.9
Michigan	7.7	2.5	1.0
Other	18.3	12.3	7.5

* Source: Comprehensive Plan for Development of Kentucky Reservoir Region, Tennessee State Planning Commission, 1964. Paris Landing Data from Tennessee Department of Highways survey, August, 1965 (one day sample—Wednesday).

Access will be greatly improved through the realignment and construction of U. S. 79 between Dover and the Kentucky Reservoir Bridge. This project, currently planned by the Tennessee Department of Highways, will lead to the now proposed major south entrance to the Land Between the Lakes Recreation Area which will be about five and one-half miles east of the Paris Landing entrance.

The Tennessee Department of Highways also has under construction or has programmed two major north-south routes that will serve the park. These include a scenic connector route (State Route 117) between New Johnsonville and Waverly on the south and the proposed entrance to Land Between the Lakes on the north. This route which is programmed in stages over the next five years will serve Lakewood Village Resort and is to eventually connect with Interstate 40. Relocation of State Route 69 connecting Paris with Interstate 40 by way of Camden is under construction in the north sector and will be completed south of Camden by 1972. The park, which heretofore has been without good access from the south, will be in a much better position to serve the areas in all directions. The overall physical relationship to other developments, especially resorts serving the Kentucky Reservoir region, will be improved.

One of more than 200 campsites already developed by TVA in the Rushing Creek Campground.

complex of recreation sites ranging downward from the 170,000 acre Land Between the Lakes Recreation Area will serve rapidly increasing numbers of people from the Mid-West and Mid-South.

The principal development and major drawing power will be the Land Between the Lakes Recreation Area, which covers parts of three counties in Kentucky and Tennessee including the isthmus south of the Barkley and Kentucky dams and north of the Paris Landing-Dover axis. The park has over 300 miles of shoreline. Emphasis on the development, now partially completed, is being placed on many phases of outdoor recreation including group and family camping, boating and water sports, natural interpretive studies, hunting, fishing and hiking. The Land Between the Lakes is planned as a demonstration or pilot project to show how a large area of relatively unproductive land may be used to meet the increasing demand for outdoor recreation facilities. Approved and commenced in 1964, there was a count of over 100,000 visitors by 1966 in limited facilities. By mid-1967 over one half of the land had been acquired and two campgrounds, a dozen picnic areas and a conservation-education center had been completed, along with roads and trails. Wildlife and forestry programs have been initiated as well.

In terms of ultimate development, TVA expects to have 5,000 improved campsites to accommodate 20,000 people in addition to an undetermined number of primitive sites' group camps barracks-type shelters in clusters handling up to 250 people each for a capacity of 1,500 persons, day use areas near the entrances including swimming beaches, playgrounds and play shelters and related facilities.

Major Route	Connecting Cities	Nearest Access	Miles from Park
Interstate 40	Memphis-Nashville	S. Of Camden, Tenn.	55
Interstate 40 connecting with I-55 and I-57	Nashville-St. Louis-Chicago	Gilbertsville, Kentucky	49
Western Kentucky Parkway—Purchase Parkway connecting with U. S. 51	Memphis-Louisville-Lexington	Mayfield, Kentucky	40

Nearby Recreation Areas: The creation of large water bodies of Kentucky and Barkley Reservoirs plus the availability of undeveloped plateau lands unsuitable for intensive uses for other purposes has led to the establishment or proposed establishment of numerous parks, wildlife refuges, resorts and campus. This

The Land Between The Lakes

In its conservation education program TVA will develop a 4,500 acre site fronting Lake Barkley aimed toward demonstrating ecological dependence of soil, trees, water, crops and wild and domestic animal life. The center will have housing for students and teachers participating in youth and adult activities.

Four other state parks, three of which are in Kentucky, are located within a relatively short distance from Paris Landing. These include the Nathan Bedford Forrest State Park in Tennessee (under development) near Camden; and Cherokee, Kentucky Dam Village, Kentucky Lake State Parks in Kentucky. Only the latter two have more or less complete facilities which include a lodge, golf course, air strip and marina. Barkley Lake State Park in Kentucky on the east shore of Barkley Reservoir is in the initial phases of development.

Wildlife refuges in the region contain almost 100,000 acres, much of which is wet land or water surface. These areas contain very little development and are managed by State and Federal agencies for the purpose of encouraging small game hunting, particularly for deer, wild ducks, geese, turkey and grouse. Managed hunts are held in a number of them.

A number of private resorts of considerable size have been developed or proposed. The Ken Bar project at Grand Rivers consists of a marina and lodge. Lakewood Village or the east side of Kentucky Reservoir and south of Paris Landing is to be a very large project built with Federal Economic Development Administration assistance. Bids have been taken and construction consisting of a 144 unit lodge, community center, two swimming pools, marina, campsites and two golf courses is to commence in late 1968.

DEMAND AND USE ESTIMATES

Measuring Demand: Many variable factors are involved in the preparation of estimates and forecasts for visitation and use in the park as proposed for expansion. Determinations of the future use, income, needs and preferences of people are always hazardous. When estimates cover a large and difficult-to-define service area, they are especially elusive. Because of rapid development of the region as a major resort, particularly Land Between the Lakes, the use of existing facilities in the past would have little validity.

Visitation estimates are determined by three steps. First, projections to 1970 and 1980 of person-day visits are arrived at for the entire Kentucky-Barkley Reservoir region. These estimates are based on past known data for Kentucky Reservoir plus TVA and U. S. Corps of Engineers' projections for Land Between the Lakes and Barkley Reservoir.

Visitations for the total region are then separated according to activity preferences based on the park's emphasis and judgment of the demand factors. In order to determine estimates for Paris Landing, a "step-down" technique is used through assignment of the share of visitations and use expected for the major resorts and parks. The share of the total visitation going to the major parks and resorts including six state parks plus Lakewood Village and Ken Bar, two private resorts, is expected to be about 36 percent of the total region or about the same as visitation to Land Between the Lakes. Projections of visits to these park and resort areas are based on available independent projections and further verified by the assumption that, for each visit to Land Between the Lakes with its more rudimentary facilities, there will be one visit to the more comfortable and varied facilities of the resorts, such as golfing or first class lodging and dining. Paris Landing is then assigned a share of major resort visitations based on the facilities that it will have to offer and its location with respect to the Land Between the Lakes. Since between 20 and 30 percent of Land Between the Lakes' visitors are expected to come into the park by way of the south entrance, which is only five and one-half miles from Paris Landing, the eight percent assignment to Paris Landing is considered to be conservative. Other major resorts on the south, either existing or under development include Lakewood Village and Nathan Bedford Forrest State Park.

The National Wildlife Refuge South of Paris Landing

Finally, the ratio of total visitation to activity-occasions is determined at 1 to 1.7, which is the same factor used by the State Department of Conservation in its recently published interim outdoor recreation plan.

Visitations And Use: This section includes actual projections for visitations and use for the Barkley-Kentucky Reservoir area, broken down according to major areas or type facilities. Three tables illustrate the "step-down" technique used to estimate actual demand at Paris Landing. These tables are supported by a narrative supporting the judgment used in breaking down the activity preferences for the major parks including Paris Landing.

The principal draw of the park should be from two sources: (a) facilities for participation in water-oriented activities, including boating, skiing, fishing, swimming and duck-hunting, and (b) facilities such as the lodge, restaurant and golf course which are not available in Land Between the Lakes, but are desired by many visitors that will be drawn to the area.

Information compiled in Tennessee's Comprehensive Outdoor Recreation Plan (An Interim Plan) published in February, 1966, shows activity preferences for participants in Middle Tennessee. Although the availability of facilities is a primary influence on the established use pattern, this information provides some indication of preference of people living and traveling in the area.

RECREATION ACTIVITY REFERENCES
BASED ON 1964 USE OF RECREATION SITES *

	Middle Tennessee Number	%	West Tennessee Number	%	Tennessee Number	%
Touring and Sightseeing	5,369,400	28.4	5,174,400	46.3	31,833,000	45.1
Fishing	3,621,600	19.2	1,693,700	15.2	9,663,400	13.7
Boating	3,112,400	16.55	1,375,600	12.3	9,491,700	13.5
Picnicking	2,046,300	10.8	1,302,200	11.7	7,753,300	11.0
Swimming	2,359,500	12.5	609,000	5.5	5,339,200	7.6
Water Skiing	998,200	5.3	365,800	3.3	2,913,900	4.1
Camping	929,300	4.9	57,600	.5	1,723,200	2.4
Other	449,600	2.4	584,400	5.2	1,817,800	2.6
	18,886,300	100.0	11,162,700	100.0	70,535,700	100.0

* *Source:* Tennessee's Plan for Outdoor Recreation, Tennessee Department of Conservation, February, 1966.

Touring and sightseeing are among the most favored activities according to State and National records and interviews over a long period of time. This high degree of interest indicates a need to include: drives, overlooks, historical markers, and a visitation

center, probably including natural and historical interpretation and a museum. Day-outing activity areas, especially for picnicking, must be included in the park plan since most visitors only expect to visit the area for a few hours. According to national trends, family and group camping facilities are a must for a park of this type. The *Tennessee State Parks Study* conducted and published as a Technical Assistance Project by the U. S. Area Development Administration in 1964 showed summer camping represents 5.1 percent of all recreation trips made in Tennessee and projected them to increase to 7.8 percent by 1975.

Population of the immediate service area is not great and includes rural and low-income families, meaning that demand for recreation facilities by people in nearby counties is comparatively low. This is borne out to some extent by past use of the park. With the development of urban areas and decline in rural population, however, this situation will change with incomes and demand for recreational facilities increasing.

About one-half of the visitation already comes from outside the immediately surrounding counties. With development of the area as a national center for outdoor recreation, this percentage will greatly increase. Population of the five state greater service area is over 27,000,000 people, and existing and projected per capita incomes are close to the national average. By 1980, the five state area population should be 32,000,000, an increase of 19 percent which also approaches the national average projection.

Because of the nature of the demand, including persons traveling great distances or persons that make secondary stops to or from Land Between the Lakes, in many cases looking for variety of activities or greater comfort, emphasis of development should be placed on varied and high quality facilities including golf course, air strip and first class lodge and restaurant.

People will have more leisure time in the future. The National Outdoor Recreation Resources Review Commission in *Outdoor Recreation for America* indicates that the average 39 hour work week in 1960 will be reduced to a 36 hour week in 1976 and by 2000 may be down to 32 hours. The development of two other features of the machine-age—increased mobility and higher incomes—means greater use of parks. With more time to spend as he chooses, the financial ability to participate and improved access to recreation areas taken together mean a fairly heavy demand for all types of recreation in the future.

VISITATION AND VISITATION PROJECTIONS IN THE BARKLEY-KENTUCKY RESERVOIR AREA—1970-1980 INCLUDING MAJOR PARKS AND RESORTS AND LAND BETWEEN THE LAKES

	1965		1970		1980	
	Percent of Total	Visita-tions	Percent of Total	Visita-tions	Percent of Total	Visita-tions
Major Resorts & Parks (excluding L.B.L.)*		3,000,000		4,000,000		12,000,000
Land Between the Lakes		600,000		4,000,000		12,000,000
Other (Commercial docks, access points and wild-life refuges)		8,360,000		10,500,000		12,000,000
Total		11,960,000		18,500,000		36,000,000

* Include Paris Landing State Park, Kentucky Dam Village State Park, Kentucky Lake State Park, Barkley Lake State Park, Lakewood Village, Nathan Bedford Forrest State Park and Ken-Bar Resort.

Source: TVA and Courses of Engineering basic estimates plus arithmetical extensions and an assignment of visitation to major parks and resorts based on a one-to-one ratio to Land Between the Lakes.

Recreational Units Required: In order to determine the extent of improvements in the park, it is necessary to translate activity-occasions into units required. The design and the number of facilities must take into consideration peak months and even peak days; therefore, it is first necessary to estimate the percentage of total activity-occasions that will be using the park from mid-May through June, July, August and early September. An average visitation per day is then arrived at, and weekend peak days are computed by using the ratio of 60 percent of the week. When this figure is divided by two, the average daily peaks in activity-occasions occurring on summer weekends are determined and used as the design standard. It should be noted, however, that extreme peak days such as the Fourth of July are not applied since it is felt that it would be impractical to design for such usage.

It is not always possible to make design proposals agree with projected demand for facilities due to limitations of space. This is particularly true for boat slip facilities which should be limited to the harbor area.

The accompanying tables are included to show the number of recreational units determined as needed to satisfy the demand estimates for the park.

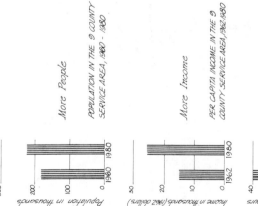

More People

POPULATION IN THE 9 COUNTY SERVICE AREA, 1960 - 1980

More Income

PER CAPITA INCOME IN THE 9 COUNTY SERVICE AREA, 1962-1980

More Leisure

WORKING HOURS PER WEEK IN THE UNITED STATES, 1955-1985

More Mobility

VEHICLE MILES DRIVEN IN TENNESSEE, 1965 - 1975

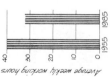

VISITATION PROJECTION TO 1980
KENTUCKY-BARKLEY RESERVOIR AREAS (Person-Day Visits)*

	1950	1955	1960	1965	1970	1975	1980
Lard Between the Lakes Recreation Area	—	—	—	600,000	4,000,000	8,000,000	12,000,000
Kentucky Reservoir Area	2,795,000	5,261,000	7,840,000	10,360,000	14,500,000	17,500,000	19,000,000
Barkley Reservoir Area	—	—	—	1,000,000	3,000,000	4,500,000	7,000,000
Total				11,960,000	21,500,000	30,000,000	38,000,000

*Source: TVA records to 1965. Projections based on arithmetical extensions plus estimates from Corps of Engineers and TVA personnel.

ACTIVITY OCCASION ESTIMATES AND VISITATION PROJECTIONS 1970-1980
PARIS LANDING STATE PARK AND KENTUCKY-BARKLEY RESERVOIR AREA

Activity	Kentucky-Barkley Reservoir Area		Major Parks and Resorts (1)			Percent of Major Parks Assigned To Paris Landing	Paris Landing State Park			% Of Total Outings Mid-May Through Mid-September	
	1970	1980	Percent of Region	1970	1980		1970	1980		1970	1980
Lodging	283,000	650,000	80	226,000	520,000	8	18,000	42,000	50%	9,000	20,800
Camping	1,697,000	3,000,000	22	373,000	660,000	8	30,000	53,000	50%	14,900	26,400
Picknicking	3,564,000	6,300,000	43	1,426,000	2,709,000	8	114,000	217,000	68%	77,520	147,560
Boating	3,395,000	6,000,000	32	1,086,000	1,920,000	8	87,000	154,000	70%	60,830	107,520
Fishing	3,847,000	6,800,000	23	885,000	1,556,000	8	71,000	125,000	38%	26,900	47,300
Swimming	4,809,000	8,500,000	60	2,885,000	5,100,000	8	231,000	408,000	90%	207,700	367,200
Water Skiing	1,697,000	3,000,000	32	543,000	960,000	8	43,000	77,000	70%	30,380	53,760
Golfing	340,000	600,000	80	272,000	480,000	8	21,000	36,000			
Hunting	1,697,000	3,000,000	12	204,000	350,000	8	16,000	29,000			
Sightseeing & Driving for Pleasure	14,620,000	25,690,000	30	4,386,000	7,707,000	8	351,000	617,000	40%	140,360	246,640
Other	600,000	1,060,000	47	282,000	512,000	8	23,000	41,000			
Total Activity Occasion (Ratio of 1.7 to 1 over Visitation)	36,550,000	64,600,000	34	12,558,000	22,484,000	8	1,005,000	1,799,000			
Total Visitation (Person Per Day Visit)	21,500,000	38,000,000	34	7,310,000	13,000,000	8	585,000	1,040,000			

(1) Excluding L.B.L.

FACILITIES REQUIREMENT ANALYSIS
PARIS LANDING STATE PARK

Activity		Annual Visitation	% of Total Outings Mid-May Through Mid-September		Average Visitation Per Day Outings 90)	Total Peak Visitation (See Note)				Units Required Peak Visitation ÷ by No. Per Unit			
Lodging	1970	18,000	50%	=	100	210	÷ by	2/unit	=	105	rooms
Lodging	1980	41,600	50%	=	230	483	÷ by	2/unit	=	242	rooms
Camping	1970	30,000	50%	=	166	348	÷ by	3.5/unit	=	100	tent & trailer units
Camping	1980	53,000	50%	=	294	617	÷ by	3.5/unit	=	176	tent & trailer units
Picknicking	1970	114,000	68%	=	862	1,810	÷ by	8/unit	=	226	units
Picknicking	1980	217,000	68%	=	1,640	3,444	÷ by	8/unit	=	430	units
Boating	1970	87,000	70%	=	675	1,400	÷ by	3.5/boat	=	400	boats
Boating	1980	154,000	70%	=	1,200	2,520	÷ by	3.5/boat	=	720	boats
Fishing	1970	71,000	38%	=	300	630				630	fishermen
Fishing	1980	125,000	38%	=	540	1,130				1,130	fishermen
Swimming	1970	231,000	90%	=	2,308	4,846				4,846	bathers
Swimming	1980	408,000	90%	=	4,080	8,568				8,568	bathers
Water Skiing	1970	43,000	70%	=	330	700				700	water skiers
Water Skiing	1980	77,000	70%	=	600	1,260				1,260	water skiers
Golfing	1970	21,000	50%	=	100	210				210	golfers
Golfing	1980	36,000	50%	=	200	420				420	golfers
Hunting	1970	29,000	—								
Hunting	1980	29,000	—								
Sightseeing	1970	350,900	40%	=	1,560	3,275				3,275	sightseers
Sightseeing	1980	616,600	40%	=	2,740	5,754				5,754	sightseers
Other	1970	23,000									
Other	1980	41,000									

Note: Total Peak Visitation = 7 days x daily average visitation x 60% occurring on weekends ÷ 2 days

BOAT SLIP ANALYSIS
PARIS LANDING STATE PARK

Activity		Annual Visitation	% of Total Outings Mid-May Through Mid-September		÷ 3.5 People/Boat		14% Kept in Slips	÷ No. of Days/Participant		No. Slips Needed 1970	No. Slips Needed 1980	No. Slips Proposed 1970	No. Slips Proposed 1980
Boating	1970	87,000	70% =	61,000	÷ by 3.5 =	17,430	2,240	÷ by 4.5 =	500	500			
Boating	1980	154,000	70% =	108,000	÷ by 3.5 =	30,850	4,320	÷ by 4.5 =	960		960		
Fishing	1970	71,000	38% =	27,000	÷ by 3.5 =	7,714	1,080	÷ by 4.5 =	240	240			
Fishing	1980	125,000	38% =	48,000	÷ by 3.5 =	13,714	1,920	÷ by 4.5 =	425		425		
Water Skiing	1970	43,000	70% =	30,000	÷ by 3.5 =	8,570	1,200	÷ by 4.5 =	270	270			
Water Skiing	1980	77,000	70% =	54,000	÷ by 3.5 =	15,430	2,160	÷ by 4.5 =	480		480		
Total Slips										1,010	1,865	500	720

BOAT LAUNCHING PER DAY

						1970	1980
470	Boats		1970			400	
720	Boats		1980				720
610	Fishermen		1970	÷ by 3.5 people/boat = 175 × 80% fishing in boats		144	
1,130	Fishermen		1980	÷ by 3.5 people/boat = 325 × 80% fishing in boats			260
700	Water Skiers		1970	÷ by 3.5 people/boat =		200	
1,260	Water Skiers		1980	÷ by 3.5 people/boat =			360
				Total Boats		744	1,340
Total x 68%	(percent of boats being launched) = launchings per day					506	910
Total x 50%	(percent of boats being launched at launch ramps) = launching at launch ramps					372	670
Total x 18%	(percent of boats being launched at marina) = launching at marina					134	240

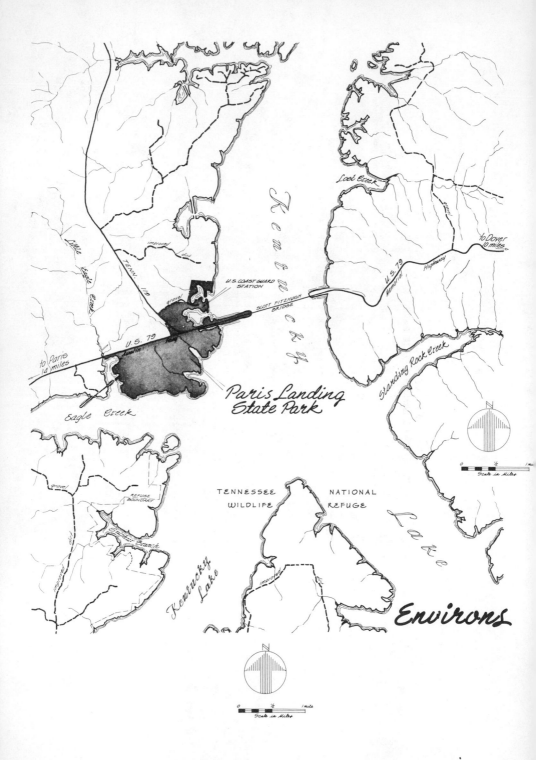

Paris Landing State Park

Environs

Evidence of shore erosion with lake at winter draw-down

Existing picnic area

SITE AND LAND USE ANALYSIS

An Environs Map is included to show the immediate vicinity of the park. As further introduction to the site analysis an organization diagram is included to relate site requirements schematically to individual facilities or areas and to portray an ideal relationship between the outdoor recreational activities.

The textual analysis is supported by the Site Analysis and Land Use Plan, a map which designates specific areas within the park in accordance with their most appropriate use.

In analyzing the park development it was determined that Paris Landing would be a resort oriented park because of its close proximity to the southern entrance to the Land Between the Lakes. The park will supplement the Land Between the Lakes activities, particularly the provision of quality facilities that would appeal to all members of the family or to portions of the family not interested in the Land Between the Lakes activities.

A factor in analyzing the land use was existing park facilities, which can hardly be abandoned because of the large capital investment already made in them. Although the relationship and the location of the existing park facilities are not always deal, they can be fitted into a logical land use pattern.

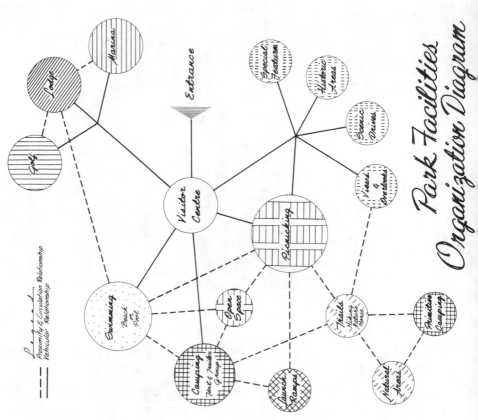

Park Facilities
Organization Diagram

Site Criteria for Park Facilities

LODGE LOCATION

Site Characteristics: buildable area, good views, suitable vegetative cover, space for parking and good accessibility. (boating, sailing, fishing, and water skiing.)
Near: swimming, golf, marina with related activities

PICNIC AREA LOCATION

Site Characteristics: gently rolling topography, suitable vegetative cover, scenic views, good drainage, space for parking, and good accessibility.
Near: swimming, trails, launch ramps, bank fishing and open spaces for active recreation.

CAMP SITE LOCATION

Site Characteristics: gently rolling topography, good drainage, adequate water supply, and sewage disposal, tree cover, and good accessibility.
Near: swimming, trails, bank fishing, and launch ramps

MARINA LOCATION

Site Characteristics: protected from prevailing winds, or deep channel to allow access to main body of water during low water periods. Close to main body of water, adequate parking and good accessibility.
Near: lodge, concession

SWIMMING LOCATION

Site Characteristics: protected area that is protected from washing action of wind. Beach area should have a edge of gradual slope. Swimming area should have a edge of approximately 2%, adequate parking, meet State water purity regulations. Park: meet State water purity regulations, good accessibility, and adequate parking.
Near: lodge, camping, picnicking

GOLF COURSE LOCATION

Site Characteristics: gently rolling topography, good soil without large rocks or stones, some streams to divide water hazards, open land with a little tree cover, adequate parking, and good accessibility.
Near: lodge

LAUNCH RAMPS

Site Characteristics: protected from prevailing winds, near deep channel to allow access to main body of water during low water periods, adequate parking and good accessibility.
Near: picnicking, camp sites.

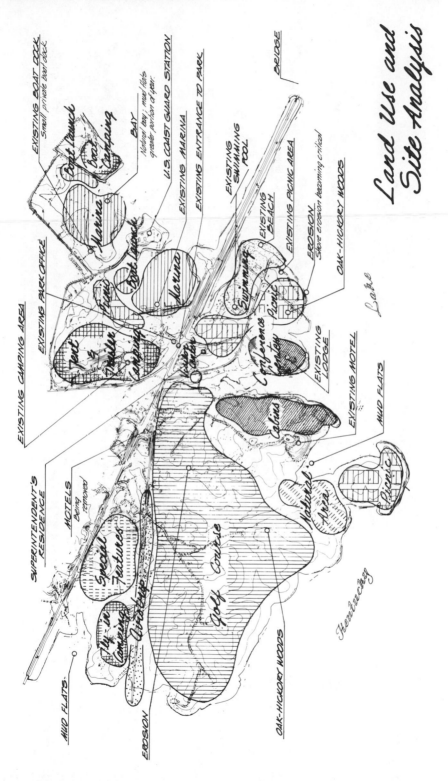

Land Use and Site Analysis

Existing Boat Dock — Small private boat dock
Boat Layout
Boat Camping
Bay — Natural bay; mud flats greater portion of year
U.S. Coast Guard Station
Existing Marina
Existing Entrance to Park
Existing Swimming Pool
Existing Beach
Existing Picnic Area
Erosion — Shore erosion becoming critical
Oak-Hickory Woods
Bridge
Marina
Boat Layout
Marina
Swimming
Picnic
Existing Park Office
Existing Camping Area
Tent & Trailer Camping
Conference Station
Existing Lodge
Existing Motel
Mud Flats
Lake
Cabins
Natural Area
Picnic
Superintendent's Residence
Motels — Being removed
Special Features
Fly-in Camping
Airstrip
Golf Course
Oak-Hickory Woods
Mud Flats
Erosion
Oak-Hickory Woods
Kentucky

Panoramic view with boat harbor at the center and picnic area to the right

In order to provide attractions for tourists and convention visitors, a convention center, golf course and airport were included in the park master plan. The airport will be located on an old existing road bed in a location which will not damage the usefulness of the remaining areas of the park.

To attract tourists and visitors from the Land Between the Lakes, an Interpretive Center is proposed which will be developed around the theme of the Indian civilizations of the Tennessee River Basin. There are a number of significant Indian sites nearby, and they will be developed and related to the park and major interpretive activity at Paris Landing State Park.

Projected visitation figures indicate heavy usage of the park and because of the limited amount of acreage available a more intensive use of land than is normally the case in state park development will be necessary. Combining the swimming pool and beach parking into a central parking facility makes it possible to utilize the land available more efficiently.

The intersection of Highway 79 and 119 along with the existing three entrances into the park form a complex and dangerous intersection. With further development of the park the situation will become extremely dangerous to regulate. To solve this problem, a rotary interchange with a single entrance into the park should be developed northwest of the present entrance.

Access to the marina and camping areas will be by means of a bridge over Route 79 from the access road.

The main park access road will be a divided roadway extending south into the existing major day use area. A visitors' center will be located along the access road 200' south of the entrance and will overlook the Par-3 golf course.

The general area to the southwest is wooded with some steep slopes and, although not ideal in terms of the amount of land used, will make an excellent site for an interesting and challenging golf course. Also, in this area a wooded peninsula provides an opportunity to develop an excellent picnic area with good views of the lake.

A natural bay north of the existing marina affords an ideal location for a well protected marina. Some dredging will be necessary to create a marina basin and also dredging of an existing channel to provide access for sail boats.

Peak visitation projected for the lodge will require an increase in the lodge from 63 units to 140 units by 1975. Capacity of the dining room (restaurant) should be increased from 150 to 300 and total private dining-meeting rooms or areas from 250 to 400.

The proposed auditorium (combining as a banquet hall or ballroom) should have a dining capacity of 400 and a seating capacity of 650. This facility should have 5,000 square feet in the main room plus a 2,000 square foot lobby and display area.

MASTER PLAN DESIGN

All proposals for park improvements are shown on the Master Plan and supporting Utility Map.

Entrance to Park: The present entrance into the park off Route 79 is a four-way intersection with access to the existing lodge and day use area to the south and access to the existing marina and camping area to the north. With further development of the park an already dangerous intersection will become too difficult to regulate.

To alleviate this problem a rotary interchange is proposed four hundred feet west of the present entrance at the intersection of U. S. Route 79 and State Route 119. There will be a single entrance into the park to the south and the access traffic to the marina and camping areas will be by means of a bridge over U. S. 79 from the entrance road.

Because of the large volume of traffic going into the main park area, a divided roadway with a varying median entrance road is proposed. A major part of an existing road will be used as the exit lane of the divided entrance road.

Visitors' Center: A visitors' center will be located approximately two hundred feet southwest of the proposed entrance. The visitors' center will contain an information center, park office and toilets. The existing park office will be used as a marina and camp registration office.

Lodge and Cabins: Development of additional lodge facilities will take place north of the existing lodge. Any development to the west of the existing lodge is undesirable because of the steep slopes and increased traffic congestion created by the addition of conference center and restaurant facilities in this area and also to the south because of obstructing the views from the existing dining room, pool and lodge units.

The proposed cabin area will be located southwest of the existing lodge facility on a heavily wooded peninsula. This site has excellent views of the lake. The majority of the cabins are within walking distance of the lodge and it will be convenient for cabin guests to use its facilities.

Conference Center: A conference center will be located south of the existing lodge lobby. The advantages of this location are: the view from the existing dining area is affected very little; the conference building ties directly to the lobby area and kitchen facilities of the main lodge building and excellent views of the lake from the meeting rooms. The conference building should be three stories high and have an auditorium, meeting rooms and private dining rooms at appropriate levels.

The Paris Landing Inn

Major Day Use Area: The existing day use area is located south of the causeway and will remain the major area for this purpose. Located in the major day use area is a recently constructed olympic size swimming pool. Reopening and expansion of the existing beach is proposed because the swimming pool will not accommodate the large number of swimmers anticipated at the park. The existing picnicking area to the south which fronts on the lake is to remain. Because of the high use of this area and erosion problems, asphalt flats or similar surfacing may be used for each picnic unit. Also, controlled paved parking areas are proposed to prevent parking in the picnicking area. Erosion of the shoreline along this same picnic area has been a very serious problem and riprapping of the banks or other controls must be continued to stop the loss of this area. Additional picnicking west of the swimming pool in the day use area is proposed. This site is wooded and rolling with some views of the lake, and it should relieve the pressure on the existing picnicking area. A concession building will be appropriately situated in the day use area at the end of the loop drive.

Tent and Trailer Camping: The existing tent and trailer camping is to be expanded to the northwest and will contain a total of 132 camp sites with 66 being pull-thru trailer spaces and 66 being spur tent spaces. A high degree of maintenance must be practiced to control the erosion problem. Paving the parking pads and a good grass cover are recommended to control the erosion problem. A buffer area of evergreens along Routes 79 and 119 will help soften traffic noises somewhat and provide more privacy for the campers.

A boat-tent camping site containing 56 spur tent spaces for boats will be located north of the existing camping area. The site is wooded and fronts on the lake, making it a very desirable site for camping, especially for those interested in boating and fishing. One washhouse with showers and flush toilets will be provided.

A fly-in camping area containing 30 sites will be provided on the west end of the runway. Tie-down spaces, camp sites and toilets will be provided.

Picnicking: In addition to the picnicking in the day use area picnicking on an isolated peninsula south of the entrance is proposed. This site is heavily wooded with excellent views of the lake and allows for a more passive type of picnicking.

Marina: The existing marina which is well protected from the prevailing winds will be enlarged to accommodate a majority of the boat visitation to the park and will contain 130 covered boat slips and 90 open boat slips. Also, launch ramps, a service dock and a fish cleaning shelter are planned. In addition, a 200-boat dry storage building is proposed.

The existing park office will serve as the marina control office. An excursion boat dock will be provided at the entrance to the marina to serve the excursion boat which will make daily trips to historical and scenic sites along the lake. A boater's picnicking area will be provided adjacent to the marina.

An additional marina is proposed in a well protected inlet north of the Coast Guard Station. This inlet will require some dredging to make it navigable. An existing channel, which also may require some dredging, provides access to deeper waters. This marina is recommended as the main mooring area for sailboats and will contain 90 sailboat slips, 164 open slips and 66 covered boat slips.

Golf Courses and Par-3 Golf: An eighteen hole regulation golf course is proposed on the southwest portion of the site. The site is wooded with steep slopes in some sections necessitating the use of a larger amount of acreage for the course layout. There are excellent views of the lake from approximately half of the holes.

Overlooking Marina Site

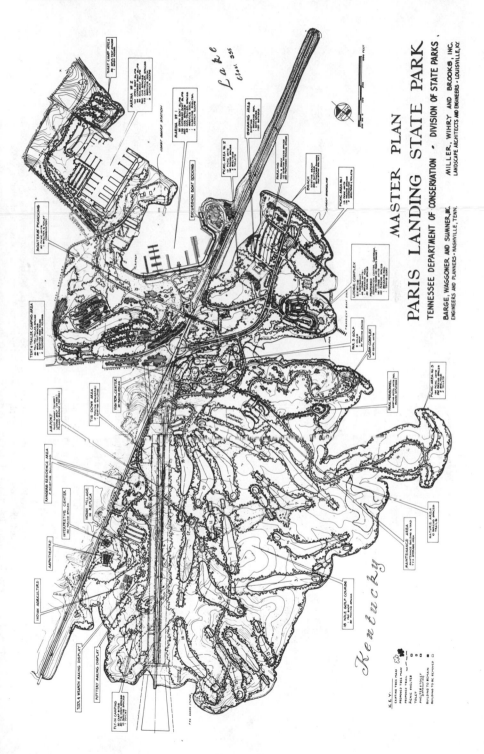

MASTER PLAN
PARIS LANDING STATE PARK
TENNESSEE DEPARTMENT OF CONSERVATION · DIVISION OF STATE PARKS

MILLER, WIHRY AND BROOKS, INC.
LANDSCAPE ARCHITECTS AND ENGINEERS · LOUISVILLE, KY.

BARGE, WAGGONER AND SUMNER, JR.
ENGINEERS AND PLANNERS · NASHVILLE, TENN.

Erosion is a problem and where drainage crosses the fairways, piping of the water and sodding will be necessary. Fairways have been located in such a way as to avoid placing fairways parallel to the valley floors where possible. The clubhouse has been located as close as feasible to the lodge and is approximately eighteen hundred feet away from the lodge by car.

A nine hole Par-3 golf course is proposed adjacent to the day use area and within walking distance of both the lodge and day use area. This facility will handle those visitors who are beginners in golf and take the pressure off the 18 hole regulation golf course.

Airport: The airport runway is located on an existing roadway bed and will require a minimum of grading and tree removal. Orientation of the runway is within the required standards and will be paved, 3,900 ft. long and 75 ft. wide. Also, there will be a 1,500 foot taxiing strip and two 250 foot by 450 foot by 1000 foot approach areas. The location of the proposed runway provides for the layout of the major park facilities without any crossing of the runway. The strip will have a 0.5 percent grade and orientation is north-northeast. This will be a recreation type facility developed by The Tennessee Aeronautics Commission under the Federal Aid Airport Program.

Interpretive Center: The proposed interpretive center will be located on a knoll approximately two thousand feet west of the proposed entrance, and is situated on the main highway so that travelers passing through on the highway could stop at the interpretive center without becoming involved with interior park traffic.

Because of the number of Indian sites within the general vicinity of the park, an interpretive center with its theme being "Indians in the Tennessee Region" is proposed for Paris Landing State Park. Along with the interpretive center will be an outdoor exhibit area which is envisioned to have a replica of an Indian village, Indian agriculture, pottery making display, tool and weapon making display, etc., which the Indians in the Tennessee Region either made or grew. Also there will be an amphitheater where daily lectures on Indian life can be held.

Another use for the amphitheater would be an outdoor drama with the story centering around the Indians of the "Temple Mound Period" who lived within the vicinity of the park. It is

Obion River Temple Mounds

felt that there will be a high visitation to the drama from the visitors who will be staying in the Land Between the Lakes area.

Obion River Temple Mounds, Duck River Temple Mounds and Dover Flint Quarries: The development of these three sites is proposed in conjunction with the interpretive center. These sites are within twenty minutes to one hour's driving time and field trips to these sites are planned as part of the interpretive program at the park center. All these sites have a highly significant Indian history dating back thousands of years and have many visible signs of Indian activity such as the temple mounds visible on two of the sites. Development of these sites will include an interpretive shelter, trails to the points of interest, and a picnic area with shelter.

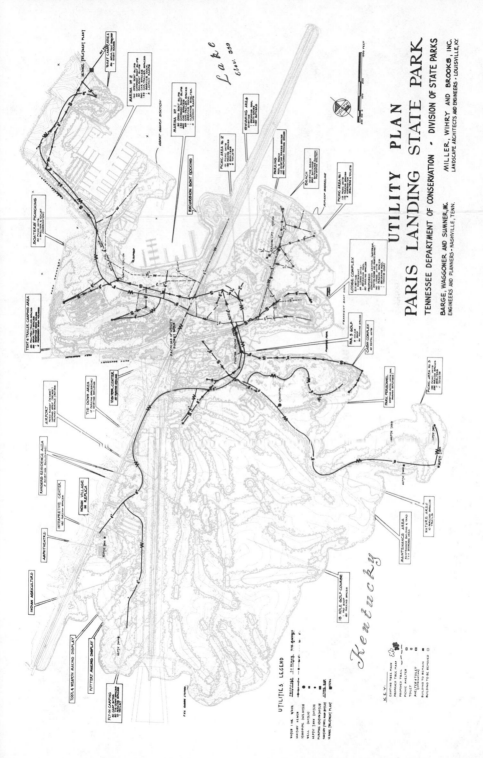

UTILITY PLAN
PARIS LANDING STATE PARK
TENNESSEE DEPARTMENT OF CONSERVATION · DIVISION OF STATE PARKS

BARGE, WAGGONER AND SUMNER, INC.
ENGINEERS AND PLANNERS · NASHVILLE, TENN.

MILLER, WIHRY AND BROOKS, INC.
LANDSCAPE ARCHITECTS AND ENGINEERS · LOUISVILLE, KY.

Maintenance Area: The proposed relocation of the maintenance area in a central location allows for easy access to the major day use area of the park. Also, this location provides storage for golf course maintenance equipment in close proximity to the 18 hole golf course and the Par-3 golf course. A TVA storage area replaced the one to be removed and because of Master Plan objectives will be provided adjacent to the maintenance building.

Park Personnel Area: An existing motel facility adjacent to the cabin area is to be used to house summer employees. Also, this facility can be used to house the actors of the proposed outdoor drama. Although this facility does not meet good park standards, with some minor repairs and restoration it can be made to fit into the surrounding park character.

Superintendent's and Rangers' Residences: The superintendent's residence will remain in its present location because of its central location to the day use area. Two existing residences along U. S. Route 79 may be used for the rangers' residences.

UTILITIES

Sanitary sewerage and water facilities, as shown on the Utilities Map, are to be installed at the main body of the park. Sewage will be collected from the cabin complex, lodge, swimming area camp sites, visitors' center, marinas, and proshops. A new treatment plant replacing the existing small plant near the lodge would be located at the north side of the park. The treated effluent would be released into Kentucky Reservoir through an outfall reaching toward the old river channel.

Water for the park will be furnished by a Utility District that has been formed to serve this area. In the event that this district's plans do not materialize, the existing water plant will have to be enlarged. An eight-inch main will be extended along the principal access road with a storage tank to be installed on the high elevation near the road to the motel for park personnel. Water will be installed to all facilities in the main park.

The Dover Flint Quarries site, the Obion River Temple Mounds site and the Duck River Temple Mounds site are too remote except for individually designed utilities and would be served by wells and individual disposal systems.

Electric power is available to the main park site by the Paris Board of Public Utilities at Paris.

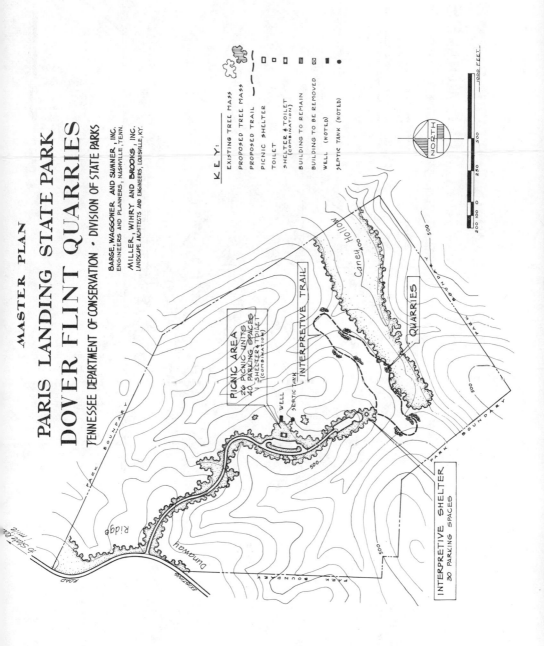

MASTER PLAN

PARIS LANDING STATE PARK

DOVER FLINT QUARRIES

TENNESSEE DEPARTMENT OF CONSERVATION · DIVISION OF STATE PARKS

BARGE, WAGGONER AND SUMNER, INC.
ENGINEERS AND PLANNERS, NASHVILLE, TENN.

MILLER, WIHRY AND BROOKS, INC.
LANDSCAPE ARCHITECTS AND ENGINEERS, LOUISVILLE, KY.

KEY:

EXISTING TREE MASS
PROPOSED TREE MASS
PROPOSED TRAIL
PICNIC SHELTER
TOILET
SHELTER & TOILET (COMBINATION)
BUILDING TO REMAIN
BUILDING TO BE REMOVED
WELL (NOTED)
SEPTIC TANK (NOTED)

NORTH

200 100 0   250   500   1000 FEET

PICNIC AREA
26 PICNIC UNITS
40 PARKING SPACES
SHELTER & TOILET
(COMBINATION)

WELL
SEPTIC TANK

INTERPRETIVE TRAIL

Caney Hollow

QUARRIES

INTERPRETIVE SHELTER
30 PARKING SPACES

Dunaway Ridge

ROAD

To State Road ½ mile

PARK BOUNDARY

PARK BOUNDARY

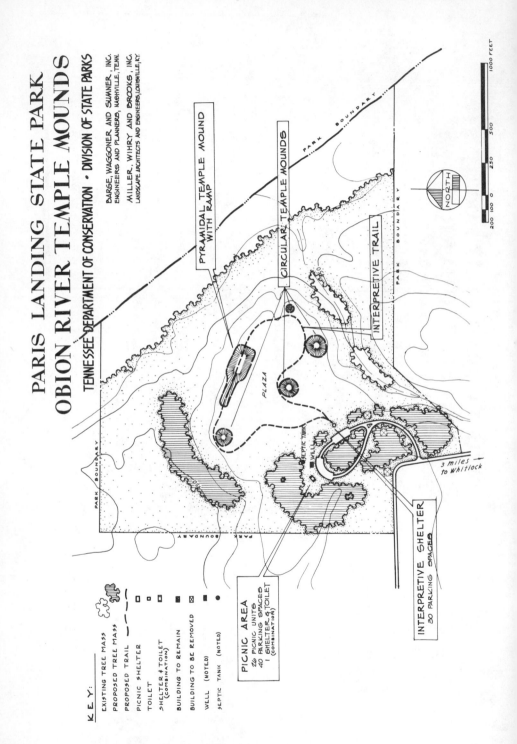

PARIS LANDING STATE PARK
OBION RIVER TEMPLE MOUNDS

TENNESSEE DEPARTMENT OF CONSERVATION · DIVISION OF STATE PARKS

BARGE, WAGGONER AND SUMNER, INC.
ENGINEERS AND PLANNERS, NASHVILLE, TENN.

MILLER, WIHRY AND BROOKS, INC.
LANDSCAPE ARCHITECTS AND ENGINEERS, LOUISVILLE, KY.

PYRAMIDAL TEMPLE MOUND
WITH RAMP

CIRCULAR TEMPLE MOUNDS

INTERPRETIVE TRAIL

PLAZA

PARK BOUNDARY

3 miles
to Whitlock

INTERPRETIVE SHELTER
30 PARKING SPACES

PICNIC AREA
26 PICNIC UNITS
40 PARKING SPACES
1 SHELTER & TOILET
(COMBINATION)

NORTH

1000 FEET
500
250
200 100 0

K.E.Y:

EXISTING TREE MASS
PROPOSED TREE MASS
PROPOSED TRAIL
PICNIC SHELTER
TOILET
SHELTER & TOILET
(COMBINATION)
BUILDING TO REMAIN
BUILDING TO BE REMOVED
WELL (NOTED)
SEPTIC TANK (NOTED)

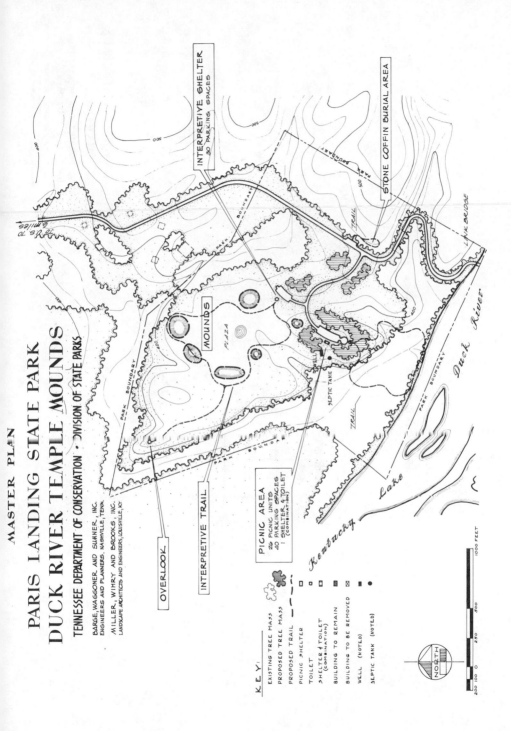

MASTER PLAN

PARIS LANDING STATE PARK
DUCK RIVER TEMPLE MOUNDS

TENNESSEE DEPARTMENT OF CONSERVATION · DIVISION OF STATE PARKS

BARGE, WAGGONER, AND SUMNER, INC.
ENGINEERS AND PLANNERS, NASHVILLE, TENN.

MILLER, WIHRY AND BROOKS, INC.
LANDSCAPE ARCHITECTS AND ENGINEERS, LOUISVILLE, KY

KEY:

EXISTING TREE MASS
PROPOSED TREE MASS
PROPOSED TRAIL
PICNIC SHELTER
TOILET
SHELTER & TOILET (COMBINATION)
BUILDING TO REMAIN
BUILDING TO BE REMOVED
WELL (NOTED)
SEPTIC TANK (NOTED)

OVERLOOK

INTERPRETIVE TRAIL

PICNIC AREA
26 PICNIC UNITS
40 PARKING SPACES
1 SHELTER & TOILET (COMBINATION)

INTERPRETIVE SHELTER
30 PARKING SPACES

STONE COFFIN BURIAL AREA

MOUNDS

PLAZA

SEPTIC TANK

WELL

PARK BOUNDARY

TRAIL

Duck River

Kentucky   Lake

LOG BRIDGE

NORTH

200 100 0   250   500   1000 FEET

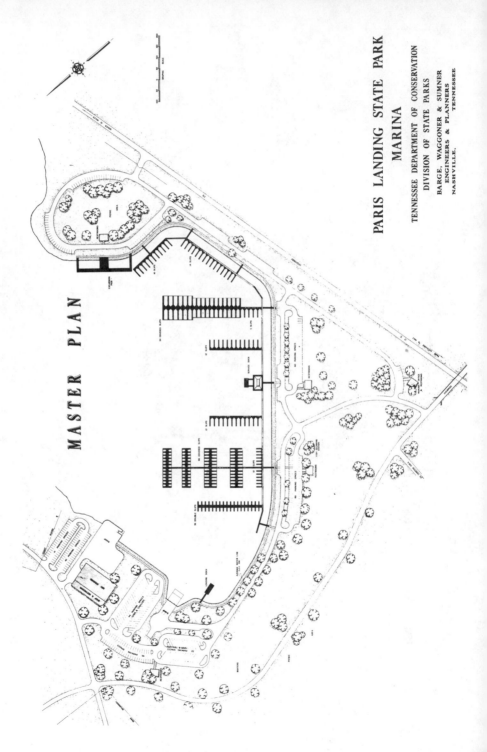

MASTER PLAN

PARIS LANDING STATE PARK
MARINA

TENNESSEE DEPARTMENT OF CONSERVATION
DIVISION OF STATE PARKS

BARGE, WAGGONER & SUMNER
ENGINEERS & PLANNERS
NASHVILLE, TENNESSEE

DEVELOPMENT PROGRAM

The Master Plan provides for the development of park facilities over a 10-year period from 1963. It is intended that the program be shown as improvements being made immediately (1968) and then improvements to be made in two-year increments to 1978.

The following steps are outlined in a priority program for action to be taken:

IMMEDIATE ACTION—1968

I. Land Acquisition

a. Previously acquired: 386.5 acres — $800,342

b. T.V.A. property transferred and Leased to the State of Tennessee — 257.0 acres — N/A.

c. T.V.A. property to be transferred to the State of Tennessee — 144.1 acres — N/A.

d. Property included in the Park Boundary but excluded from Park (U. S. Coast Guard) — 7.0 acres — N/A.

e. Three related Indian sites Not included in park acreage — 420 acres — 110,500 estimated

	Acres	Cost
Total for Park (Paris Landing)	827.6	800,342
Excluded (U. S. Coast Guard)	7.0	
Indian Mounds (3 sites)	420.0	110,500
Total All Land	1254.6	910,842
		say 911,000

2. Partial construction of Lower Harbor including dredging, riprap, access roads, parking, service dock, cleaning shelter, and boat slips.

3. Provide croquet, shuffleboard and tennis facilities at the Lodge Complex.

4. Provide water and sewer improvements for lower Harbor.

5. Landscape existing facilities and install shoreline improvements.

6. Construct Concession Building.

7. Repair existing roads.

PHASE I—1969-1971

1. Provide remaining Lower Harbor facilities.
2. Construct Golf Course including pro shop.
3. Construct addition to existing lodge.
4. Construct visitation center.
5. Construct airstrip.
6. Construct 80 units for boater picnicking.
7. Provide 115 picnic units at Picnic Area No. 1.
8. Provide access roads including new entrance and utilities to golf course, lodge, visitation center, airstrip and picnic areas.

PHASE II—1971-1973

1. Construct maintenance area and remodel existing Rangers' residences.
2. Provide parking area for pool and beach.
3. Construct 100 campsites (50 tent and 50 trailer).
4. Construct first 20 units of rental cabins.
5. Provide access road and utilities to maintenance area, campsites, and rental cabins.
6. Acquisition of Indian sites.

PHASE III—1973-1975

1. Construct fly-in campsites.
2. Provide 154 picnic units at Picnic Area No. 3.
3. Construct remaining 32 campsites at the tent and trailer camping area.
4. Provide access and utilities to Picnic Area No. 3, fly-in campsites and tent and trailer campsites.

PHASE IV—1975-1977

1. Provide remaining 20 units of rental cabins.
2. Provide 101 more picnic units at Picnic Area No. 2.
3. Construct remaining 56 tent campsites.
4. Construct Golf Course (Par-3—9 holes) including pro shop.
5. Construction of Nature Area including trails.
6. Provide access roads and utilities to rental cabins, Picnic Area No. 2, and remaining campsites.

PHASE V—978

1. Construct amphitheatre and interpretive center including related facilities.
2. Construct Upper Harbor facilities.
3. Construct facilities on Duck River Temple Mounds Site, Obion River Mounds Site, and Dover Flint Quarries Site.

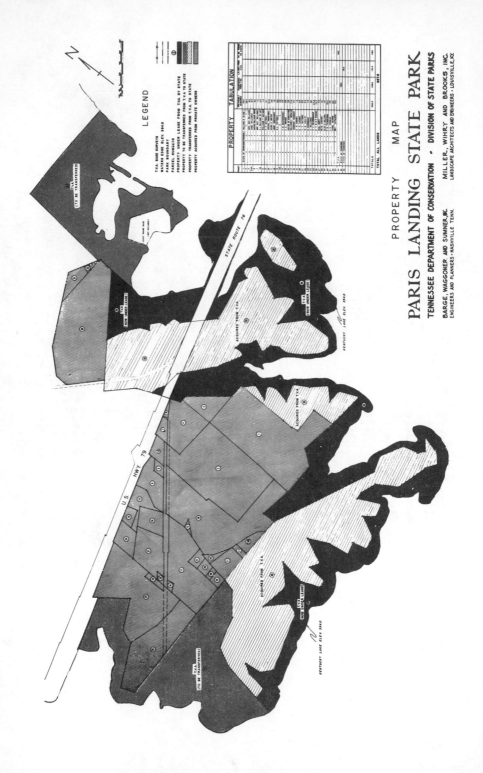

PROPERTY MAP

PARIS LANDING STATE PARK

TENNESSEE DEPARTMENT OF CONSERVATION · DIVISION OF STATE PARKS

BARGE, WAGGONER AND SUMNER, INC.
ENGINEERS AND PLANNERS · NASHVILLE TENN.

MILLER, WIHRY AND BROOKS, INC.
LANDSCAPE ARCHITECTS AND ENGINEERS · LOUISVILLE, KY.

COST ESTIMATE

Cost estimates are included for all facilities proposed in the Master Plan. These costs reflect the expenditures for the current program as well as for five two-year periods extending to 1979. All estimates are based on current construction and do not take into account increases or changes occurring over future years. Equipment is included as well as land improvements.

	Total	Immediate 1967-68	Phase I 1969-71	Phase II 1971-73	Phase III 1973-75	Phase IV 1975-77	Phase V 1977-79
A. LAND ACQUISITION							
*911,000 (All under immediate program except $110,500 for Indian sites which are in Phase II).							
B. IMPROVEMENTS							
(1) Roads and Drives							
(6" Base and bituminous surface includes roadside landscaping, signs and markers) 50,000 lin. feet @ $7.50	$ 375,000		$ 145,000	$ 60,000	$ 65,000	$ 85,000	$ 20,000
Resurface existing roads	20,000	20,000					
Overpass	125,000		125,000				
(2) Picnic Areas							
(Average 100 tables — includes toilet and parking area)							
4 @ $25,000 ....$100,000			30,000	20,000	30,000	20,000	
7 Shelters @ $8,000 56,000	206,000		16,000	8,000	16,000	16,000	
Shoreline Stabilization & Landscaping	50,000	50,000					
(3) Visitor Center Office (Includes exterior and parking)	40,000		40,000				
(4) Interpretive Center Area—							
Museum (Includes parking and Landscaping)	175,000						175,000
Amphitheater	125,000						125,000
	300,000						
(5) Lodge Complex Addition							
140 additional lodge units @ $10,000 1,400,000	1,400,000		1,400,000				
convention center	250,000		250,000				
Pool, parking and landscaping games area, and Tennis Court	130,000	30,000	100,000				
	1,780,000						
(6) Cabin Complex 40 cabins @ $15,000	600,000			300,000	300,000		
(7) Tent and Trailer Camping Area							
188 Sites @ $2,250 ... 423,000				225,000	72,000	126,000	
3 wash houses @ $25,000 ... 75,000	498,000			25,000	25,000	25,000	
(8) Marinas							
Lower Harbor							
Dredging, Shore Improvements	565,000	170,000	395,000				
and Utilities	805,000	350,000	455,000				
Piers and slips							
Service Docks & Fueling Barge	170,000	80,000	90,000				
	1,540,000						
Upper Harbor							
Site work—excavation, riprapping and utility	240,000						
Ramps, parking, landscaping	100,000						
Buildings	60,000						
Piers and slips	600,000						
	1,000,000						1,000,000

Cost Estimate (continued)

Item	Cost	Total	Immediate 1967-68	Phase I 1969-71	Phase II 1971-73	Phase III 1973-75	Phase IV 1975-77	Phase V 1977-79
(9) Swimming Area								
Parking and landscaping ...	20,000				20,000			
Bath House (converted) shelter ...	10,000	30,000			10,000			
(10) Maintenance Area								
Includes exterior and parking		100,000			100,000			
(11) Rangers' Residence Area ...		20,000	10,000		10,000			
(12) Airport								
*Runway, Taxiway, Apron, lighting, fencing, parking ...	407,500			407,500				
30 Campsites @ $2,250 ...	67,500							67,500
1 Wash House @ $25,000 ...	25,000	500,000						25,000
(13) Golf Course								
18 Holes @ $15,000 ...	270,000			270,000				
Pro-Shop and parking ...	100,000	370,000		100,000				
9 holes—Par 3 @ $7,500 ...	67,500							67,500
Shop and parking ...	40,000	107,500						40,000
(14) Concession Bldg. ...		25,000	25,000					
(15) Utilities								
Water—24,000 ft. water lines ...	72,000		5,000	7,500	10,000	31,000	17,000	1,500
Storage Tanks ...	25,000				25,000			
**Plant Expansion ...	50,000			50,000				
Sanitary Sewers—21,000 l.f. lines ...	95,000			51,000	20,000	4,500	19,500	
3 Pumping Stations @ $20,000 ...	60,000			60,000				
Sewage Treatment Plant ...	75,000			75,000				
6 Septic Tanks @ $1,100 ...	6,600					6,600		
Electrical Distribution System ...	20,000	403,600		10,000	5,000	5,000		
Subtotal		$8,040,100	$740,000	$4,077,000	$838,000	$555,100	$308,500	$1,521,500

* Cost of this facility is borne 50% by the Federal Aviation Agency and 50% by the Tennessee Aeronautics Commission.

** There will be no expenditure for this facility if water is furnished by Utility District.

Cost Estimate (continued)

Duck River Temple Mounds Site

	Total	Immediate 1967-68	Phase I 1969-71	Phase II 1971-73	Phase III 1973-75	Phase IV 1975-77	Phase V 1977-79
Land Acquisition—135 acres @ $300..$ 40,500 Phase II incl. under "A" above							
Improvements							
(1) Roads and Drives 6" Base and bituminous surface (includes roadside landscaping, signs and markers) 1,000 l.f. @ $7.50	7,500						7,500
(2) Foot Trails	3,000						3,000
(3) Picnic Area 26 picnic units (includes parking) ......$ 15,000 1 shelter @ $8,000 8,000	23,000						23,000
(4) Interpretive Shelter (includes parking)	15,000						15,000
(5) Utilities 1 well @ 2000 ...... 2,000 1 septic tank @ 1100 1,100	3,100						3,100
Sub-Total Improvements	$ 51,600						$ 51,600

Obion River Temple Mounds Site

	Total	Immediate 1967-68	Phase I 1969-71	Phase II 1971-73	Phase III 1973-75	Phase IV 1975-77	Phase V 1977-79
Land Acquisition—130 acres @ $300..$ 39,000 in Phase II, incl. under "A" above							
(1) Roads and Drives 6" Base and bituminous surface (includes roadside landscaping, signs and markers) 1,700 l.f. @ $7.50	12,750						12,750
(2) Foot Trails	2,500						2,500
(3) Picnic Area 26 picnic units (includes parking) ......$ 15,000 1 shelter @ $8,000 8,000	15,000						15,000 8,000
(4) Interpretive Shelter (includes Parking)	15,000						15,000
(5) Utilities 1 well @ 2000 ...... 2,000 1 septic tank @ 1100 1,100	3,100						3,100
Subtotal Improvements	$ 56,350						$ 56,350

Cost Estimate (continued)

Dover Flint Quarries Site

	Total	Immediate 1967-68	Phase I 1969-71	Phase II 1971-73	Phase III 1973-75	Phase IV 1975-77	Phase V 1977-79
Land Acquisition—155 acres @ $200 ..$ 31,000 (In Phase II, incl. under "A" above)							
Improvements							
(1) Roads and Drives (6" Base and bituminous surface includes roadside landscaping, signs and markers)	2,000						2,000
(2) Foot Trails 2,400 l.f. @ $7.50	18,000						18,000
(3) Picnic Area — 26 picnic units (includes parking) $ 15,000; 1 shelter @ $8,000 ... 8,000	23,000						23,000
(4) Interpretive Shelter (includes Parking)	15,000						15,000
1 well @ 2000 ... 2,000; 1 septic tank @ 1100 ... 1,100	3,100						3,100
Subtotal Improvements	61,100						61,100
TOTAL Improvements	8,209,150	740,000	4,077,000	838,000	555,100	308,500	1,690,550
PROFESSIONAL FEES	815,000	75,000	400,000	85,000	55,000	30,000	170,000
C. Equipment							
(1) Lodge Convention Center and Vocation Cabins — 140 rooms @ $600 ..$ 84,000; 40 cabins @ $3,000 ... 120,000; Conference center (includes auditorium, meeting rooms and private dining room) 40,000 say $ 244,000	244,000		$ 244,000				
(2) 2 Golf Courses and 2 Pro Shops	35,000		25,000				$ 10,000
(3) Furnishings (other than for above facilities)	50,000		10,000	10,000	$ 10,000	$ 10,000	$ 10,000
(4) Marinas (includes rental equipment)	125,000	25,000	25,000				75,000
(5) General Maintenance—vehicles and miscellaneous	40,000	5,000	5,000	5,000	5,000	10,000	10,000
Subtotal—Equipment	$ 494,000	$ 30,000	$ 309,000	15,000	$ 15,000	$ 20,000	$ 105,000
TOTAL—IMPROVEMENTS AND EQUIPMENT	9,518,150	845,000	4,786,000	938,000	625,100	358,500	1,965,550
GRAND TOTAL—LAND, IMPROVEMENTS AND EQUIPMENT	10,429,150	1,645,500	4,786,000	1,048,500	625,100	358,500	1,965,550
say	10,430,000	1,645,000	4,785,000	1,050,000	625,000	360,000	1,965,000

OPERATIONS

Estimates have been prepared for annual revenues and expenditures associated with park facilities after three full years of operation. These projections are shown on the accompanying tables.

Gross receipts are based on visitation and use projections in a previous section of this report. Charges for selected services are based on current or anticipated state park practices in Tennessee.

Total income after three years' operation is estimated to be about $865,000; at the same time, expenditures should be expected to amount to $600,000. These recurring costs include salaries, utilities, maintenance, supplies and stores for resale. They are primarily based on expenses at similar state parks in the system.

While the ratio of income to expenditures is shown to be very favorable in the projections, it must be noted that no provision is made for payment of the original capital investment for land and improvements. If it were appropriate to make allowance for retirement of the state bond issue and repayment or reimbursement of other sources of capital, the facility would not show a favorable operating situation. Moreover, there is no reason to expect that it should since such basic park services and facilities for sightseeing, picnicking, hiking, and the interpretive program are offered without charge to the people of Tennessee and its visitors.

ESTIMATED ANNUAL GROSS RECEIPTS
PARIS LANDING STATE PARK *
(After 3 years of Operation)

1. Lodge and Cabins (based on 45% occupancy annually)

130 doubles @	$12.00	$255,840
73 singles @	9.00	107,748
40 cabins @	15.00	98,400
		$-61,988

2. Tent and Trailer Camping (based on 30,000 visitation days)

8,530 Tents or trailers @ $2.50	21,325

3. Swimming (based on 231,000 activity-occasions—1/3 in pool)

50,000 adults @ $0.75	$ 37,500	
25,000 children @ $0.50	12,500	50,000

4. Boating

Slip Rentals (500 slips with $150 average income)	75,000
Boat and Motor Rental	
4480 occasions @ $7.50 (based on 18% boating-fishing visitations @ 3.5 persons per boat)	33,600

5. Restaurant

150 persons per meal @ $1.50— 200 days	135,000

6. Golf Course

14,000 occasions @ $2.50	$35,000	
7,000 occasions @ 1.25	8,750	
Cart and Equipment Rental	2,500	$ 46,250

7. Gifts, Beverages, Gas Oil, and Other Sales incl. marina and concession — 40,000

8. Boat Cruise (May be concession— not net income)

Total Income	say	$863,165
		$865,000

* Note: Does not include Upper Harbor Marina since it is included for long range development.

ESTIMATED ANNUAL EXPENDITURES
PARIS LANDING STATE PARK *
(After 3 years Operation)

1. Wages and Salaries

Park Superintendent		$ 8,000
Clerks—4 @ $3,600		14,400
2 Senior Park Ranger @ $6,000		12,000
4 Junior Park Ranger @ 4,800		19,200
Park Attendants		
10 Full time @ $3,600	$36,000	
10 Part time @ $1,200	12,000	48,000
3 Utility Men		9,000
Lodge and Restaurant Manager		6,000
Lodge and Restaurant Personnel		

20 @ $3,200		64,000	
Naturalist		7,000	
Interpretive Center Manager		7,000	
Airport Manager		7,000	
Marina Manager		6,000	
Marina Attendants			
10 Seasonal @ $1,200		12,000	
Lifeguards			
25 Seasonal @ $1,200		30,000	
Golf Pro		7,000	
Greenkeeper		7,000	
7 Seasonal @ $1,200		8,400	
Golf Course Attendants and Labor			
7 @ $3,600		25,200	
Subtotal		$297,200	
7½% Employee Benefits		22,290	
Total		$319,490	
2. Variable Expenses			
Golf Course Maintenance, Supplies			
and Equipment		$ 24,000	
Utilities			
Telephone ($100 per mo.)	$ 1,200		
Elec. & Heating ($400 per mo.)	4,800		
Water ($600 per mo.)	7,200		
Other	1,000		
Maintenance, Repairs & Service	$12,000		14,200
Laundry—$1.00 per room			
per room	33,000		
Supplies and Materials	12,000		
Motor Vehicle Operation	5,000		
Rentals and Insurance	2,000		
Fees, Miscellaneous and			
Contingencies	75,000		177,200
3. Stores for Resale			
Restaurant	$ 67,500		
Gifts, Beverages, Groceries,			
Gas and Other	30,000		
Total		$ 97,500	
		$594,190	
say		$600,000	

*Note: Does not include Upper Harbor Marina or "Theme Area" since it is included for long range development.

SELECTION D

CRITERIA FOR EVALUATING QUALITY OF RECREATION LANDS*

Occupancy and Observation Sites

A. *Attraction*. Water attractions will include lakes, impoundments, major streams, cascades, and scenic rapids. Slow sluggish streams and small springs would be considered poor attractions. Land features would include unusual scenic views, outstanding timber stands or groves, histori cal areas, archeological areas, geological areas such as caves and rock formations, botanical areas with rare plant life, or zoological areas having unusual animal life. In some cases the attraction will be a combination of both land and water features.

The attraction must be within reasonable distance of the potential site. Usually this will mean about 700 feet for occupancy sites exclusive of waterfront or buffer zones. On those forests where suitable national forest land under the above specification will not be available to meet the projected demand, it will be necessary to consider lands up to one half mile or more from an attraction. Certain sites might be very attractive which may serve as a base from which fishing, swimming, or boating can be enjoyed on one or more nearby lakes or streams. Opportunity to hike along trails to observe some interesting scenery, or to enjoy historical, geological or other features, would enhance the attractiveness of such sites.

Both water and land features on a combined scale will be used for rating the attraction. The area limitations of 10 acres more or less for a lake

---

*Developed by Region 9, U. S. Forest Service.

or reservoir shown on U. S. Forest Service Form 17, will not be a factor in this region. As a guide for our purposes, the water attractions should be rated as follows:

Lake or reservoir, two or more recreational uses such as swimming, fishing, and boating possible.   1

Fast flowing rivers and other major nonpolluted streams.   2

Waterfalls, cascades, sizable springs, or small live streams.   3

Slow moving rivers, reservoirs, and lakes which because of size, heavy weed growth, or shallow waters are suitable only for fishing and/or waterfowl hunting.   4

Bog lakes, polluted rivers, and streams which can be made productive.   5

As on Form 17.   6

The rating items for land features shown under A–2 will be used as listed. Examples of unusual scenery might include areas along the Great Lakes, views overlooking several lakes, or scenic stretches of rivers. Examples of other outstanding features might include certain historical sites such as the Bay Furnace, old forts, trading posts, etc; archeological areas such as painted rocks, Indian mounds, and exceptional big game, bird, or waterfowl hunting areas. Parks or meadows in the second item are confined to the West. Here we will consider exceptional groves or timber stands, and other pleasing views, vistas, or features that are uncommon but not necessarily outstanding. On a combined rating scale the minimum acceptable attraction would have a rating of 8. Quality prescriptions would be as follows:

	Minimum Acceptable Conditions
Fair attraction	7–8 Slow rivers and lakes suitable only for fishing or waterfowl hunting w/o scenic land features, or bog lakes, polluted streams w/common scenery.
Good atttraction	5–6 Waterfalls, cascades, small scenic streams w/common scenery. Fast flowing major stream w/o scenic features.
Outstanding attraction	1–4 Lake or reservoir suitable for 2 recreation uses w/common scenery, or unusual scenery w/small live stream or cascades.

B. *Climatic Relief.* Most of the forest areas of the region have an agreeable climate during the summer season, more so than nearby population centers. These areas, therefore, afford a good degree of climatic relief.

The ratings as shown on the work plan and on U.S. Forest Service Form 17 will be used. The minimum acceptable rating for this criterion will be a 4. Quality prescriptions will be as follows:

		Minimum Acceptable Conditions
Fair	4	0–5°
Good	3	6–10°
Outstanding	1–2	11–15°

C. *Forest Environment.* Environment means the general surroundings and "atmosphere" of the site. It is affected by physical conditions in and around it. Environment is not measurable in precise terms, but it can be expressed in relative terms. The order of desirability as shown on the inventory Form 17 will be used. Interpretation will depend upon the skill of the examiner.

To assist in rating this criterion, a hypothetical set of conditions are presented here:

Grade 1 The site is relatively undisturbed, the timber is fairly uniform in character, mostly of large poles to saw timber size, not necessarily a closed stand. Very little evidence of recent logging present. The site is not within sight and sound of a noisy highway, nearby commercial enterprise such as a gas station, resort, tavern or farm. Very little erosion evident. Wildlife species varied but not necessarily abundant.

Grade 2 The timber stand would be generally similar to above. Minor detractions might include proximity to a main highway with fairly heavy traffic the noise of which is audible, or evidence of last logging job present in the form of small scattered and half rotted tops on the ground, or a group of summer homes is present near by.

Grade 3 The timber is scattered or patchy or a very young age class. Some evidence of recent partial cut is present. Crop, land pasture, or private development bound one side of the site.

Grade 4 Serious detractions might include: the surrounding area has just been subjected to a heavy cut of timber with a poorly stocked residual stand, or the site is small and is surrounded by crop land, pasture, or other private development, or the site is open and without cover but is otherwise suitable.

Grade 5 In this class would be included areas that in their present state are not acceptable for recreation use, but with correction of the conditions would be. Examples of such situations might include sites that are low, poorly drained, shallow swamp areas which can be made usable by drainage or filling; sites where most of the ground area is covered with poison ivy; or sites subject to sand blows, which can be stabilized by establishment of ground cover.

Grade 6 An example of an unacceptable area would be one that is subject to flooding due to frequent fluctuation of water levels during the use season and where correction of the situation is not possible.

The minimum acceptable rating for this criterion will be 5. Quality prescriptions will be as follows:

		Minimum Acceptable Conditions
Fair	4–5	Unacceptable but correction feasible.
Good	3	Detractions substantial.
Outstanding	1–2	Well preserved w/minor detractions.

D. *Terrain.* Picnicking probably is the least demanding occupancy use insofar as terrain is concerned. In many cases the terrain can be modified to make it usable for occupancy use. It is considered that slopes of over 30% are generally unsuitable for occupancy development.

Terrain usually will not be a limiting factor in rating observation sites, as many of these sites will be small, involving only minor developments, and may be accessible only by foot trail. However, terrain is an important factor where parking, picnic, and sanitary facilities will be necessary in connection with observation sites. This criterion should be rated for observation sites in the same manner as for occupancy use.

The minimum acceptable rating will be *3*. Quality prescriptions will be as follows:

		Minimum Acceptable Conditions
Fair	3	20–30% slope.
Good	2	10–20% slope.
Outstanding	1	0–10% slope.

E. *Soil. Fertility*—this term is intended to express the relative difficulty of establishing or retaining the vegetative cover. The type of soil, aspect, and topography all have an influence on fertility. For the purpose of this survey, the following classification of fertility has been made:

Good Medium to well drained silts, sandy clay and clay loams, heavy clay and muck soils.

Fair Gravelly and sandy loams, moist but well drained sands.

Poor Dry sands, gravels, rock, and eroded soils.

Stability—this term means the resistance of the soil to damage by erosion or compaction as a result of use. Steepness and length of slope, kind of soil, amount of cover are all factors that affect stability. The following conditions describe the various ratings for this term:

Good Not more than 3% slope. Length of slope not more than 100 feet. The soil is sandy clay or clay loam, heavy clay, or rock.

Fair Slope less than 3% but over 100 feet long. Slopes over 3% but not more than 10% and not over 200 feet in length. The soil is sand or gravelly loam, or heavy sand.

Poor Slopes are not over 10% but more than 200 feet long, and all slopes over 10%. The soil is silt, fine sand, or severely eroded.

Depth—the depth of soil affects the supply of water and nutrients to plants as well as the ability of the forest to withstand winds. In this part of the region the depth of soil will refer to distance to bed rock or the water table. This factor will be rated as follows:

Good Soils more than three feet deep.

Fair Soils between one and three feet deep.

Poor Less than one foot deep.

Permeability—this term in intended to express the ability of the soil to absorb or to allow water to percolate through it. The texture of the soil has a direct bearing on this capacity. The coarser the soil, the greater the permeability. For the purpose of the survey, the soils will be classed as follows:

Good Sands, gravel, gravelly or sandy loam.

Fair Stony loam, clay and silt loam.

Poor Heavy clay, or silt. Soil compacted as a result of heavy use such as logging.

Damp, poorly drained, bog or swamp — The soil would not be given this classification unless most of the site would fall into this class.

Extensive rock exposures, ledges, etc. —extensive rock exposures may make it prohibitive to develop a potential area for occupancy. Development may be limited to a small picnic area. If the potential site can be developed for $3,000.00 per development acre or less, then it can be considered as feasible. In situations such as this, give this factor an arbitrary rating of *3*.

The minimum acceptable rating for the soil criterion will be *3*. Quality prescriptions will be as follows:

		Minimum Acceptable Conditions
Fair	3	Fair fertility, stability, permeability; thin.
Good	2	Good stability; fair fertility, permeability and depth.
Outstanding	1	Good fertility, stability, permeability; fair depth.

F. *Shade or Shelter.*   High shade in this criterion means shade from trees over 30 feet in height. Low shade is from trees 30 feet or less in height. When the canopy is composed of both high and low shade, rate it on the basis of that which is in greatest proportion. Seven conditions of shade are recognized in order of desirability. No rating will be done on the basis of a direct shelter or constructed basis. This is for certain western conditions.

The inventory does not provide for consideration of the composition of the canopy providing the shade. It is felt that this should receive consideration. Four sets of canopy conditions have been set up which are added to Form 17. Briefly, the conditions in order of quality are described as follows:

Thrifty mature stands of northern hardwoods, hemlock, pine types, and various mixtures of these.

Pole types would be the same as above, including paper birch, thrifty aspen, and spruce fir below small sawlog size.

Overmature hardwoods, overmature spruce fir; mature aspen. These would include the overmature, decadent, hollow, unthrifty hardwood and spruce fir stands where more than a fairly high danger exists from windfall breakage and snow damage, along with mature aspen.

Saplings and undesirable species would include young stands less than thirty feet high. Very unthrifty, overmature, and off-site aspen, open fields that are being taken over by scrub oak, cherry, aspen, etc., and open areas where planting is necessary.

Form 18 for this criterion has been amended to include the composition rating. It will be scored along with the shade factor. The minimum acceptable rating will be a *4*. The quality prescriptions will be as follows:

		Minimum Acceptable Conditions
Outstanding	1	High shade 50–100%; pole types.
Good	2	Low shade 25–50%; pole types. High shade 25–50%; overmature, aspen. High shade 10–25%; thrifty mature fir.

Fair   3–4   High and low shade less than 10% w/sapling
                                               or undesirable hardwood or open areas.

G. *Cover (Composition and Density)*.   The term "cover" as used here
includes the vegetation below the shade producing level. It includes the
grasses, shrubs, and reproduction. This type of cover serves to protect the
site from erosion, provide screening, and may contribute to its general
beauty. It also may have a bearing on the cost of site development and
maintenance.

It is difficult to define exact conditions of composition and density of
this low cover. *It means having the right amount of a desirable mixture
of species that will provide enough screening between family units or on the
buffer strip around the area, and still allow for adequate circulation of
air.* The presence of flowering shrubs would add to the general beauty
of the site. On the other hand, too dense a stand of desirable species of
reproduction in the form of a thicket all over the site would be undesirable.

The following are broad guides which may be of assistance in rating
this criterion:

Composition

Excellent—The reproduction may consist of any mixture of the more desirable hardwoods, hemlock, spruce and fir, or pine along with such shrubs such as dogwood, blue-
berry, serviceberry, snowberry, honeysuckle. Ferns and grasses may be found in the
openings. Poison ivy is present in a small quantity which can be readily eradicated with
herbicides.

Good—Conifers, the more desirable hardwoods, and shrubs are present in quantity,
but almost 50 percent of the ground cover consists of such species as hazel, scrub oak,
rose, hawthorn, or sweet fern. Poison ivy is present as above.

Fair— Desirable hardwoods and conifers scarce or absent. The cover consists of a variable mixture of scrub oak, aspen, hazel brush, buckbrush, sweet fern. Small patches
of poison ivy and raspberry or blackberry may be present.

Unsatisfactory—Poison ivy, blackberry, raspberry, nettles, or prickly ash occupy most
of the site in various mixtures.

Density

Excellent—At least 60 percent but not more than 80 percent of the area not occupied
by overstory trees is stocked with desirable cover species. Points on the site at a distance
of 100′ are intervisible but not clearly so.

Good—30–60 percent of the ground area not occupied by overstory trees is stocked with
a good or better composition of species. Points on the area at a distance of 100′ are readily
visible.

Fair—10–30 percent of the ground area not occupied by overstory trees is stocked with a
fair or better composition of species. There are situations where the stocking of reproduction even of desirable species is too dense, walking over the site may be difficult,
with visibility being limited to a very short distance. This is an undesirable but not entirely unsatisfactory situation which can be corrected by cutting. It is classified here.

Unsatisfactory—Less than 10 percent of the site is occupied by a fair or better composition of species.

The minimum acceptable rating for this criterion will be a *4*. Quality prescriptions are as follows:

Minimum Acceptable Conditions

Fair	3–4	Composition and density unsatisfactory but correction feasible.
Good	2	Composition and density fair or composition excellent w/unsatisfactory density.
Excellent	1	Excellent composition—good density. Good composition—excellent density.

H. *Domestic Water.* The rating of this criterion needs no explanation. The formula in the work plan instructions which is also indicated on Form 17 (Instr. 12) is applicable to R–9 situations. An examiner of a site may not be in a good position to make this evaluation. The advice of the ranger, forest engineer, or other qualified person familiar with problems of local wells should be consulted before the costs are calculated. The best water source may not be a well but a lake, stream or nearby spring.

The minimum acceptable rating will be a *4*. Quality prescriptions are as follows:

Minimum Acceptable Conditions

Outstanding	1	Available at low cost.
Good	2	Available at moderate cost.
Fair	3–4	Unavailable.

Accessibility

The relative accessibility of each site will be rated. This will be done independently of the physical rating. Relative accessibility is based upon the cost per development (usable) acre of providing access from the nearest existing road or road planned for construction by the year 2000 to the potential site being examined. Internal service roads within the site will not be considered here.

The following accessibility guidelines will be used in making this evaluation:

Outstanding accessibility — A site that is accessible by means of an existing road or water route, or if not accessible, the cost of construction of an access road will not be more than $1500 per development acre.

Good accessibility — A site that is not accessible and the estimated access road costs will be not more than $1500 to $2500 per development acre.

Fair accessibility — An unaccessible site to which access is considered feasible, provided road cost will be not more than $2500 to $4000 per development acre.

Unsatisfactory accessibility — Sites which do not meet the above conditions due to access road costs in excess of $4000 per development acre.

In general, in this region most of the potential sites will be within one-half mile of either the planned primary or the secondary transportation system. A SN22 road will generally be standard for providing access to rec-

reation areas. Assistance of the forest engineer should be obtained in providing estimated average road construction costs for different conditions
that may be encountered on the forest.

Determination of per acre costs are derived as follows:

$$\frac{\text{road length (mi.)} \times \text{ave. construction cost/mi}}{\text{usable area}} = \text{access road cost per development acre}$$

Data concerning accessibility is recorded in the access road block on the
first page of Form 17. Indicate the information as it applies to the various
statements. In those situations where the site is over ½ mile away from
an existing or planned road but access is feasible, modify the next to the
last statement to show this. Under item (9) in the last statement, show the
estimated cost per development acre.

The relative accessibility rating that is obtained will be compared with
the site quality rating. The final rating will be that assigned to site quality,
unless it is higher than the accessibility rating, in which case the latter will
be the final rating.

Potential Waterfront Sites

In making evaluations of the criteria for these sites, keep in mind that
both swimming and boating sites are being considered. Swimming and
boating sites in most cases will be adjunct to occupancy sites. In some
situations, a boating site will serve only as an access point for the launching
of boats. Similarly there may be potential swimming sites suitable for
development not in connection with an occupancy use.

Where the waterfront development site is part of the same area being
examined for occupancy, only the 100 foot waterfront zone will be evaluated for this use. Do not consider part of the occupancy area as to suitability for bathhouse or parking purposes. In those cases where the potential
waterfront sites are not in conjunction with a potential occupancy site such
as involving only a swimming or a boat access site to a fishing or waterfowl
lake, the land required for bathhouses and parking areas will also be evaluated.

A. *Water Temperatures.* Average water temperatures during the
summer season may be a limiting factor for swimming activities in some
of the waters in this part of the region. Literature on the subject of water
temperature in swimming pools indicates that the average low temperature
should be about 70°. Temperature insofar as a boating site is concerned is
not significant. These sites will be used not only by water sports enthu-
siasts but by fishermen and waterfowl hunters as well.

Quality prescriptions for these two uses will be as follows:

	Swimming	Minimum Acceptable Conditions	Boating	Minimum Acceptable Conditions
Outstanding	1	73° + F	1–2	68–73°F
Good	2	68–73°F	3	60–67°F
Fair	3*	60–67°F	4*	less than 60°F

*Minimum acceptable rating.

B. *Shoreline or Flow Fluctuation.*   This criterion is well explained in the work plan. It is especially of concern with reservoirs or impoundments that may be subject to drawdown for flood control or power purposes.

A knowledge of the type of bottom and steepness of the slope would have a bearing as to whether a fluctuation in water levels would constitute a detraction. For example, a sandy, gentle slope would still be an attractive swimming or boating site with more fluctuation than a steeper slope or one that may have clay, rocks, mud, or stumps exposed when water is drawn down. This should be kept in mind when these sites are being examined.

Quality ratings are as follows:

	Swimming	Boating	Minimum Acceptable Conditions
Outstanding	1	1	Fluctuation little or none.
Good	2	2	Fluctuation moderate or immaterial.
Fair	3*	3*	Major detractions less than ½ the season.

*Minimum acceptable rating.

C. *Shoreline—First 20' Above Water.*   On this region most of the lakes do not have a clear beach of up to fifty feet. We have arbitrarily set a distance of twenty feet for consideration here as this might be closer to the average. As explained in the work plan instructions, this criterion is a measure of suitability of the site in its natural state as well as an indicator of development costs. It is recognized that developments can be made to overcome almost any deficiency.

The various elements to be rated are self-explanatory except the soil-mud item. Include here heavy soil types as well as mud. In rating this criterion, a timbered site will be defined as one that has a stocking of 50% or more of poles or larger trees. If the stocking of timber is less than 50%, it will be considered as nontimbered. A timbered site may have sandy, gravelly, or clay soil. In those situations where a timbered site is underlaid with clay, rate the site as 4. Quality prescriptions are as follows:

	Swimming	Minimum Acceptable Conditions	Boating	Minimum Acceptable Conditions
Outstanding	1	Sand	1–2	Gravel
Good	2	Gravel	3	Timbered
Fair	3*	Timbered	4–5*	Rock

*Minimum acceptability.

D. *Bottom, Below Waterline to a 5' Depth.*   The nature of the bottom affects the suitability of a site for boating and swimming. In rating this criterion for boating, consider the nature of the bottom to a depth of 2 to 3 feet. For swimming, rate the bottom to a wading depth of 5 feet. Quality prescriptions are as follows:

	Swimming	*Minimum Acceptable Conditions*	*Boating*	*Minimum Acceptable Conditions*
Outstanding	1	Sand	1–2	Gravel
Good	2	Gravel	3–4	Mud
Fair	3*	Rock	5*	Rock

*Minimum acceptability.

E. *Distance, Shoreline.*   The requirements for this criterion as explained in the work plan are satisfactory and will fit most of the conditions in this region. It is a measure of drop-off from the water line to maximum wading depth. In those areas where canoeing is a popular sport, it may be desired to rate a potential boating site for canoeing, particularly a stream that is not suitable for all around boating. In such situations the distance to about a three-foot depth will be rated. When a site is rated with this in mind, appropriate notes should be made in the comments on Form 18. Quality prescriptions are as follows:

	Swimming		*Boating*	
100' or more	1	Outstanding	4	
50–100'	2	Good	3*	Fair
25–50'	3*	Fair	2	Good
0–25'	4		1	Outstanding

*Minimum acceptability.

F. *Industrial or Domestic Pollution.*   The terms as defined in the work plan for this criterion need no further explanation and will apply in this region. Quality prescriptions are as follows:

	Swimming	*Boating*	*Minimum Acceptable Conditions*
Outstanding	1	1	Uncontaminated.
Good	2*	2	Contaminated.
Fair		3*	Light pollution.

*Minimum acceptability.

G. *Color and Turbidity.*   These characteristics as defined in the work plan will apply to this part of the region. The brown "tea-colored" condition in many of the waters of the Lake States resulting from tannins in solution are not a deterrent to water activities. Quality prescriptions are as follows:

	Swimming	Boating	Minimum Acceptable Conditions
Outstanding	1	1	See U.S. Forest Service Form 18 P–26a.
Good	2*	2	See U.S. Forest Service Form 18 P–26a.
Fair		3*	See U.S. Forest Service Form 18 P–26a.
Unsatisfactory	3		

*Minimum acceptability.

H. *Wind Velocity and Constancy.* Unfavorable winds would be winds of such velocity as to create conditions on a body of water so as to make it very difficult or unsafe for the majority of small boats to stay out for the purpose of general boating, water sports, or fishing. Small boats would be generally defined as those using outboard motors common today. Swimming, on the other hand, may be enjoyed in spite of windy conditions on the lake.

It is doubtful that unfavorable wind conditions are much of a factor except in certain locations along the Great Lakes. Quality prescriptions are as follows:

	Swimming	Boating	Minimum Acceptable Conditions
Outstanding	1	1	See U.S. Forest Service Form 18 P–26a.
Good	2	2	See U.S. Forest Service Form 18 P–26a.
Fair	3–4*	2*	See U.S. Forest Service Form 18 P–26a.
Unsatisfactory		3–4	See U.S. Forest Service Form 18 P–26a.

*Minimum acceptability.

I. *Classification of Waters.* This classification is meant to show the management of the waters being considered. Various management may affect or limit developments that may be contemplated.

Navigable waters according to law are those that are navigable-in-fact. If a boat can be floated, then the waters are navigable, and they are public waters. Navigable interstate waters such as the Mississippi and Ohio Rivers and tributaries thereto are under the jurisdiction of the federal government. The agency in charge is the Corps of Engineers.

Other public waters would include impoundments under the jurisdiction of the Corps of Engineers, Bureau of Reclamation, Fish and Wildlife Service, Soil Conservation Service, states, other public agencies, as well as certain natural lakes.

National forest waters would be those impoundments constructed by the Forest Service and natural lakes entirely surrounded by national forest ownership. In these cases, the Forest Service controls the developments on these lands.

Private waters would include private impoundments and for this classification all natural lakes surrounded by private land.

On navigable and public waters usually there are no restrictions to an abutting owner in development or use of a swimming or boating site. For our purposes in this part of the region, navigable and other public waters are equally satisfactory for these developments. Quality prescriptions for this criterion are as follows:

	Swimming and Boating	Minimum Acceptable Conditions
Outstanding	1–3*	Other public.
Unsatisfactory	4	Private waters.

*Minimum acceptable rating.

Winter Sports Sites

Criteria for this use are explained on pages 88–92 of the work plan. Additional explanations are given below for those criteria necessary to cover conditions as they apply to Region 9.

Acres. In general, areas of less than about 100 acres would not be considered as a potential winter sports site. This would include parking, improvements such as a central shelter, as well as suitable ski terrain.

A. *Snow cover or Ice.*

1. Period of sufficient snow to make sports feasible. Quality prescriptions:

		Minimum Acceptable Conditions
Outstanding	1–2	Snow cover 3 months.
Good	3	Snow cover 2 months.
Fair	4*	Snow cover 1 month.

*Minimum acceptability.

2. Snow texture.

		Minimum Acceptable Conditions
Outstanding	1	Dry snow 2/3 of season.
Good	2	Dry snow 1/2 of season.
Fair	3*	Dry snow 1/3 of season.

*Minimum acceptability.

3. Snow depth during peak period.

		Minimum Acceptable Conditions
Outstanding	1–3	Depth 2–3 feet.
Good, Fair	4*	Depth 1–2 feet.

*Minimum acceptability.

4. Snowfall as an adverse factor.

		Minimum Acceptable Conditions
Outstanding	1	No problems.
Good	2	Occasional problems.
Fair	3*	Problems at least 1/2 of season.

*Minimum acceptability.

5.   Period of satisfactory open ice.   We have little or none of this use. It is not necessary to rate this item.

B.   *Vertical Rise of Slopes.*   In this region we do not have potential ski areas with slopes having a vertical rise of more than a few hundred feet. In making ratings of different sites, cross out the last zero of all the slope classes shown on Form 19. The range of slope height will then be from 300 feet to 30 feet. Quality prescriptions will then be as follows:

		Minimum Acceptable Conditions
Outstanding	1–2	250–300 foot rise.
Good	3–4	150–200 foot rise.
Fair	5	100–150 foot rise.

C.   *Steepness of Slope.*   The guidelines of what are novice, intermediate, and advanced slopes are indicated on page 89 of the work plan as well as on Form 19. Quality prescriptions will be as follows:

		Minimum Acceptable Conditions
Outstanding	1	40–60% intermediate; w/adequate novice and expert slopes.
Good	2	Majority intermediate, adequate novice, some expert slopes.
Fair	3*	Majority intermediate, no expert slopes.

*Minimum acceptability.

D.   *Aspect of Slopes.*   Quality prescriptions:

		Minimum Acceptable Conditions
Outstanding	1	North slope.
Good, Fair	2*	East or west slope.

*Minimum acceptability.

E.   *Wind Conditions.*   Quality prescriptions:

		Minimum Acceptable Conditions
Outstanding	1–2	Occasional winds and drifting.
Good	3	Occasional high winds.
Fair	4*	Frequent high winds.

*Minimum acceptability.

F.   *Temperatures.*   Quality prescriptions:

		Minimum Acceptable Rating
Outstanding	1	Generally above 0°F.
Good	2	Above 0°F on majority of days.
Fair	3*	Below 0°F.

*Minimum acceptability.

G.   *Avalanche Possibilities.*   It is believed that there are no avalanche problems in this region; therefore, all potential winter sports sites can be given a rating of *1* for this.

H.   *Slope Protection.*   Adequate protection would be timber or terrain that would afford protection by cutting down the wind, thereby keeping the snow from blowing from the slope, or by keeping the slope shaded, thus cutting down the possibility of undue thawing. Quality prescriptions:

Minimum Acceptable Conditions

Outstanding	1	Adequate or not needed.
Good, Fair	2*	Adequate for most.

*Minimum acceptability.

I. *Cost of Slope Clearing.* The relative costs of clearing will be judged on the basis of the timber cover on the site as follows:

High Costs	Medium well stocked stands of mature hardwoods and pine saw timber. Well stocked stands of merchantable pole timber.
Moderate Costs	Operable, poorly stocked stands of mature hardwood and pine saw timber. Medium stocked stands of merchantable pole timber.
Lower Costs	Poorly stocked stands of merchantable pole timber, nonmerchantable pole and sapling stands of variable stocking, open areas.

Quality prescriptions:

Minimum Acceptable Conditions

Outstanding	1	Costs low.
Good	2	Costs moderate.
Fair	3*	Costs high.

*Minimum acceptability.

J. *Ground Surface Conditions.* Quality prescriptions:

Minimum Acceptable Conditions

Outstanding	1–2	Some work needed.
Good	3	Moderate work needed.
Fair	4*	Heavy work needed.

*Minimum acceptability.

K. *Availability of Electric Power.* For the purpose of rating this item, consider that electric power is at the site if an existing power line is within one mile. Quality prescriptions:

Minimum Acceptable Conditions

Outstanding	1	At site.
Good	2	Available, moderate cost.
Fair	3*	Available, high cost.

*Minimum acceptability.

The following criteria as listed on Form 19 will be rated similarly as shown:

L Parking development costs.

M Convenience of parking location.

O Year-long or seasonal recreation.

Outstanding	1
Good	2
Fair	3 (Minimum acceptability)

The following criteria as listed on Form 19 will be rated similarly as shown:

N Appurtenant service development possibilities.

P Damage to aesthetic view.

　Outstanding　　　1

　Good, Fair　　　2 (Minimum acceptability)

Accessibility—accessibility will be considered and rated under the same standards as prescribed for occupancy development sites.

SELECTION E

SELF-EVALUATION CHECKLIST FOR COMMERCIAL OUTDOOR RECREATION PLANNING AND DEVELOPMENT*

This checklist is designed to systematically consider factors which might affect the success of the contemplated development. Thus, the decision to continue with the planning/development should be based on facts and sound judgment.

The main purpose of this publication is to cause one to consider many facets of the prospective development in relation to local conditions. No checklist can answer your questions; it can only pose them. You must then answer the questions based on your knowledge of the local situation. Place a check beside each question after you have answered it to your satisfaction. When you have completed the checklist, you should be in a better position to judge the possible success of the planned development.

---

*This was developed by Alan Jubenville. Acknowledgment is made to Byron Haley, Cooperative Extension, Washington State University, for his contribution to this planning instrument. Other extension and professional personnel, too numerous to list by name, contributed to the development of this checklist.

Part I. ORIENTATION

____A. What type of recreation enterprise do I want?

(List) _____

____B. Why do I want to get into this business?

_____

____C. What types of activities will be offered?
(Check all activities to be offered.)

____ 1. Archery
- ____Field
- ____Hunting
- ____Target

____ 2. Beach combing

____ 3. Bicycling

____ 4. Boating

____ 5. Camping
- ____Trailer
- ____Tent

____ 6. Canoeing

____ 7. Exploring

____ 0. Fishing

____ 9. Golf
- ____Miniature golf
- ____Driving range
- ____Par 3
- ____Pitch and putt
- ____Full course

____10. Group activities
- ____Group camping
- ____Group picnicking
- ____Group programs

____11. Group meetings
- ____Conferences
- ____Sales meetings

____Executive retreats
____Seminars & workshops

____12. Group outings
- ____Family reunions
- ____Hiking clubs
- ____Camping clubs
- ____Bike clubs
- ____Square dance clubs
- ____Trailer clubs
- ____Civic or fraternal clubs

____13. Hayrides

____14. Hiking

____15. Hobby crafts

____16. Horseback riding

____17. Hunting
- ____Bow only
- ____Gun
- ____Big game
- ____Small game
- ____Upland birds
- ____Waterfowl

____18. Mountain climbing

____19. Nature study

____20. Outdoor games

____21. Pageants

____22. Parachute jumping

____23. Photography

____24. Picking wild food

____25. Picnicking

____26. Piloting (airplane)

____27. Programs

    ____Campfire

    ____Games

    ____Movies

    ____Singing

    ____Stories

    ____Talks

____28. Racing

____29. Rockhounding

____30. Sailing

____31. Skating

____32. Skiing

____Snow

____Water

____33. Sliding (tobogganing)

____34. Snowshoeing

____35. Spelunking

____36. Sports

____37. Swimming

____38. Tows and lifts

____39. Trail riding

    ____Bike

    ____Dune buggies

    ____4-wheel drive

    ____Snowmobiles

    ____All-terrain vehicles

____40. _____

____41. _____

____D.   What types of sales and services will be provided?

____ 1. Bait

    ____Grasshoppers

    ____Minnows

    ____Worms

    _____

____ 2. Boat and motor rental

____ 3. Boat and motor services

    ____Gas and oil

    ____Launching

    ____Moorage

    ____Repair

    ____Show-me trips

    ____Storage

____ 4. Cleaning fish

____ 5. Cook guest's fish, game

____ 6. Decoy rental

____ 7. Dog boarding

____ 8. Dressing game

____ 9. Duck blind rental

____10. Equipment sales

    ____Boats, motors trailers

    ____Camera equipment

    ____Camping equipment

    ____Sporting goods

    ____Tents, campers,

____11. Farm products

____12. Filling station

____13. Firewood

____14. Grocery store

____15. Guide service

    ____Exploring

    ____Fishing

_____Hunting   _____20.   Outfitting

_____Local attrac- _____21.   Snack shop
tions
          _____22.   Souvenir shop
_____Nature Study

_____Pleasure   _____23.   Sports instruction

_____Spelunking   _____24.   Tent rental

_____16.   Horse boarding   _____25.   Trailer rental

_____17.   Horse rental   _____26.   _____

_____18.   Meals (family style)   _____27.   _____

_____19.   Natural landscaping
materials

_____E.   Based on the items checked under C and D, list the major developments that are anticipated and their components. (Develop the list using the functional diagram discussed in the text.)

_____F.   What sources of information have I sought?

   _____ 1.   Publications—for example:

     Cooperative Extension Service
     Virginia Polytechnic Institute
     Blacksburg, Virginia 24060

     Bulletin 301— Guidelines to Planning, Developing, and Managing Rural Recreation Enterprises

     Cooperative Extension Service
     University of New Hampshire
     Durham, New Hampshire 03824

     Extension Folder 64—*Evaluating Forest Campground Sites*

   _____ 2.   Professional assistance:

     _____Association of Illinois Rural Recreation Enterprises (or similar organization)
     _____County Adviser (Cooperative Extension Service)
     _____Soil Conservation Service
     _____Division of Forestry, State Department of Conservation
     _____Division of Game, State Department of Conservation
     _____Division of Fisheries, State Department of Conservation

_____Department of Business and Economic Development
_____Professional Planner
_____State Department of Health

_____G.   What are my qualifications? Brief resume:

_____

_____ 1.   Am I interested in the following?

_____People   _____Camping activities
_____Entertainment   _____Supervising
_____Recreation   _____Enforcing
programs   regulations
_____Nature study   _____Maintenance of
_____Hunting and   area
fishing   _____Service
_____Business adminis-   _____Trying new things
tration   _____Advertising
_____Organizing recrea-   _____Teaching
tion   _____
_____Public relations
_____

_____ 2.   What are my personal characteristics?

_____Personable   _____Always on time
_____Decisive   _____Always remain calm
_____Clean and neat   _____Good leader
_____Willing to learn   _____Desire to succeed
_____   _____

_____ 3.   In what areas do I have experience and training?

_____Farming   _____Area maintenance
_____Conservation   _____Traffic control
_____Hunting and fishing_____Program leadership
_____Bookkeeping   _____Personnel
_____Dealing with   management
people   _____Camping
_____Public speaking   _____Business adminis-
_____Park design   tration
_____Public safety   _____Construction
_____Promotion   _____First aid
_____Sewer and water   _____Equipment opera-
systems   tion/repair
_____   _____

Major Development	*Components*
Example:	
Campground	1. Road and parking spurs. 2. Unit equipment (fireplace, table, garbage can, etc.). 3. Comfort station. 4. Road barricades. 5. Dumping station. 6. Water and electric system. 7. Office and maintenance building. 8. Signs.

Part II. SUITABILITY OF SITE

Suitability is the initial step in decision-making. The planner judges whether to proceed with the project, based on a preliminary inspection of the area, not on a detailed site analysis. This is the process that he goes through in the acquisition phase as well as in initial planning.

Questions arise, such as: Is it accessible? Is it large enough? Is there room for expansion? What are the zoning requirements? Is the terrain too rough? Are the soils unstable? Does it have good natural landscaping? Is it suitable for water development? Is sufficient water available? Are great numbers of potential customers within reasonable driving distances? What are the attractions? These are but a few that should be considered on a preliminary basis.

Comment on the suitability of the particular site:

SUITABILITY OF SITE

	Comments
Size: (Is it large enough?)	
Location: (Is it in a good location?)	
Adaptability: (Is it suitable for the type of development I want? Expansion?)	
Site Conditions: (What problems do I foresee? Good points?)	

Part III. INVENTORY OF RESOURCES

_____A.   Aesthetics and natural beauty (general).

_____ 1.   Attractive natural surroundings

_____ 2.   Planned facilities will blend with surroundings

_____ 3.   Abundance and variety of trees, shrubs, and wild flowers

_____ 4.   Interesting geological features (waterfalls, caves, etc.)

_____ 5.   Vista points available

_____ 6.   Many scenic attractions

_____ 7.   Bodies of clean water

_____ 8.   Varied topography

_____B.   Natural resources.

_____ 1.   How large is the area? Number of acres _____.
(Is this large enough for the development plus future expansion?)

_____ 2.   How would I best describe the terrain in the area?

_____Steep and rugged   _____Flat to rolling
_____ Very hilly   _____Flat
_____ Rolling   _____ Variable

(Variable topography that has some flat land is best.)

_____ 3.   What are the major drainages (streams, rivers, etc.)?
(Sketch these into the site design.)

_____ 4.   What types of vegetation are present?

_____Trees   _____Marshes
_____Meadows   _____Bogs and swamps
_____Abandoned fields   _____Cropland
_____ Dense brush   _____Variety (Combination of several)

(Variety with majority in open woodland is best for most recreational activities.)

_____ 5.   What is the size of the trees?

_____No trees
_____Young (to 10 ft.)
_____Immature (15–35 ft.)
_____ Mature (40–70 ft.)
_____Overmature (over 75 ft.)

_____ 6.   What is the condition of the trees?

_____Look healthy
_____Some broken tops
_____Some with large numbers of dead limbs
_____A large number of diseased trees
_____A few scattered dead ones
_____A large number of dead ones

(Be very suspicious if trees do not look completely healthy.)

_____ 7. What recreational waters are available on the property?

____City water   ____Pond
____Springs   ____Lake
____Intermittent streams   ____River
____Year around   ____No good sources
    streams   of water

(Water is essential for every type of recreational enterprise—for activities, scenic beauty, and cooking and washing. Plan on developing a body of water if not available.)

_____ 8. What are the shoreline conditions?

____Stable   ____Dense cover
____Eroding   ____Open
____Bog areas   ____Steep bank
____Sandy soil   ____Level ground
____Heavy clay soil   ____Gently sloping

_____ 9. What are the bottom conditions of the bodies of water?

____Muddy   ____Solid rock
____Sandy   ____Gravel
____Rocky   _____

_____10. What are the water conditions?

____Clear   ____Algae present
____Cloudy   ____Sedges present
____Murky   ____Reeds and cattails
____Stagnant   _____

_____11. What fishing is available?

____Managed trout pond
____Well-stocked (warm-water fish) pond
____Over-stocked pond
____Clean river or stream with adequate stocking
____Don't know condition of fishery
____There is none

(Fishing is a popular outdoor recreation activity—an attraction to many visitors.)

_____12. What game and upland birds are present?

____Deer   ____Turkey   ____Rabbit
____Squirrels   ____Black bear ____Wild boar
____Quail   ____Pheasant   ____Waterfowl

_____Grouse   _____Woodcock _____Snipe

_____   _____   _____

(People are interested in seeing animals in their native habitats.)

_____13.   Are the game animals and birds in sufficient numbers
to allow hunting?

(Hunting may be one way to extend the season of the
recreation enterprise.)

_____14.   What type of soils are present?

_____Sand   _____Loam   _____Clay
_____Gravel   _____Solid rock _____

(Avoid heavy clay material because of the compaction from heavy recreational use.)

_____15.   What is the weather like during the four seasons?
_____Spring   (list: _____)
_____Summer   (list: _____)
_____Fall   (list: _____)
_____Winter   (list: _____)

(Is the weather a deterrent or an attraction during the
general recreation season? Sunny and warm during
summer? Cold and good snow and ice during winter?
Consult local weather bureau office.)

_____16.   What special attractions are present?

_____Waterfall   _____Unusual plants
_____Cave   _____Unusual overlooks
_____Rock formations   _____Historical sites
_____Gems   _____Local legends
_____Anadromous fish   _____
(Salmon, steelhead,
etc.)

_____C.   Previous developments.

_____ 1.   Are there any historical sites on the land?   _____
Nearby?   _____

Site	Development	Condition	Potential Use

_____ 2.   Is written information available about the history of
the area? Site? Please list.

_____ 3. What other developments are present on the site?

Type of Development	Condition	Potential Use

_____ D. Health and safety.

    _____ 1. What natural or artificial hazards exist at the proposed site?

        _____ High cliffs

        _____ Fire hazard

        _____ Open mine shafts, quarries, old buildings, or other man-made hazards

        _____ Whirlpools, undertows, swift streams, underwater obstructions, drop-offs, or muck bottom in swimming area

        _____ Manufacturing plants

        _____ Does other water, unsuitable for swimming, provide undue hazards?

        _____ Poisonous reptiles

        _____ Poisonous plants

        _____ Biting insects—low-lying swampy areas for breeding

        _____ Garbage or manure dumps

        _____ Railroads, trolley, or bus lines

        _____ Junk piles

        _____ Run-down buildings

        _____ Equipment

    _____ 2. Is ventilation adequate in existing structures?

    _____ 3. Are there enough shaded grounds, as well as open sunny spaces?

    _____ 4. Is the site within a reasonable distance from medical services?

    _____ 5. Has health department clearance been established?

Part IV. APPRAISAL OF LOCAL CONDITIONS

_____ A. What are the attitudes of the local people toward the development?

_____ 1. Local government officials   _____ 6. Local businessmen

_____ 2. Recreation clubs   _____ 7. Social organizations

_____ 3. Youth organizations   _____ 8. Service organizations

_____ 4. State agencies   _____ 9. Conservation organizations

_____ 5. Special interest groups   _____ 10. _____

_____B. What tourist and recreational attractions and developments are available? Are contemplated for the future?

_____ 1. Complementary (may attract people to my development)

_____ 2. Competitive (will compete strongly with the contemplated development)

_____C. What community services are available at the development site? (Check each one thoroughly.)

_____ 1. Garbage dumping
_____ 2. Garbage collection
_____ 3. Sewer system
_____ 4. City water system
_____ 5. Public utilities (gas and electricity)
_____ 6. Church services

_____ 7. Tourist information
_____ 8. Public recreation facilities
_____ 9. Telephone
_____10. Post office
_____11. Law enforcement
_____12. Fire protection
_____14. _____

_____D. What privately owned services are available?

_____1. Vehicle service stations   _____2. Restaurants
_____3. Repair shops   _____4. Taxi Service
_____5. _____   _____6. _____

_____E. Is the appearance of the surrounding community and landscape attractive to the visitor? Why? Why not?

_____F. What are the major transportation systems in the area?

_____ 1. Major commercial airport   _____ 5. Interstate highway
_____ 2. Commuter airport   _____ 6. Major highway artery
_____ 3. Major bus terminal   _____ 7. _____
_____ 4. Major passenger train depot

_____G. What are the conditions of the highway immediately adjacent to the development?

_____ 1. Road width _____
_____ 2. Load limit _____
_____ 3. Distance to main artery _____
_____ 4. Condition of pavement _____

_____ 5. Condition of road shoulders _____

_____ 6. Straightness of road _____

_____ 7. Periodic flooding _____

_____ 8. Condition of bridges _____

_____ 9. _____

_____H. Are there any planned future developments which might affect the development?

    _____ 1. Private   _____ 4. State

    _____ 2. Community   _____ 5 Federal

    _____ 3. County

_____I. What are the present labor market conditions?

    _____ 1. Supervisory   _____ 3. Management

    _____ 2. Maintenance   _____ 4. General labor

_____J. What are the local zoning law requirements?

_____K. What are the health standards for the particular development?

_____L. What environmental regulations apply to the development?

_____M. What insurance companies would extend coverage on the proposed development? List.

Part V. DEMAND

_____A. What general type of visitor is the development being designed for?

_____B. What type of person do you anticipate using the facilities?

_____C. Where (areas, cities, etc.) do I expect the visitors to come from? List.

_____D. How far will most of the people travel?

    _____1. 0–25 miles   _____3. 100–200 miles

    _____2. 25–100 miles   _____4. More than 200 miles

_____E. What do managers of complementary recreational develop-
         ments think of your proposed development?

         _____ 1. Definitely needed; people always asking for this
                   type of development

         _____ 2. Possibly needed; some people inquire

         _____ 3. Not sure; few inquiries

         _____ 4. _____

_____F. What do managers of competing developments think?

         _____ 1. Needed; turns away groups because facilities fill up
                   early

         _____ 2. Needed; offers just a little different type of service

         _____ 3. Possibly needed; increasing numbers of visitors

         _____ 4. Not needed; too much competition

         _____ 5. _____

                   (Evaluate conversations carefully.)

_____G. Have any agencies been contacted about demand for the pro-
         posed type of development?

         _____ 1. Chambers of commerce

         _____ 2. Highway department

         _____ 3. State department of conservation

         _____ 4. Regional planning commission

         _____ 5. Division of tourism, state bureau of economic de-
                   velopment

         _____ 6. College or university

         _____ 7. Federal agencies

                   _____U.S. Fish and Wildlife Service
                   _____U.S. Forest Service
                   _____National Park Service
                   _____Corps of Engineers
                   _____Bureau of Outdoor Recreation
                   _____Soil Conservation Service

                   _____

         _____ 8. _____

_____H. What observations have you made about demand in the local area? (Example—an average of 23 families per weekend were turned away from the campground at Soccittoomee State Park during the month of July.) List.

Part VI.   THE SITE PLAN

The written plan is the next step in the planning process. The preceding sections were steps used in projecting the success or failure of the proposed development. If after careful consideration of all data, the decision is to continue with the development, then a site plan should be developed. Included in this is the purpose or goals, who will use the developments, types of facilities needed, coordinating structures (roads, trails, parking lots, etc.), diagram of relationships on the site, scale drawing of all facilities in relation to the site, detailed construction plans for each facility, and finally a justification for each decision one makes. Also, one must consider future expansion of programs and facilities. Finally, a plan of action should give a construction time schedule, cost involved, and how the plan should be implemented.

The guidelines for planning the various recreation areas and facilities are given in the text. This step is necessary before the financial situation can be assessed (Part VII).

Part VII.   FINANCIAL STATEMENT

_____A.   What will be the sources of income?

_____ 1.   Single entrance fee covering all charges

_____ 2.   Entrance fee (plus additional charges for each major activity)

_____ 3.   Single component fee; charge based on type of equipment, number of people, etc.

_____ 4.   Equipment repair

_____ 5.   Equipment rental

_____ 6.   Restaurant

_____ 7.   Laundry

_____ 8.   Farm store

_____ 9.   Annual lease (camping area, hunting area, etc.)

_____10.   General store

_____11.   Gift shop

_____12.   Excursion trips

_____13. Reservation system

_____14. Lodge and cabins

_____15. _____

_____B. What should be included under construction costs? List all facilities to be constructed (see page 7 of this selection), type and amount of material and equipment for each facility, and the construction diagrams. Then get bids from contractors within the region. Get total construction bids and also bids by individual facility. It may be cheaper and better if you do your own contracting and contract out each facility or major operation (electrical, plumbing, etc.). The final decision must be based on local conditions, your background, the complexity of the task, and the bids received.

_____C. What equipment would be necessary for initial operation? With future expansion? Ask dealers for bids on each piece of equipment.

_____D. What are the annual operating expenses?

_____ 1. Maintenance and repair of equipment and facilities and related structures

_____ 2. Taxes (business, property, income, etc.)

_____ 3. Utilities (gas, electric, water)

_____ 4. Labor costs

_____ 5. Land acquisition payments

_____ 6. Insurance premiums

_____ 7. Legal counsel

_____ 8. Advertising

_____ 9. Fuel

_____10. Concession supplies

_____11. Gasoline

_____12. Depreciation of facilities and equipment

_____13. Interest on investment

_____14. Management salaries

_____15. Food and drink supplies

_____16. Care of animals

———17. Cost of producing farm products

———18. Road maintenance

———19. _____

———E. What does the layout of a financial evaluation sheet look like?

Enterprise _____ Owner _____

Location _____ Acreage _____

Dollar Value

1. Gross income
   Detailed fees
   Detailed charges $(A)

2. Annual Operating Expenses $(B)

3. Net income $(A − B)

SELECTION F

LEISURE ATTITUDE-INTEREST QUESTIONNAIRE*

---

*This questionnaire was used for planning the LaSalle County Conservation District, Illinois. Developed by the Office of Recreation and Park Resources, Department of Recreation and Park Administration, University of Illinois, Urbana, Illinois.

LASALLE COUNTY STUDY

Please ignore the dark numbers beside the questions. They are for office use only.

1. How many **hours** do you work in an average week? If you do some work at home related to your job, include those hours too. Housewives should figure time spent doing household activities. (Check one)

    1 ☐ None   4 ☐ 25 to 34 hours   7 ☐ 45 to 49 hours

    8   2 ☐ Less than 15   5 ☐ 35 to 39 hours   8 ☐ 50 to 59 hours

    3 ☐ 15 to 24 hours   6 ☐ 40 to 44 hours   9 ☐ 60 or more hours

2a. How much vacation time do you **usually** have each year? (Check one)

    1 ☐ None   4 ☐ 2 weeks   7 ☐ Varies

    9   2 ☐ Less than 1 week   5 ☐ 3 weeks

    3 ☐ One week   6 ☐ More than 3 weeks

  b. When do you **usually** take your vacation? (Check one)

    10   1 ☐ Jan. - Feb.   3 ☐ May - June   5 ☐ Sept. - Oct.

    2 ☐ Mar. - April   4 ☐ July - Aug.   6 ☐ Nov. - Dec.

  c. What part of your vacation time **last year** was spent in LaSalle County? (Check one)

    11   1 ☐ None   3 ☐ One-half   5 ☐ All

    2 ☐ One-fourth   4 ☐ Three-Fourths

  d. How do you **most often** spend your vacation? (Check one)

    01 ☐ Traveling   05 ☐ Resort areas

    02 ☐ Visiting relatives and friends   06 ☐ Camping

    12-13   03 ☐ At home   ☐ Other (List)_____

    04 ☐ Outdoor water sports

3a. Do you **usually** have weekends free?

    1 ☐ No (If no, continue to 4)

    14   2 ☐ Yes

  b. How do you most often spend your weekend? (Check one)

    01 ☐ Traveling

    02 ☐ Visiting relatives and friends

    15-16   03 ☐ At home

    04 ☐ Outdoor water sports

    05 ☐ Resort areas

    06 ☐ Camping

    ☐ Other(List)_____

    _____

4. What time or times of day, **during the week,** would you most often have free for participation in activities that you would consider recreational? (Check all that apply)

    17 ☐ Before 9 a.m.   20 ☐ 3 p.m. – 6 p.m.   22 ☐ After 8 p.m.

    18 ☐ 9 a.m. – 12 noon   21 ☐ 7 p.m. – 8 p.m.   23 ☐ None of these

    19 ☐ 1 p.m. – 3 p.m.

5. How many **hours** were spent in each of the following activities **yesterday** (week-day) from 6:00 a.m. to 12:00 midnight? (18 hours)

    Hours

    | 24-25 | a. Work (occupation) | _____ |
    | 26 | b. Sleep | _____ |
    | 27 | c. Work around the house | _____ |
    | 28 | d. Leisure activities | _____ |
    | 29 | e. Personal grooming | _____ |
    | 30 | f. Other | _____ |

6. How many **hours** were spent in each of the following activities **last Saturday** from 6:00 a.m. to 12:00 midnight? (18 hours)

    Hours

    | 31. | a. Work (occupation) | _____ |
    | 32-33 | b. Sleep | _____ |
    | 34 | c. Work around the house | _____ |
    | 35-36 | d. Leisure activities | _____ |
    | 37 | e. Personal grooming | _____ |
    | 38 | f. Other | _____ |

7a. Do you work with any youth programs?

     1 ☐ No (If no, continue to 8)

     39   2 ☐ Yes

b. If **yes,** which ones? (check all that apply)

     40 ☐ Scouting for boys   44-7 ☐ Other (List) ___

     41 ☐ Scouting for girls   _____

     42 ☐ 4–H   _____

     43 ☐ Y Indian Guides   _____

8. Which of the following items of recreational equipment do you own? (Check all that apply)

    | 48 ☐ Power boat | 54 ☐ Golf clubs |
    | 49 ☐ Sail boat | 55 ☐ Tennis racket |
    | 50 ☐ Canoe | 56 ☐ Tent and other camping gear |
    | 51 ☐ Outboard motor | 57 ☐ Camera |
    | 52 ☐ Shotgun or rifle | 58 ☐ Toboggan or sled |
    | 53 ☐ Bow and arrow | 59 ☐ None |
    | 60 Other_____ | 62 _____ |
    | 61   _____ | 63 _____ |

9. To which outdoor organizations do you belong? (Check all that apply)

    | 64 ☐ Audubon Society | 67 ☐ Sportsmens Club |
    | 65 ☐ Izaak Walton League | 68 ☐ Garden Club |
    | 66 ☐ Outboard Boat Club | 69 ☐ None |
    | 70-3 ☐ Other (List) _____ | _____ |
    | _____ | _____ |

HEAD OF HOUSEHOLD: 10. 46-47 Age _____   11. 48 1□ Male   2□ Female

Please answer the following for each activity in which the head of the household participates in a 30 day period and during the proper season.

12. Do you: **13. With whom**   **14. Where (most often)**

	Approximate number of days in 30 day period / Not at all	Alone	Family or Friends	Organized Group	Lake	River	Creek		Name of Facility	State
a. Go power boating?	49-50 00	51 1	2	3 52	1	2	3		53-54	55
b. Go sailing?	56-57 00	58 1	2	3 59	1	2	3		60-61	62
c. Canoe?	63-64 00	65 1	2	3 66	1	2	3		67-68	69
d. Swim?	70-71 00	72 1	2	3 73	1	2	3	Pool 4	74-75	76
e. Fish?	77-78 00	79 1	2	3 80	1	2	3		8-9	10
f. Waterski?	11-12 00	13 1	2	3 14	1	2	3		15-16	17

		Alone	Family or Friends	Organized Group	Big Game	Small Game	Water Fowl	Wilderness or Remote Area (check one)	Public Area	Private Area
g. Hunt (firearm)?	18-19 00	20 1	2	3	21 1	22 2	23 3 → 24		□ 1	□ 2
h. Hunt (bow and arrow)?	25-26 00	27 1	2	3	28 1	29 2	30 3 → 31		□ 1	□ 2
i. Target or trap shoot?	32-33 00	34 1	2	3			→ 35		□ 1	□ 2

		Alone	Family or Friends	Organized Group	Developed Area	Wilderness or Remote Area (check one)	Public Area	Private Area
j. Go camping (overnight)?	36-37 00	38 1	2	3	39 1		□ 2	
k. Picnic?	40-41 00	42 1	2	3	43 1		□ 2	

		Alone	Family or Friends	Organized Group	Public Area	Private Area (check one)
l. Walk or hike for pleasure?	44-45 00	46 1	2	3	47 1	□ 2
m. Go horseback riding?	48-49 00	50 1	2	3	51 1	□ 2
n. Play team sports?	52-53 00	54 1	2	3	55 1	□ 2
o. Golf?	56-57 00	58 1	2	3	59 1	□ 2
p. Play tennis?	60-61 00	62 1	2	3	63 1	□ 2
q. Go driving for pleasure?	64-65 00	66 1	2	3		
r. Go bicycling?	67-68 00	69 1	2	3		

SPOUSE

15. 70-71 ☐ No spouse (If none skip to next page)   Age of Spouse _____

Please answer the following for each activity in which the spouse participates.

16. Do you: 17. With whom   18. Where (most often)

	Not at all	Approximate number of days in 30 day period	Alone	Family or Friends	Organized Group	Lake	River	Creek	Name of Facility	State
a. Go power boating?	72-73 00☐		74 ☐1	☐2	75 ☐3	☐1	☐2	☐3	76-77	78
b. Go sailing?	79-80 00☐		8 ☐1	☐2	9 ☐3	☐1	☐2	☐3	10-11	12
c. Canoe?	13-14 00☐		15 ☐1	☐2	16 ☐3	☐1	☐2	☐3	17-18	19
d. Swim?	20-21 00☐		22 ☐1	☐2	23 ☐3	☐1	☐2	☐3 (Pool 4☐)	24-25	26
e. Fish?	27-28 00☐		29 ☐1	☐2	30 ☐3	☐1	☐2	☐3	31-32	33
f. Waterski?	34-35 00☐		36 ☐1	☐2	37 ☐3	☐1	☐2	☐3	38-39	40

	Not at all	days in 30	Alone	Family or Friends	Organized Group	Big Game	Small Game	Water Fowl	Public Area	Private Area (check one)
g. Hunt (firearm)?	41-42 00☐		43 ☐1	☐2	☐3	44 ☐1	45 ☐	46 ☐	47 ☐1	☐2
h. Hunt (bow and arrow?)	48-49 00☐		50 ☐1	☐2	☐3	51 ☐1	52 ☐	53 ☐	54 ☐1	☐2
i. Target or trap shoot?	55-56 00☐		57 ☐1	☐2	☐3			58		

	Not at all	days in 30	Alone	Family or Friends	Organized Group	Developed Area	Wilderness or Remote Area		Public Area	Private Area (check one)
j. Go camping (overnight)?	59-60 00☐		61 ☐1	☐2	☐3	62 ☐1	☐2		☐2	
k. Picnic?	63-64 00☐		65 ☐1	☐2	☐3	66 ☐1			☐2	

	Not at all	days in 30	Alone	Family or Friends	Organized Group	Public Area	Private Area (check one)
l. Walk or hike for pleasure?	67-68 00☐		69 ☐1	☐2	☐3	70 ☐1	☐2
m. Go horseback riding?	71-72 00☐		73 ☐1	☐2	☐3	74 ☐1	☐2
n. Play team sports?	75-76 00☐		77 ☐1	☐2	☐3	78 ☐1	☐2
o. Golf?	79-80 00☐		8 ☐1	☐2	☐3	9 ☐1	☐2
p. Play tennis?	10-11 00☐		12 ☐1	☐2	☐3	13 ☐1	☐2
q. Go driving for pleasure?	14-15 00☐		16 ☐1	☐2	☐3		
r. Go bicycling?	17-18 00☐		19 ☐1	☐2	☐3		

OLDEST CHILD (Living at home)

19. 20-21 □ None (If none skip to page 7)   Age of child _____   20. 22 1□ Male   2□ Female

Please answer the following for each activity in which the oldest child (living at home) participates.

21. Do you:

	Approximate number of days in 30 day period	Not at all	22. With whom — Alone	Family or Friends	Organized Group	23. Where (most often) — Lake	River	Creek	Name of Facility	State
a. Go power boating?	23-24	00	25 1	2	3 26	1	2	3	27-28	29
b. Go sailing?	30-31	00	32 1	2	3 33	1	2	3	34-35	36
c. Canoe?	37-38	00	39 1	2	3 40	1	2	3	41-42	43
d. Swim?	44-45	00	46 1	2	3 47	1	2	3 (Pool 4)	48-49	50
e. Fish?	51-52	00	53 1	2	3 54	1	2	3	55-56	57
f. Waterski?	58-59	00	60 1	2	3 61	1	2	3	62-63	64

	days	Not at all	Alone	Family or Friends	Organized Group	Big Game	Small Game	Water Fowl	Name of Facility	State
g. Hunt (firearm)?	65-66	00	67 1	2	3	68 1	69 1	70 1	71 1	2
h. Hunt (bow and arrow)?	72-73	00	74 1	2	3	75 1	76 1	77 1	78 1	2
i. Target or trap shoot?	79-80	00	8 1	2	3				9	2

	days	Not at all	Alone	Family or Friends	Organized Group	Developed Area	Wilderness or Remote Area (check one)	Name of Facility	State
j. Go camping (overnight)?	10-11	00	12 1	2	3	13 1	3	2	2
k. Picnic?	14-15	00	16 1	2	3	17 1	3	2	2

	days	Not at all	Alone	Family or Friends	Organized Group	Public Area	Private Area (check one)	Name of Facility	State
l. Walk or hike for pleasure?	18-19	00	20 1	2	3	21 1	3	2	2
m. Go horseback riding?	22-23	00	24 1	2	3	25 1	3	2	2
n. Play team sports?	26-27	00	28 1	2	3	29 1	3	2	2
o. Golf?	30-31	00	32 1	2	3	33 1	3	2	2
p. Play tennis?	34-35	00	36 1	2	3	37 1	3	2	2
q. Go driving for pleasure?	38-39	00	40 1	2	3				
r. Go bicycling?	41-42	00	43 1	2	3				

SECOND OLDEST CHILD (Living at home)

24. **44-45** ☐ None (If none skip to page 7)   Age of child _____   25. **46** 1 ☐ Male   2 ☐ Female

Please answer the following for each activity in which the second oldest child (living at home) participates.

26. Do you:

27. **With whom**

28. **Where** (most often)

	Not at all	Approximate number of days in 30 day period	Alone	Family or Friends	Organized Group	Lake	River	Creek	Name of Facility	State
a. Go power boating?	00 ☐ 47-48	→ 49 1 ☐	2 ☐	3 ☐	50 1 ☐	2 ☐	3 ☐	51-52	53
b. Go sailing?	00 ☐ 54-55	→ 56 1 ☐	2 ☐	3 ☐	57 1 ☐	2 ☐	3 ☐	58-59	60
c. Canoe?	00 ☐ 61-62	→ 63 1 ☐	2 ☐	3 ☐	64 1 ☐	2 ☐	3 ☐	65-66	67

								Pool		
d. Swim?	00 ☐ 68-69	→ 70 1 ☐	2 ☐	3 ☐	71 1 ☐	2 ☐	3 ☐	4 ☐ 72-73	74
e. Fish?	00 ☐ 75-76	→ 77 1 ☐	2 ☐	3 ☐	78 1 ☐	2 ☐	3 ☐	79-80	8
f. Waterski?	00 ☐ 9-10	→ 11 1 ☐	2 ☐	3 ☐	12 1 ☐	2 ☐	3 ☐	13-14	15

						Big Game	Small Game	Water Fowl	Public Area	Private Area
									(check one)	
g. Hunt (firearm)?	00 ☐ 16-17	— 18 1 ☐	2 ☐	3 ☐	19 1 ☐	20 ☐	21 ☐	22 1 ☐	2 ☐
h. Hunt (bow and arrow)?	00 ☐ 23-24	→ 25 1 ☐	2 ☐	3 ☐	26 1 ☐	27 ☐	28 ☐	29 1 ☐	2 ☐
i. Target or trap shoot?	00 ☐ 30-31	→ 32 1 ☐	2 ☐	3 ☐	33 ↑				

						Developed Area	Wilderness or Remote Area	
						(check one)		
j. Go camping (overnight)?	00 ☐ 34-35	→ 36 1 ☐	2 ☐	3 ☐	37 1 ☐	2 ☐	
k. Picnic?	00 ☐ 38-39	→ 40 1 ☐	2 ☐	3 ☐	41 1 ☐	2 ☐	

						Public Area	Private Area	
						(check one)		
l. Walk or hike for pleasure?	00 ☐ 42-43	→ 44 1 ☐	2 ☐	3 ☐	45 1 ☐	2 ☐	
m. Go horseback riding?	00 ☐ 46-47	→ 48 1 ☐	2 ☐	3 ☐	49 1 ☐	2 ☐	
n. Play team sports?	00 ☐ 50-51	→ 52 1 ☐	2 ☐	3 ☐	53 1 ☐	2 ☐	
o. Golf?	00 ☐ 54-55	→ 56 1 ☐	2 ☐	3 ☐	57 1 ☐	2 ☐	
p. Play tennis?	00 ☐ 58-59	→ 60 1 ☐	2 ☐	3 ☐	61 1 ☐	2 ☐	
q. Go driving for pleasure?	00 ☐ 62-63	→ 64 1 ☐	2 ☐	3 ☐			
r. Go bicycling?	00 ☐ 65-66	→ 67 1 ☐	2 ☐	3 ☐			

29. Which words best describe **LaSalle County** as a whole (not your own geographic location)?

Place a check in the square according to the best description.

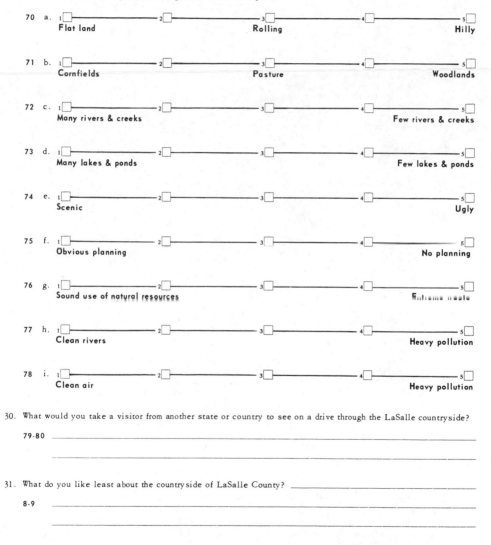

70 a. 1☐——————2☐——————3☐——————4☐——————5☐
      Flat land   Rolling   Hilly

71 b. 1☐——————2☐——————3☐——————4☐——————5☐
      Cornfields   Pasture   Woodlands

72 c. 1☐——————2☐——————3☐——————4☐——————5☐
      Many rivers & creeks   Few rivers & creeks

73 d. 1☐——————2☐——————3☐——————4☐——————5☐
      Many lakes & ponds   Few lakes & ponds

74 e. 1☐——————2☐——————3☐——————4☐——————5☐
      Scenic   Ugly

75 f. 1☐——————2☐——————3☐——————4☐——————5☐
      Obvious planning   No planning

76 g. 1☐——————2☐——————3☐——————4☐——————5☐
      Sound use of natural resources   Extreme waste

77 h. 1☐——————2☐——————3☐——————4☐——————5☐
      Clean rivers   Heavy pollution

78 i. 1☐——————2☐——————3☐——————4☐——————5☐
      Clean air   Heavy pollution

30. What would you take a visitor from another state or country to see on a drive through the LaSalle countryside?

79-80 _____

_____

31. What do you like least about the countryside of LaSalle County? _____

8-9 _____

_____

32. Now we would like to know how you feel regarding the function of a Conservation District and other related items. Here are a few statements. Check the box which corresponds to how **you feel.** (Answer every question as best you can.)

	Completely Disagree	Partially Disagree	Partially Agree	Completely Agree
10 a. The conservation district should purchase lands and leave them natural for wildlife refuges, nature study, and scenic enjoyment	1 ☐	2 ☐	3 ☐	4 ☐
11 b. The conservation district should acquire lands and preserve them in a completely undisturbed state	1 ☐	2 ☐	3 ☐	4 ☐
12 c. The conservation district should develop facilities such as swimming areas, campgrounds, marinas, golf courses, etc., on the lands it acquires ..	1 ☐	2 ☐	3 ☐	4 ☐
13 d. The conservation district should charge user-fees at its facilities.............	1 ☐	2 ☐	3 ☐	4 ☐
14 e. Fees should be higher for non-residents of LaSalle County.....................	1 ☐	2 ☐	3 ☐	4 ☐
15 f. Private enterprise can do a better job of developing such facilities as lodging, marinas, golf courses, etc...	1 ☐	2 ☐	3 ☐	4 ☐
16 g. Lands suitable for recreational use should be under public ownership............	1 ☐	2 ☐	3 ☐	4 ☐
17 h. Federal assistance should be sought to help pay for the acquisition and development of conservation district facilities............................	1 ☐	2 ☐	3 ☐	4 ☐
18 i. The conservation district should assume the park and recreation function in parts of the county not served by an existing Park District or Recreation Commission	1 ☐	2 ☐	3 ☐	4 ☐
19 j. The conservation district should become involved in pollution control	1 ☐	2 ☐	3 ☐	4 ☐
20 k. The conservation district should become involved in lands which they do not own (through lease, easement, etc.)	1 ☐	2 ☐	3 ☐	4 ☐

33. Here are some additional statements. Check the box which tells how **you feel** about each statement.

		Not True	True
21 a.	There are enough outdoor-oriented organizations in LaSalle County	₁☐	₂☐
22 b.	There are plenty of outdoor recreational facilities in LaSalle County	₁☐	₂☐
23 c.	The conservation district should hire personnel to conduct programs in outdoor education and recreation	₁☐	₂☐
24 d.	Borrowing money is an appropriate way for a conservation district to secure funds for the development of facilities	₁☐	₂☐
25 e.	I prefer to be more of a participant in leisure rather than a spectator	₁☐	₂☐
26 f.	There should be more man made bodies of water in LaSalle County	₁☐	₂☐
27 g.	Children have adequate opportunities to learn about nature	₁☐	₂☐

34a. Should the conservation district provide outdoor recreation facilities on the lands it shall acquire?

   ₁☐ No (If no continue to 35)

28 ₂☐ Yes

b. If **yes,** which of the following? (check)

29☐ Picnic areas complete with shelter houses
30☐ Hiking trails
31☐ Bridle paths
32☐ Playground equipment in the picnic areas
33☐ Softball and baseball diamonds
34☐ Playfields that can be used for football, badminton, volleyball, croquet, or other similar games
35☐ Fishing and boating lakes
36☐ Natural swimming area with sand beach
37☐ Swimming pool
38☐ Golf course
39☐ Overnight lodging
40☐ Regulated hunting
41☐ Group camp areas
42☐ Archery and rifle ranges
43☐ Boat ramps
44☐ Nature centers
45☐ Winter sports such as ice skating, sledding and tobogganning
46☐ Tent and/or trailer campgrounds for short-term use (one week or less)
47☐ Tent and/or trailer campgrounds for long-term use (one week or longer)

48-49 Other: _____

50-51 _____

52-53 _____

Skip to next page

35a. Should the conservation district conduct organized programs on the lands it shall acquire?

        1☐ No (If no continue to 36)

    54   2☐ Yes

b. If **yes,** which of the following? (check all that apply)

        55☐ Competitive sports

        56☐ Handicrafts

        57☐ Instructions in fishing, boating, swimming, etc.

        58☐ Overnight group camping

        59☐ Bicycle trips

        60☐ Canoeing trips

        61☐ Day camps

        62☐ Outdoor education

        63☐ Other (List)_____

_____

_____

36a. Do you go out occasionally on overnight camping trips?

        1☐ No (If no continue to 37)

    64   2☐ Yes

b. If **yes,** which type of campground do you prefer?

      65   1☐ Primitive type with no marked sites where you set up at random within a specified area.

        2☐ Primitive type with marked sites including driveway and picnic table, pit toilets, hand pumped wells, and no electrical outlets.

        3☐ Improved type with marked sites including driveway and picnic table, flush toilets, running water, shower and laundry facilities, and electrical outlets.

37. Would you support a network of bicycle trails that connect the major population centers in the county with the Conservation District's properties and possibly other public recreational areas?

    66   1☐ No   2☐ Yes

Please answer the following questions for **yourself** even though you are included earlier.

    8-9   38. What is your age? _____

    10   39. Are you: 1☐ Male?   2☐ Female?

    11   40. Are you: 1☐ Married?

                        2☐ Single (never married)?

                        3☐ Divorced or separated?

                        4☐ Widowed?

41. Are there children living at home for which you did not have an answer sheet for activity estimates?

  ₁☐ No (If no continue to 42)

12   ₂☐ Yes

13   a. Age of third child_____

14   b. Age of fourth child_____

15   c. Age of fifth child_____

42. How many years of education have **you** completed? (Circle the number of years.)

16-17   Grade school: 1   2   3   4   5   6   7   8

  High school: 9   10   11   12

  College: 1   2   3   4   5

43. What is the occupation of the **chief wage earner** of the household?

18-19 _____

44. How much was earned by all the adult members of the household last year? (check one)

20   ₁☐ Under $5,000   ₄☐ $11,000 to $13,999   ₇☐ $20,000 to $24,999

  ₂☐ $5,000 to $7,999   ₅☐ $14,000 to $16,999   ₈☐ $25,000 to $29,999

  ₃☐ $8,000 to $10,999   ₆☐ $17,000 to $19,999   ₉☐ $30,000 or more

45. How long have you lived in LaSalle County? (check one)

21   ₁☐ less than 1 year   ₄☐ 3 - 4 years   ₇☐ 9 - 10 years

  ₂☐ 1 year   ₅☐ 5 - 6 years   ₈☐ 10 - 15 years

  ₃☐ 2 years   ₆☐ 7 - 8 years   ₉☐ over 15 years

46a. Are there properties or natural features in LaSalle County that **you feel** are worthy of preservation and which should be in public ownership?

  ₁☐ No

22   ₂☐ Yes

b. If **yes**, please name them

23-24 _____

_____

_____

Additional Comments:

INDEX

Note: Page numbers in *italics* indicate illustrations; (t) indicates a table.